SCRIPTURAL TRACES
CRITICAL PERSPECTIVES ON THE RECEPTION AND
INFLUENCE OF THE BIBLE

28

Editors
Matthew A. Collins, University of Chester, UK
Michelle Fletcher, King's College London, UK
Andrew Mein, Durham University, UK

Editorial Board
Michael J. Gilmour, David Gunn, James Harding, Jorunn Økland

Published under

LIBRARY OF NEW TESTAMENT STUDIES

651

Formerly Journal for the Study of the New Testament Supplement Series

Editor
Chris Keith

Editorial Board
Dale C. Allison, Lynn H. Cohick, R. Alan Culpepper, Craig A. Evans,
Jennifer Eyl, Robert Fowler, Simon J. Gathercole, Juan Hernández Jr., John
S. Kloppenborg, Michael Labahn, Matthew V. Novenson, Love L. Sechrest,
Robert Wall, Catrin H. Williams, Brittany E. Wilson

PATRISTIC PERSPECTIVES ON LUKE'S TRANSFIGURATION

Interpreting Vision

Peter Anthony

LONDON • NEW YORK • OXFORD • NEW DELHI • SYDNEY

T&T CLARK
Bloomsbury Publishing Plc
50 Bedford Square, London, WC1B 3DP, UK
1385 Broadway, New York, NY 10018, USA
29 Earlsfort Terrace, Dublin 2, Ireland

BLOOMSBURY, T&T CLARK and the T&T Clark logo are trademarks of
Bloomsbury Publishing Plc

First published in Great Britain 2022
Paperback edition published 2024

Copyright © Peter Anthony, 2022

Peter Anthony has asserted his right under the Copyright, Designs and Patents Act, 1988, to be identified as Author of this work.

For legal purposes the Acknowledgements on p. vii constitute an extension of this copyright page.

Cover image © Giuseppe Masci/AGF/Universal Images Group via Getty Images

All rights reserved. No part of this publication may be reproduced or transmitted in any form or by any means, electronic or mechanical, including photocopying, recording, or any information storage or retrieval system, without prior permission in writing from the publishers.

Bloomsbury Publishing Plc does not have any control over, or responsibility for, any third-party websites referred to or in this book. All internet addresses given in this book were correct at the time of going to press. The author and publisher regret any inconvenience caused if addresses have changed or sites have ceased to exist, but can accept no responsibility for any such changes.

A catalogue record for this book is available from the British Library.

Library of Congress Cataloging-in-Publication Data
Names: Anthony, Peter, 1979– author.
Title: Patristic perspectives on Luke's transfiguration : interpreting vision / by Peter Anthony.
Description: London ; New York : T&T Clark, 2022. | Series: Scriptural traces ; 28 | Includes bibliographical references and index. |
Summary: "Peter Anthony explores how visionary elements in Luke's Gospel had a particular influence on early interpretation of the Transfiguration, by exploring the rich hermeneutical traditions that emerged - particularly in the Latin West - as the Transfiguration was first depicted visually in art"– Provided by publisher.
Identifiers: LCCN 2021043808 (print) | LCCN 2021043809 (ebook) |
ISBN 9780567699756 (hb) | ISBN 9780567699794 (pb) | ISBN 9780567699763 (epdf) |
ISBN 9780567699787 (ebook)
Subjects: LCSH: Bible. Luke–Criticism, interpretation, etc. | Jesus Christ–Transfiguration–Biblical teaching. | Jesus Christ–Transfiguration–Art.
Classification: LCC BS2595.52 .A58 2022 (print) | LCC BS2595.52 (ebook) | DDC 226.4/06–dc23/eng/20211005
LC record available at https://lccn.loc.gov/2021043808
LC ebook record available at https://lccn.loc.gov/2021043809

ISBN: HB: 978-0-5676-9975-6
PB: 978-0-5676-9979-4
ePDF: 978-0-5676-9976-3
eBook: 978-0-5676-9978-7

Series: Scriptural Traces 28

Series: Library of New Testament Studies, volume 651
ISSN 2513-8790

Typeset by Newgen KnowledgeWorks Pvt. Ltd., Chennai, India

To find out more about our authors and books visit www.bloomsbury.com
and sign up for our newsletters.

CONTENTS

List of illustrations	vi
Acknowledgements	vii
List of abbreviations	viii

Chapter 1
INTRODUCTION — 1

Chapter 2
AN EXAMINATION OF THE NEW TESTAMENT SYNOPTIC TRANSFIGURATION NARRATIVES — 19

Chapter 3
MODERN INTERPRETATION OF THE SYNOPTIC TRANSFIGURATION NARRATIVES — 35

Chapter 4
RECEPTION OF THE TRANSFIGURATION IN 2 PETER, THE *APOCALYPSE OF PETER*, THE *ACTS OF PETER* AND THE *ACTS OF JOHN* — 49

Chapter 5
THE TRANSFIGURATION IN TERTULLIAN AND ORIGEN — 71

Chapter 6
INTERPRETATION OF THE TRANSFIGURATION IN THE GREEK EAST AFTER ORIGEN — 103

Chapter 7
INTERPRETATION OF THE TRANSFIGURATION IN THE LATIN WEST AFTER TERTULLIAN — 125

Chapter 8
THE EARLIEST DEPICTION OF THE TRANSFIGURATION — 151

Chapter 9
CONCLUSION — 205

Bibliography	215
Index	233
Index of biblical references	237

ILLUSTRATIONS

1	Saint Catherine's monastery in Sinai, Egypt – Mosaic of the Transfiguration (sixth century)	155
2	Transfiguration apse over high altar, St Apollinare in Classe, Ravenna	158
3	Ss. Nereo ed Achilleo, Rome	168
4	Close up of Transfiguration image, Ss. Nereo ed Achilleo, Rome	169
5	Close up of Annunciation scene, Ss. Nereo ed Achilleo, Rome	172
6	Close up of virgin and child, Ss. Nereo ed Achilleo, Rome	173
7	S. Prassede, Rome	176
8	Close up of heavenly Jerusalem, S. Prassede, Rome	176
9	Moses figure in the heavenly Jerusalem scene, S. Prassede, Rome	177
10	Close up of Elijah figure in heavenly Jerusalem scene, S. Prassede, Rome	178
11	Close up of Christ in the heavenly Jerusalem, S. Prassede, Rome	181
12	Transfiguration image, St Zeno Chapel, S. Prassede, Rome	184
13	Close up of the Transfiguration image, St Zeno Chapel, S. Prassede, Rome	186
14	S. Maria in Domnica, Rome	188
15	John the Baptist/Elijah figure close up in S. Maria Domnica, Rome	189
16	S. Maria in Domnica, Moses figure close up	190
17	Close up of chancel arch, S. Maria in Domnica	191
18	Utrecht Psalter, Ms. 32, for 1 83v, reverse	193
19	Close up of Transfiguration scene in Utrecht Psalter, Ms. 32, for 1 83v, reverse	194
20	Ivory, Victoria and Albert Museum, Catalogue number 253-1867	197

ACKNOWLEDGEMENTS

I would like to thank the large number of people who have supported, taught and helped me in the process of writing this monograph.

In origin, this book is largely the fruit of the doctoral thesis I defended at the University of Oxford in 2015. I would like, first and foremost, to thank my doctoral supervisor the Revd Prof. Christopher Rowland. His wisdom, knowledge and experience were such a blessing to me, and I am very grateful indeed to him for his encouragement and insight through the process of researching and writing my thesis.

I am grateful to a number of people who helped and advised me academically in a more informal way through my time as a graduate student. Prof. Ian Boxall was an unfailing source of crucial advice and help. It was his teaching that first gave me my love of New Testament study, and I will always be grateful to him for what I learned as his student. Thanks must also be given to the Revd Dr Jane Baun who read my thesis in its last stages and provided excellent advice and sage recommendations in terms of further reading and editing.

I would like to thank the institutions whose support made this monograph possible. The Arts and Humanities Research Council funded my doctoral studies, and I am hugely grateful to them for the crucial bursary which I received from them. During my time as a graduate student, I was Junior Dean at Stephen's House, Oxford, and Junior Chaplain at Merton College, Oxford. I want to thank the fellows, staff and students of both colleges for the wonderful home they gave me and for the stimulating academic community they provided.

My DPhil thesis was redrafted into the form it now has in this monograph thanks to a period of sabbatical study leave, which I took whilst I was vicar of St Benet's, Kentish Town. I want to thank the churchwardens and people of St Benet's for making that possible, and especially my then colleague the Revd Nigel Palmer for holding the fort whilst I was absent for three months.

Amongst those who have helped and encouraged me during the process of writing this book, I would also like to thank the Revd Dr Anders Bergquist, who read my DPhil thesis and offered some first thoughts on how it might be re-edited to make a publishable work.

My thanks are also due to all at Bloomsbury who helped with the process of publishing, especially Sarah Blake, my editor.

Above all, I would like to thank Richard Zavitz for his love, support and endless patience with me.

ABBREVIATIONS

Primary sources

Apoc. Pet.	*The Apocalypse of Peter*
	Ethiopic text: D. Buchholz, *Your Eyes will be Opened: A Study of the Greek (Ethiopic) Apocalypse of Peter* (Atlanta, GA: Scholars Press, 1988), 162–243.
	Greek, Akhmim text: GCS, Neue Folge 11, 104–17.
	Elliot and James, *The Apocryphal New Testament* (Oxford: Clarendon Press, 1993).
Act. Pet.	*The Acts of Peter*
	Latin text: *Acta Apostolorum Aprocrypha*, vol. 1, ed. Richard Lipsius (Hildesheim: Georg Olms Verlag, 1959), 45–103.
Act. Joh.	*The Acts of John*,
	Acta Apostolorum Aprocrypha, vol. II/1, ed. Richard Lipsius (Hildesheim: Georg Olms Verlag, 1959), 151–216.
Ad Theo. Laps.	John Chrysostom, *Paraenesis sive Adhortatio Ad Theodorum Lapsum*, Patrologia Graeca 47, 278–316.
Adv. Marc.	Tertullian, *Adversus Marcionem*, Corpus Christianorum Series Latina 1 (Turnhout: Brepols, 1956), 441–725.
Adv. Prax.	Tertullian, *Adversus Praxean*, Corpus Christianorum Series Latina 2 (Turnhout: Brepols, 1956), 1159–1205.
Amb. Lib.	Maximus the Confessor, *Ambiguorum Liber*, Patrologia Graeca 91.1125-8.
Bab.	John Chrysostom, *Discours sur Babylas,* Sources Chrétiennes 362, ed. M. Schatkin (Paris: Editions du Cerf, 1990).
CCSL	*Corpus Christianorum Patristic Series Latina*
Com. in Mat.	Hilary, *Commentarius in Matthaeum*, Patrologia Latina 9, 917–1078.
Com. in Ev. Mat.	Jerome, *Commentarorium in Evangelium Matthaei* 3.17.1-9; Patrologia Latina 26, 17–218.
Com. in Ioh.	Cyril of Alexandria, *Commentarii in Iohannem* (P. E. Pusey, *Sancti patris nostril Cyrilli arch. Alexandrini in d. Joannis Evangelium*, Oxford, 1872).
Com. in Luc.	Eusebius of Caesarea, *Comentarii in Lucae Evangelium quantum superset in Codicibus Vaticanis*, Patrologia Graeca, 24, 529–605.
Com. Mat.	Origen, *Commentarorium In Evangelium Secundum Matthaeum*, Patrologia Graeca 13, 835–1600.
Comm. Matt.	Hilary of Poitiers, *Commentarius in Matthaeum*, Patrologia Latina 9, 917–1078.
Contra Cels.	Origen, *Contra Celsum*, Patrologia Graeca 11, 651–1632.

Contra Haer.	Irenaeus, *Contra Haereses*, Patrologia Graeca 7, 437–1224.
De Anima	Tertullian, *De Anima*, Corpus Christianorum Series Latina 2, 781–869.
De Div. Nom.	Pseudo-Dionysius the Areopagite, *De Divinis Nominibus* 1.4, Patrologia Graeca 3, 585–996.
De Prin.	Origen, *Peri Archon* (De Principiis), Patrologia Graeca 11, 115–414.
Explan. in Luc.	Cyril of Alexandria, *Explanatio in Lucae Evangelium*, Patrologia Graeca 72, 475–950.
Expos. in Luc.	Ambrose, *Expositio Evangelii secundum Lucam*, Patrologia Latina 15, 1527–1850.
Frag. Luc.	Origen, *Fragmenta in Lucam*, ed. Max Rauer, Die Griechischen Christlichen Schriftsteller, Origenes Werke 9 (Berlin: Akademie Verlag, 1959) 227–336.
GCS	Die Griechischen Christlichen Schriftsteller der ersten Jahunderte (Berlin-Brandenburgische Akademie der Wissenschaften; Berlin: Walter de Gruyter).
Hom. 21	John Chrysostom, Homilia XXI, *Ecloga de Imperio, Poteste et Gloria*, Patrologia Graeca 63, 696–716.
Hom. 24	The Venerable Bede, *Homilia 24 in Quadragesima: Quia Dominus Ac Redemptor*, ed. David Hurst and J. Faipont, Corpus Christianorum 122, 170 ff. (1955).
Hom. 56	John Chrysostom, *Hom XLV, Commentarius In S. Matthaeum Euangeliam*, Patrologia Graeca 58, 549–58.
Hom. in Trans.	Ambrose Autpert, *Homilia in Transfiguratione Domini*, Patrologia Latina 89, 1305–20.
Hom. Div. 9	Cyril of Alexandria, *Cyrilii Homilae Diversae, Homilia IX*, Patrologia Graeca 77, 1109–1016.
Hom. Gen.	Origen, *Homélies sur la Genèse*, ed. Henri de Lubac and Louis Doutreleau, Sources Chrétiennes 7 (Paris: Editions du Cerf, 1976).
Hom. in Io.	John Chrysostom, *In Ioannem Homiliae*, Patrologia Graeca 59, 23–483.
Hom. in Ps. 44	Basil of Caesarea, *Homilia in Psalmum XLIV*, Patrologia Graeca 29, 387–414.
Hom. Lev.	Origen, *In Leviticum Homilia*, Patrologia Graeca 12, 404–574.
Hom. Luc.	*Homélies sur S. Luc*, SC 87, ed. Henri Crouzel (Paris: Editions du Cerf, 1962), 94–459.
Hom. Nom.	Origen, *In Numeros Homilia*, Patrologia Graeca 12, 585–806.
Hom. Ps.	Basil, *Homilae in Psalmos*, Patrologia Graeca 29, 209–493.
In Ps. 45	Ambrose, *In Psalmum XLV Enarratio*, Patrologia Latina 14, 1133–46.
Joh. Com.	Origen, *Origenes Johannescommentar* (Commentary on St John's Gospel), ed. Erwin Preuschen, Die Griechischen Christlichen Schriftsteller 10 (Origenes 4) (Leipzig: J.C. Hinrichs'sche Buchandlung, 1903), 3–480.
Orat. 7	Andrew of Crete, *Sancti Andreae Archiepiscopi Cretensis Cognomento Hierosolymitani Orationes Oratio VII: In Domini nostri Transfiguratione*, Patrologia Graeca 97, 932–57.

Paed.	Clement of Alexandria, *Paedogogos*, ed. O. Stählin, Die Griechischen Christlichen Schriftsteller 15 (Berlin: Akademie Verlag, 1972), 87–292.
PG	*Patrologia Graeca*, J. P. Migne (Paris, 1857–66).
PL	*Patrologia Latina*, J. P. Migne (Paris, 1841–55).
Prim. Reg. Expos.	Gregory the Great, *In Primum Regium Expositiones*, Patrologia Latina 79, 21–468.
Sch. in Luc.	Athanasius, *Scholia in Lucam* Patrologia Graeca 27, 1397D–1400A.
Ep. ad Episc.	*Epistola ad Episcopos Aegypti et Libyae 13*, Patrologia Graeca 25, 568C–569A.
SC	Sources Chrétiennes (Paris: Editions du Cerf).
Serm. 1	Anastasius I of Antioch, *Sancti Anastasii Sermones Quator*, Sermo I, Patrologia Graeca 89, 1365–76.
Serm. 51	Leo, *Sermo LI*; Patrologia Latina 54, 308–13.
Serm. 78	Augustine, *Sermo LXXVIII*, Patrologia Latina 38, 490-3.
Tract. Adv. 5 Haer.	*Tractatus Adversus Quinque Haereses*, Patrologia Latina 42, 1101 ff.

Other abbreviations

DACL	*Dictionnaire d'archéologie chrétienne et de liturgie*, ed. Fernand Cabrol and Henri Leclercq, 15 vols (Paris: Letouzey et Ané, 1953).
Danker	*A Greek-English Lexicon of the New Testament and other Early Christian Literature*, ed. Frederick Danker, 3rd edn (Chicago: Chicago University Press, 2000).
EDNT	*Exegetical Dictionary of the New Testament*, 3 vols, ed. Horst Balz and Gerhard Schneider (Grand Rapids, MI: Eerdmans, 1993).
Good News	*Good News Bible*, 2nd edn (London: Bible Society/Harper Collins, 1994).
Jerusalem Bible	*The Jerusalem Bible*, edn Alexander Jones (London: Darton, Longman and Todd, 1966).
Lewis and Short	*A Latin Dictionary: Founded on Andrews' Edition of Freund's Latin Dictionary*, ed. E. A. Andrews, William Freund, Charlton Lewis and Charles Short (Oxford: Clarendon Press, 1975).
Liddell and Scott	*A Lexicon Abridged from Liddell and Scott's Greek-English Lexicon* (Oxford: Clarendon Press, 1998).
Oxford Latin Dictionary	*Oxford Latin Dictionary*, ed. P. G. W. Glare (Oxford: Clarendon Press, 1982).
NEB	*The New English Bible* (Oxford: Cambridge: Oxford University Press, 1970).
NIV	*The Holy Bible: The New International Version* (London: Hodder and Stoughton, 1974).
NRSV	*The Holy Bible, New Revised Standard Version, Containing the Old and New Testaments with the Aprocrypha, or

	Deuterocanonical Books (Cambridge: Cambridge University Press, 1989).
Patristic Greek Lexicon	*A Patristic Greek Lexicon*, ed. G. W. H. Lampe (Oxford: Oxford University Press, 1968).
REB	*The Revised English Bible: New Testament* (Oxford: Oxford University Press, 1990).
RSV	*The Holy Bible, Revised Standard Version, Containing the Old and New Testaments with the Aprocrypha, or Deuterocanonical Books* (London: Thomas Nelson, 1952).
TDNT	*Theological Dictionary of the New Testament*, 10 vols, trans. and ed. Geoffrey W. Bromiley (Grand Rapids, MI: Eerdmans, 1964–74).
Translator's NT	*The Translator's New Testament*, ed. W. D. McHardy (London: British and Foreign Bible Society, 1973).

Chapter 1

INTRODUCTION

People saw things differently in antiquity. There is a huge difference between how vision was conceived in the patristic age and our understanding of it now.

The ancients expected to be able to see a wide range of phenomena which we consider irrational, invisible or non-existent, such as phantasms, deities, ghosts and portents. We, by contrast, have visual access to a thousand and one things which the ancients could never have conceived as perceptible to sight, like telescope imagery of far distant planets, cells under a microscope, or two friends in different continents chatting by Zoom.

Our popular culture frequently relegates claimed vision of anything that cannot be measured by empirical science to the realm of crankdom, mental illness or fraud. Modern scientific theories on vision, sight, memory and perception, however, increasingly assert the subjective, illusory and inconstant character of our understanding of the things we think we see. There is an all-too-fickle overlap between vision, memory, fantasy and imagination.[1]

This study seeks to examine the way in which one of the New Testament's most extraordinary accounts of miraculous vision was interpreted in the patristic period. When contrasted with the academic and hermeneutic approach of our own age, we see a considerable divergence in the way in which the incident is assessed, what it signified, parallels drawn with it and the way in which it is depicted.

I argue that there is much worth in that earlier perspective. Considerable insight can be gained concerning the meaning, value and hermeneutic potential which early readers, hearers and artists saw in this narrative. A diachronic approach reveals ways in which much modern historical-critical scholarship on the Transfiguration focuses on a very narrow field of questions, frequently to the

---

1. An excellent example of this is the exhibition mounted by the Wellcome Trust in 2019 entitled 'Smoke and Mirrors: The Psychology of Magic'. The exhibition explored the complex interaction between psychology, science and the art of deception and magic. The exhibition's accompanying book, *The Spectacle of Illusion: Magic, the Paranormal, and the Complicity of the Mind* (London: Thames and Hudson, 2019), by Matthew Tompkins is a fascinating account of ways in which human perception can be moulded, abused and manipulated.

exclusion of the rich tradition of interpretive creativity, homiletic speculation and artistic depiction which we see in the patristic period.

The purpose of this study

This study seeks to make three broad contributions to knowledge. The first is to focus on the distinct character of Luke's version of the Transfiguration narrative. I argue that the narrative found in that gospel exploits certain themes, phrases and images to emphasize the visionary character of the incident. These include the following: mention of the disciples' drowsiness, hints at Peter being out of his mind, Luke's different sequence of events and description of space and movement, cultic language of prayer and evocation of the Jerusalem Temple, terms such as 'glory' and 'exodus', and evocation of other visionary scenes in Luke's texts through shared vocabulary.

It is notable how sensitive early interpretation was to these visionary characteristics and apocalyptic imagery. I argue that Luke's version of the narrative has a significant influence on depiction of the narrative in the Latin West. I also hope to reveal just how inventive, lithe and complex Latin hermeneutic traditions were when the Transfiguration was interpreted in the light of other visionary or prophetic texts by early theologians. This monograph is in part, therefore, also a call for the re-evaluation of the worth of early Western traditions of interpretation concerning the Transfiguration.

A second contribution to knowledge made by this work is the proposition of further evidence for the worth of reception history approaches to biblical scholarship. I argue that this is particularly useful with visionary texts which claim to be an account of visionary experience. The cultural difference between modern and ancient understandings of vision is considerable. By attending to the many voices which commented on the Transfiguration in the patristic period, we realize how different our hermeneutic assumptions are and how distant our visual culture is from theirs. A reception history approach reveals the different cultural contexts in which readings and depictions of the Transfiguration narrative have taken place and gives us deeper understanding of what these texts meant to early readers, hearers and beholders of the Transfiguration. The insight afforded by a reception history approach contextualizes our own assumptions and perspectives on the Transfiguration. It challenges the hegemony of the postmodern intellectual culture we inhabit and the value judgement it makes concerning experience of the ecstatic, the miraculous, the visionary and the apocalyptic.

A third contribution to knowledge made in this monograph is an emphasis on the value of artistic depiction in the history of biblical interpretation. I argue that this is particularly the case with visionary texts which claim to be a verbalized, written record of an experience apprehended or experienced visually by the eyes and/or mind. Textual comment on biblical narratives is good at expressing categorized meaning, linear order and rhetorical, reasoned argument. Visual depiction, however, can sometimes express better a sense of the more allusive meaning at the heart of visionary experiences, characterized by paradox, simultaneity and verbal ellipsis. Indeed, artistic depiction allows visionary passages to be brought into conversation with other biblical texts, which might otherwise be considered to have little in common from a historical-critical perspective. Later chapters of this study will reveal a range of prophetic, visionary and apocalyptic biblical texts which the Transfiguration is used to elucidate through visual depiction. Artists reveal unexpected parallels, curious similarities and intriguing points of contact with other biblical texts through innovative depiction of the Transfiguration which allows these texts to sit side by side. We will undertake an extensive survey of written patristic comment on the Transfiguration narratives' status as vision, but we will then use that survey to offer readings of a number of ancient images whose meaning has sometimes been opaque to modern commentators. The approach of this study is not one in which either textual comment or artistic depiction is seen as superior to the other. Rather, I seek an approach in which both have a fruitful role to play in revealing how early Christians understood the Transfiguration narratives.

Some hermeneutical questions and points of first principle

When one examines modern scholarly comment on the Transfiguration, one is struck by a sense of disjuncture between the expansive significance the narrative had in the history of theological and liturgical reflection, and the narrow focus of modern historical-critical scholarship's questions. The questions this study seeks to answer were prompted by an incisive comment made by Ulrich Luz on the Transfiguration in his commentary on Matthew's gospel:

> The modern exegesis of our text leads us into a different world. It asks not how hearers and readers participate in this story; it primarily asks historical questions about the origin of our story ... While I would by no means dispute such interpretations, what they have in common is that they experience the story as *alien* and try to rationalise this *strangeness*. It is surprising by contrast how vivid our story is in the exegesis of the church and how relevant it is to life.[2]

His critique highlights two significant issues. The first is the way in which modern scholarship experiences the Transfiguration narratives as 'alien' and as characterized by 'strangeness'. He points here to a tension inherent in historical-critical approaches. On the one hand, modern scholarship sees as its aim ascertaining the historical 'origin of our story'. In other words, it focuses on the events which lie behind it and how we account for the creation of our narrative in the light of that. On the other hand, however, the fact that our narrative claims to

---

2. Ulrich Luz, *Matthew 8–20* (Minneapolis, MN: Fortress Press, 2001), 403. Italics mine.

be an account of a subjective visionary experience means that, to some extent, the 'origin of our story' will always remain resistant to historical enquiry.

A number of voices have come to similar conclusions in more recent comment on this question. In an essay comparing modern interpretation of the Transfiguration with that offered by Origen and Chrysostom, Frederick Norris speaks about the way in which the Transfiguration throws into particularly acute relief some of the tensions within modern biblical studies:

> NT studies is a sub-discipline that too often depends on rather narrow views of reality, parts of which were learned from the age of Western Enlightenment rationalism, which have now been discredited by contemporary physics, biology and chemistry, as well as historical and literary investigations. Such outlooks occasionally struggle with the accounts of the Transfiguration of Christ ... The miraculous is frequently defined poorly and treated as suspect.[3]

This monograph will argue that one of the reasons historical critics find the Transfiguration 'alien' and 'strange' is that they are operating with a very different model of what it meant to experience such a vision from that embraced by those who wrote the gospels.

A second problem highlighted by Luz's words is the gap between the tightly focused desire of much modern scholarship to account historically for the Transfiguration narrative's origins and the hugely creative influence our narratives have had in the history of Christian theology, spirituality, liturgy and artistic expression. To put it bluntly, a large number of historical-critical scholars quite simply don't believe the Transfiguration happened and their study of it is as a fictive literary construct. By contrast, Norris[4] shows in the essay quoted above, a consistent hermeneutic agenda characterizing patristic interpretation was a concern to relate the Transfiguration narratives to theological questions concerning the transformation of the Christian church and of the human subject. Luz argues that this wider influence by the Transfiguration on Christian theology and spirituality is so great that to set one's investigative horizons no wider than simple historical accounting for the 'origin of our story' would only offer a partial account of the meaning and significance of the Transfiguration narratives.[5] For Luz, there is a disjuncture between the richness and complexity of the reception history of the Transfiguration and the narrow focus with which historical scholarship has often approached a much smaller number of critical questions, frequently resulting in little consensus. His observation prompts the question whether an examination of

---

3. Frederick Norris, 'The Transfiguration of Christ: The Transformation of the Church', in *Reading in Christian Communities: Essays on Interpretation in the Early Church*, ed. Charles Bobert (Notre Dame, IN: University of Notre Dame Press, 2002), 196.

4. Ibid., 188–96.

5. Luz, *Matthew 8-20*, 403.

that history of interpretation might, in fact, reveal exegetical insights which offer a wider account of the Transfiguration's meaning and significance.

Cosmin Pricop[6] comes to similar conclusions and responds to some of Luz's ideas in an excellent monograph comparing modern and patristic comment on the Transfiguration from a Romanian Orthodox perspective. He finds himself caught between a tradition of orthodox exegesis deeply rooted in patristic interpretation, but sometimes lacking in critical ingenuity and ossified in its attachment to tradition,[7] and a Western critical outlook which all too often ignores the riches of early interpretation and the significance of the narrative's actualization in the life of the believing reader.[8] In an attempt to bring out the most worthwhile perspectives in both traditions, he brings commentary by Origen, Chrysostom and Jerome into conversation with a thorough examination of the Transfiguration texts using the tools of critical examination, revealing some intriguing similarities as well as points of tension and difference.

A narrowness of focus can also be detected in comment by modern patrologists and art historians on the Transfiguration. Substantial surveys exist which catalogue the broad contours of Greek[9] and Latin[10] comment on the Transfiguration, but they rarely focus on visionary elements, the hermeneutics

---

6. Cosmin Pricop, *Die Verwandlung Jesu Christi, historisch-kritische und patristische Studien*, Wissenschaftliche Untersuchungen zum Neuen Testament, 2 Reihe (Tübingen: Mohr Siebeck, 2016).

7. See esp. ibid. 6–18, 151–67.

8. Ibid., 127–49.

9. E.g. Michel Coune, *Joie de la Transfiguration d'après les Pères d'Orient*, Spiritualité Orientale no. 39 (Bégrolles-en-Mauges: Abbaye de Bellefontaine, 1985); Brian E. Dailey, S.J., *Light on the Mountain: Greek Patristic and Byzantine Homilies on the Transfiguration of the Lord* (Yonkers, NY: St Vladimir's Seminary Press, 2013); Edouard Divry, *La Transfiguration selon l'orient et l'occident*, Croire et Savoir vol. 54 (Paris: Pierre Tequi, 2009); Georges Habra, *La Transfiguration selon les pères grecs* (Paris: Editions S.O.S, 1974); John Anthony McGuckin, *The Transfiguration of Christ in Scripture and Tradition* (Lewiston, NY: Edwin Mellen Press, 1986); Pricop, *Die Verwandlung Jesu Christi*, 170–279; Michael Ramsey, *The Glory of God and the Transfiguration of Christ* (London: Longmans, Green, 1949), 128–39; Kenneth Stevenson, *Liturgy and Interpretation* (London: SCM Press, 2011), 86–102; Christopher N. Veniamin, 'The Transfiguration of Christ in Greek Patristic Literature: From Irenaeus of Lyons to Gregory Palamas' (DPhil. diss., University of Oxford, 1991).

10. Aaron Canty, *Light and Glory: The Transfiguration of Christ in Early Fransiscan and Dominican Theology* (Washington, DC: Catholic University of America Press, 2011), 11–15; Michel Coune, *Grace de la Transfiguration d'après les Pères d'Occident*, Vie Monastique no. 24 (Bégrolles-en-Mauges: Abbaye de Bellefontaine, 1990); Jean Leclercq, *Regards Monastiques sur le Christ au Moyen Age*, Jésus et Jésus-Christ, no. 56 (Paris: Mame-Desclée, 1993), 89–100; Pricop, *Die Verwandlung Jesu Christi*, 280–326; McGuckin, *Transfiguration of Christ*, 99–125; Kenneth Stevenson, *Rooted in Detachment: Living the Transfiguration* (London: Darton, Longman and Todd, 2007), 25–9.

of vision, or the key role of Luke's version of the narrative. One important voice to recognize notable gaps in patristic Transfiguration scholarship was Kenneth Stevenson in his work on patristic interpretation of the Transfiguration.[11] One of his most important observations was a call for further scholarly examination of the reception history of the Transfiguration, and the recognition that Latin interpretation is an area which has particularly suffered from a degree of academic neglect.[12] In many respects this study represents a fleshing out of the questions he points to as in need of further exploration and is a response to his call for further study in this area.

Similar shortcomings can be noted in art history commentary on early depictions of the Transfiguration. A number of admirable surveys exist of early depiction of the Transfiguration,[13] frequently with a focus on Eastern traditions of iconography.[14] However, this emphasis on Eastern traditions throws into relief the relative lack of discussion of Western portrayals and the creative, often more allusive, hermeneutic connections made by artists from the Latin West with other visionary texts.

In an attempt to respond to these gaps in scholarship, this study will examine afresh the Transfiguration narratives, with a particular focus on Luke's version, and seek to trace the way in which some of the distinct visionary motifs found in his gospel are interpreted in early comment. That survey of patristic interpretation will then be used as a springboard to examine the very earliest depictions of the Transfiguration. It will be seen that these complex images, whose meaning has sometimes been a cause of confusion or uncertainty to scholars, can often then be read more easily in the light of the hermeneutic outlook we will have traced in early written comment.

---

11. Stevenson, *Rooted in Detachment*, 25–9; *Liturgy and Interpretation*, 71–85, 103–22.

12. Stevenson, *Liturgy and Interpretation*, 103.

13. Andreas Andreopoulos, *Metamorphosis: The Transfiguration in Byzantine Theology and Iconography* (Crestwood, NY: St Vladimir's Seminary Press, 2005); Erich Dinkler, *Das Apsismosaik von S. Apollinare in Classe* (Köln: Westdeutscher Verlag, 1964), 25–50; Manfred Krüger, *Die Verklärung auf dem Berge: Erkenntnis und Kunst* (Hildesheim: Georg Olms Verlag, 2003); Solrunn Nes and Arlyne Moi, *The Uncreated Light: An Iconographical Study of the Transfiguration in the Eastern Church* (Grand Rapids, MI: Eerdmans, 2007); Gertrud Schiller, *Iconography of Christian Art* (London: Lund Humphries, 1971), 145–52.

14. John Baggley, *Doors of Perception: Icons and their Spiritual Significance* (London: Mowbray, 1987), 40, 81, 93, 136–7, 146–7; John Baggley, *Festival Icons for the Christian Year* (London: Cassell, 2000), 58–71; Paul Evdokimov, *L'art de L'icône: théologie de la beauté* (Paris: Desclée De Brouwer, 1970), 249–56; Konrad Onasch, *Icons* (London: Faber and Faber, 1963), 362, 367, 370, 384; Leonide Ouspensky and Vladimir Lossky, *The Meaning of Icons* (Boston: Boston Book and Art Shop, 1969), 210–13; Kurt Weitzmann, *The Icon: Holy Images, Sixth to Fourteenth Century* (London: Chatto & Windus, 1978), 86–7, 94–6.

Some important interlocutors

In order to examine the differences between ancient and modern interpretation, a number of ideas elaborated by theorists in the realm of visual culture and hermeneutics will be of significant use as a heuristic lens through which to examine the material we cover. This focus on the interplay between the theory of visual culture and the interpretation of visionary texts will be one of the principal drivers behind the argument and focus of this study. I outline these pivotal ideas in this first chapter in order to sketch the main theoretical contours of the approach I intend to take as we trace different responses to the Transfiguration narrative in contrasting times and places.

'Scopic regime'

Stephen Pattison's excellent work on vision, *Seeing Things: Deepening Relations with Visual Artefacts*, is particularly helpful in pinpointing some of the dynamics which characterize the different understandings of vision and visual culture in the patristic age and our own. He argues that sight can be understood in three different ways:[15]

1. The first is as a *perceptual experience*. This is the physiological process whereby the eyes apprehend the physically visible world and transmits that information to the brain. This also includes psychological questions concerning how the brain interprets that information, or is capable of misinterpreting it, or imagining other realities and attributing them to sight.
2. A second way of understanding vision is as a *social practice*. This refers to the historical, philosophical and cultural influences that affect how we understand sight: how we value vision; the things we choose to see and the things we forbid being seen; how we represent and describe the visual; the things we regard as credible for someone to claim to see and the things we don't think it possible to witness; the different scientific and philosophical theories of light and sight that we produce. These change depending on time and place, and Pattison uses Martin Jay's phrase, 'scopic regime',[16] to describe the 'integrated complex of visual theories and practices'[17] which exist at any one time.
3. The third element of sight is its status as a *discursive construct*. By this Pattison means the wide range of visual metaphors used by the Western intellectual

---

15. Stephen Pattison, *Seeing Things: Deepening Relations with Visual Artefacts* (London: SCM Press, 2007), 25–7.
16. Ibid., 26.
17. Martin Jay, 'Scopic Regimes of Modernity', in *Vision and Visuality*, ed. Hal Foster (Seattle: Bay Press, 1988), 4.

tradition to describe knowledge, reasoning and experience of the divine. These revolve around understanding seen as sight and light, and ignorance as darkness, or blindness. In these, an analogy is drawn between our experience of reason, spiritual growth or mystical ecstasy, and human sight as defined by a particular 'scopic regime'.

It strikes me that much modern New Testament scholars' interpretation of the Transfiguration is overwhelmingly governed by the understanding of vision we see in category 1, as a purely *perceptual experience*. Very few explore what Pattison would describe as the scopic regime within which the gospel writers work, and within which their first audience read and understood them. It is clear that modern and New Testament writers inhabit two completely different scopic regimes. Patristic writers share a scopic regime much closer to those who created the New Testament and so understand the wider range of meaning which claims to vision had in the ancient world. I argue that this notion of scopic regime is useful in explaining many of the interpretative differences we will explore through this study between ancient and modern interpretation.

Pattison shows that pre-Cartesian understandings of vision were fundamentally 'haptic'. In other words, sight was understood to establish a participatory, reciprocal relationship between the viewer and that which is seen. This was partly due to the many theories in antiquity explaining the physiological processes of sight in terms of a physical relationship.[18] Amongst the ancient Greeks, the Atomists Leucippus and Democritus held a theory of *intromission* in which physical objects gave off an *eidolon*, an effulgence made of air which reached out to the object and communicated a simulacrum of it back to the eye.[19] Others, including Plato (and later Augustine), by contrast, held a theory of *extramission* in which a form of fire came out of the eye and comingled with daylight coming from the object seen, forming a connection with it.[20] Though frequently very different in their mechanics, most ancient theories of vision involved a connection being established between the eye and the object seen through invisible, but nonetheless physical, particles. These theories came to be extended conceptually to undergird all sight as having a relational, almost tactile quality. Pattison asserts, 'Sight was not abstract, passive

---

18. David C. Lindberg, *Theories of Vision from Al-Kindi to Kepler* (Chicago: University of Chicago Press, 1976), 1–17; David Park, *The Fire Within: A Historical Essay on the Nature and Meaning of Light* (Princeton, NJ: Princeton University Press, 1997), 33–50; Pattison, *Seeing Things*, 42; Martin Jay, *Downcast Eyes: The Denigration of Vision in Twentieth Century Thought* (Berkeley: University of California Press, 1993), 21–32.

19. See David Chidester, *Word and Light: Seeing, Hearing, and Religious Discourse* (Urbana: University of Illinois Press, 1992), 3–6; Lindberg, *Theories of Vision*, 2–3.

20. Chidester, *Word and Light*, 3–5; Francis Cornford, *Plato's Cosmology: The Timaeus of Plato* (London: Routledge and Kegan Paul, 1937), 153; Lindberg, *Theories of Vision*, 3–6; Pattison, *Seeing Things*, 42.

and distant, it was physically relational, a kind of active touching, penetrating and being penetrated.'[21]

Pattison contrasts the scopic regime of antiquity with that of modernity.[22] He notes a significant change brought about by John Locke and René Descartes, in which vision is increasingly divorced from the activity of the mind. The mind becomes the true seat of sight, separate from the physical world, and the eye simply a perceptual organ feeding it with the information it needs to interpret its surroundings. The viewer increasingly stands at an objective distance from what is seen, as a dispassionate, forensic observer of what is physically present. A complete divorce has taken place by the nineteenth century between sight and touch, now seen as entirely separate realms of sense. With the reasoning mind as the organ of vision interpreting its surroundings, claims to subjective vision of something not seen by others becomes categorized as misinterpretation or psychological disturbance. The range of things which may legitimately be described as 'seen' is, therefore, much narrower in modernity than in antiquity. In this way, the modern world's 'ocularcentric' understanding of vision excludes ecstatic vision. Pattison judges the modern view of vision to be an impoverished one: 'This dismissal of "extraordinary" sight may simply be another kind of blindness which confines Westerners' vision to a thin, limited view of reality. ... The arbitrary censorship of apparently non-material "seeing" might be another instance of our unwillingness to deal with vision in its pluriformity.'[23]

These differences in understanding of vision go to the heart of some of the difficulties inherent in modern critical scholarship's treatment of the Transfiguration and its ignoring of pre-critical comment. For the writers of the New Testament, vision was not just an objective judging or measuring of reality external to the human subject. The writers of the New Testament would necessarily see in the Transfiguration's status as a miraculous vision an important *participatory* element largely overlooked in modern criticism. In this, the role of the disciples as witnesses and participants in this experience takes on a much greater importance, in the context of a much more haptic understanding of vision. I argue, therefore, that patristic interpretation is much more sensitized to interpretation of the ways in which the disciples *participate* in our narrative and gives this element a much greater significance.

Patristic comment also lays stress on the Transfiguration as a metaphor for knowledge and vision of the divine in those who read the narrative. The cleavage we have noted between modern and ancient interpreters' theories of vision becomes even more pronounced when we examine the third category of vision described by Pattison, that of vision as a *discursive construct*. Modern historical-critical New Testament scholarship is almost universally uninterested in exploring in the Transfiguration narratives any kind of metaphor or analogy which might

---

21. Pattison, *Seeing Things*, 42.
22. Ibid., 31–6.
23. Ibid., 30–1.

appertain to epistemological questions touching on knowledge, understanding of God or spiritual growth. Critical scholars are concerned more with establishing the historical origins of the text, or with giving a cultural and historical account of theological motifs within our narratives. Ancient commentators, by contrast, see a rich range of analogies between the Transfiguration story and the processes whereby the faithful reader of the narratives experiences God, interprets the scriptures and 'sees' the divine.

A further difference between the scopic regime of our time and that of antiquity is the privileging of words over image in modernity, and of sight over hearing in antiquity, an idea laid out in in Hans Jonas's seminal examination of the question, 'The Nobility of Sight'.[24] Pattison elaborates modernity's scepticism concerning the reliability and value of images, and exaltation of words as communicators of true meaning.[25] David Chidester's fascinating study of sight and hearing in theological discourse comes to similar conclusions. He argues that the ancient world valued sight as a metaphor for connection, continuity, simultaneity, immediacy and relationship. By contrast, hearing was a signifier of discontinuity, temporal delay and ordered sequence. Because of the immediate way in which sight can bestow a panoramic view or infinite vista, it was also seen as the sense which bestowed foreknowledge or insight into the future. Hearing, by contrast, was the linear recorder of past events. Chidester's main focus is on pre-modern theologians' use of synaesthesia as a way of describing experience of the divine which goes beyond and frustrates the categories of sense perception. However, he convincingly shows the priority which sight had in the thinking of the patristic world, especially in writers such as Philo[26] and the principal focus of his work, Augustine.[27] He contrasts this patristic perspective with the exaltation of hearing and words in the Reformation and from the nineteenth century onwards.[28]

Other theorists, too, trace developments in which the value and reliability of sight becomes increasingly questioned and problematized in the twentieth century. Jay's work, *Downcast Eyes*, for example, elaborates the way in which the twentieth-century French philosophical tradition departs from the convictions of antiquity about the primacy of vision and becomes fundamentally sceptical about the epistemological reliability of sight. He reveals changes in theories of vision in a wide range of discourses from Impressionist and post-Impressionist art,[29] to the emergence of feminist critiques of the acquisitive male gaze,[30] to phenomenological

---

24. Hans Jonas, 'The Nobility of Sight: A Study in the Phenomenology of the Senses', *Philosophy and Phenomenological Research* 14, no. 4 (June 1954): 507–19.

25. Pattison, *Seeing Things*, 87–95; see also Barbara Stafford, *Looking Good – Essays on the Virtues of Images* (Cambridge, MA: MIT Press, 1998), esp. 1–17.

26. Chidester, *Word and Light*, 30–43.

27. Ibid., 53–128.

28. Ibid., esp. 121–8; 132–45.

29. Jay, *Downcast Eyes*, 149–70.

30. Ibid., 523–42.

critics such as Jean-Paul Sartre and Maurice Merleau-Ponty.[31] For many of these philosophers, sight is seen as a compromised, fallible and sometimes potentially abusive sense. James Elkins sums up well the scepticism concerning the worth of vision of many recent commentators, when he states,

> Seeing is irrational, inconsistent, and undependable. It is immensely troubled, cousin to blindness and sexuality, and caught up in the threads of the unconscious. Our eyes are not ours to command; they roam where they will and then tell us they have only been where we sent them. No matter how hard we look, we see very little of what we look at.[32]

We see a twofold development in modern thinking about vision. First, the basic scopic regime of post-Enlightenment European discourse shifts to be a Cartesian ocularcentric one (i.e. one which understands seeing much less as tactile participation and more as clinical observation). Second, much examination of vision and sight in the twentieth century has tended to denigrate its worth, questioned its capacity to communicate reality or shown it to be potentially exploitative. These two developments must be recognized as the fundamental cultural background against which historical-critical scholars have commented of the Transfiguration narratives, even if those very critics are unaware of the significance of these shifts, or the degree to which their thinking is influenced by them.

Carruthers: The visual character of memory and thought

The fascinating work Mary Carruthers has undertaken in the area of memory is of huge use to this study, especially in pinpointing ways in which pre-modern readers and hearers of the Transfiguration will have sought to remember, understand and visualize the text and interact with it using the imagination and memory.

Carruthers proposes two important ideas which are crucial for this study. Firstly, she emphasizes the previously underestimated *visual* nature of memory for the ancient and medieval mind. She asserts all memorizing, recalling and thinking to be conceived in the Middle Ages as involving the visualization of image and the use of the imaginative faculties.[33] Second, she argues memory to have been conceived of as a remarkably *creative* concept. Modern understandings of memory tend to prize it simply as the processes by which facts are recalled from

---

31. Ibid., 264–328.
32. James Elkins, *The Object Stares Back: On the Nature of Seeing* (New York: Simon and Schuster, 1996), 11.
33. Mary J. Carruthers, *The Book of Memory: A Study of Memory in Medieval Culture*, 2nd edn, Cambridge Studies in Medieval Literature (Cambridge: Cambridge University Press, 2008), 18–56, 153–95.

the mind like files from a computer. By contrast, in the medieval period, memory was understood as a key nexus in a wide range of ideas such as growth in virtue, speculative thought, meditative prayer and artistic creativity, in addition to the simple recalling of facts.[34]

Carruthers argues that in the ancient world, the memorization of information, ideas and experiences was thought to involve turning sense data into *memory-images* or *phantasmata* which then lodged the information in the brain.[35] This involved turning abstracted ideas, feelings or thoughts into images to be stored physically in the brain. Recalling those ideas, therefore, was about the retrieval of things which had been *visualized*.[36] Indeed, thought was conceived of as the creative constructing, bringing together or collating of visualized memories.

Carruthers explores Augustine's understanding of vision found in his *Commentary on Genesis*.[37] There Augustine outlines three forms of vision: first, the sensible, mortal vision we experience with the physical eyes; second, the direct vision of God accomplished by the mind, which he describes as true *theoria*, the contemplation of true reality which the saints experience in heaven and which few experience in this life; but between those two, mediating a third way is what he describes as 'spiritual' vision, which involves the use of the imaginative faculties to visualize divine realities. This is the form of vision he argues the prophets had when they saw images and forms.

We will notice that the interaction of ancient readers and hearers with the Transfiguration text will frequently involve these Augustinian processes which Carruthers outlines. Use of the imaginative faculties of the mind is a means by which ancient commentators, such as Chrysostom and Anastasius of Sinai, explore the Transfiguration narrative, as we will show in Chapter 6. We will also note in Chapter 5 the way in which Tertullian sees a form of visualized imaginative vision as characterizing the prophets' foreseeing of the Transfiguration. In addition, Chapter 8 will reveal mnemonic devices used by the Utrecht Psalter to conjure the Transfiguration text to mind using visualized memory prompts.

Vision, location and liturgy

A further crucial factor in the reception of visionary texts such as the Transfiguration is also the connection between vision and place, and the culture of religious 'viewing' of the divine which existed in the ancient world.[38] This will

---

34. Mary J. Carruthers, *The Craft of Thought: Meditation, Rhetoric, and the Making of Images, 400–1200*, Cambridge Studies in Medieval Literature (Cambridge: Cambridge University Press, 1998), 7–60, 116–70; *The Book of Memory*, 195–233.

35. Carruthers, *The Book of Memory*, 18–98.

36. Carruthers, *The Craft of Thought*, 56–98.

37. Ibid., 172.

38. Extensive accounts of the rich culture of religious vision, prophecy and encounter with the divine in the ancient world can be found in Robin Lane Fox, *Pagans and Christians*

be of significance when we come to examine early monumental depictions of the Transfiguration in churches. Both the location of the church and the fact that the imagery is located in a liturgical setting affect the way in which viewers in antiquity interacted with those depictions.

Jas Elsner's work on this dynamic reveals the way in which images placed in locations of worship participate in a visuality of reciprocal gaze with the worshipper with a more participatory form of viewing. He identifies two sorts of viewing of art in ancient times. The first is the precursor of Renaissance verisimilitude, where the viewer stands at a distance from an object whose purpose is to look like the thing depicted.[39] However, he contrasts this with what he describes as 'religious' or 'ritual viewing'.[40] This kind of interaction is dependent on the location an image is to be found in, the journey to find it or the rituals of preparation which have taken place before the image is viewed.[41] In this circumstance, the distance between viewer and viewed is broken down and the witness beholds a deity who looks back. Elsner argues as follows:

> In ritual-centred viewing, the grounds for a direct relationship have been prepared. The viewer enters a sacred space set apart from ordinary life, in which the god dwells. In this liminal site, the viewer enters the god's world and likewise the deity intrudes directly into the viewer's world in a highly ritualised contact. The reciprocal gaze of this visuality is a kind of epiphanic fulfilment [for] the pilgrim-viewer, who discovers his or her deepest identity in the presence of the god.[42]

Elsner's idea of 'religious viewing' points to the importance of location and ritual as key determiners of how viewers relate to images and see the divine. This notion of religious viewing will become an important idea for this study when we come to examine early depictions of the Transfiguration, such as those found in St Catherine's Monastery, Sinai, Sant'Apollinare in Classe, Ravenna, or depictions in Roman churches such as Santa Prassede. The location and liturgical context in which images of the Transfiguration were viewed can play a significant role in influencing how they are experienced, what other images or narratives they are

(London: Penguin, 1988), 102–67, 375–418; and Jeffrey B. Pettis, *Seeing the God: Ways of Envisioning the Divine in Ancient Mediterranean Religion*, Perspectives on Philosophy and Religious Thought (Piscataway, NJ: Gorgias Press, 2013).

39. Jas Elsner, 'Between Mimesis and Divine Power', in *Visuality before and beyond the Renaissance: Seeing as Others Saw*, ed. Robert Nelson (Cambridge: Cambridge University Press, 2000), 45–52.

40. Ibid., 52–60.

41. See also Georgia Frank, 'The Pilgrim's gaze in the age before Icons', in *Visuality before and beyond the Renaissance*, 98–109.

42. Elsner, 'Between Mimesis and Divine Power', 61.

placed with and the theological ideas that viewing draws from the experience. Robert Nelson emphasizes this dynamic when commenting on vision in ancient Byzantium:

> Unlike the omnipresent photographic eye of our world, vision ... was not merely mechanistic or physical. It was also moral and situational, so that the act of seeing, like our notion of interpretation, depended upon who you were and when, where, and how you saw.[43]

Judith Kovacs and Christopher Rowland's ideas concerning what they term the 'actualization'[44] of visionary texts are also useful. Kovacs and Rowland's work on the book of Revelation distinguishes between two approaches. First, there are allegorical attempts to interpret the visions described in the book of the Apocalypse which are intended to 'decode' an unchanging, clear message. However, they also detect interpreters who use its descriptions of apocalyptic vision as a lens through which to understand their present circumstances. It is during this second process that Kovacs and Rowland argue that the visionary text of the book of Revelation is 'actualized' in the lives of those contemplating it. I argue that ancient images of the Transfiguration frequently undergo similar processes of 'actualization' during the celebration of the liturgy in which the eschatological and physical divide between the life of heaven and earth is held to be broken down for the worshipper, often in locations decorated with imagery from the book of Revelation.

Although commenting on later apocalyptic writings in a Byzantine context, Jane Baun has also pointed to the way in which the imagery employed by ancient visionary texts sometimes makes more sense to the modern mind when 'viewed' as if in a sacred building. She speaks of 'thinking "architecturally"' as a 'way to approximate the experience of time and space within apocalypses'.[45] She argues that a liturgical context provides a series of episodic glimpses in which imagery, words, action and ideas are momentarily brought together coherently.[46]

The eucharistic context of many of the mosaic depictions of the Transfiguration which will be examined in this study represents a crucial perspective in which those present in the church celebrating the liturgy conceive of themselves as experiencing the reality depicted before them.

---

43. Robert Nelson, 'To Say and to See', in *Visuality before and beyond the Renaissance*, 158.
44. Judith Kovacs and Christopher Rowland, *Revelation: the Apocalypse of Jesus Christ* (Oxford: Blackwell, 2004), 7–11.
45. Jane Baun, *Tales from another Byzantium: Celestial Journey and Local Community in the Medieval Greek Apocrypha* (Cambridge: Cambridge University Press, 2007), 152.
46. Ibid., esp. 151–62.

Visionary visual exegesis

A further question prompted by examination of the reception of the Transfiguration is whether there is something about visual depiction which can interpret, present and explore visionary texts better than verbal description or written analysis. Both Chidester and Natasha O'Hear have written extensively in this area.

Chidester points to the capacity for visual depictions of narratives to communicate several ideas, narratives and motifs at once. One of the most important ideas he formulates is that a dichotomy existed in the patristic mind between two modes of perception. The reading, hearing and understanding of words was orientated towards expressing or presenting ideas in terms of *order* and *sequence*. Vision, however, and the seeing of light was orientated towards expressing ideas in terms of a sense of *simultaneity*. Chidester reveals many examples of ancient comment in which verbal perception expresses discontinuity, distance, difference, temporal sequence and prioritized order. By contrast, vision is shown by him to convey a sense of continuity, union, connection, and to be capable of expressing the spatial rather than the temporal.[47] Baun has made similar points in her work on medieval Greek apocalypses. She points to the way in which description of visionary experience often frustrates modern scholars' attempts to order, define and categorize those accounts in terms of linear time and space.[48]

A characteristic of many early Western images of the Transfiguration is their ability to express several theological motifs *simultaneously*. Indeed, I would argue it is precisely their ability to present many ideas at once that has frequently made them difficult for modern commentators to interpret. A writer can only comment on the Transfiguration as evoking ideas in a temporal order, which will inevitably be prioritized by the sequence in which they are discussed. Visual interpreters, by contrast, can create an image which evokes them simultaneously in a way which resists prioritizing and categorizing, and which is frequently more allusive and suggestive in the way in which it accomplishes that. We will see this dynamic present in the great apse mosaic depictions of the Transfiguration in Classe, Santa Prassede and Santi Nereo e Achilleo where different biblical and visionary texts are interpreted in the light of each other and help in a creative, if at times complex, hermeneutic tension.

Chidester reveals the act of viewing a series of images in the ancient world to have involved a presupposition of continuity, simultaneity, cohesion and compatibility in the way in which they relate to each other. It was less concerned with the forensic diagnosing of origins, the pinpointing of one single theme to the

---

47. He notes this distinction, in chapter 2 of *Word and Light*, particularly in Philo, and in debate around the Arian controversy. See Chidester, *Word and Light*, 25–50.
48. Baun, *Tales from another Byzantium*, esp. 133–51.

exclusion of others, or the spotting of inconsistencies and theological tensions, in the way that modern comment on those images sometimes is.

The excellent work of O'Hear has also shed great light on some of the findings of this study in relation to the depiction of texts reporting visionary experience. O'Hear convincingly shows in her studies of the reception of the book of the Apocalypse that exegesis of the book of Revelation has all too often taken place without recognition of the visual nature of the imagery the text uses to express itself, and the visionary character of the experience the narrator claims lies behind it.[49] O'Hear wonders whether there is something about the idiom of visual artistic interpretation which is better suited to expressing the content of the book of Revelation in a way that textual, verbal interpretation cannot. She goes further, though, and asks whether 'images of the text may offer a particular insight that a text either has not or cannot'.[50] She asks, in other words, whether there is something about the *visionary* nature of the text (i.e. that it claims to be the product of a vision, of something seen) that visual interpretation is capable of communicating best. O'Hear skilfully uses Hans-Georg Gadamer's distinction between *Vorstellung* (literalistic representation) and *Darstellung* (an image which brings forth in the mind the essence – the *Sache selbst* – of the thing being visualized)[51] as a useful tool to categorize and analyse several images of the book of Revelation. She concludes that in some depictions of the book of Revelation we can detect what she coins as 'visionary visual exegesis'. This is imagery which has the ability to 'connect the viewer with the visionary essence of the Book of Revelation'.[52]

I want to ponder whether, within O'Hear's terms, we see a form of visionary visual exegesis emerge in early depictions of the Transfiguration, especially when we see it compared with portions of Revelation 21 and 22 in churches explored in Chapter 8, such as Santa Prassede, Santa Maria in Domnica and in the Utrecht Psalter. By combining Revelation 21 with elements from the Transfiguration narratives, artists point to a quality within both texts which can be articulated *visually* and which is *visionary* in origin. In other words, both Revelation 21 and the Transfiguration narratives should be seen as reporting in words a visionary experience of a visual nature. There exists behind the text a visionary experience, recounted, possibly imperfectly by a narrative, which the artist chooses now to express using a visual medium. By doing this, the artist judges the character of the two narratives to be defined not just by imagery which may be expressed or depicted visually but also that this visual character stems from a similar or parallel visionary experience.

---

49. Natasha O'Hear, *Contrasting Images of the Book of Revelation in Late Medieval and EarlyModern Art: A Case Study in Visual Exegesis*, Oxford Theological Monographs (Oxford: Oxford University Press, 2011).

50. Ibid., 226.

51. Ibid., 213–18.

52. Ibid., 226.

Conclusions

An examination of a range of theorists in the realm of visual culture and hermeneutics reveals important insights which will characterize the approach of this study and act as a lens through which material will be examined.

The first and most important is an awareness of the cultural differences that exist between our age and antiquity, especially with regard to understandings of vision and sight. This revolves around, in Jay's terminology, different scopic regimes: a modern one which claims to value only sight of that which can be empirically proven but which in the twentieth century paradoxically became more and more sceptical about the epistemological worth of sight; and a pre-Cartesian one which emphasizes vision as a mode of participation, connection and relationship.

Second, when one appreciates the 'scopic regime' of the culture in which the New Testament emerged, one notes the way in which the Transfiguration becomes a nexus for a wider range of interpretive discourse in antiquity than in modernity. It is seen as an analogy for ideas such as participation in the divine, the exercise of human reason, divine revelation and spiritual growth in virtue. Patristic commentators speak from within a scopic regime which is much closer to that of the New Testament. This prompts them to be more sensitive to visionary elements within that story, especially those found within Luke's version, whose significance is sometimes overlooked or misunderstood by historical-critical scholars.

Third, it is clear that ancient interaction with visionary texts involves processes of thought, reflection and interpretation which are dependent on very 'visual' understandings of those processes. Thought and memory were conceived as the creative process of visualizing ideas. In addition, the location or liturgical context in which an image of the Transfiguration is experienced plays a crucial part in how the narrative is visualized by early readers, hearers and viewers. This dynamic is very important for ancient interpretation but is attended to seldom in historical-critical approaches to the narrative.

Fourth, we should not be surprised to see a tendency in the patristic period which interprets one visionary text in terms of another. We should expect to see the Transfiguration compared with passages from texts such as the book of Revelation and prophetic narratives from the Old Testament. Whilst historical-critical scholars see little historical connection between these texts, ancient commentators see deep connections between the claimed visionary origins of such narratives and the visual imagery used by them. Depiction of these texts participates in a process of visionary visual exegesis, in which the visionary character of the incident is expressed through visual representation and interpretation.

These insights into the presuppositions of ancient commentators and artists will be crucial to the way in which this study explores patristic engagement with the Transfiguration text. As we embark on an extensive survey of the synoptic Transfiguration texts themselves, and early comment and depiction of the Transfiguration, this study will keep constantly in mind the key characteristics of the different scopic regimes from which the texts and its reception emerges.

It will also be necessary to acknowledge the power of image to express complex hermeneutic engagement and the importance of liturgical and geographic contexts. In other words, we will keep at the forefront of our minds the vivid creativity of the imaginative processes which ancient readers used to engage with visionary texts.

Chapter 2

AN EXAMINATION OF THE NEW TESTAMENT SYNOPTIC TRANSFIGURATION NARRATIVES

Our examination of the Transfiguration and its reception must begin with a careful study of the New Testament narratives themselves. Substantial redactional differences exist between the three synoptic accounts. I argue that the Lucan version is not only very distinct from the Matthean and Marcan accounts but also exercises a particularly strong influence on Latin interpretation and depiction of the Transfiguration. This influence can be seen through the detection of theological themes, narrative elements and particular vocabulary which are only present in Luke and which frequently appertain to his understanding of vision. These, in turn, reveal the scopic regime within which Luke is working. The following chapter seeks to delineate, therefore, the differences and particular theological focuses of the synoptic narratives with particular attentiveness to visionary language and what it tells us about the visual culture and scopic regime within which the gospel writers lived. We begin with the first written account of the Transfiguration created, that of the Gospel of Mark.

Mk 9.2-8

Mark places his Transfiguration narrative within the context of Peter's Confession at Caesarea Philippi, along with speculation concerning Jesus' identity, the suffering and Resurrection he must undergo and his return in judgement. Mark's Transfiguration is preceded by the assertion, at Mk 9.1, that some of those standing around will not taste death before seeing 'the Kingdom of God has come with power'. Interpretation of the Transfiguration as embodying the Kingdom coming with power will be a frequent one in patristic interpretation.[1] By contrast, historical-critical comment frequently denies any historical connection

---

1. For a summary of patristic reception of the verse with regard to the Transfiguration, see Martin Künzi, *Das Naherwartungslogion Markus 9,1* (Tübingen: Mohr, 1977), esp. 9–11 (Greek patristic reception) and 23–4, 35–6 (Latin patristic reception).

between the two, seeing the logion at Mk 9.1 referring, in origin, to the Parousia,[2] the Resurrection[3] or to the revealing of the Kingdom through Jesus' miracles.[4] Modern commentators tend to deny that the two episodes are historically linked.[5]

The location of the mountain of Transfiguration in Mark is unclear. According to Mk 8.27, Peter's Confession takes place somewhere on the road in the region of Caesarea Philippi. The Transfiguration happens six days later and so could be anywhere within six days' travel of that place. Origen is the first to identify the hill as Tabor, largely as the result of speculation in the light of Ps. 89.12,[6] which establishes a broad patristic consensus. By contrast, modern critical scholarship has been much more reticent about identifying the Mount of Transfiguration. However, arguments have been made for Mount Hermon as a candidate, particularly because of its height, closer location to Caesarea Philippi and association with visionary cultic activity in the past,[7] as have arguments for Mount Meron for similar reasons.[8] Mounts Sinai (and Moriah) and Carmel have been proposed simply because of their association with Moses and Elijah, though these suggestions have not gained support.[9]

We see emerge in Mark 9 the basic Transfiguration narrative which Matthew and Luke in their turn will redact. Mark 9.2 recounts Jesus taking Peter, James and John up to a high mountain in order to be alone. Patristic commentators will frequently speculate about the reason for the choice of those three, but no canonical gospel explicitly comments on the question. This question has evoked very little interest in modern interpretation. Mark then describes in the same verse a change which takes place to Jesus' appearance in the passive, as being 'metamorphosed'

---

2. Adela Yarbro Collins, *Mark: A Commentary* (Minneapolis, MN: Fortress Press, 2007), 412; Norman Perrin, *The Kingdom of God in the Teaching of Jesus*, New Testament Library (London: SCM Press, 1963), 67–8.

3. Erich Klostermann, *Das Markusevangelium Erklärt* (Tübingen: Mohr, 1950), 86.

4. Craig A. Evans, *Mark 8:27-16:20* (Nashville: Thomas Nelson, 2001), 28–9.

5. The only voice I have been able to find in modern scholarship to argue for the reading of the Transfiguration as a fulfillment of Mk 9.1 is Bruce Chilton, 'The Transfiguration: Dominical Assurance and Apostolic Vision', *New Testament Studies* 27 (1980): 115–24.

6. Origen, *Hom Ps 88*, 13 (PG 12, 1548).

7. Joseph Klausner, *Jesus of Nazareth: His Life, Times, and Teaching* (London: George Allen & Unwin, 1925), 303; George Nickelsburg, 'Enoch, Levi, and Peter: Recipients of Revelation in Upper Galilee', *Journal of Biblical Literature* 100, no. 4 (1981): 575–600; Henry Barclay Swete, *The Gospel According to St. Mark* (London: Macmillan, 1927), 187.

8. Walter Liefeld, 'Theological Motifs in the Transfiguration Narrative', in *New Dimensions in New Testament Study*, ed. R. N. Logenecker and M. C. Tenney (Grand Rapids, MI: Zondervan, 1974), esp. 167, footnote 27.

9. For a summary of this debate, see W. D. Davies and Dale C. Allison, *A Critical and Exegetical Commentary on the Gospel According to Saint Matthew* (Edinburgh: T&T Clark, 1988), vol. 2, 695.

before his chosen witnesses. Mark describes this metamorphosis in terms of outward appearance and as solely concerning the colour and aspect of Jesus' clothing. He describes this at Mk 9.3 as becoming 'dazzling, very white'. Though there is no direct mention of light or glory in Mark, there is possibly implicit in the insistence on Jesus' clothes being 'dazzling' some notion of light in the sense of intense whiteness. The narrator also qualifies this brightness as having a non-earthly origin, being of a quality that no human fuller could achieve.

Mark continues to use language appertaining to the sense of sight to punctuate his narrative, as Moses and Elijah are described as appearing before the disciples. Although depiction of this scene throughout art history will frequently place Moses and Elijah on either side of Jesus, with the disciples below,[10] no mention is made by Mark of their relative position.

Mark then describes Peter ejaculating, 'Rabbi, it is good for us to be here,' and proposing at Mk 9.5 the construction of three 'σκηνάς' ('tents' or 'tabernacles'), one each for Jesus, Moses and Elijah (Mk 9.5). The range of references this word 'tabernacles' could be evoking is the focus of extensive speculation in both modern and ancient exegesis. Some commentators point to traditions associated with vision of the dwelling of God in heaven described as a tabernacle, such as we see in Rev. 21.3, and of these tents being reference to the dwellings of the just in heaven such as we see in *1 Enoch* 39;[11] others see echoes of Sukkoth motifs, and through those some sort of comparison with the Jerusalem Temple;[12] further echoes of Moses have also been discussed in relation to possible evocation of the Tent of Meeting.[13] Mark's only response to this suggestion is the comment that Peter didn't

---

10. See Andreas Andreopoulos, *Metamorphosis: The Transfiguration in Byzantine Theology and Iconography* (Crestwood, NY: St Vladimir's Seminary Press, 2005), 677–82.

11. E.g. John PaulHeil, *The Transfiguration of Jesus: Narrative Meaning and Function of Mark 9:2-8, Matt 17:1-8 and Luke 9:28-36* (Rome: Editrice Pontificio Istituto Biblico, 2000), 115-27; E. Lohmeyer, 'Die Verklärung Jesu nach dem Markus-Evangelium', *Zeitschrift für Neutestamentliche Wissenschaft* 21 (1922): 185–215, esp. 194.

12. E.g. Heinrich Baltensweiler, *Die Verklärung Jesu; Historisches Ereignis Und Synoptische Berichte* (Zürich: Zwingli-Verlag, 1959), 37–61 and 130; Crispin Fletcher-Louis, 'The Revelation of the Sacral Son of Man: The Genre, History of Religions Context, and Meaning of the Transfiguration', in *Auferstehung-Resurrection: 4th Durham-Tübingen Research Symposium: Resurrection, Transfiguration, and Exaltation in the Old Testament, Ancient Judaism, and Early Christianity*, ed. H. Lichtenberger (Tübingen: Mohr Siebeck, 2001), 261–7; Lohmeyer, 'Die Verkärung Jesu', 191–6; Harald Riesenfeld, *Jésus Transfiguré: L'arrière-plan récit évangélique de la Transfiguration de Notre-Seigneur* (Copenhagen: E. Munksgaard, 1947), esp. 146–205, 265–80; William Stegner, 'The Use of Scripture in Two Early Narratives of Early Jewish Christianity (Mt 4.1-11; Mk 9.2-8)', in *Early Christian Interpretation of the Scriptures of Israel: Investigations and Proposals*, ed. Craig A. Evans and James Sanders, JSNT Suppl. 148, SSEJC 5 (Sheffield: Sheffield University Press, 1997), 116.

13. E.g. Davies and Allison, *Gospel According to Saint Matthew*, 699–700; Heil, *Transfiguration of Jesus*, 117.

know what to say, for he and the other disciples were afraid (Mk 9.6). This has frequently been seen as a narratorial criticism of Peter's comment.[14] However, the only thing Mark categorically says is that fear was the reason he did not know what to say. Mark does not explicitly state that Peter's comment was misguided or inappropriate. The exact reason for the sudden appearance of this fear is unclear in Mark's text. It could be a response to the change in Jesus' appearance which has already happened, or it could be a development in the narrative responding to the appearance of the cloud.

Mark then describes the appearance of a cloud which overshadows 'them'. It is unclear who precisely this 'them' is. It could refer to Jesus, Moses and Elijah, the subject of Peter's proposal.[15] It could also refer just to the disciples, who are the subject of the previous clause ('for they were terrified'). Alternatively it could describe the cloud as engulfing the whole group on the mountain, and refer to everyone mentioned from v. 4 onwards.[16] In Mark's narrative, all movement is on the part of the cloud which does the overshadowing, whilst the disciples remain static.

From this cloud emerges a voice addressed to those witnessing the Transfiguration referring to Jesus in the third person as 'my son, the Beloved' and instructing them to listen to him. This closely echoes the words Mark recounts heard at Mk 1.11, except that at the Baptism, they are addressed to Jesus in the second person and declare him to be, in addition, the one in whom the Father delights. These words have prompted some to hear echoes of the Isaac narrative from Genesis 22 in the Transfiguration.[17]

Finally, Mark renews reference to the sense of sight. The disciples look around but find they no longer see anyone with them other than Jesus. Mark seems to understand the Transfiguration as concluded by the point at which Moses and

---

14. E.g. Evans, *Mark 8:27-16:20*, 37; Joel Marcus, *Mark 8-16: A New Translation with Introduction and Commentary*, The Anchor Yale Bible (New Haven, CT: Yale University Press, 2009), 638.

15. As argued by Joachim Gnilka, *Das Evangelium nach Markus* (Zürich: Benziger, 1978), vol. 2, 35; Marcus, *Mark 8-16*, 634; M. Öhler, 'Die Verklärung (Mk 9.1-8): die Ankunft der Herrschaft Gottes auf der Erde', *Novum Testamentum* 38 (1996): 210–11; and Albrecht Öpke, 'Νεφέλη', in *Theological Dictionary of the New Testament*, vol. 4, ed. Gerhard Kittel (Grand Rapids, MI: Eerdmans, 1969), 908.

16. As argued by R. T. France, *The Gospel of Mark: A Commentary on the Greek Text*, The New International Greek Testament Commentary (Grand Rapids, MI: Eerdmans, 2002), 354; and Dieter Zeller, 'Bedeutung und religionsgeschichtlicher Hintergrund der Verwandlung Jesu', in *Authenticating the Activities of Jesus*, ed. Bruce Chilton and Craig A. Evans (Leiden: Brill, 1999), 308–9.

17. Ernest Best, *The Temptation and the Passion: The Markan Soteriology* (Cambridge: Cambridge University Press, 1965), 169–73; David Flusser, *Jesus* (New York: Herder, 1969), 95–7.

Elijah are no longer to be seen. Nothing whatsoever is said by Mark about Jesus' appearance reverting back to that which he had before the Transfiguration.

Mark concludes his Transfiguration with a descent from the mountain, in which Jesus instructs the disciples to tell nobody of the experience until the Son of Man rises from the dead. Mark again makes reference to the incident in terms of visual apprehension, by describing the Transfiguration at Mk 9.9 as 'ἃ εἶδον', 'things which they had seen'. There then ensues a discussion concerning Elijah's coming. Mark, by contrast with Luke, who will remove this whole section, identifies Elijah with John the Baptist. Matthew will make this identification all the more clear by his narratorial comment at Mt. 17.13.

Conclusions

From this initial outlining of the earliest Marcan Transfiguration narrative, several important elements should be noted. First, language appertaining to the human senses of sight and hearing recurs frequently and is something the temporal sequence of the narrative is dependent on. The key moments of progression in the narrative are always accompanied by renewed sensual perception: first Jesus' clothing changes *colour and appearance* (Mk 9.3); then Moses and Elijah *appear* before the disciples (Mk 9.4); they *hear* the voice from the cloud (Mk 9. 7); then they look around themselves and *see* nobody but Jesus (Mk 9.8); finally, Jesus refers to the whole experience as 'things seen' (Mk 9.9) by them; in addition, reading the Transfiguration in fulfilment of Mk 9.1 as *seeing* the Kingdom come is a frequent patristic topos, but one rejected by many modern commentators. A series of ambiguities also exists within Mark's text which will not necessarily be resolved by later redaction by Matthew and Luke. There remains, for example, uncertainty concerning who the 'them' of Mk 9.7 refers to, and whom and how the cloud overshadows. In addition, the range of ideas or scriptural parallels which the mention of 'tabernacles' could be intended to evoke is debated. It is also unclear whether we are to understand Peter's comment as gravely inappropriate or as an inoffensive comment made in a moment of confusion.

Mt. 17.1-8

The account we read in Matthew of the Transfiguration has had significant influence in the history of interpretation by virtue of that gospel's canonical primacy. This has meant that in both East and West it has tended to be the version read at the Eucharist on the Feast Day of the Transfiguration[18] and on other occasions such as the Saturday of the second week of Lent in the West.

18. See Richard Pfaff, *New Liturgical Feasts in Later Medieval England* (Oxford: Clarendon Press, 1970), 13–39.

Matthew's account preserves much of Mark's narrative context. Matthew adds Jesus' more extended interaction with Peter after his Confession, conferring on him the Keys of the Kingdom of Heaven (Mt. 17.19). Matthew also makes more explicit some of Mark's eschatological speculation. He links the coming of the Son of Man with the Parousia at Mt. 16.28. He also makes clearer the reference to John the Baptist in the discussion of Elijah after the Transfiguration (Mt. 17.10-13). Matthew retains Mark's ambiguity concerning location, stating only that it was six days after Peter's Confession, which was in the district of Casearea Philippi (Mt. 16.13; cf. Mt. 17.1).

Matthew introduces a series of new elements to the narrative. The most significant is his insistence that Jesus' metamorphosis is not just restricted to his clothing but also involves his body shining brightly. Matthew describes Jesus' face as shining 'like the sun' (Mt. 17.2) and removes Mark's mention of an earthly fuller, instead describing Jesus' clothing as bright as the light. It is Matthew, therefore, who most explicitly introduces the language of light to the Transfiguration narratives. His association of this with Jesus' face will be seen by both modern and patristic authors to evoke a wide range of interpretations associated with Sinai and Moses traditions.[19]

Matthew treats Peter's words differently from Mark. He removes any mention of Peter not knowing what to say and adds 'if you wish' to Peter's suggestion. That the three booths are not created implies it is *not* what Jesus wishes. This is the first explicitly negative comment on the appropriateness of Peter's suggestion. Peter's comment is much more closely linked with the appearance of the cloud, which is now described as appearing *whilst* Peter is speaking at Mt. 17.5.

Matthew continues his addition of motifs connected with light when he describes the overshadowing cloud as 'bright' (Mt. 17.5). However, the ambiguity seen in Mark's narrative concerning precisely who is overshadowed is maintained by Matthew. Matthew's removal of Peter not knowing what to say means that the last people to be referred to before the 'them' of Mt. 17.5 are Moses and Elijah. One could argue, therefore, Matthew implies the cloud only overshadows Moses and Elijah, though this is ultimately unclear. Matthew alters Mark's words uttered from the cloud, so that Jesus is declared not just to be the beloved Son but also the one in whom the Father delights. Of all the synoptic evangelists, Matthew most closely ties the Baptism to the Transfiguration by conforming the words spoken at his Baptism narrative and those heard at the Transfiguration to each other.

The hearing of this voice is then followed by a motif only found in Matthew, namely the disciples' falling on their faces to the ground with fear. This will be a crucial element of many artistic depictions of the Transfiguration.[20] It is important

---

19. For a brief summary of patristic comment, see, John Anthony McGuckin, *The Transfiguration of Christ in Scripture and Tradition* (Lewiston, NY: Edwin Mellen Press, 1986), 12-19, 46-7; for an excellent summary of modern comment on this subject, see, Marcus, *Mark 8-16*, 1114.

20. Andreopoulos, *Metamorphosis*, 155-60; Manfred Krüger, *Die Verklärung auf dem Berge: Erkenntnis und Kunst* (Hildesheim: Georg Olms Verlag, 2003), 59-60.

to note, however, that in Matthew it concludes the episode. Depictions which show the disciples on their faces, therefore, are representing a moment at the *end* of the narrative. It is also important to note the emergence in Matthew of the notion that this is a visionary experience which overwhelms sight. Matthew's text itself presents the falling down as a consequence of terror at *hearing* the voice (Mt. 17.6) rather than having their vision overwhelmed. Matthew does, however, signal the end of the vision by having the disciples raise their eyes once Jesus touches them and calls them to rise. The end of the Matthean Transfiguration vision is signalled paradoxically by the restoration of the disciples' ability to raise and use their eyes. We have in the Matthean version the seeds of an important strand of interpretation seeing the Transfiguration as an experience whose visionary quality leads to the overwhelming of the physical faculties of sight and hearing, or which needs special grace to make it bearable.

Of great significance is Matthew's interpretation at Mt. 17.9 of the Transfiguration as 'ὅραμα', a 'vision', a *hapax legomenon* amongst the synoptic gospels. The precise meaning of this word is debated by many modern commentators: some point to Matthew's use of it as implying nothing more than a concrete terrestrial sight, or spectacle;[21] whereas others see it as interpreting the Transfiguration as an ecstatic revelation pointing forward to the Resurrection.[22] It is intriguing that Luke uses the word 'ὅραμα' extensively to refer to a wide range of ecstatic, visionary and dreamlike incidents in Acts[23] yet does not use it to describe his Transfiguration narrative.

Conclusions

Although the basic narrative in Matthew's Transfiguration remains very similar to Mark's, we see in his redaction the addition of a number of new motifs such as an emphasis on light in the description of Jesus' face shining, with its evoking of Moses and Sinai, and the topos of the disciples' falling down in fear. Both of these elements will play an important role in the history of artistic interpretation. Matthew foregrounds, but also problematises, the Transfiguration's visionary status and the disciples' participation in it. He describes, for example, the whole experience explicitly as a 'vision'. However, he invests this term with a considerable degree of complexity by hinting that this vision experience actually overwhelms

---

21. Davies and Allison, *Gospel According to Saint Matthew*, 713; Donald Alfred Hagner, *Matthew 14-28*, Word Biblical Commentary (Dallas, TX: Word Books, 1995), 498.

22. Daniel J. Harrington, *The Gospel of Matthew*, Sacra Pagina Series (Collegeville, MN: Liturgical Press, 1991), 254; Wolfgang Wiefel, *Das Evangelium nach Matthäus* (Leipzig: Evangelische Verlagsanstalt, 1998), 310.

23. These include description of Moses's experience of the Burning Bush (Acts 7.31), several elements of Paul's conversion (Acts 9.10; 9.12), Peter's house top vision (Acts 10.3, 17, 19; 11.5) and escape from prison (Acts 12.9), along with various revelations to Paul in dreams (Acts 16.9, 10; 18.9).

the disciples' faculty of physical sight. He also retains ambiguity concerning who is overshadowed by the cloud.

Lk. 9.28-36

Luke uses the Transfiguration, just as Mark does, as a narrative turning point, but for him, this is part of the conclusion of the Galilean ministry and the turning to Jerusalem. For Luke, therefore, the Transfiguration confirms Jesus' identity as declared by Peter (Lk. 9.20) but defines that against the backdrop of his rejection, death and 'taking up' in Jerusalem, to which the narrative turns decisively at Lk. 9.51.

Luke introduces a number of new motifs to the Transfiguration narrative and also marks a significant reorganization of the sequence of events making this a much more radical redaction of Mark's text than Matthew's.

Luke removes the discussion concerning Elijah from the descent from the mountain.[24] He also alters Mark's mention of six days at the beginning of his narrative and replaces it with reference to the events happening on the eighth day. This will be the focus of much patristic comment, which will argue that the synoptic accounts are, contrary to surface appearances, not in disagreement with each other on this matter. Patristic writers will often read a wide range of complex numerologies or allusions to the Resurrection and eighth-day recreation motifs into Luke's reference to eight days.[25] By contrast, modern scholarship tends to see this as a simple Lucan re-expressing in different terms of the same period of time mentioned by Mark and consequently to be of little significance.[26] Heinrich Baltensweiler[27] and Harald Riesenfeld,[28] for whom, in different ways, the six-day

---

24. Luke inhabits an ambiguous position somewhere between the assertions by Mark and Matthew that John is Elijah returned (Mt. 17.10-13; Mk 10-13), and the insistence on the part of the writer of the Fourth Gospel that John is not Elijah (Jn 1.21). For further discussion, see Raymond Edward Brown, *The Gospel According to John*, The Anchor Bible (Garden City, NY: Doubleday, 1966), xliv–xlvii; Joseph A. Fitzmyer, *The Gospel According to Luke (I-IX)*, The Anchor Bible (Garden City, NY: Doubleday, 1981), 87–9; Barbara Shellard, *New Light on Luke: Its Purpose, Sources and Literary Context* (London: Sheffield Academic Press, 2002), 215–18.

25. See McGuckin, *Transfiguration of Christ*, 122–3.

26. Fitzmyer, *Gospel According to Luke (I-IX)*, 797; I. Howard Marshall, *The Gospel of Luke: A Commentary on the Greek Text* (Exeter: Paternoster, 1978), 382; John Nolland, *Luke*, Word Biblical Commentary (Dallas, TX: Word Books, 1989), vol. 2, 497.

27. Baltensweiler, *Die Verklärung Jesu*, 46–51, sees the reference to six days as pointing to Jesus wanting to spend the seventh day of Sukkoth on the mountain.

28. Riesenfeld, *Jésus Transfiguré*, 276–7, sees the six days as a reference to the length of time between the Day of Atonement and Feast of Tabernacles.

reference is a crucial pointer to Sukkoth connections, similarly play down Luke's mention of eight days as unimportant.

A significant Lucan characteristic is his introduction of the motif of prayer. This is described as the purpose of Jesus' retreat up the mountain with the Three. Prayer is the very activity which Luke claims accompanies the alteration in Jesus' appearance at Lk. 9.29. Luke also removes Mark's language of metamorphosis. Instead, he describes the 'appearance' of Jesus' face altering and becoming 'different' or 'other'. Luke retains the mention of Jesus' clothing becoming bright but describes it as 'ἐξαστράπτων', 'sparkling like lightening'. So, whilst Luke does, therefore, mention a change in Jesus' body, he doesn't describe what it was like other than 'different', and he only attaches mention of light to Jesus' clothing.

The most significant difference in the Lucan narrative is a substantial alteration of the sequence concerning Moses's and Elijah's appearance, in which the vision is divided into two by a period of sleepiness on the part of the disciples. Two men are described at Lk. 9.30 appearing in conversation with Jesus, introduced with the words 'ἰδοὺ ἄνδρες δύο', 'behold two men'. On two other occasions, Luke uses this phrase[29] to introduce angelic men in his Resurrection and Ascension accounts.[30] The narratorial voice then describes these two men as Moses and Elijah. These two are then referred to in 9.31 as appearing 'in glory'. Luke is the only evangelist to introduce the term 'δόξα'. This first mention of glory does not refer to Jesus directly, but rather to the two prophets.

Luke then introduces one of the most enigmatic references in his narrative, namely the topic of conversation on the mountain, referring to it as 'τὴν ἔξοδον', the 'exodus' Jesus will accomplish in Jerusalem. The precise meaning of this is debated. In patristic comment it will generally be seen as a reference to Christ's passion and death.[31] Modern scholars have tended to see a wider range of possible references. Some simply see the language of Lk. 9.31 as portraying Jesus as a Mosaic prophet-like figure and evoking an Exodus typology.[32] Others have used this Exodus motif as part of feminist liberationist readings.[33] Some have seen the Exodus being one

---

29. c.f. Lk. 24.4 and Acts 1.10.

30. For several examples of Luke linking the Transfiguration to the Ascension, see J. G. Davies, 'Prefigurement of the Ascension in the Third Gospel', *Journal of Theological Studies* 6, no. 2 (1955): 229–33.

31. See McGuckin, *Transfiguration of Christ*, 115–16.

32. Luke Timothy Johnson, *The Literary Function of Possessions in Luke-Acts* (Missoula, MT: Scholars Press, 1977), 70–6; J. Manek, 'The New Exodus in the Books of Luke', *Novum Testamentum* 2 (1958): 8–23; David Moessner, 'Luke 9.1-50: Luke's Preview of the Journey of the Prophet Like Moses of Deuteronomy', *Society of Biblical Literature* 102 (1983): 575–605; David Moessner, 'Jesus and the "Wilderness Generation": The Death of the Prophet Like Moses According to Luke', in *S.B.L. 1982 Seminar Papers*, ed. Kent Richards (Chico, CA: Scholars, 1982), 319–40; David W. Pao, *Acts and the Isaianic New Exodus* (Tübingen: Mohr Siebeck, 2000), 87.

33. S. H. Ringe, 'Luke 9.28-36: The Beginning of an Exodus', *Semeia* 28 (1983): 81–99.

of bondage to Satan.[34] Although some see it as merely a synonym for Jesus' death,[35] echoing usage in 2 Pet. 1.15 and Wis. 3.2 and 7.6, large numbers of modern scholars assert that it probably includes Jesus' Resurrection and Ascension.[36] This interpretation would seem to reflect Luke's emphasis on the Ascension as the point of his going to Jerusalem, and his use of the language of being 'taken up' as short hand for his Passion, Resurrection and Ascension at Lk. 9.51.

After this discussion, Luke adds an interlude in which the disciples are described as weighed down by sleepiness. It is unclear whether this description refers back to the disciples' state before the beginning of the episode (in other words, whether we should understand them as waking at the beginning of the Transfiguration) or whether it describes something happening halfway through the Transfiguration, after their first glimpse of glory. It is also unclear whether Luke's use of 'διαγρηγορήσαντες' at Lk. 9.32 to describe their becoming wakeful after being 'weighed down by sleep' implies they actually fall fully asleep[37] and are awoken,[38] or whether it suggests, rather, they enter a drowsy state[39] in which they are sleepy but nonetheless manage to stay awake.[40] Violet MacDermot has pointed

34. Susan Garrett, 'Exodus from Bondage: Luke 9.31 and Acts 12.1-24', *Catholic Biblical Quarterly* 52 (1990): 656–80.

35. Wilhelm Michaelis, 'Είσ– Έξ– Διεξοδος', in *Theological Dictionary of the New Testament*, vol. 5, trans. and ed. Geoffrey Bromley (Grand Rapids, MI: Eerdmans, 1964), 107; Heinz Schürmann, *Das Lukasevangelium*, Herders Theologischer Kommentar zum Neuen Testament (Freiburg: Herder, 1969), vol. 1, 558.

36. E. EarleEllis, *The Gospel of Luke*, The Century Bible (London: Oliphants, 1974), 143; A. Feuillet, 'Les perspectives propres à chaque évangéliste dans les récits de la Transfiguration', *Biblica* 39 (1958): 290; Fitzmyer, *Gospel According to Luke (I-IX)*, 800; Luke Timothy Johnson and Daniel J. Harrington, *The Gospel of Luke* (Collegeville, MN: Liturgical Press, 1991), 153; Manek, 'The New Exodus', 12; Marshall, *The Gospel of Luke*, 384–5.; G. Schneider, *Das Evangelium nach Lukas*, vol. 1 (Güttersloh: G. Mohn, 1977), 216.

37. This is implied by the translation offered by the *REB*: 'Peter and his companions had been overcome by sleep; but when they awoke …'; the *RSV*: 'Now Peter and those who were with him were heavy with sleep, and when they wakened …'; and the *NIV*: 'Peter and his companions were very sleepy, but when they became fully awake …'.

38. See also Johnson and Harrington, *The Gospel of Luke*, 150; Jacob Kremer, *Lukasevangelium*, Neue Echter Bibel (Würzburg: Echter, 1988), 108; John B. F. Miller, *Convinced That God Had Called Us: Dreams, Visions and the Perception of God's Will in Luke-Acts*, Biblical Interpretation Series (Leiden: Brill, 2007), 155; Schürmann, *Das Lukasevangelium*, 558; Wolfgang Wiefel, *Das Evangelium nach Lukas*, Theologischer Handkommentar Zum Neuen Testament (Berlin: Evangelische Verlagsanstalt, 1988), 181.

39. This is implied by the translation offered by the *NRSV*: 'Now Peter and his companions were weighed down by sleep, but since they had stayed awake …'; and the Jerusalem Bible: 'Peter and his companions were heavy with sleep, but since they kept awake …'.

40. See also François Bovon, *Luke 1: A Commentary on the Gospel of Luke 1:1–9:50* (Minneapolis, MN: Fortress Press, 2002), 377; Fitzmyer, *Gospel According to Luke (I-IX)*,

to the connection frequently made in the ancient world between prayer, attempts to abstain from sleep and visionary experience, often involving heavenly journeys and admission to the divine presence in paradise.[41] Patristic commentators, such as Tertullian, Origen and Anastasius of Sinai, will be shown in Chapters 5 and 6 of this study to point to this drowsiness as characteristic of entry into the sort of ecstatic state that MacDermot claims frequently accompanied visionary experience.

The depiction of this sleepiness will become a very complex part of visual portrayal of the Transfiguration. Some images will show the disciples asleep in the Lucan posture, whereas others will show them falling on their faces as Matthew describes. Other depictions seem intentionally to elide these two characteristics and to make it difficult to establish whether the disciples are shown to be falling or sleeping. It is important to note that Luke's sleepiness is mentioned halfway through the Transfiguration, at a very different point from Matthew's falling on their faces, which takes place at the very end of the incident. If, therefore, an image unequivocally shows Lucan sleeping, it depicts a very different point in the narrative from that being shown in the classic Eastern image which tends much more regularly to depict the disciples falling down the mountain.

When they awake, the disciples are no longer described as seeing Jesus but his 'glory' and the two men standing with him. 'Glory' has now ceased to be simply the aura surrounding Moses and Elijah which it seemed to be in Lk. 9.31, and it becomes at Lk. 9.32 closely associated with Jesus alone, something which belongs to him and which appears now to outshine Moses's and Elijah's.

Luke introduces a much more precise sense of temporal sequence, space and movement to his narrative which is absent in Matthew and Mark. The first element of this is his reference to Moses and Elijah *standing* with Jesus in 9.32. This notion of the two prophets standing with Jesus, separate from the disciples who are either fallen on the floor (cf. Mt. 17.6) or sleeping (cf. Lk. 9.31) will form a crucial foundation for the depiction of the Transfiguration.

Luke then adds a distinct element not found in Mark or Matthew, namely a sudden separation of Jesus, and possibly Moses and Elijah, from the disciples. One consequence of this is a fuller awareness of spatial movement. Luke is the only evangelist to say Peter's tents suggestion is triggered by a movement of separation when he adds at Lk. 9.33 that Peter spoke, 'ἐν τῷ διαχωρίζεσθαι αὐτοὺς ἀπ'αὐτοῦ.' Most translations interpret this phrase to mean Moses and Elijah beginning to

---

791; Walter Liefeld, *Luke* (Grand Rapids, MI: Regency Reference Library, 1984), 925; Marshall, *The Gospel of Luke*, 385; Nolland, *Luke*, vol. 2, 489.

41. Violet MacDermot, *The Cult of the Seer in the Ancient Middle East: A Contribution to Current Research on Hallucinations Drawn from Coptic and Other Texts*, Publications of the Wellcome Institute of the History of Medicine (London: Wellcome Institute of the History of Medicine, 1971), 43–8, 338–40.

leave.[42] Indeed, some actually *add* a specific reference to Moses and Elijah not present in the Greek to remove this ambiguity.[43] This interpretation of the text is presumably intended to explain Peter's tents suggestion as an attempt to prolong their presence. It is far from clear, however, that the 'they' of Lk. 9.33a has to refer to Moses and Elijah. They were certainly the object of the verb of the last sentence (εἶδον). However, this 'they' at Lk. 9.33a could also include Peter, or all three disciples, as they are the subjects of verbs in both the sentence before and after this one (διαγρηγορήσαντες, εἶδον and εἶπεν). The 'they' of Lk. 9.33, therefore, could refer to Moses and Elijah, or the disciples, or both. A second problem concerns the supposition that διαχωρίζω means 'to leave'. Liddell and Scott's Greek Lexicon[44] defines it as 'to separate'. Lampe's Patristic Greek Lexicon gives two meanings, 'to separate' and 'to distinguish'.[45] Frederick Danker[46] defines the verb as 'to cause a distance to be put between objects or persons, separate'. 'Ἐν τῷ διαχωρίζεσθαι αὐτοὺς ἀπ'αὐτοῦ' could, therefore, be translated, 'as they were separating from him',[47] as A. R. C. Leaney renders it.[48] A translation involving a sense of departure necessarily means that this 'they' is more likely to be interpreted as Moses and Elijah only, as there would be no sense in the disciples beginning to leave. Once the ambiguity of the meaning of εν τῷ διαχωρίζεσθαι is realized, however, a wider range of possible meaning involving a broader sense of separation of Jesus from the others, rather than of departure by Moses and Elijah, becomes apparent. Whoever 'they' are, the moment at Lk. 9.32 when the disciples see Jesus as the sole embodiment of glory is one in which he is beginning to be separated from those around him. The third gospel creates, therefore, a sense of expanded space

---

42. *RSV*: 'And as the men were parting from him …'; *NRSV*: 'Just as they were leaving him …'; *NIV*: 'As the men were leaving Jesus …'; *NEB*: 'And as these were moving away from Jesus …'; *Jerusalem Bible*: 'As these were leaving him …'.

43. E.g. *Translator's NT*: 'While Moses and Elijah were parting from Jesus …'; *REB*: 'As these two were moving away from Jesus …'.

44. 'διαχωρίζω', *A Lexicon Abridged from Liddell and Scott's Greek-English Lexicon* (Oxford: Clarendon Press, 1909), 169.

45. 'διαχωρίζω', *A Patristic Greek Lexicon*, ed. G. W. H. Lampe (Oxford: Oxford University Press, 1962), vol. 2, 364.

46. Frederick W. Danker, 'διαχωρίζω', in *A Greek-English Lexicon of the New Testament and other early Christian Literature*, 3rd edn (Chicago: Chicago University Press, 2000), 240.

47. A. R. C. Leaney, *A Commentary on the Gospel According to St. Luke*, Black's New Testament Commentaries (London: Black, 1966), 168.

48. It is noteworthy that German translators tend to retain the ambiguity of the Greek because they have at their disposal the verb *sich trennen*, which conveys not only a sense of separation but also of departure, or leaving. See François Bovon, *Das Evangelium nach Lukas*, Evangelisch-Katholischer Kommentar Zum Neuen Testament (Zurich: Benziger, 1989), vol. 1, 488: 'als sie sich von ihm trennten …'; and Wiefel, *Das Evangelium nach Lukas*, 179: 'als sie von ihm getrennt wurden …'.

between Christ and the other figures in this scene at the very point at which they are overshadowed by the cloud.

In Luke, it is this movement of separation which triggers Peter's word concerning tents. Luke adds a subtle alteration of Mark's verdict on Peter. Luke asserts not that he did not know what he was to say (Mk 9.6: οὐ γὰρ ᾔδει τί ἀποκριθῇ) but rather that he did not know *what he was saying* (Lk. 9.33: μὴ εἰδὼς ὃ λέγει). We will show in Chapter 5 of this study that the nature of Peter's mental state was debated extensively by Tertullian and Origen, who see in this not knowing what he said some degree of ecstasy and even madness. This Lucan change is very infrequently commented upon by modern commentators, and I have found none who detects any visionary significance in it.

There then follows a very different sequence of events from those recounted by Matthew and Mark, in which Luke describes a precise moment of entry into the overshadowing cloud at Lk. 9.34. This exploits the fuller sense of space and movement which Luke has been careful to create and describes the overshadowing cloud as something the disciples *enter into*.

Luke 9.34 is characterized by a number of textual variants, some of which may be attempts to remove ambiguity present in the Greek text. It is once again unclear who the 'they' is that enter the cloud: possibly Moses and Elijah; the disciples; or both groups. The variant at Lk. 9.34 found in A, D, W, Θ and Ψ that reads 'ἐκείνους εἰσελθεῖν' makes it much clearer that Moses and Elijah are envisaged as the ones entering the cloud, pointing to the subject of εἰσελθεῖν not being that of the last verb, ἐφοβήθησαν. There are, however, significant problems with accepting this variant over the reading preferred by the Nestle-Aland 26th edition (N-A 26) and UBS. Not only is the N-A 26/UBS reading attested in ℵ, B and L, but the disciples' reaction of fear would also make little sense if only Moses and Elijah enter the cloud; fear on the disciples' part would be a much more natural response to their own entry. Second, Joseph Fitzmyer[49] points to the early evidence of P[75], which, by omitting αὐτούς, implies it is those who were afraid who enter the cloud. It is highly likely, as John Nolland asserts,[50] that 9.34 refers to the disciples entering the cloud.

A verdict that the 'they' in Lk. 9.34b refers to the disciples entering into the cloud also has an impact on our interpretation of who the 'they' are that are overshadowed by the cloud in the first half of 9.34. The text is, again, ambiguous as to who is overshadowed. It could be just Moses and Elijah; Moses and Elijah with Jesus; the disciples; or everyone present. Again, the witness of P[75], ℵ, B and L could be significant: a variant here places the verb 'overshadow' in the imperfect (ἐπεσκίαζεν) rather than the aorist (ἐπεσκίασεν) as attested by P[45], A, D, W, Θ and Ψ. This imperfect verb could be read as describing a process whereby the cloud *began* to overshadow the disciples. In other words, the entry into the cloud could be a description of the overshadowing. By contrast with this, the aorist verb would

---

49. Fitzmyer, *Gospel According to Luke (I-IX)*, 802.
50. Nolland, *Luke*, vol. 2, 501.

produce a more clearly delineated sequence, in which the cloud's overshadowing is complete, halts and then the disciples enter it. If this latter reading is accepted, the more natural sense might be to presume that as the overshadowing, and the fear which accompanies entry, are two separate actions, the following happens: the cloud overshadows Jesus, Moses and Elijah; then after this, the three apostles enter the cloud.

Luke's treatment of the scene is very different, therefore, from that of Mark and Matthew. The first two gospels retain a similar ambiguity over who the overshadowed αὐτούς (Mt. 17.5)/αὐτοῖς (Mk 9.7) might be but do not have a verb mentioning fear whose subject shows the object of the verb 'overshadow' to include the disciples. Three possible conceptions, therefore, of the Lucan scene are possible:

1. First, Jesus appears in glory. He is then separated from everyone else. When this glory-filled space is overshadowed, Moses and Elijah are included in it with Jesus. Then the terrified disciples enter into this cloud and join Jesus, Moses and Elijah there.
2. Second, it is the disciples who are separated from Jesus, Moses and Elijah. Jesus, Moses and Elijah are together in a space which is overshadowed and then finally entered by the terrified disciples (if P[45], A, D, W, Θ and Ψ's use of the aorist is accepted).
3. Third, the process of the overshadowing of the glory-filled space in which Jesus, Moses and Elijah are standing could be understood to be the same as the disciples' entry (if P[75], ℵ, B and L's imperfect is accepted).[51]

In all three, Luke has created a scenario in which the disciples *enter* a cloud which has overshadowed a glory-filled space. The most significant thing revealed by this examination of the text, however, is that this overshadowing takes place *after* the distancing of Jesus from those around him in 9.34. In other words, Luke creates a space which the cloud can be conceived of as filling. The three apostles then enter into this cloud- and glory-filled space. It is unclear whether Moses and Elijah are with Jesus in that space, or on the apostles' side of the divide. Whereas Matthew associates the disciples' fear with the *voice*, Luke's mention of fear coincides with the disciples' *going into* the cloud.

This distinct sense of space, with a key point of entry into it, which Luke develops has been largely overlooked by modern commentators. This increased sense of space and entry could represent an echoing of the entry of the seer into the heavenly tabernacle of God seen in many apocalyptic texts, or of the priest into the Holy of Holies in the Jerusalem Temple. If this is the case, then Luke could be emphasizing the Transfiguration's status as a visionary experience similar to that recounted in many apocalyptic texts, a theological point which, as we will see in

---

51. This would seem to be the interpretation offered by the *Good News Bible's* translation: 'And the disciples were afraid as the cloud came over them.'

Chapters 5 and 8 of this study, is noticed and developed by Origen and a number of artists working in the Italian peninsula in the sixth and ninth centuries.

Luke's narrative then concludes by omitting the instruction from Jesus not to tell anyone of the event on the mountain top. Instead, the disciples voluntarily keep silence. There is also a hint at the end of Luke's narrative, not to be found in any other version, that the Transfiguration possibly took place at night. Lk. 9.37 speaks of the party descending from the mountain first thing the next morning. Such a possibility would seem to make sense of the sleepiness of the disciples. It is intriguing that this verse has been the subject of remarkably little speculation indeed both in Christian antiquity and modern comment.

Conclusions

Luke's version adds a number of elements not found in any other gospel. First, he creates a Transfiguration narrative much more frequently linked to other episodes in his gospel through shared language. These episodes often involve the presence of angelic beings, such as in the Lucan Gethsemane, Resurrection and the Ascension recounted in Acts. Second, Luke expands the language of vision used of the Transfiguration. Luke describes the Transfiguration as the 'ὧν ἑώρακαν' – 'the things they had seen' – in Lk. 9.36 and includes the motif of sleep followed by wakefulness and a refreshed ability to see in Lk. 9.32. He also introduces hints at the disciples being in some sort of liminal visionary state through their passing from sleepiness to vision and through suggestion that Peter was somehow unable consciously to understand what he said. A third element is the different sense of movement and space which characterizes his narrative, creating a feeling of separation and space between Jesus and the others, followed by a specific mention of entry into the cloud. Fourth, Luke adds two motifs closely associated with liturgical worship and the temple, in the mention of prayer and δόξα, a term closely linked with God's presence both in the Tent of Meeting and in the Jerusalem Temple. One of the most important elements to emerge from Luke's account, therefore, is the way in which the disciples' *participation* in the Transfiguration is foregrounded and made more complex both through more explicit description of their movements and entry into the cloud, through motifs such as their *hearing* and *understanding* more of the conversation on the mountain top and hints at ecstatic, liminal states of awareness.

Synoptic narratives: Conclusions

Our outlining of the main characteristics of the Transfiguration narratives has shown a number of complexities, differences and ambiguities to exist in the three synoptic versions. These include a difference in the narrative order of events, the sense of space and movement, and uncertainty about how the cloud overshadows and who is included in that overshadowing. Luke's version is distinct in that it uses language of glory, mentions the disciples feeling sleepy, describes the content of the conversation with Moses and Elijah, and creates a very different succession of events associated with entry into the cloud.

A repeated motif emphasized in different ways by the gospel writers is its status as a vision. That is to say, our narrative presents the experience as something *seen*, a revelation perceived through the sense of sight, of something which is usually hidden or unavailable to perception by the eyes. The Transfiguration is also linked through shared language, especially in Luke, with other revelatory moments in the New Testament, which are frequently presented as visionary, or which involve entry into the divine presence in heaven, such as the Ascension.

A renewed awareness of this dynamic within our narratives reveals two things. First, the Lucan narrative particularly emphasizes these visionary elements through some of its most distinctive characteristics. Second, questions concerning the *participation* of the disciples in this vision lie in the New Testament narratives themselves and are not merely later interpretive concerns. If the Transfiguration is presented as a visionary experience, then questions concerning who it is seen by, and how, are important ones and lie at the heart of many of the complexities in the gospel texts which we have outlined.

In our next chapter we proceed to examine how modern scholarship has understood these complexities along with the broad sweep of different interpretive approaches which have characterized the critical reception of the Transfiguration narratives in twentieth- and twenty-first-century scholarship.

Chapter 3

MODERN INTERPRETATION OF THE SYNOPTIC TRANSFIGURATION NARRATIVES

Having outlined the main contours of the synoptic Transfiguration narratives, and the way in which they are different from each other, we now need to look at how those narratives were interpreted by scholars in the modern era. This survey reveals much about the scopic regime within which that scholarship has taken place. The questions which form the focus of historical-critical comment and the kind of answers it provides reveal a number of assumptions about what constitutes human vision: that it is about the empirical observation of physical phenomena; that any description of vision beyond those bounds resides in the separate realm of mythic literary invention, and with little focus on vision as a broader metaphor for human thought, imagination, connection or participation in the divine. The history of Transfiguration interpretation by 'critical' scholars is one in which initial attempts were briefly made in the nineteenth century to account for the narrative in terms of a historically verifiable event. However, this quickly gives way to a consensus that the story's meaning and origin are to be found in a series of mythic or historically contingent metaphors, frequently with a strong emphasis on questions concerning textual sources and editing as a way of accounting for the shape of the narrative.

That sense which Ulrich Luz noted of scholars experiencing a certain 'strangeness' in the Transfiguration narratives is particularly evident. Twentieth-century scholarship frequently focuses on a narrow series of historical questions concerning the origin of our texts but displays less interest in the way in which they were interpreted by preceding generations or the rich seam of interpretation offered by visual depiction. An overwhelming sense emerges amongst modern biblical scholars of the Transfiguration as a series of created, literary, metaphorical texts, rather than a powerful account of visionary experience. The most appropriate way of analysing and making sense of it seems all too often in modern biblical scholarship to be through desiccated textual, historical and linguistic analysis and less through a valuing of its potential as a visually depicted image or a liturgically lived out narrative, which situates it within a living history of reception and interpretation.

Early historical-critical theories

The advent of historical-critical approaches to exegesis of the New Testament in the nineteenth century prompted a series of attempts to establish whether it was reasonable to suppose that a historically verifiable incident could lie behind the Transfiguration narratives. A large number of these attempts saw it necessary to posit some sort of event, possibly visionary, in the life of Jesus or the disciples as triggering the creation of the synoptic accounts. Some of these theories revolved around tricks of the light, or early morning meteorological phenomena. These supposedly gave the disciples, upon awaking from sleep, a glorious, though entirely terrestrial, vision of Jesus.[1] Similar theories abounded which saw, at the prompting of Luke's mention of sleepiness, the Transfiguration as a dream.[2] Others, such as Heinrich Baltensweiler, posited some sort of mystical experience in Jesus' own experience of prayer as the historical kernel around which the Transfiguration was created.[3] Adolf von Harnack saw the Transfiguration's origins lying in a pre-Resurrection visionary experience comparable with that of Peter in 1 Cor. 15.3.[4] The popularity of these approaches waned through the second half of the twentieth century, though a small minority of scholars has persisted which sees some sort of visionary experience on the part of the disciples as lying behind our narrative.[5]

Even amongst those who assert a historical kernel, there is no consensus concerning how the Transfiguration should be understood as vision: for some, this could be subjective psychological disturbance; for others a dream or an optical experience physically apprehended with the eye, dependent on surrounding physical phenomena. At the heart of many of these historical-critical examinations of the Transfiguration lies uncertainty about what counts as 'vision' and how such a vision might count as verifiable or historically plausible.

---

1. David Strauss, George Eliot and Otto Pfleiderer list Paulus and Schleiermacher advocating such a rationalization, in *The Life of Jesus, Critically Examined*, 2nd edn (London: S. Sonnenschein; Macmillan, 1892), 539–40.

2. Strauss, Eliot and Pfleiderer list Rau, Gabler, Kuinöl and Neander as holding some version of this idea: ibid., 538.

3. Heinrich Baltensweiler, *Die Verklärung Jesu: historisches Ereignis und Synoptische Berichte* (Zürich: Zwingli-Verlag, 1959), 134–5.

4. Adolf von Harnack, 'Die Verklärung Jesu, der Bericht des Paulus (1 Kor 15,3)', in *Sitzung der philosophisch-historischen Klasse vom 2. März, 1922* (Sitzungen der Königlichen Preussischen Akademie der Wissenschaften, Berlin, 1922), 62–80.

5. Joseph Blinzler, *Die neutestamentlichen Berichte über die Verklärung Jesu* (Münster: Aschendorff, 1937); C. E. B. Cranfield, *The Gospel According to Saint Mark* (Cambridge: Cambridge University Press, 1963), 292–4; Vincent Taylor, *The Formation of the Gospel Tradition* (London: Macmillan, 1949), 150; Vincent Taylor, *The Gospel According to St Mark: The Greek Text* (London: Macmillan, 1966), 387.

A misplaced Resurrection account

One of the most popular theories to emerge amongst form critics was the assertion that the Markan Transfiguration might be a misplaced Resurrection narrative. Julius Wellhausen[6] was the first to propose this theory, which was then more fully fleshed out by Rudolf Bultmann and taken up by others.[7] However, an influential article by R. Stein[8] convincingly undermined many of these theories and reasserted that whatever the narrative's historical origins, the pre-Markan Transfiguration account was principally one of a glorification of Jesus during his pre-Resurrection earthly life. Stein pointed out that Bultmann's theory was in part popular because it tallied with the presupposition many critical scholars brought to biblical study that visionary or supernatural phenomena such as the Transfiguration simply don't happen. Much scholarship written after Stein has rejected Bultmann's ideas.

Source- and redaction-critical questions

Speculation concerning the Transfiguration as a misplaced Resurrection account prompted further questions concerning the relationship between the synoptic accounts, which have tended to focus on two questions: first, how to account for the remarkably high number of minor agreements between Luke and Matthew; and second, how to explain the distinct character of the Lucan text. One of the most significant consequences of this was the popularity for a time of a theory suggesting that Luke had access to some sort of distinct, separate Transfiguration source in the construction of his gospel.

The first investigations of the redaction history of Luke's Transfiguration tended to focus on the examination of the high number of minor agreements of Matthew and Luke against Mark. Many concluded that the most reasonable solution to this question was positing use by Matthew and Luke of some sort of

---

6. Julius Wellhausen, *Das Evangelium Marci* (Berlin: Reimer, 1909), 71.

7. The following see the Transfiguration as originally a resurrection narrative: C. Carlston, 'Transfiguration and Resurrection', *Journal of Biblical Literature* 80 (1961): 233–40; Rudolf Bultmann, *The History of the Synoptic Tradition*, 2nd edn (Oxford: Blackwell, 1968), 259–61; F. McCurley, '"And after Six Days," (Mark 9.2): A Semitic Literary Device', *Journal of Biblical Literature* 93 (1971): 79; W. Schmithals, 'Der Markusschluss, Die Verklärungsgeschichte Und Die Sendung Der Zwölf', *Zeitschrift für Theologie und Kirche* 95 (1976): 79–96; Gerd Theissen, *The Miracle Stories of the Early Christian Tradition* (Edinburgh: T&T Clark, 1983), 96–7; M. Thrall, 'Elijah and Moses in Mark's Account of the Resurrection', *New Testament Studies* 16 (1969–70): 305–17, esp. 310; Theodore J. Weeden, *Mark: Traditions in Conflict* (Philadelphia: Fortress Press, 1971), 118–26.

8. R. Stein, 'Is the Transfiguration (Mark 9.2-8) a Misplaced Resurrection Account?', *Journal of Biblical Literature* 95, no. 1 (1976): 79–96.

non-Markan Transfiguration source.[9] More wind was put in the sails of this theory particularly in relation to Luke's version in the 1980s and 1990s by Barbara Reid[10] and J. Murphy-O'Connor.[11]

In response to these ideas, two impressive critiques have been offered by Frans Neirynck[12] and John Miller,[13] which have led to a substantial decline in the popularity of this theory. Neirynck's article from the 1970s simply examines two of the minor agreements[14] and shows them to be only apparent agreements, and to be perfectly explicable as independent redaction. As a small test case study, he is successful at showing how overly eager source-critical scholars can be in interpreting evidence as proof for the use of shared, written sources. In a more extensive methodological assessment, Miller seriously undermines the foundations of many of Reid's and Murphy-O'Connor's assumptions, showing them frequently to be based on contradictory logic.

Miller is the only recent commentator to focus on visions in Luke-Acts in a more extensive work, and in his review of scholarship in that study he notes that whilst a few individual investigations of visionary events in Luke-Acts exist, no work before him has examined the question of vision within the Lucan corpus as a whole.[15] In the light of this, we might conclude that many scholars' positing

---

9. Blinzler, *Die neutestamentlichen Berichte*, 32–62; Eugeniusz Dabrowski, *La Transfiguration de Jésus*, Scripta Pontificii Instituti Biblici (Rome: Pontifical Biblical Institute, 1939), 21; Wolfgang Dietrich, *Das Petrusbild der lukanischen Schriften*, Beiträge zur Wissenschaft vom alten und neuen Testament (Stuttgart: W. Kohlhammer, 1972), 104–9; E. E. Ellis, 'The Composition of Luke 9 and the Source of its Christology', in *Current Issues in Biblical and Patristic Interpretation: Studies in Honour of Merrill C. Tenney*, ed. Gerald F. Hawthorne (Grand Rapids, MI: Eerdmans, 1975), 122–4; Walter Grundmann and Friedrich Hauck, *Das Evangelium nach Lukas*, Theologischer Handkommentar Zum Neuen Testament (Berlin: Evangelische Verlagsanstalt, 1964), 191; Karl Heinrich Rengstorf, *Das Evangelium nach Lukas*, Neue Testament Deutsch (Göttingen: Vandenhoeck & Ruprecht, 1962), 121; Tim Schramm, *Der Markus-Stoff bei Lukas: Eine literakritische und redaktionsgeschichtliche Untersuchung* (Cambridge: Cambridge University Press, 1971), 139.

10. Barbara E. Reid, *The Transfiguration: A Source- and Redaction-Critical Study of Luke 9: 28-36*, Cahiers De La Revue Biblique (Paris: Gabalda, 1993), esp. 29–75, 145–8.

11. J. Murphy-O'Connor, 'What Really Happened at the Transfiguration?' *Bible Revue* 3 (1987), 8–21.

12. Frans Neirynck, 'Minor Agreements Matthew-Luke in the Transfiguration Story', in *Orientierung an Jesus: zur Theologie der Synoptiker*, ed. Paul Hoffmann, Norbert Brox and Wilhelm Pesch (Freiburg: Herder, 1973), 253–66.

13. John B. F. Miller, 'Source Criticism and the Limits of Certainty', *Ephemerides Theologicae Lovanienses* (1998): 127–44.

14. Mt. 17.2; cf. Lk. 9.29: Neirynck, 'Minor Agreements', 256–60; Mt. 17.5; cf. Lk. 9.34: Ibid., 260–4.

15. John B. F. Miller, *Convinced That God Had Called Us: Dreams, Visions and the Perception of God's Will in Luke-Acts*, Biblical Interpretation Series (Leiden: Brill, 2007), 66–90, esp. 90.

of Lucan access to a third Transfiguration source allowed them to avoid seeing in Luke's Transfiguration visionary tendencies which might need explaining in the context of a wider Lucan theology of vision.

Hellenistic myth theories

Many of those who have judged there to be no historical foundation to our narratives, such as Hans Conzelmann, Martin Dibelius, Werner Kümmel and, more recently, Dieter Zeller, have seen the Transfiguration as influenced by Hellenistic epiphany traditions.[16] In these readings, the Transfiguration is seen as modelled on episodes found in the literature of the Greek-speaking world in which gods residing on earth in human form reveal their divine identity.[17] Interpretations of the kind exemplified by Dibelius and Conzelmann, influenced by a strong early-twentieth-century history-of-religions approach, have tended to see the principal conceptual background to the Transfiguration narratives as the Greek idea of divinization in which the *theos-aner* Jesus is empowered and revealed as Christ. E. Lohmeyer saw the Transfiguration's background as a mixture

16. Klaus Berger, 'Die Verklärung Jesu', *IKaZ* 37 (2008): 3–9, esp. 8–9; Hans Dieter Betz, 'Jesus as Divine Man', in *Jesus and the Historian: Written in Honor of Ernest Cadman Colwell*, ed. Thomas Trotter (Philadelphia: Westminster, 1968), 114–33, esp. 122–3; Hans Conzelmann, *An Outline of the Theology of the New Testament* (London: S.C.M. Press, 1969), 128–9; Martin Dibelius, *From Tradition to Gospel* (London: Ivor Nicholson and Watson, 1934), 267–76; Marco Frenschkowski, *Offenbarung und Epiphanie*, WUNT2/79-80 (Tübingen: Mohr Siebeck, [1995] 1997), vol. 2, 184–7; Ferdinand Hahn, *The Titles of Jesus in Christology: Their History in Early Christianity* (New York: World, 1969), 300–2, 334–7; Werner Georg Kümmel, *The Theology of the New Testament: According to Its Major Witnesses, Jesus, Paul, John* (London: SCM Press, 1974), 123; M. David Litwa, *Iesus Deus: The Early Christian Depiction of Jesus as a Mediterraenean God* (Minneapolis, MN: Fortress, 2014), 111–40; Candida Moss, 'The Transfiguration: An exercise in Marcan Accommodation', *BibInt* 12 (2004): 69–89; Randall E. Otto, 'The Fear Motivation in Peter's Offer to build Τρεῖς Σκηνάς', *WTJ* 59 (1997): 101–12, esp. 104–5, 108; Ludger Schenke, 'Gibt es im Markusevangelium eine Präexistenzchristologie?', *ZNW* 91 (2000): 45–71, esp. 59–62.

Dieter Zeller, 'Die Menschwerdung des Sohnes Gottes im Neuen Testament und die antike Religionsgeschichte', in *Menschwerdung Gottes – Vergöttlichung von Menschen*, ed. Dieter Zeller (Göttingen: Vandenhoeck & Ruprecht, 1988), 141–76; Dieter Zeller, 'La Métamorphose de Jésus comme Épiphanie (Mc 9, 2-8)', in *L'évangile exploré*, ed. Alain Marchendour (Paris: Cerf, 1996), 167–86; Dieter Zeller, 'Bedeutung und religionsgeschichtlicher Hintergrund der Verwandlung Jesu', in *Authenticating the Activities of Jesus*, ed. Bruce Chilton and Craig A. Evans (Leiden: Brill, 1999), 303–21.

17. For an extensive list of examples, see Adela Yarbro Collins, *Mark: A Commentary* (Minneapolis, MN: Fortress Press, 2007), 416–19.

of Hellenistic motifs, magical elements and Jewish eschatological material.[18] More recently, Dennis MacDonald has renewed interest in Hellenistic influence through his argument that the gospels are influenced by Homer's *Odyssey* and sees in the Transfiguration echoes of Odysseus' transformation in *Odyssey* 16.[19]

These theories have gradually been undermined and gone out of favour for a number of reasons. Some, such as H. C. Kee and W. Gerber,[20] have highlighted eschatological motifs present in the Transfiguration narratives which don't form any part of the Hellenistic epiphany tradition.[21] Others, such as W. D. Davies and Dale C. Allison, see Pentateuchal and Mosaic echoes showing the Transfiguration's imaginative milieu to be more appropriately described as Jewish than Greek.[22] More recent scholarship, though, has sought to overcome the assumption of a rigid dichotomy between Jewish and Hellenistic influences. Adela Collins, for example, still detects a significant influence by Greek epiphany traditions but regards them as reinterpreted in the light of Old Testament theophanies.[23]

Moses

Further significant strands of interpretation have revolved around reading the Transfiguration in the light of Moses themes and the Exodus Sinai narrative.[24] However, many of these theories revolving around Mosaic echoes involve a

---

18. E. Lohmeyer, 'Die Verklärung Jesu nach dem Markus-Evangelium', *Zeitschrift für Neutestamentliche Wissenschaft* 21 (1922): 185–21, 203–8.

19. Dennis R. MacDonald, *The Gospels and Homer* (Lanham, MD: Rowman & Littlefield, 2015), 264–6; Dennis R. MacDonald, *Luke and Vergil* (Lanham, MD: Rowman & Littlefield, 2015), 148.

20. H. C. Kee, 'The Transfiguration in Mark: Epiphany or Apocalyptic Vision?', in *Understanding the Sacred Text*, ed. J. Reumann (Valley Forge: Judson, 1972), 135–52; W. Gerber, 'Die Metamorphose Jesu, Mk 9.2f', *Theologische Zeitschrift* 23 (1967): 385–95.

21. Kee, 'Transfiguration in Mark', 140–9.

22. W. D. Davies and Dale C. Allison, *A Critical and Exegetical Commentary on the Gospel According to Saint Matthew* (Edinburgh: T&T Clark, 1988), vol. 2, 691.

23. Collins, *Mark: A Commentary*, 416–17.

24. For a good summary, see Joel Marcus, *Mark 8-16: A New Translation with Introduction and Commentary*, The Anchor Yale Bible (New Haven, CT: Yale University Press, 2009), 1114–15. See also Bruce Chilton, 'The Transfiguration: Dominical Assurance and Apostolic Vision', *New Testament Studies* 27 (1980): 115–24, esp. 122; William Richard Stegner, 'The Use of Scripture in two Narratives of Early Jewish Christianity (Matthew 4.1-11; Mark 9.2-8)', in *Early Christian Interpretation of the Scriptures of Israel: Investigations and Proposals*, ed. Craig A. Evans and James Sanders, JSNT Suppl. 148, SSEJC 5 (Sheffield: Sheffield Academic, 1997), 98–120, esp. 110–20; J. A. Ziesler, 'The Transfiguration Story and the Markan Soteriology', *ExpTim* 81 (1970): 263–8.

very wide range of connections and frequently come to divergent conclusions concerning their significance.

Many commentators recognize numerous connections between the Transfiguration narratives and Exodus 24.[25] Some see the Transfiguration as a reworking of an event or narrative in the light of Exodus 24.[26] Many see the eschatological significance of Jesus' fulfilment of Deut. 18.15[27] as particularly important, whilst others highlight Jesus' and Moses's shared status as mystical figures privileged with mountain-top vision of God, or with ascent to heaven involving some degree of possibly angelic glorification.[28] John Lierman has undertaken extensive discussion of the different ways in which Moses was understood in early Christian and Jewish writings. He argues, amongst other things, that Moses was seen as a priestly figure.[29]

However, a number of complications exist in this Jesus-Moses connection. Luz, for example, points out that the cloud motif found at Sinai is also associated with the Tent of Meeting (Exod. 40.34-38), where it *prevents* Moses from entering God's presence.[30] In addition, the shining face motif of the Transfiguration fits ill with Exodus 34, where it only appears *after* Moses has spoken with God (a

---

25. For a summary, see Craig Evans, *Mark 8:27-16:20* (Nashville: Thomas Nelson, 2001), 34; Ulrich Mauser, *Christ in the Wilderness: The Wilderness Theme in the Second Gospel and Its Basis in the Biblical Tradition* (London: SCM, 1963), 110–19.

26. Davies, Allison, and Hagner propose a visionary experience rewritten in the light of Exodus 24, and McCurley posits an Ascension reworked using Exodus 24. See Davies and Allison, *A Critical and Exegetical Commentary on the Gospel According to Saint Matthew*, 693; Donald Alfred Hagner, *Matthew 14-28*, Word Biblical Commentary (Dallas, TX: Word Books, 1995), 493; McCurley, 'And after Six Days', 67–81.

27. Collins, *Mark: A Commentary*, 423 and 426; Evans, *Mark 8:27-16:20*, 38; Hagner, *Matthew 14-28*, 494; Marcus, *Mark 8-16*, 1114; Howard Merle Teeple, *The Mosaic Eschatological Prophet* (Philadelphia: Society of Biblical Literature, 1957), 83–94.

28. François Bovon, *Luke 1: A Commentary on the Gospel of Luke 1:1-9:50* (Minneapolis, MN: Fortress Press, 2002), 372; Collins, *Mark: A Commentary*, 423; Evans, *Mark 8:27-16:20*, 36; J. E. Fossum, 'Ascensio, Metamorphosis: The Transfiguration of Jesus in the Synoptic Gospels', in *The Image of the Invisible God: Essays on the Influence of Jewish Mysticism on Early Christology*, ed. J. E. Fossum (Göttingen: Vandenhoeck & Ruprecht, 1995), 71–97; Hagner, *Matthew 14-28*, 493; John Paul Heil, *The Transfiguration of Jesus: Narrative Meaning and Function of Mark 9:2-8, Matt 17:1-8 and Luke 9:28-36* (Rome: Editrice Pontificio Istituto Biblico, 2000), 95–113, 129–48; M. Öhler, 'Die Verklärung (Mk 9.1-8): Die Ankunft der Herrschaft Gottes auf der Erde', *Novum Testamentum* 38 (1996): 197–217.

29. John Lierman, *The New Testament Moses: Christian Perceptions of Moses and Israel in the Setting of Jewish Religion*, Wissenschaftliche Untersuchungen zum Neuen Testament, 2 Reihe (Tübingen: Mohr Siebeck, 2004), 65–78, 272.

30. A similar motif is echoed at the consecration of the Temple (1 Kgs 8.10-11), where the glory-filled cloud prevents the priests from entering the Sanctuary.

point Michael Mach[31] also makes) and continues *after* Moses's descent in a way which is not seen with Jesus. A further complication concerns Moses's presence on the mountain with Jesus. Does he point to Jesus as a prophet like him, or does his presence signify Jesus' replacing him and transcending his greatness? In other words, is Jesus' glory borrowed, like Moses's was, or is it something he possesses in an altogether different way as the embodiment of God's presence with his people? A. D. A. Moses[32] argues that Matthew portrays Jesus not as a prophet *like* Moses but as *superior* to him in the Transfiguration, an idea Howard Teeple also argues is present more broadly in the New Testament.[33]

Whilst many commentators see Mosaic echoes and typological connections with Moses narratives, there is a lack of consensus concerning precisely how these work, what is being compared and how those typologies work.

Eschatological and apocalyptic readings

A small number of more recent scholars have sought to interpret the Transfiguration in the light of Jewish eschatological or apocalyptic thought. Most still work within a historical-critical paradigm, seeing the creation of our narratives as best explained by comparison with a particular body of more eschatologically orientated literature. However, the fact that much of this literature claims to be the product of visionary experience and ascent into heaven has produced some worthwhile reflection on visionary dynamics within the Transfiguration narratives.

G. H. Boobyer[34] provided a more eschatological reading in order to disprove Dibelius's theories concerning mythic Hellenistic influence. Kee[35] shares Boobyer's eschatological emphasis and reads Mark's Transfiguration principally in the light of Daniel 10 and as a foretaste of the Parousia. Richard Bauckham,[36] too, has argued against a Hellenistic interpretation, claiming that it is the 2 Peter account that makes the apocalyptic milieu of the narrative most clear. For Baltensweiler, it is the motif of tabernacles, and their connection to Sukkoth, which makes the Transfiguration's eschatological focus evident.[37]

---

31. Michael Mach, 'Christus Mutans: Zur Bedeutung der Verklärung Jesu im Wechsel von jüdischer Messianität zur neutestamentlichen Christologie', in *Messiah and Christos*, ed. Ithamar Grunwald (Tübingen: Mohr Siebeck, 1992), 185.

32. A. D. A. Moses, *Matthew's Transfiguration Story and Jewish-Christian Controversy* (Sheffield: Sheffield Academic Press, 1996), esp. 114–60, 239–44.

33. Teeple, *The Mosaic Eschatological Prophet*, 594–7.

34. G. H. Boobyer, *St. Mark and the Transfiguration Story* (Edinburgh: T&T Clark, 1942), esp. 64–87.

35. Kee, 'Transfiguration in Mark', 135–52.

36. Richard Bauckham, *Jude, 2 Peter*, Word Biblical Commentary (Waco, TX: Word Books, 1983), 212.

37. Baltensweiler, *Die Verklärung Jesu*, 37–61, esp. 61.

M. Sabbe[38] and Delbert Burkett[39] have gone further and see the Transfiguration as a fully apocalyptic revelation of Jesus' enthronement as Son of Man. Sabbe underlines the apocalyptic significance of the theme of revealed and guarded mysteries, something Christopher Rowland[40] has also particularly emphasized. Sabbe also sees the location of the Confession in Mark and Matthew in the place of Enoch's vision as significant, giving Caesarea Philippi 'une allure apocalyptique'.[41]

George Nickelsburg[42] has expanded on this last idea of Sabbe's, that Caesarea Philippi was associated with a tradition of apocalyptic vision, though he seems to be unaware of his work and does not quote him at any point. Nickelsburg argues that the location of Peter's Confession and the Transfiguration in Caesarea Philippi, near Mount Hermon, draws on the place's associations with pagan vision and oracle, and the location of the heavenly visions of Enoch and Levi in *The Testament of Levi*.

In a related area, Mach has explored questions of angelomorphic presentation. He sees, for example, the Transfiguration as evidence of a series of developments within Jewish apocalyptic angelology in which the righteous are increasingly portrayed as having communion with the angels and, indeed, eventually as being transformed into angelic beings.[43] At the same time, he detects a trend in messianic thought increasingly seeing the Messiah in angelic terms.[44]

Amongst those who read the Transfiguration within an apocalyptic context, a minority emphasize the narrative as one principally concerning entry into the presence of God in the heavenly sphere and as evoking heavenly ascent narratives. M. Öhler, for example, reads the Transfiguration as a revelation of Jesus' enthronement and consequently to be akin to an experience on earth of the life of heaven, expressed in language similar to that used in heavenly journey traditions.[45] Gerber has compared the Transfiguration with the Hekhalot writings, showing that those who journey into heaven are changed by their experience of God's presence.[46] J. E. Fossum, too, sees the Transfiguration as evoking an ascent

38. M. Sabbe, 'La rédaction du récit de la Transfiguration', in *La venue du messie: messianisme et eschatologie*, ed. E. Massaux (Bruges: Desclée de Brouwer, 1962), 65–100.

39. Delbert Burkett, 'The Transfiguration of Jesus (Mark 9:2-8): Epiphany or Apotheosis?', *JBL* 138 (2019): 413–32.

40. Christopher Rowland and Christopher R. A. Morray-Jones, *The Mystery of God: Early Jewish Mysticism and the New Testament* (Leiden: Brill, 2009), 106–9.

41. Sabbe, 'La rédaction du récit de la Transfiguration', 96.

42. George Nickelsburg, 'Enoch, Levi, and Peter: Recipients of Revelation in Upper Galilee', *Journal of Biblical Literature* 100, no. 4 (1981): 575–600.

43. Mach, 'Christus Mutans', 184–9. Examples include Dan. 12.2, Wis. 3.6, 1 *En*. 51.5.

44. Mach, 'Christus Mutans', 189–92. Examples include 11GMelch showing Melchizedek starting to assume a role similar to the Angel of Light of 1QS 3.2, and 1QSb 4.25's reference to an eschatological figure referred to as an angel of the presence.

45. Öhler, 'Die Verklärung (Mk 9.1-8)', 215.

46. Gerber, 'Die Metamorphose Jesu, Mk 9.2f', 395.

to heaven,[47] as does Morton Smith, who sees the narrative's origins in ecstatic visionary experience on the part of Jesus orientated to showing him as a powerful magician or shaman figure.[48]

Temple, priestly and tabernacle motifs

A strand of interpretation, advocated by a small number of modern scholars, has read the synoptic Transfiguration narratives in the light of a series of motifs evoking the Jerusalem Temple and its High Priest.

Some, such as Crispin Fletcher-Louis, see connections between the Transfiguration narratives and apocalyptic writings, especially ones which describe a seer's visionary entry into heaven, or which describe the worship of the celestial city found there.[49] Fletcher-Louis agrees with Harald Riesenfeld and Nickelsburg in positing in the history of the Transfiguration some sort of originating event around the time of Sukkoth. He expands on Nickelsburg's work by pointing to an association between springs near Mount Hermon, the Transfiguration and the feast of Sukkoth in the *Gospel of Thomas*.[50] He goes on to argue that the Son of Man of Daniel 7 was understood in a priestly light. Consequently, Jesus himself is presented in the Transfiguration, according to Fletcher-Louis, as a priestly figure worthy of worship.[51] Here, a *conceptual* analogy is drawn, in which the Transfiguration is seen as akin to entry into the heavenly tabernacle in which the glorified Jesus appears as a High Priestly figure.

47. Fossum, 'Ascensio, Metamorphosis', 71–94.

48. Morton Smith, *Clement of Alexandria and a Secret Gospel of Mark* (Cambridge, MA: Harvard University Press, 1973), 237–44; Morton Smith, 'The Origin and History of the Transfiguration Story', *Union Seminary Quarterly Review* 36 (1980): 39–44; Morton Smith, 'Ascent to the Heavens and the Beginnings of Christianity', *Eranos* 50 (1981): 403–29.

49. Crispin Fletcher-Louis, 'The Revelation of the Sacral Son of Man: The Genre, History of Religions Context, and Meaning of the Transfiguration', in *Auferstehung-Resurrection: 4th Durham-Tübingen Research Symposium: Resurrection, Transfiguration, and Exaltation in the Old Testament, Ancient Judaism, and Early Christianity*, ed. H. Lichtenberger (Tübingen: Mohr Siebeck, 2001), 261–71.

50. Ibid., 264–5.

51. Crispin Fletcher-Louis, 'The Worship of Divine Humanity as God's Image and the Worship of Jesus', in *The Jewish Roots of Christological Monotheism: Papers from the St. Andrews Conference on the Historical Origins of the Worship of Jesus*, ed. Carey C. Newman, James R. Davila, and Gladys S. Lewis (Leiden: Brill, 1999), 112–28; 'The Revelation of the Sacral Son of Man', 272; Crispin Fletcher-Louis, 'Jesus as the High Priestly Messiah Part 1', *Journal for the Study of the Historical Jesus* 4, no. 2 (2006): 155–75; Crispin Fletcher-Louis, 'Jesus as the High Priestly Messiah Part 2', *Journal for the Study of the Historical Jesus* 5, no. 1 (2007): 57–79.

However, others, principally Riesenfeld,[52] see evidence of a *historical* connection between Temple traditions associated with Sukkoth and the Transfiguration's mention of tabernacles. However, Reisenfeld makes connections spanning considerable periods of time, without defining how these connections are judged to have been discerned. This lack of analytic rigour seems to be the principal reason for the almost complete dismissal of his ideas by modern scholars.

A further voice which has interpreted the Transfiguration in terms of temple ideas is Margaret Barker. Just as with Riesenfeld, the historical connections she claims to have made back to the first Jerusalem Temple and its cultic life are difficult to prove.[53] However, Barker's work has produced some important insights in related areas. Principal amongst these is the importance of a range of motifs connected with the Temple present in the New Testament, even if one chooses not to see them, as she argues, as the vestiges of a cruelly suppressed First Temple theology. In addition, Barker has reasserted, as a result of considerable study of the Enochic tradition, the connection between apocalyptic writing and the conceptual world of the temple, frequently expressed through accounts of visionary experience of the heavenly temple dwelling of God.[54] She has, like Fletcher-Louis, underlined a number of connections between the Transfiguration narratives and the texts of the Enoch tradition, especially parallels with *2 Enoch* 22.[55] In addition, her work on the role of the High Priest has emphasized many elements which conceivably cohere closely with the Transfiguration accounts, such as his angelic, possibly divine status; the significance of his garments; and the symbolism of light associated with Resurrection.[56]

Working in a similar area as Barker, Rachel Elior's work makes, in a more tentative and scholarly convincing way, a series of similar but less speculative assertions. Elior argues that conceptions of heaven found in apocalyptic works and the Hekhalot literature as a temple space, and of priests as angelic figures, emerge from the mystical speculation of groups of priests excluded at various points from

---

52. Harald Riesenfeld, *Jésus Transfiguré: l'arrière-plan récit évangélique de la Transfiguration de Notre-Seigneur* (Copenhagen: E. Munksgaard, 1947).

53. Margaret Barker, *The Hidden Tradition of the Kingdom of God* (London: SPCK, 2007), esp. 4–28; Margaret Barker, *Temple Themes in Christian Worship* (London: T&T Clark, 2007), 1–18; Margaret Barker, *The Gate of Heaven: The History and Symbolism of the Temple in Jerusalem* (Sheffield: Sheffield Phoenix Press, 2008).

54. Margaret Barker, *The Lost Prophet: The Book of Enoch and Its Influence on Christianity* (Sheffield: Sheffield Phoenix Press, 2005), 29–53.

55. Barker, *The Hidden Tradition of the Kingdom of God*, 44; *Temple Themes in Christian Worship*, 113–14.

56. Margaret Barker, *On Earth as it is in Heaven: Temple Symbolism in the New Testament* (Edinburgh: T&T Clark, 1995), 13–25, 61–72; *The Hidden Tradition of the Kingdom of God*, 54–76; *Temple Themes in Christian Worship*, 160–5; *The Gate of Heaven*, 111–14, 148–50.

the life of the Jerusalem Temple. She argues for a widespread conceptual parallel drawn by many in the first century AD between the life of the Jerusalem Temple and conceptions of heaven as a similar cultic space, and for the frequent conception of heavenly figures as both priestly and angelic.[57]

Rhetorical- and narrative-critical readings

A number of commentators have subjected the Transfiguration narratives to readings informed by the concerns of literary theory and rhetorical- and narrative-critical approaches.

John Paul Heil, for example, has focused on the narratives' genre in order to explore how the gospels' readers might expect to interpret the Transfiguration. He categorizes the incident as a 'pivotal mandatory epiphany',[58] which gives a proleptic view of Christ's future glory.

A further approach to the Transfiguration narratives is that taken by Simon Lee,[59] in which he sees the Transfiguration narratives of the synoptic gospels as part of the way in which the broader concept of transfiguration and transformation was received by the earliest followers of Jesus. His work represents an analysing of the history of a concept rather than of three discrete narratives. He sees the Transfiguration to be the expression in narrative form by Mark, and then the later synopticists, of a number of ideas explored by Paul in 2 Corinthians 3,[60] concerning Jesus' exaltation and triumph over suffering, and the transfiguration which the Christian believer hoped for both in this life and in the world to come.

The treatment which the Transfiguration narrative receives in Edith Humphrey's work on the rhetoric of vision in the New Testament should be noted. She argues that reports of visions are used by the writers of the New Testament to achieve a number of rhetorical ends in terms of completing, directing and shaping the narrative. Her small section on the Transfiguration[61] points appositely to ways in which Luke's narrative emphasizes visionary elements, such as the disciples' sleep.

---

57. Rachel Elior, *The Three Temples: On the Emergence of Jewish Mysticism* (Oxford: Littman Library of Jewish Civilization, 2004), esp. 165–231.

58. Heil, *The Transfiguration of Jesus*, 43–92.

59. Simon S. Lee, *Jesus' Transfiguration and the Believers' Transformation: A Study of the Transfiguration and its Development in Early Christian Writings*, Wissenschaftliche Untersuchungen Zum Neuen Testament (Tübingen: Mohr Siebeck, 2009).

60. For an exploration of 2 Corinthians 3 in relation to the Transfiguration, see ibid., 49–91.

61. Edith McEwan Humphrey, *And I Turned to See the Voice: The Rhetoric of Vision in the New Testament* (Grand Rapids, MI: Baker Academic, 2007), 135–50.

Conclusions

In this chapter, I have pointed to a number of areas where a lack of consensus is to be found in modern scholarly discussion of our topic, which, in turn, reveal much about the scopic regime within which it takes place.

The first is a lack of clarity concerning precisely what critical study of the Transfiguration narratives is attempting to uncover. For some, it is an attempt to establish what historical event or series of events lies behind the text. For others, it is simply a question of explaining the cultural milieu which produced a fictional narrative claiming to be the fruit of visionary experience. A majority of modern critics bring to their study of the Transfiguration a critical presupposition that the event as recounted simply cannot have happened. This results in a value judgement which neglects the significance of visionary motifs, or which judges them to be a fictive construct or the fruit of unsoundness of mind. It also prompts a near universal ignoring of patristic comment as being of any use in the answering of critical questions to do with the Transfiguration narratives. The perspectives of earlier commentators are rarely seen as a worthwhile source of insight. The narrower range of questions that modern critics are interested in also means many other historical questions have not been investigated by them. These neglected questions include how these narratives were interpreted differently in changing periods of Christian history; the role they played in dogmatic, liturgical and ascetic speculation; and the influence which visual depiction of the Transfiguration had on hermeneutic and homiletic discourse.

In addition to a neglect of patristic comment, we also see considerable variation in what the visionary experience of the Transfiguration is understood to be within modern comment. For some, it stands as recognition of the existence of the supernatural breaking in on the terrestrial. For others, it is seen as a psychological phenomenon, or as an example of either ecstatic religious experience or a culturally conditioned metaphor. A majority of modern New Testament scholarship dismisses outright the possibility that the Transfiguration is rooted in any historically verifiable visionary event. Many historical-critical examinations have failed to examine the participatory role of the disciples in the narrative as viewers, and the ambiguity which exists concerning their entry into the cloud. As part of these tendencies, the distinctive Lucan version has regularly been either unsatisfactorily explained, or its distinct elements overlooked.

We have noted a small number of critics who have sought to explain the Transfiguration in the context of apocalyptic traditions. Their work has revealed a number of parallels with heavenly ascent narratives, the Enochic corpus, developing angelologies and temple and High Priestly echoes, but has often failed to gain widespread scholarly recognition. Because of the claim made by most apocalyptic writings to be the product of visionary experience, these scholars have often been more ready to recognize the importance of motifs associated with ecstatic religious experience.

I argue, therefore, that there are shortcomings in four areas of modern scholarship's appraisal of the Transfiguration narratives. The first concerns the best methodology and critical approach to be adopted in study of the Transfiguration, and what that approach is intended to discover. This has resulted in the almost universal neglect by modern critics of pre-critical comment as having any use in the elucidation of the Transfiguration narratives. It has also prompted an ignoring of their reception history as having any role in a full account of these texts' historical significance and meaning. A second problem concerns what is understood by the notion of vision, especially as presented in the Transfiguration, and how the ancient world understood sight as a physical faculty and a wider metaphor for experiences in the lives of those who read these narratives. Third, few have adequately accounted for a number of visionary elements, such as ambiguity concerning the disciples' participation in the Transfiguration as spectators who enter the overshadowing cloud, and the presence of priestly, tabernacle and temple echoes. Fourth, it appears that few have accounted for the distinct nature of the Lucan version and the particularly prominent role these visionary, participatory, priestly and temple themes may have in it.

I wish to suggest that one way through the impasses we have outlined in modern interpretation is to survey patristic interpretation and artistic depiction of the Transfiguration, as a way of supplementing the insights of modern New Testament scholarship and as a way of establishing how the Transfiguration narratives were first interpreted and understood within the scopic regime of antiquity.

Chapter 4

RECEPTION OF THE TRANSFIGURATION IN 2 PETER, THE *APOCALYPSE OF PETER*, THE *ACTS OF PETER* AND THE *ACTS OF JOHN*

Having outlined the need for a surveying of the reception history of the Transfiguration, this chapter explores its earliest reception in the Second Epistle of Peter, the *Apocalypse of Peter*, the *Acts of Peter* and the *Acts of John*. These are the first documents to discuss, use and interpret the Transfiguration in narratives written either about the lives of the apostles or pseudonymously in their name. In documenting this early reception, we see evidence of a scopic regime which prises highly the *participation* of the disciples in the Transfiguration vision and asks questions about the character and consequences of that participation. In the texts examined in this chapter, a repeated trope is the conviction that the disciples' vision needed to be altered to make possible their witnessing of the Transfiguration.

I show that the writer of 2 Peter uses language capable of evoking the Transfiguration as an ecstatic, visionary experience which bestows privileged authority on its seer. In addition, the *Apocalypse of Peter* interprets the Transfiguration as a visionary entrance into heaven which draws on Luke's narrative. The *Acts of Peter* and *Acts of John* show the Transfiguration being used in more docetic discourse about the appearance of Jesus, which requires the apostles' vision to be altered. Although all these texts make very different rhetorical and theological points, the status of the Transfiguration as a text describing visionary experience is crucial to their arguments.

2 Pet. 1.16-18

The account of the Transfiguration found in 2 Pet. 1.16-18 differs in many respects from that found in the synoptic narratives. It contains neither a direct reference to an overshadowing cloud nor any description of a change in the appearance of Jesus or the presence of Moses and Elijah. The number of disciples who witness the Transfiguration is not recounted in 2 Peter. This text replaces all descriptions of Jesus' change of appearance by reference to his receiving 'honour and glory', and describes this glory being bestowed on Jesus by the voice which comes from heaven, directed to Jesus. All mention of Peter's confusion, sleep, fear or his suggestion concerning tabernacles is absent, and the account seems to be marshalled as evidence in arguments concerning the certainty of Christ's Parousia.

A significant question addressed by modern scholarship is whether this account represents an independent tradition concerning the Transfiguration, as argued by Richard Bauckham,[1] or whether it is dependent on the synoptic gospel accounts, as Robert Miller[2] and Michael Gilmour[3] have proposed. Miller has shown the evidence of Bauckham's argument to be so finely balanced as to be difficult to prove conclusively. In the absence of a more robustly proven theory positing anything other than the *possibility* of independence for 2 Peter, Miller suggests that the simplest explanation is to assume reliance on Matthew. Gilmour sees the presence of allusions to Matthew's Transfiguration as tipping the scales of likelihood in the direction of reliance by 2 Peter on that gospel. I find Miller's and Gilmour's logic convincing in that they do not offer an exhaustively comprehensive answer but simply point to the difficulty of proving independence conclusively and the importance of a series of likely, though not unassailably, proven allusions to Matthew's Transfiguration. I will regard 2 Pet. 1.16-18, therefore, as an example of the earliest reception of the gospels' accounts of the Transfiguration.

We will focus in this study on the language 2 Peter uses of 'eyewitness' to describe Peter's experience of the Transfiguration and show that the writer may be aware of a range of meaning that language is able to evoke concerning the way in which Peter's vision was altered to perceive the event. An assumption lying behind 2 Peter's account could be that Peter experienced some sort of ecstatic vision which bestowed upon him privileged knowledge and sight. We see in 2 Peter the first hints at speculation concerning the precise nature of Peter's vision, a topos which becomes a frequent focus of debate in later comment.

Most modern scholars of 2 Peter see the writer marshalling the Transfiguration as evidence to support belief in the return of Jesus, with Peter's experience of the Transfiguration seen as a foretaste of the glory Jesus will have on the Last Day as eschatological judge.[4] For them, the writer's polemical aims explain his leaving out elements from the gospel accounts as a jettisoning of anything not focused on Jesus' future eschatological glory. Of crucial importance is the writer's claim at 2 Pet. 1.16 to be amongst the 'eyewitnesses of his majesty' (ἐπόπται ... τῆς ἐκείνου μεγαλειότητος).

---

1. Richard Bauckham, *Jude, 2 Peter*, Word Biblical Commentary (Waco, TX: Word Books, 1983), 205–10.

2. Robert Miller, 'Is there Independent Attestation for the Transfiguration in 2 Peter?', *New Testament Studies* 42 (1996): 620–5.

3. Michael J. Gilmour, *The Significance of Parallels between 2 Peter and Other Early Christian Literature* (Atlanta: Society of Biblical Literature, 2002), 99–100.

4. See, e.g., Bauckham, *Jude, 2 Peter*, 212; Jerome H. Neyrey, 'The Apologetic Use of the Transfiguration in 2 Peter 1.16-21', *Catholic Biblical Quarterly* 42 (1980): 504–19; Jerome H. Neyrey, *2 Peter, Jude: A New Translation with Introduction and Commentary* (Garden City, NY: Doubleday, 1993), 172–4.

Jerome Neyrey emphasizes the pseudepigraphical character of the letter and sees this language of eyewitness as simply intended to increase the credibility of the narrator's voice.[5] However, Bauckham asserts that the eyewitness claim is best explained by the theological assertions it makes about the character of the Transfiguration and the Parousia as sure events which could be apprehended by human sight.[6] For him, the author evokes the claim by Peter to have seen the Transfiguration in order to argue that the reader's seeing of the Parousia is just as likely.

However, the term 'eyewitnesses' (ἐπόπται) evokes a range of meaning in ancient discourse and has a history of signifying those initiated into esoteric mystical traditions. It does not simply describe uncommitted, dispassionate viewing but necessarily includes some sense of comprehension. Wilhelm Michaelis translates the word's basic sense as 'one who sees and notes something'.[7] It can also have a hierarchical and cultic meaning indicating one set in oversight over others in which vision communicates authority. Josephus uses the word to describe the Temple priests,[8] for example, as the 'overseers of all things'. Some scholars have pointed to the way in which this New Testament *hapax* is used to describe those initiated into the highest of the Eleusinian mysteries, a usage Clement of Alexandria was aware of.[9] Although the content of these mysteries is much debated, the dramas which took place only for the view of the initiates had a highly visual and dramatic form.[10] In addition, initiation into the Greater Mysteries seems frequently to have involved claims to dreams and ecstatic vision, often associated with the taking of a drink called the *kykeon*. Mention of this potion has led to considerable speculation as to whether it might have contained some sort of hallucinogenic agent.[11] We must conclude that the word can, in certain circumstances, carry a sense of initiated knowledge of the divine, especially revealed through ecstatic vision.

Many New Testament commentators have been suspicious of seeing this ecstatic sense present in 2 Pet. 1.16.[12] However, Horst Balz and Gerhard Schneider

---

5. Neyrey, *2 Peter, Jude*, 129–41.

6. Bauckham, *Jude, 2 Peter*, 216.

7. Wilhelm Michaelis, 'Ἐπόπτης', in *Theological Dictionary of the New Testament* (Grand Rapids, MI: Eerdmans), vol. 5, 373.

8. *Contra Apionem*, 2.187 H, St J. Thackeray, *Josephus*, Loeb Classical Library (Cambridge, MA: Harvard University Press, 1958), vol. 1, 366.

9. Clement of Alexandria, *Stromateis*, 3.3.17, Wilhelm Dittenberger, *Sylloge Inscriptionum Graecarum* (Lipsiae: apud S. Hirzelium, 1898), 42, 48ff.

10. Harold R. Willoughby, *Pagan Regeneration: A Study of Mystery Initiations in the Graeco-Roman World* (Chicago: University of Chicago Press, 1929), 37–67.

11. Walter Burkert, *Ancient Mystery Cults* (Cambridge, MA: Harvard University Press, 1987), 93–5, 108; R. Gordon Wasson, Carl A. Ruck and Albert Hofmann, *The Road to Eleusis: Unveiling the Secret of the Mysteries* (Los Angeles: William Dailey Rare Books, 1998), 21–60.

12. E.g. Simon Lee, *Jesus' Transfiguration and the Believers' Transformation: A Study of the Transfiguration and its Development in Early Christian Writings*, Wissenschaftliche

show it is difficult to prove it is completely absent.[13] Much hangs on whether one interprets the mention of following 'cleverly concocted myths' to be an argument of the writer's opponents being answered[14] or an accusation of the writer.[15] Neyrey convincingly shows the rhetorical significance of the 'Οὐ ... ἀλλα' construction used by the writer to make best sense if seen as the first reply to his opponents' arguments. It is unclear whether these opponents themselves make claim to exclusive gnostic revelation, or whether they argue that the Parousia is akin to it. Their argument would seem to be that Christian expectation concerning the Parousia is to be dismissed as fanciful and not provable by evidence of any sort. The writer introduces the Transfiguration as the evidence he needs to prove the likelihood of the future event he defends and holds himself out as amongst the 'ἐπόπται' who witnessed it. Either this is intended to trump the gnostic knowledge of his opponents by showing them to be outside the initiated circle he shares with his readers or to argue against their protestations concerning the authenticity of his revealed witness. Either way, his claim to legitimate authority over them is rooted in his claim to have received authentic revelation at the Transfiguration.

Conclusion

It seems difficult entirely to exclude the possibility that something more than the simple forensic reliability of sense vision is being evoked by use of the phrase 'eyewitnesses of his majesty' (ἐπόπται ... τῆς ἐκείνου μεγαλειότητος). I agree

Untersuchungen Zum Neuen Testament (Tübingen: Mohr Siebeck, 2009), 136; Michaelis, 'Εποπτης', 375; Neyrey, *2 Peter, Jude,* 176; Donald Senior and Daniel J. Harrington, *1 Peter, Jude and 2 Peter,* Sacra Pagina Series (Collegeville, MN: Liturgical Press, 2003), 255–6.

13. As argued in *Exegetical Dictionary of the New Testament,* ed. Horst Balz and Gerhard Schneider, vol. 2, 46; Michael Green, *The Second Epistle General of Peter and the General Epistle of Jude: An Introduction and Commentary,* Tyndale New Testament Commentaries (London: Tyndale Press, 1968), 83; J. N. D. Kelly, *A Commentary on the Epistles of Peter and of Jude* (London: Black, 1969), 318.

14. As argued by Bauckham, *Jude, 2 Peter,* 205; Tord Fornberg, 'An Early Church in a Pluralistic Society: A Study of 2 Peter' (Uppsala: CWK Gleerup, 1977), 60; Green, *The Second Epistle General of Peter and the General Epistle of Jude,* 81–2; Kelly, *Commentary on the Epistles of Peter and of Jude,* 316; Neyrey, *2 Peter, Jude,* 170; Terence V. Smith, *Petrine Controversies in Early Christianity: Attitudes towards Peter in Christian Writings of the First Two Centuries,* Wissenschaftliche Untersuchungen Zum Neuen Testament, 2 Reihe (Tübingen: J.C.B. Mohr, 1985), 78.

15. As argued by Walter Grundmann, *Der Brief Des Judas Und Der Zweite Brief Des Petrus,* Theologischer Handkommentar Zum Neuen Testament (Berlin: Evangelische Verlagsanstalt, 1974), 59–64, 80; Karl Hermann Schelkle, *Die Petrusbriefe; Der Judasbrief: Auslegung* (Freiburg: Herder, 1961), 197; Wolfgang Schrage, *Die 'Katholischen' Briefe: Die Briefe des Jakobus, Petrus, Johannes und Judas,* Neue Testament Deutsch (Göttingen: Vandenhoeck & Ruprecht, 1993), 135.

with J. N. D. Kelly that it implies the writer is, at least, 'aware that it suggests privileged admission to a divine revelation.'[16] The language of eyewitness could be capable of evoking the ecstatic, visionary practices of the mystery cults. For the writer of 2 Peter, the Transfiguration similarly requires altered perception and bestows revealed insight upon its witnesses. If some degree of extraordinary vision is implied by the word 'eyewitnesses' (ἐπόπται), then 2 Peter points to the Transfiguration as an experience which requires vision beyond the sense faculty of sight. In other words, the narrator assumes the only way one would believe the evidence of someone claiming to have experienced the Parousia before its time would be if they were in a state of altered, privileged vision. Although 2 Peter says little explicitly about the precise nature of the epistemic state Peter may have been in, it foregrounds a question which will return time and time again throughout patristic comment, namely whether the disciples' vision needed to be altered in order to perceive the Transfiguration. The narrator assumes the authority of a figure who received privileged vision which gave him a distinct authority to report something which is otherwise unavailable to the sight of others, but which in the Parousia will be made known to all.

The Apocalypse of Peter

The *Apocalypse of Peter* is a second-century text whose origins and precise dating have been the focus of recent discussion. A widely held theory that its reference to a 'Liar' figure is Simon Bar Kokhba, who revolted against Roman rule in 132,[17] is being challenged and has become a lively focus of debate.[18] Until the nineteenth century, the *Apocalypse of Peter* was only known about through a number of fleeting patristic quotations and its listing in the Muratorian canon as an apocryphal text. However, a Greek version was found in Akhmim, Upper Egypt, in 1886, and a fuller version in Ethiopic was recovered in 1910.

The 'Transfiguration' scene in the Ethiopic and Greek 'Akhmim' texts of the Apocalypse of Peter

The Ethiopic version recounts an extended Olivet discourse, which draws heavily on Matthew 24. After Jesus' prediction of the end time, a description of hell and allusions to Peter's martyrdom in Rome, there follows a transfiguration scene of

---

16. Kelly, *Commentary on the Epistles of Peter and of Jude*, 318.

17. Richard Bauckham, 'The Two Fig Tree Parables in the Apocalypse of Peter', *Journal of Biblical Literature* 104, no. 2 (1985): 269–87; Richard Bauckham, 'The Apocalypse of Peter: A Jewish Christian Apocalypse from the Time of Bar Kokhba', *Apocrypha* 5, no. 1 (1994): 7–111.

18. See Jörg Frey, Matthijs den Dulk and Jan van der Watt (eds), *2 Peter and the Apocalypse of Peter: Towards a New Perspective* (Leiden: Brill, 2019).

sorts.[19] Jesus addresses Peter suggesting he and the whole group of disciples ascend 'the holy mountain' to pray. On this mountain, Peter sees two men of appearance so glorious that they could hardly be gazed upon. Nothing is said at all concerning Jesus' appearance. Upon asking Christ who they are, Peter is informed that they are Moses and Elijah. Jesus then shows the seer a beautiful garden, full of fruits with a tree. Those who rest there are described as having 'honour' and 'glory'. At this point, Peter makes his suggestion concerning three tabernacles. This is dismissed by Christ, who describes Peter's understanding as being veiled by Satan. As a result, Peter is told his 'eyes therefore must be opened' and his, 'ears unstopped' so that he can see 'a tabernacle, not made with men's hands, which my heavenly Father has made for me and for the elect'.[20] This Peter then sees, whereupon a celestial voice is heard, and a white cloud carries Jesus, Moses and Elijah off into heaven.

The Akhmim text is much shorter. There is no ascension scene, no apocalyptic discourse at the beginning, and no mention of Peter's martyrdom. It simply contains the 'Transfiguration' scene, which happens as a result of the disciples asking to see the fate of those who had died.[21] However, the two glorious men are *not* described as Moses and Elijah but rather the 'righteous brethren whose appearance you wished to see'.[22] They are then shown 'a very great region outside this world, exceedingly bright with light',[23] full of blossoms and fruits in which the righteous dwell in angelic appearance. Following this, Peter sees a tour of hell, at the end of which the text finishes.

There are two significant differences between the two 'transfiguration' texts. First, in the Akhmim, the tour of hell is in the form of a vision experienced by Peter, which follows on from the 'transfiguration' vision. In the Ethiopic, however, hell is simply *described* by Jesus to Peter, and leads up to the final transfiguration vision and ascension scene. Second, the Akhmim 'transfiguration' and heavenly tour appears to be more concerned with the *present* state of Christians who have *already* died. By contrast, the Ethiopic version sees its 'transfiguration' narrative in terms of the *future* eschatological fate of Jewish Christian believers. Indeed, the 'transfiguration' in the Akhmim version seems more distant from the synoptic narratives than the Ethiopic, and to be much closer to a description of the righteous in heaven, than a narrative drawing on an incident in the earthly life of Jesus. Largely because early work on the *Apocalypse of Peter* was focused on the Akhmim

---

19. Dennis D. Buchholz, *Your Eyes Will Be Opened: A Study of the Greek (Ethiopic) Apocalypse of Peter*, Society of Biblical Literature (Atlanta: Scholars Press, 1988), 232–43.

20. Ibid., 241; J. K. Elliott and M. R. James, *The Apocryphal New Testament: A Collection of Apocryphal Christian Literature in an English Translation* (Oxford: Clarendon Press, 1993), 611.

21. Die griechischen christlichen Schriftsteller der ersten Jahrhunderte (GCS), Neue Folge, 11, 104–9.

22. Die griechischen christlichen Schriftsteller der ersten Jahrhunderte (GCS), Neue Folge, 11, 106; Elliott and James, *The Apocryphal New Testament*, 610.

23. Elliott and James, *The Apocryphal New Testament*, 610.

text, many scholars such as Martin Dibelius and Rudolf Bultmann saw the Greek as the earlier version.[24] Since then, scholarly consensus has moved considerably and now widely sees the Ethiopic version as the more reliable witness[25] to an original Greek text underlying both of these manuscripts, not least because of its closer conformity to known patristic quotations.[26] Simon Lee convincingly suggests that the Akhmim version represents a reworking in a context outside Jewish Palestine where mention of the patriarchs or Moses and Elijah would carry less weight, and that the Ethiopic text is probably a translation of an original intended for a more Jewish audience.[27] Hereafter, it will be assumed that any mention of the *Apocalypse of Peter* refers to the Ethiopic version unless otherwise stated.

The Apocalypse of Peter's relationship with New Testament texts

The relationship between the 'transfiguration' in the *Apocalypse of Peter* and the synoptic gospels and 2 Peter is a complex one. Earlier scholars[28] saw the *Apocalypse of Peter* for many years as evidence of a tradition more primitive to that

---

24. Rudolf Bultmann, *The History of the Synoptic Tradition*, 2nd ed. (Oxford: Blackwell, 1968), 432–433; Martin Dibelius, *Die Geschichte der urchristlichen Literatur* (Munich: Chr. Kaiser, 1975), 84.

25. Dennis Buchholz offers the most recent case for the reliability of the Ethiopic text, based in part on his careful examination of Manuscripts B and R, which frequently agree with the Ethiopic against the Akhmim text. See Buchholz, *Your Eyes will be Opened*, 107–109, 145–52, 418–22.

26. See also Richard Bauckham, *The Fate of the Dead: Studies on the Jewish and Christian Apocalypses*, Supplements to Novum Testamentum (Leiden: Brill, 1998), 163; Gilmour, *Parallels between 2 Peter and Other Early Christian Literature*, 107; M. R. James, 'A New Text of the Apocalypse of Peter', *Journal of Theological Studies* (1911): 367–75, 573–83; M. R. James, 'The Rainer Fragment of the Apocalypse of Peter', *Journal of Theological Studies* 32 (1931), 270–9; Erich Klostermann, 'Zur Petrusapokalypse', in *Hundert Jahre A. Marcus und E. Webers Verlag*, ed. A. Marcus und E. Webers Verlag (Bonn: A. Marcus and E. Webers Verlag, 1921), 77–8.; Lee, *Jesus' Transfiguration and the Believers' Transformation*, 146; K. Prumm, 'De Genuine Apocalysis Petri Textu Examen Testium Ian Notorum Et Novi Fragmenti Raineriani', *Biblica* 10 (1929): 62–80; P. Van Minnen, 'The Greek Apocalypse of Peter', in *The Apocalypse of Peter*, ed. Jan N. Bremmer and Istvan Czachesz (Leuven: Peeters, 2003), 15–39.

27. Lee, *Jesus' Transfiguration and the Believers' Transformation*, 146.

28. K. G. Goetz, *Petrus als Gründer und Oberhaupt der Kirche und Schauer von Gesichten nach den altchristlichen Berichten und Legenden* (Leipzig: J.C. Hinrichs, 1927), 76–92; Maurice Goguel, *La foi à la résurrection de Jésus dans le christianisme primitif* (Paris: Leroux, 1933), 326–30; Adolf von Harnack, *Geschichte der altchristlichen literatur bis Eusebius* (Leipzig: J.C. Hinrichs, 1893), Part 2, 470–2; Howard Merle Teeple, *The Mosaic Eschatological Prophet* (Philadelphia: Society of Biblical Literature, 1957), 84–6; Julius Wellhausen, *Das Evangelium Marci* (Berlin: Reimer, 1909), 71.

found in the gospels, since it has no direct description of Jesus' metamorphosis. This was frequently, however, part of now discounted theories conjecturing the Transfiguration as a misplaced Resurrection narrative. F. Spitta,[29] G. H. Boobyer[30] and most commentators following them have tended to see the *Apocalypse of Peter* as representing a more developed interpretation of the synoptic Transfiguration traditions, especially as the text seems to expand or explain elements in the synoptic accounts.

Many elements in the *Apocalypse of Peter*, however, seem to cohere more closely with the 2 Peter account of the Transfiguration than with synoptic accounts,[31] such as interpreting the Transfiguration in the light of Parousia ideas, a focus on false teachers, mention of 'honour and glory'[32] and ethical concerns described in terms of the 'way of righteousness'.[33] It is likely that a literary relationship exists between 2 Peter and the *Apocalypse of Peter*. Many have seen them as penned by the same writer,[34] or by writers of an identical theological school.[35] The debated question is whether 2 Peter is dependent on the *Apocalypse of Peter*, or the other way around. Although Bauckham sees 2 Peter as also influenced by a tradition independent from the gospels, a considerable range of scholars agree with his assertion of literary reliance by the *Apocalypse of Peter* on 2 Peter.[36] Lee sees 2 Peter and the *Apocalypse of Peter* in a looser relationship, with both dependent on common

---

29. F. Spitta, 'Die Petrusapokalypse und der Zweite Petrusbrief', *Zeitschrift für Neutestamentliche Wissenschaft* 12 (1911): 237–42.

30. G. H. Boobyer, *St. Mark and the Transfiguration Story* (Edinburgh: T&T Clark, 1942), 13–14.

31. Bauckham, *The Fate of the Dead*, 294–303; Buchholz, *Your Eyes Will Be Opened*, 97, footnote 3; J. Armitage Robinson and M. R. James, *The Gospel According to Peter, and the Revelation of Peter* (London: C. J. Clay, 1892), 52–3; Smith, *Petrine Controversies in Early Christianity*, 49–50.

32. Buchholz, *Your Eyes Will Be Opened*, 238; *Apoc. Pet.* 16, cf. 2 Pet. 1.17.

33. Akhmim *Apoc. Pet.* 28, cf. 2 Pet. 2.21.

34. Ernst Richard T. Kühl, *Die Briefe Petri und Judae* (Göttingen: Kritischexegetischer Kommentar über das Neue Testament, Vandenhoeck & Ruprecht, 1897), 375–6; W. Sanday, *Inspiration: Eight Lectures on the Early History and Origin of the Doctrine of Biblical Inspiration, being the Bampton Lecture for 1893* (London: Longmans, Green, 1894), 346–8, 384.

35. F. H. Chase, 'Peter, Second Epistle', in *Dictionary of the Bible* (New York: Schibner and Sons, 1900), vol. 3, 814–16; M. R. James, *The Second Epistle General of Peter and the General Epistle of Jude* (Cambridge: Cambridge University Press, 1912), xxvi–xxviii.

36. Bauckham, *The Fate of the Dead*, 303; Charles Bigg, *A Critical and Exegetical Commentary on the Epistles of St. Peter and St. Jude* (Edinburgh: T&T Clark, 1902), 207–9, 242–4, 265; Joseph Blinzler, *Die neutestamentlichen Berichte über die Verklärung Jesu* (Münster: Aschendorff, 1937), 73–6; Green, *The Second Epistle General of Peter and the General Epistle of Jude*, 34; Kelly, *Commentary on the Epistles of Peter and of Jude*, 236–7; Joseph B. Mayor, *The Epistle of St Jude and the Second Epistle of St Peter: Greek Text* (London: Macmillan, 1907), cxxx–cxxxiv; A. E. Simms, 'Second Peter and the Apocalypse

Petrine traditions.[37] However, a convincing challenge has been made recently by Jörg Frey,[38] Jan Bremmer,[39] Terrance Callan[40] and Wolfgang Grünstäudl[41] to Bauckham's theory in an attempt to resurrect the idea that the *Apocalypse of Peter* is actually the older text, on which 2 Peter is dependent.[42] They point to a number of elements which make better sense if the *Apocalypse of Peter* is assumed to be older, such as the way in which the eschatological delay so important in 2 Peter is not present in the *Apocalypse of Peter* at all, and the absence of any reference to Jude. Frey notes the 2 Peter Transfiguration differs from Matthew only in the areas where 2 Peter and the *Apocalypse of Peter* agree. If 2 Peter draws on the synoptic tradition rather than being independent, Frey argues that 2 Peter's Transfiguration is a combination of synoptic elements from Matthew with features from the already existing *Apocalypse of Peter*. Frey argues that 2 Peter is, therefore, a later text that responds to the *Apocalypse of Peters* assertions that Peter's death will usher in the end times, a view I find compelling.

The principal significance of the *Apocalyse of Peter* for this study is the way in which it explores imaginatively the sort of interpretation put forward by Crispin Fletcher-Louis, J. E. Fossum, M. Sabbe, W. Gerber and M. Öhler, which we explored in Chapter 3, that sees the Transfiguration as an apocalyptic opening of heaven, or even entry into it, pointing to Jesus as a High Priestly figure entering the celestial tabernacle. In the *Apocalypse of Peter*, the transfiguration scene is used as the opening of an ascension into heaven and is presented as a fulfilment of Psalm 24, with its entry of the King of Glory.[43] These new assessments of the *Apocalypse of Peter* led by Frey which date it earlier have renewed a sense of its importance as an example of reception of the Transfiguration which is earlier than that recorded in canonical 2 Peter.

of Peter', *Expositor* 8, Fifth Series (1898): 460-71; Smith, *Petrine Controversies in Early Christianity*, 53-4; Spitta, 'Die Petrusapokalypse und der zweite Petrusbrief', 237-43.

37. Lee, *Jesus' Transfiguration and the Believers' Transformation*, 163.

38. Frey, Dulk and Watt, *2 Peter and the Apocalypse of Peter*, esp. 15-23.

39. Jan Bremmer, 'The Apocalypse of Peter as the First Christian Martyr Text: Its Date, Provenance and Relationship with 2 Peter', in Frey, *2 Peter and the Apocalypse of Peter*, 75-98.

40. Terrance Callan, 'The Second Letter of Peter, Josephus, and Gnosticism', in Frey, Dulk and Watt, *2 Peter and the Apocalypse of Peter*, 128-46.

41. Grünstäudl, Wolfgang, *Petrus Alexandrinus: Studiun zum historischen und theologischen Ort des Zweiten Petrusbriefes*, WUNT 2/315 (Tübingen: Mohr Siebeck, 2013), 114-21.

42. Harnack, *Geschichte der altchristlichen Literatur bis Eusebius*, 470; M. Porter, *The Message of the Apocalyptical Writers* (New York: C. Scribner's Sons, 1905), 355; Robinson and James, *Gospel According to Peter, and the Revelation of Peter*, 819-20.

43. For an examination of the use of Psalm 24 in the *Apocalypse of Peter*, see Ernst Kähler, *Studien zum Te Deum and zur Geschichte des 24. Psalms in der alten Kirche*, Veröffentlichungen der evangelischen Gesellschaft für Liturgieforschung (Göttingen: Vandenhoeck & Ruprecht, 1958), 53-5.

However, the text of the *Apocalypse of Peter* also presents a large number of complications. It must be asked if the transfiguration in the *Apocalypse of Peter* actually is a transfiguration in the sense understood by the synoptic gospel writers.[44] After all, the *Apocalypse of Peter*'s focus is on Moses and Elijah with no interest in describing any change to Jesus' appearance. There seems to be a much stronger concentration on the Transfiguration as a sign of the eschatological destiny of the righteous, as exemplified by Moses and Elijah, rather than as a scene in which Jesus is revealed as glorified Son of Man. A further difference is that the *Apocalypse of Peter* describes the whole band of Twelve as present.

The *Apocalypse of Peter* is an important piece of evidence for this study as it reveals one way in which visionary traditions rooted in the synoptic Transfiguration narratives were interpreted and explored at a very early stage. I explore in the rest of this section the way it evokes temple and tabernacle motifs, its links to Revelation 11 and the influence of the Lucan narrative over it. I also look at the reception history of the *Apocalypse of Peter* to suggest that its influence in the interpretation of the Transfiguration could be more important than previously estimated.

Temple and tabernacle motifs

A distinguishing characteristic of the *Apocalypse of Peter* is the way in which it presents the Transfiguration as a vision of the heavenly tabernacle, the worship of those within it as priestly, and evokes a number of motifs associated with the Jerusalem Temple and Mount Zion.

Much comment has focused on Jesus' suggestion in the Ethiopic text 'Let us go to the holy mountain',[45] widely seen to be a reference to 2 Pet. 1.18. Some see the mountain mentioned in 2 Peter as holy, simply because the Transfiguration took place there.[46] Others see evidence of Sinai echoes.[47] Bauckham has suggested, however, that the holy mountain of 2 Pet. 1.18 could be Zion.[48] In the *Apocalypse of Peter*, the setting for the first half of the opening discourse is already the Mount of Olives in Jerusalem. To proceed from there to 'the holy mountain' most logically points to Zion as the destination. This also makes sense of the association of quotations from Ps. 24.6-9, with Jesus', Moses's and Elijah's ascension in *Apoc. Pet.* 17. Although the exact location of the mount in the *Apocalypse of Peter* is never explicitly resolved, it seems likely that an evocation of Zion is taking place.

---

44. F. Spitta asserts that the *Apocalypse of Peter* does not contain a Transfiguration at all but rather a revelation of the heavenly world ('Die evangelische Geschichte von der Verklärung Jesu', *Zeitschrift für Wissenschaftliche Theologie* 53 (1911): 126–30).

45. Buchholz, *Your Eyes will be Opened*, 233; *Apoc. Pet.* 15, Elliott and James, *The Apocryphal New Testament*, 609.

46. Senior and Harrington, *1 Peter, Jude and 2 Peter*, 256.

47. M. Sabbe, 'La rédaction du récit de la Transfiguration', in *La venue du messie: messianisme et eschatologie*, ed. E. Massaux (Bruges: Desclée de Brouwer, 1962), 75.

48. Bauckham sees a particular reference in 2 Pet. 1.18 to Ps. 2.6: *Jude, 2 Peter*, 221.

The *Apocalypse of Peter* also presents the Transfiguration as the revelation of a heavenly tabernacle. Jesus reproves Peter's suggestion concerning tents, saying Satan has 'veiled your understanding ... your eyes, therefore, must be opened and your ears unstopped that you may see a tabernacle, not made with men's hands, which my heavenly Father has made for me and for the elect'.[49] The narrator continues, 'And we beheld it, and were full of gladness.' Bauckham has made connections between this vision and the Jerusalem Temple. For him, the vision of a truer, heavenly tabernacle should be read as a critique of Bar Kokhba's intention to rebuild the earthly Jerusalem Temple.[50] However, it might be useful to make two further important points of clarification.

The first is to note how Jesus' reply interprets Peter's words. The connection made by Peter between the experience of the Transfiguration and the idea of tabernacles is not the thing being criticized. The focus of critique is the idea that they could be built with human hands. The *Apocalypse of Peter* interprets Peter's mention of tabernacles not as evidence of an inappropriate wanting to stay longer on the mountain but as correctly evoking the life of the heavenly tabernacle.

Second, it could be that the experience of the Transfiguration is itself being described as that viewing of God's tabernacle. It is unclear whether this viewing of the heavenly tabernacle is a second vision of something different, following on from the Transfiguration, or whether it represents an interpretation of that first vision. It would seem the most obvious reading is one in which the Transfiguration scene is apprehended imperfectly by Peter's sense of sight. Following this, Peter's 'eyes must be opened and ... ears unstopped that [he] might see a tabernacle not made with men's hands'. Peter's understanding is unveiled, and the disciples' vision of the heavenly tabernacle is their seeing of the same sight they viewed before. This viewing of the paradise garden as a temple space coheres with the conception found in many inter-testamental texts of Eden as a Holy of Holies.[51] The disciples are thus enabled to perceive with renewed sight that the 'transfiguration' they are witnessing is in fact a vision of the heavenly tabernacle dwelling of God and his elect. For the writer of the *Apocalypse of Peter*, the altering of Peter's vision enables his seeing the Transfiguration to become a vision of the heavenly tabernacle.

Further evidence of temple echoes is the language the *Apocalypse of Peter* uses to describe those in heaven as priests. In the Akhmim version, the disciples ask

---

49. Buchholz, *Your Eyes will be Opened*, 241; *Apoc. Pet.* 16, Elliott and James, *The Apocryphal New Testament*, 611.

50. Richard Bauckham, 'Jews and Jewish Christians in the Land of Israel at the Time of the Bar Kochba War with Special Reference to the Apocalypse of Peter', in *Tolerance and Intolerance in Early Judaism and Christianity*, ed. Graham Stanton and Guy Stroumsa (Cambridge: Cambridge University Press, 1998), 228-35.

51. E.g. *Jub.* 3.12 describes Eden as the holiest place on earth; *Jub.* 8.19 calls it the 'Holy of Holies'; *Jub.* 3.27 describes Adam offering incense; and *Jub.* 4.26 shows Enoch offering sacrifice in Eden. See also *1 En.* 25, *T. Levi* 18.6-14; *T. Dan* 5.12.

Jesus to show them 'one righteous person who had gone forth out of the world, in order that we might see of what manner of form they are'.[52] They then see 'the place of your *high priests*, the righteous men'.[53] However, a number of complexities are associated with this verse.

The first concerns how this mention of ἀρχιερεων should be translated. J. K. Elliott and M. R. James see the word as having no cultic significance at all and translate it as 'The Lord said to us, this is the place of your leaders, the righteous men'.[54] They seem to be taking their lead from the parallel Ethiopic text, 'And my Lord and God Jesus Christ said to me, "Have you seen the companies of the fathers?"'[55] Dennis Buchholz, too, is sceptical of giving this reference to high priests too much significance. He sees the presence of ἀρχιερεων as a corruption brought about by the presence of the word πατριαρχων both in the Rainer fragment of *Apoc. Pet.* 4.1-14 and in the Ethiopic version's mention of fathers at ch. 16.[56] He prefers a reading in the Greek text in which ἀρχιερεων is replaced with πατριαρχων. In many respects, Buchholz's conclusion is a reasonable hypothesis. However, I wish here to conjecture two further possibilities, which might also be considered. The first is to say that if ἀρχιερεων does represent a corruption of the Greek Akhmim text, the presence of temple and tabernacle motifs which we have outlined in the Ethiopic would seem to stand as a good explanation for it. It could either be a subliminal slip of the hand by a scribe who had noticed the presence of tabernacle themes in the original. Alternatively it could be a *deliberate* attempt to preserve in his Greek redaction some hint or sign post towards this reading of the Transfiguration, which his abbreviated narrative would otherwise be in danger of losing.

Second, I wish to raise the question of whether we need necessarily to see ἀρχιερεων as a corruption. In the light of the tabernacle and temple themes, whose presence I have outlined, might we not reconsider the possibility that Akhmim *Apoc. Pet.* 20 reads the paradise inhabited by the righteous as a temple-like tabernacle, just as Ethiopic *Apoc. Pet.* 16 does? The idea that the vindicated righteous share a priestly character as they worship in heaven is, after all, a common place in the New Testament.[57] Although I don't claim to have mustered overwhelmingly convincing evidence for the retention of ἀρχιερεων, I hope to have at least provided a theological rationale, which has not been proposed before, which allows us to speculate that retaining ἀρχιερεων might make theological sense in the context of the Ethiopic version.

---

52. GCS, Neue Folge, 11, 104; Akhmim *Apoc. Pet.* 5, Elliott and James, *The Apocryphal New Testament*, 609-10.

53. GCS Neue Folge, 11, 108; Akhmim *Apoc. Pet.* 20, Elliott and James, *The Apocryphal New Testament*, 611.

54. Elliott and James, *The Apocryphal New Testament*, 611.

55. *Apoc. Pet.* 20, J. K. Elliott and James, *The Apocryphal New Testament*, 601.

56. Buchholz, *Your Eyes will be Opened*, 236-8.

57. E.g. Rev. 1.6; 1 Pet. 2.4-8.

Possible evocation of Revelation 11 in the Apocalypse of Peter

In *Apoc. Pet.* 2, after Jesus has explained the fig tree parable, we are told, 'Enoch and Elijah shall be sent to teach them that this is the deceiver who must come into the world and do signs and wonders in order to deceive. And therefore, those who die by his hand shall be martyrs.'[58] At first glance this seems simply to be an evocation of well-known eschatological traditions concerning the advent of Elijah and Enoch before the end time. Bauckham reads this verse simply as pointing to Bar Kokhba as the deceiver concerned.[59] However, Seth Turner's work[60] has revealed that the two witnesses of Revelation 11 were almost universally interpreted as Enoch and Elijah throughout the patristic period and much less frequently as Moses and Elijah. We need to ask the question whether there might be any evocation of Revelation 11 detectable in the *Apocalypse of Peter*.

One problem is that further similarities between the *Apocalypse of Peter* and Revelation 11 are very few. The principal one, though, is the correlation between the way in which the Two Witnesses of Revelation 11 are taken up into heaven on a cloud after hearing a voice beckon them into heaven, and the description in *Apoc. Pet.* 17 of Moses, Elijah and Jesus being similarly taken up into heaven on the white overshadowing cloud, this time after hearing a heavenly voice declare Jesus to be the Father's beloved son. More broadly, Elliott sees allusions to the book of Revelation in other parts of the *Apocalypse of Peter*, especially in concepts such as God's judgement being 'true and just',[61] and seems to assume the writer knew Revelation. However, differences also abound. In the *Apocalypse of Peter* Transfiguration, Moses and Elijah are not eschatological prophets like the Witnesses of Revelation 11, whose advent presages the end time. In the *Apocalypse of Peter*, they simply stand as examples of the life of heaven which humanity will experience after the Parousia.

There seem also to be few correlations between Revelation 11 and the mention of Enoch and Elijah in *Apoc. Pet.* 2. There, Elijah and Enoch's vocation is pedagogic, teaching Israel who the real deceiver is and showing those who die at his hands therefore to be martyrs. By contrast, the Two Witnesses of Revelatioin 11 fight violently against their enemies, die and are resurrected, something of which there is no hint in the *Apocalypse of Peter*.

In sum, it is almost impossible to establish whether there is direct use of Revelation 11 in *Apoc. Pet.* 2, or whether the writer simply draws on similar traditions concerning eschatological prophet-witnesses as those that influenced John of Patmos. However, it is also difficult entirely to dismiss the possibility

---

58. Buchholz, *Your Eyes will be Opened*, 174; *Apoc. Pet.* 2, Elliott and James, *The Apocryphal New Testament*, 601.

59. Bauckham, 'The Apocalypse of Peter', 177-94.

60. Seth Turner, 'Revelation 11:1-13: History of Interpretation' (D.Phil. diss., University of Oxford, 2004), esp. 12-44.

61. Buchholz, *Your Eyes will be Opened*, 202; *Apoc. Pet.* 7; cf. Rev. 16.7; 19.2; Elliott and James, *The Apocryphal New Testament*, 604, footnotes 29 and 30.

of some sort of echo of Revelation 11 in the ascension scene of *Apoc. Pet.* 17. If Revelation 11 is an influence, then we see in the *Apocalypse of Peter* an early bringing of it together with a Transfiguration narrative. Revelation 11 could be an important text, which allows the writer of the *Apocalypse of Peter* to reinterpret the Transfiguration as part of an ascent into heaven. We will see this dynamic at work frequently when we examine visual depiction of the Transfiguration in Chapter 8 of this study. Reading the Transfiguration in the light of portions of the book of Revelation could be a remarkably early practice in its history of reception, and Revelation 11 could be one of the triggers which allow the writer of the *Apocalypse of Peter* to reinterpret the Transfiguration in terms of an ascent into heaven.

Links with Luke

I wish now to challenge the widely held view that Matthew's is the principal gospel to exert influence over the *Apocalypse of Peter*. Bauckham has convincingly proved that Matthew 24 is the principal influence behind the *Apocalypse of Peter*'s Olivet discourse.[62] In *Apoc. Pet.* 16, Peter states, 'I rejoiced and believed and understood that which is written in *the book* of my Lord Jesus Christ.'[63] The fact that only one book is mentioned here has moved Buchholz and Lee to think that the writer has access to only one principal gospel, which they assume to be Matthew.[64] While I do not wish to claim that Matthew's gospel is not an influence, this single mention of 'the book of my Lord Jesus Christ' cannot on its own count as convincing proof that the writer had access to only one gospel.

There are a number of motifs present in the *Apocalypse of Peter* only found in Luke's Transfiguration narrative. Amongst these, the mention of prayer,[65] both as the point of ascending the mountain (cf. Lk. 9.28) and as associated with the appearance of the two men in the Akhmim text (cf. Lk. 9.29), must count as significant. Further similarities between Luke's narrative and the *Apocalypse of Peter* include the fact that Luke links his Transfiguration with the betrayal at Olivet by making both incidents involve ascent of a hill to pray and the disciples falling asleep. Luke also draws connections between the Transfiguration and the Ascension, an instinct shared with the writer of the *Apocalypse of Peter*.[66] In

---

62. Bauckham, 'The Apocalypse of Peter', 168–76.

63. Buchholz, *Your Eyes will be Opened*, 239; *Apoc. Pet.* 16.6, Elliott and James, *The Apocryphal New Testament*, 611. Italics mine.

64. Buchholz, *Your Eyes will be Opened*, 370; Lee, *Jesus' Transfiguration and the Believers' Transformation*, 159–60.

65. Buchholz, *Your Eyes will be Opened*, 233–5 (Ethiopic *Apoc. Pet.* 15); GCS Neue Folge 11, 104 (Akhmim *Apoc. Pet.* 4); Elliott and James, *The Apocryphal New Testament*, 609.

66. Many have seen the discussion of the 'exodus' Jesus would accomplish in Jerusalem (Lk. 9.31) as a reference to the Ascension, not least because of its proximity to mention of Jesus' 'taking up' at Lk. 9.51 and because of the coincidence in the two narratives of use of the phrase 'behold two men' (Lk. 9.30; cf. Acts 1.10). See J. G. Davies, 'Prefiguration of the Ascension in the Third Gospel', *Journal of Theological Studies* 6, no. 2 (1955): 229–33.

addition, some account has to be made of the fact that the Greek *Apocalypse of Peter* uses the word 'glory' (only used by Luke) to describe the two men who appear and the heavenly world revealed in the vision. Akhmim *Apoc. Pet.* 6's description of Moses and Elijah's first appearance is also close to Luke's: both texts refer to Moses and Elijah as 'two men'; both describe them as appearing in, or clothed with 'glory'; and both refer to them as *standing*, a motif not mentioned in Mark or Matthew.

It must be acknowledged that the question of what constitutes the Gospel of Luke in the early stages of its redaction is debated. Recent scholarly voices have advocated the idea that Luke does not reach its final canonical form until later in the second century.[67] This theory posits an early Lucan text to which elements such as the birth narratives and the second volume of Acts are added much later in response to Maricon. Proponents of this theory would clearly be inclined to argue that the *Apocalypse of Peter* shows evidence of reliance on this 'early' Luke rather than its later canonical version. It lies beyond the scope of this study to add to this debate other than to comment on evidence touching the Transfiguration narratives. As will be discussed at greater length in the next chapter, the distinctive characteristic of canonical Luke's Transfiguration which is not found in Marcion's text is the discussion of Christ's exodus in Jerusalem. Whilst it is true that this is not echoed in the *Apocalypse of Peter*, this does not decisively prove either the existence

---

67. Scholars who have argued in favour of a late dating of Luke and Acts in the second century: Mark G. Bilby, 'Pliny's Correspondence and the Acts of the Apostles: An Intertextual Relationship', in *Luke on Jesus, Paul and Christianity: What Did He Really Know?*, ed. Joseph Verheyden and John S. Kloppenborg, BTS 29 (Leuven: Peeters, 2017), 171–89; Mark G. Bilby, 'The first Dionysian Gospel: Imitational and Redactional Layers in Luke and John', in *Classical Models of the Gospels and Acts: Studies in Mimesis Criticism*, ed. Mark G. Bilby, Michael Kochenash and Margaret Froelich, Claremont Studies in new testament and Christian Origins 3 (Claremont, CA: Claremont Press, 2018), 49–68; Mary Rose D'Angelo, 'The ANHP Question in Luke-Acts: Imperial Masculinity and the Deployment of Women in the Early Second Century', in *A Feminist Companion to Luke*, ed. Amy-Jill Levine (Sheffield: Sheffield Academic Press, 2002), 44–69; John S. Kloppenborg, 'Literate Media in Early Christ Groups: The Creation of a Christian Book Culture', *JECS* 22, no. 1 (2014): 21–59; Shelly Matthews, *Perfect Martyr: The Stoning of Stephen and the Construction of Christian Identity* (Oxford: Oxford University Press, 2010); Christopher Mount, *Pauline Christianity: Luke-Acts and the Legacy of Paul*, NovTSup 104 (Leiden: Brill, 2002); Laura Nasrallah, 'The Acts of the Apostles, Greek Cities, and Hadrian's Panhellenion', *JBL* 127, no. 3 (2008): 533–66; Richard I. Pervo, *Dating Acts: Between the Evangelists and the Apologists* (Santa Rosa, CA: Polebridge Press, 2006); Richard I. Pervo, *Acts*, Hermeneia (Minneapolis, MN: Fortress Press, 2009), 5–7; Joseph B. Tyson, 'The Date of Acts: A Reconsideration', *Forum* 5, no. 1 (2002): 33–51; Joseph B. Tyson, 'Why Dates Matter: The Case of the Acts of the Apostles', *The Fourth R* 18, no. 2 (2005): 8–14; Dennis Smith and Joseph B. Tyson, eds, *Acts and Christian Beginnings: The Acts Seminar Report* (Salem: Polebridge, 2013).

of an 'early Luke' or that the *Apocalypse of Peter* was solely influenced by it to the exclusion of a later canonical text. I judge it to be difficult, therefore, to prove that the *Apocalypse of Peter* was influenced by a version of Luke substantially different from its canonical form. Of all the possible connections between the *Apocalypse of Peter* and Luke, the mention of prayer is probably the most significant piece of evidence, as its presence in the *Apocalypse of Peter* is so unequivocal and its status as a specifically Lucan motif so secure. When considered in conjunction with the other Lucan echoes present in the *Apocalypse of Peter* which I have outlined, it would seem reasonable to detect greater influence by Luke's Transfiguration narrative on both the Ethiopic and Akhmim versions of the *Apocalypse of Peter* than has previously been assumed.

Reception history and influence of the Apocalypse of Peter

I now wish to make an initial assessment of the extent of the influence exerted by the *Apocalypse of Peter*. A chapter by Attila Jakab[68] traces evidence of use of the *Apocalypse of Peter* through the patristic period, in response to Bauckham's assertion that 'the Apocalypse of Peter evidently became a very popular work in the church as a whole, from the second to the fourth centuries.'[69] It becomes clear that Bauckham's assessment is broadly correct. Jakab points to evidence of initial popularity in the West, in Rome, Syria, Palestine and North Africa in the second and third centuries. The text only spreads to the great centres of Greek learning such as Constantinople by the fifth century. The last mention of it we possess is the evidence of Sozomen in early-fifth-century Constantinople: 'Thus the book entitled "The Apocalypse of Peter", which was considered altogether spurious by the ancients, is still read in some churches of Palestine, on the day of preparation, when the people observe a fast in memory of the passion of the Saviour [on Good Friday].'[70] It is evident that the question of its canonicity was increasingly being resolved in favour of exclusion from the New Testament, but local liturgical use in Palestine remained. After the fifth century the *Apocalypse of Peter* completely disappeared until the archaeological discoveries of the nineteenth century.

There is, however, a problem with the methodology employed by Jakab. His otherwise very thorough survey of the reception history of the *Apocalypse of Peter* only touches on written comment and excludes artistic depiction, and particularly the apse mosaic of the Transfiguration in the early-sixth-century church of Sant'Apollinare in Classe, Ravenna. I will argue in Chapter 8 that the *Apocalypse*

---

68. A. Jakab, 'The Reception of the Apocalypse of Peter Is Ancient Christianity', in *The Apocalypse of Peter*, ed. Jan N. Bremmer and Istvan Czachesz (Leuven: Peeters, 2003), 174–86.

69. Bauckham, *The Fate of the Dead*, 160.

70. Church History 7.19, *A Select Library of the Nicene and Post-Nicene Fathers of the Christian Church*, 14 vols (Grand Rapids, MI: T&T Clark, 1988), series 2, vol. 2, 390.

of Peter plays a significant role in the artistic conception of this apse mosaic.[71] Part of my argument in Chapter 8 is that this mosaic, in turn, exerts influence on later depictions in Rome. If one includes artistic depiction in one's survey of the *Apocalypse of Peter*'s reception history, it becomes clear its influence in Italy is possibly greater than Jakab thinks. Jakab's conclusion that its popularity in Rome declines from the second or third century onwards must be questioned. I will argue that the mosaic in Classe provides evidence that the *Apocalypse of Peter.* may have had a continued influence until at least the ninth century on depiction of the Transfiguration in Ravenna and Rome.

Conclusion

The 'transfiguration' narrative found in the *Apocalypse of Peter* contains a complex mixture of theological impulses and traditions. Its focus is not on a glorified presentation of Jesus but on the eschatological fate of the righteous, particularly prophets such as Moses and Elijah. However, the *Apocalypse of Peter* does seem to represent an early attempt to draw out a number of more apocalyptically orientated elements within the New Testament Transfiguration narratives which emphasize vision and entry into heaven, and which use cultic language appertaining to the experience of God's presence in the Jerusalem Temple and heavenly tabernacle. It is also possible that we see here early connections being made between the Transfiguration narratives and portions of the book of Revelation. It is possible that the *Apocalypse of Peter* draws on elements from Revelation 11 to conceive of the Transfiguration as a sort of ascension, or prelude, to it. I have also made a case for considering the possibility that Luke's gospel exercises a greater influence over the *Apocalypse of Peter* than has often been thought. When one includes visual depiction within an examination of the reception history of the *Apocalypse of Peter*, it is probable that it exercised more influence than has been imagined.

Acts of Peter and the Acts of John

Scenes drawing upon the Transfiguration narratives are also to be found in the *Act. Pet.* 20,[72] a text originating from Asia Minor probably around the end of the second century.[73] The complex relationship between *Act. Pet.* and *Act. Joh.*, a text in which a transfiguration scene of sorts is also to be found, has been the focus of

---

71. See especially Erich Dinkler, *Das Apsismosaik von S. Apollinare in Classe*, Wissenschaftliche Abhandlungen der Arbeitsgemeinschaft für Forschung des Landes Nordrhein-Westfalen (Köln: Westdeutscher Verlag, 1964), 90-5.

72. From now on, *Act. Pet.* and *Act. Joh.*

73. For discussion of dating and origins, see Lee, *Jesus' Transfiguration and the Believers' Transformation*, 171-2.

much scrutiny and little consensus.[74] I do not intend to make any contribution to that debate other than to compare the two Transfiguration scenes, which are very different.

Act. Joh. 90[75] recounts two transformations in the appearance of Jesus, which take place in the presence of Peter, James and John on a mountain. The first very sparely describes John beholding 'such a light on him that it is not possible for a man who uses mortal speech to describe what it was like'.[76] A second incident is then recounted in which Jesus is seen naked by John, with his feet lighting the ground. Jesus grows, so that his head touches heaven, then shrinks to pygmy proportions. When John cries out in astonishment, Jesus playfully tugs at John's beard, which causes him agony for thirty days.

The scene in *Act. Pet.* 20,[77] however, is very different. In Rome, Peter is invited to Marcellus's house and heals the sight of one of the many blind widows who have gathered there, by touching her. As he walks into Marcellus's dining room, a reading of the Transfiguration gospel is taking place for the blind widows. Peter then explains the reading in a little homily to those gathered and describes his experience on the mountain. He recounts how each of the disciples saw 'as his capacity permitted'.[78] He then describes falling down as if dead, overwhelmed by the brilliance of the light emitted by Jesus and imagining he had been blinded. Indeed, he wonders if the experience was deliberately designed to blind him. Upon being touched by Jesus, he is enabled to see him but in a 'form which [he] could comprehend'.[79] The room in which Peter is speaking, full of blind widows, suddenly fills with blinding light. The light cures the widows' sight, and only they are enabled to see it. They report seeing a vision of a man who appeared to some as an old man, to some as a young man and to some as a boy. Peter then gives a further speech in which he compares many paradoxes and opposites drawn from the scriptures which describe Christ.

---

74. See P. J. Lalleman, 'The Relation between the Acts of John and the Acts of Peter', in *The Apocryphal Acts of Peter*, ed. Jan Bremmer (Leuven: Peeters, 1998), 161–8, esp 168; Lee, *Jesus' Transfiguration and the Believers' Transformation*, 171–5; Dennis R. MacDonald, 'Which Came First? Intertextual Relationships amongst the Apocryphal Acts of the Apostles', *Semeia* 80 (1997): 11–41; R. F. Stoops, 'The Acts of Peter in Intertextual Context', *Semeia* 80 (1997): 57–86.

75. Richard Lipsius, ed., *Acta Apostolorum Apocrypha*, vol. II/1 (Hildesheim: Georg Olms Verlag, 1959), 195; Elliott and James, *The Apocryphal New Testament*, 317–18.

76. Lipsius, *Acta Apostolorum Apocrypha*, vol. II/1, 195; Elliott and James, *The Apocryphal New Testament*, 317.

77. Lipsius, *Acta Apostolorum Apocrypha*, vol. I, 66–9; Elliott and James, *The Apocryphal New Testament*, 413–15.

78. Lipsius, *Acta Apostolorum Apocrypha*, vol. I, 67; Elliott and James, *The Apocryphal New Testament*, 413.

79. Lipsius, *Acta Apostolorum Apocrypha*, vol. I, 67; Elliott and James, *The Apocryphal New Testament*, 317–18.

Many motifs present in the canonical accounts of the Transfiguration are absent from both of these 'transfigurations'. There is no mention of either Moses and Elijah, the cloud, tabernacles or a heavenly voice. The second transfiguration narrative found in *Act. Joh.* presents a miraculous polymorphy which only resembles the Transfiguration in the sense that it takes place on the top of a mountain. *Act. Pet.*, however, explicitly claims to present the narrative of the Transfiguration as it is found in the New Testament. It describes Peter explaining the narrative in a homily, which then seems to be experienced and exemplified in the vision the widows receive of Christ.

P. J. Lalleman feels the writer of *Act. Joh.* probably knew the synoptic gospel Transfiguration narratives but did not consider them 'authoritative'.[80] D. R. Cartlidge, by contrast, denies that there is any connection at all between the *Act. Joh.* transfigurations and the synoptic versions.[81] It is certainly the case that the second transfiguration in *Act. Joh.* is more distanced from the synoptic account than the first one, which is only the briefest of mentions. The *Act. Joh.* narrative displays a significantly more docetic impulse than that found in the *Act. Pet.* Transfiguration. The two texts also present very different notions of polymorphy. In *Act. Joh.*, Jesus' appearance during his earthly life changes in front of the eyes of one viewer, John, whereas in *Act. Pet.*, the polymorpy is a post-resurrection vision which is separately different to each of the blind widows. In the light of uncertainty amongst scholars concerning whether the *Act. Joh.* transfigurations should even be considered a version of the synoptic Transfiguration at all, I will simply note the possibility that they very freely and loosely rework a small number of elements from the Transfiguration narratives. These include the three disciples being present and the idea of ascending a mountain, and are used to create a very different polymorphous revelation of a docetic Christ.

A number of points can be made, however, about the narrative found in *Act. Pet.* which are pertinent to this study. The first is to note the degree to which it emphasizes an alteration of Peter's sense of sight. Peter insists that the three disciples present saw only in relation to their capacity to see, and Peter needed Jesus to touch him before he could witness Jesus in the form he could comprehend. It is unclear which gospel this detail is drawing from. Only Matthew mentions a falling down and a touching of the disciples by Jesus, but this moment is usually seen to signal the end of the vision. It could be that the writer interprets the words 'but they saw no-one but Jesus only'[82] as a further vision, the one which Peter could comprehend. The themes of blindness and sight are also carefully interwoven. Peter, for example, imagines he has been blinded during his vision of Jesus, whilst the blind widows are the only ones who see the light which fills the rooms after Peter's homily. In his sermon, Peter's principal point is that the incident was one in

---

80. See P. Lalleman, *The Acts of John* (Leuven: Peeters, 1998), 126.
81. D. R. Cartlidge, 'Transfigurations and Metamorphosis Traditions in the Acts of John, Thomas and Peter', *Semeia* 38 (1986): 54.
82. Mt. 17.8.

which he first lost his sense of mortal sight and then regained the ability to see the greater wonder of Jesus in a form he could comprehend, a process which seems then to be echoed in the experience of the blind widows.

A second point worth noting is the way in which Peter's speech after the curing of the blind widows raises a particular hermeneutic tradition also found in Origen. Both Origen and *Act. Pet.* hold that Jesus could present himself in different forms to different people at different times, and both *Act. Pet.* and Origen speak of the disciples seeing in accordance with their spiritual capacity.[83] In addition to this, they share a similar interpretation dependent on comparing the exaltation of the Transfiguration with the kenosis of the incarnation. Peter's speech presents a number of binary opposites, which exemplify Jesus' life. The first opposite he presents is that between the Transfiguration and Isa. 53.4. He contrasts the exaltation of the Transfiguration with the kenosis of the Suffering Servant who 'bore our sufferings and carried our transgressions'. In the next chapter, we will note how Origen also makes a similar contrast, using Isa. 53.4 and the Philippians hymn.[84]

The Transfiguration we see in *Act. Pet.* presents the Transfiguration as an incident in which Peter's sight needed to be altered in order to give him true sight. This emphasis on the need for transformation of sight is then exemplified in the vision experienced by the blind widows. Vision of the transformed Christ, be that on the Mount of Transfiguration or in Marcellus's dining room, paradoxically emerges both in Peter's and in the widows' experience from a state of blindness. However, even then, what is seen with that renewed sight is problematic and resists reporting, for Peter recounts nothing of what he saw, simply that he could comprehend it, whilst the blind widows offer contradictory stories concerning what image of Christ was revealed to them. *Act. Pet.* presents this miraculous sight not only as the product of miraculous transformation in the viewer but also as an equivocal phenomenon which resists human ability to describe in words. *Act. Pet.*, nonetheless, represents a further example of the Transfiguration being reused and reinterpreted as part of a narrative involving Peter in which the transformation of his sight is emphasized as a prerequisite of his witnessing the Transfiguration.

Conclusion

I argue in this chapter that the question of the visionary status of the Transfiguration forms a very significant part of the earliest reception of the narrative, especially in texts which describe the life of Peter, or which are written pseudonymously in his name.

In 2 Peter, Peter is described as an eyewitness of the event, yet uses language which could be capable of evoking an understanding of that vision as an ecstatic

---

83. Cf. *Contra Cels.* 2.64 (PG 11, 897, B).
84. *Contra Cels.* 6.76. (PG 11, 1413) and *Hom. Luc.* 18.1 (SC 87, 264).

experience in which Peter's vision is altered to reveal to him privileged knowledge. Such an assertion makes rhetorical sense and bestows on the Petrine narrator authority to speak of mysteries unseen by his readers.

In the *Apocalypse of Peter*, we see a very different reworking of the Transfiguration in which it is portrayed as a visionary entry into heaven. Here, too, the writer insists that Peter's sight needs to be changed and his perception altered in order to see and enter heaven. We see the Transfiguration presented in the light of motifs appertaining to the Jerusalem Temple, the heavenly tabernacle and language describing priestly figures in heaven. I have argued that many of these motifs draw on details from the Lucan narrative. I show in Chapter 8 that the influence of the *Apocalypse of Peter* on visual depiction of the Transfiguration as a visionary entry into heaven is greater than many have thought.

Brief allusion to the Transfiguration found in *Act. Joh.* shows the Transfiguration used in more docetic and gnostic circles to comment on the appearance of Jesus as miraculously being able to change and alter. *Act. Pet.* also emphasizes the need for change within the disciples' own vision in order for them to be able to witness this, and it offers a miraculous healing of several blind widows as an exemplifying of this.

We see in these very different texts a scopic regime highly sensitized to the question of how the disciples participate in the vision before them, and which explores the idea that the disciples' vision is somehow altered in order that realities unseen by others might be revealed to them. The visionary status of the Transfiguration raises for the writers of these texts a range of questions to do with an alteration in the faculty of sight in those witnessing it. We will see in the next chapter these broad concerns explored further by Tertullian and Origen, who both use the Transfiguration as evidence in a range of discourses about ecstatic vision, human reason, divine revelation and prophetic utterance.

Chapter 5

THE TRANSFIGURATION IN TERTULLIAN AND ORIGEN

In our survey so far of the earliest reception of the Transfiguration narratives we have seen evidence of an understanding of vision very different to that espoused by modern historical-critical scholars. This ancient scopic regime prises the participation of the witnesses of the Transfiguration and asks questions about the theological and epistemological significance of the miraculous sight bestowed upon them. This continues in the reflection offered by Tertullian and Origen, which we examine in this chapter. Both Tertullian and Origen, for example, employ the Transfiguration as an important exemplification of how the Christian scriptures should be read and interpreted. Both see the presence of ecstatic vision within the Transfiguration narrative, even though they judge its worth differently. They both, to different degrees and in different ways, see temple and cultic motifs within the text. In all these reflections, both writers focus on visionary and ecstatic motifs only present in Luke's version of our narrative. This allows both Tertullian and Origen to see the Transfiguration, and especially Luke's version, as a crucial hermeneutic nexus that exemplifies how the faithful Christian should read the scriptures, interpret prophetic utterance in the Church and, through those processes, conceive of the vision of God. Through their writings, we learn something of the scopic regimes which Tertullian and Origen inhabited. They focus on similar visionary elements within Luke's narrative but often draw very different conclusions about how the disciples were able to witness the Transfiguration and the consequences that has for a wider epistemology.

Tertullian

Tertullian was born in Carthage, in Roman Africa, in the latter half of the second century. He converted to Christianity around 200 AD but was later attracted to the teachings of the 'New Prophecy' of Montanus, a charismatic movement wedded to the significance of new prophetic revelation. He also engaged, however, in strong polemic criticism of the teachings of Marcion. He implacably opposed Marcion's disparaging of the witness of the Old Testament and the gospel he advocated to legitimize his theological convictions. We find that Tertullian, therefore, uses the

Transfiguration in these two significant arguments, against Marcionite opponents, but in favour of Monatanist claims. The Transfiguration's character as a visionary text plays an important role in both those discourses.

Tertullian's discussion of the Transfiguration is intriguing as it reveals what Marcion's rival version of the narrative may have looked like. One of the ambiguities characterizing the Lucan narrative, namely uncertainty concerning what it meant for Peter not to know what he said (Lk. 9.33), is crucial for Tertullian in explaining how the Transfiguration is apprehended by the disciples. It becomes clear that the Transfiguration's status as an ecstatic vision is fundamental to Tertullian's understanding of its significance. The Transfiguration becomes for him a legitimizing example of ecstatic prophetic activity in the contemporary church of Tertullian's time. In addition, the Transfiguration becomes a key text in his interpretation of Old Testament prophecy.

In the first half of this chapter, we will outline Tertullian's comment in *Adv. Marc.* 4.22 and establish the likely appearance of the Marcionite text he was commenting on. Tertullian evidently regards the concept of ecstasy as crucial to understanding the Transfiguration, so we will then establish what can be known about Tertullian's use of this term and how this relates to Peter's experience of the Transfiguration. We then explore how Tertullian's relating of several Old Testament texts to the Transfiguration exemplifies how he used it as a key interpretative lens for explaining the prophetic coherence of the Old and New Testaments. Finally, a summary will be pieced together of what Tertullian believed happened at the Transfiguration and what he understood by the significance of its ecstatic character.

Marcion's Transfiguration text

Marcion was born around 85 AD in Sinope, Roman Asia Minor, and died in the mid-second century. One of his most notable contributions to early Christian discourse concerned the canon of scripture and his advocating of a gospel text which was historically claimed by his opponents to be an abridged version of Luke edited with a Pauline scalpel.

The precise make up and origin of Marcion's gospel remains much debated.[1] The traditional view of Marcion's text as an abridgment of canonical Luke has much historical scholarship behind it reaching from patristic assertions by

---

1. For an extensive review and evaluation of different attempts to reconstruct Marcion's gospel see Andrew F. Gregory, *The Reception of Luke and Acts in the Period before Irenaeus: Looking for Luke in the Second Century*, Wissenschaftliche Untersuchungen Zum Neuen Testament, 2 Reihe (Tübingen: Mohr Siebeck, 2003), 175–83; Sebastian Moll, *The Arch-Heretic Marcion*, Wissenschaftliche Untersuchungen zum neuen Testament (Tübingen: Mohr Siebeck, 2010), 1–10; Dieter T. Roth, 'Marcion's Gospel and Luke: The History of Research in Current Debate', *Journal of Biblical Literature* 127 (2008): 513–27; Dieter T. Roth, 'Marcion and the Early New Testament Text', in *The Early Text of the New*

Irenaeus[2] and Tertullian,[3] through to the era of 'critical' biblical study in which this paradigm was re-established by G. Volckmar,[4] Adolf Hilgenfeld,[5] Adolf von Harnack[6] and more recently by Sebastian Moll.[7] Shifts in scholarship in recent years, however, have led to a number of voices questioning this earlier consensus, especially in relation to the dating of Luke and proposals that Luke and Acts in its final form be dated to the second century.[8] John Knox and then Joseph B. Tyson

---

Testament, ed. Charles E. Hill and Michael Kruger (Oxford: Oxford University Press, 2012), 302–12; Dieter T. Roth, *The Text of Marcion's Gospel* (Leiden: Brill, 2015).

2. *Contra Haer.* 1.27.2 (PG 7, 688); 3.12.12 (PG 7, 906).

3. *Adv. Marc.* 4.2.4 (CCSL 1, 548).

4. G. Volckmar, 'Über das Lukas-Evangelium nach seinem Verhältnis zu Marcion und seinem dogmatischen Charakter, mit besonderer Beziehung auf die kritischen Unter-Suchungen F. Ch. Baur's und A. Ritschl's', *Theologische Jahrbücher* 9 (1850): 110–38, 185–223.

5. Adolf Hilgenfeld, *Kritische Untersuchungen über die Evangelien Justin's, Der clementinischen Homilien und Marcion's* (Halle: C.A. Schwetschke, 1850), 394–475.

6. Adolf von Harnack, *Marcion: das Evangelium vom fremden Gott: eine Monographie zur Geschichte der Grundlegung der katholischen Kirche* (Leipzig: J.C. Hinrichs'sche Buchhandlung, 1921), esp. 32–68.

7. Moll, *The Arch-Heretic Marcion*, 89–102.

8. Scholars who have argued in favour of a late dating of Luke and Acts in the second century: Mark G. Bilby, 'Pliny's Correspondence and the Acts of the Apostles: An Intertextual Relationship', in *Luke on Jesus, Paul and Christianity: What Did He Really Know?*, ed. Joseph Verheyden and John S. Kloppenborg, BTS 29 (Leuven: Peeters, 2017), 171–89; Mark G. Bilby, 'The First Dionysian Gospel: Imitational and Redactional Layers in Luke and John', in *Classical Models of the Gospels and Acts: Studies in Mimesis Criticism*, ed. Mark G. Bilby, Michael Kochenash and Margaret Froelich, Claremont Studies in New Testament and Christian Origins 3 (Claremont, CA: Claremont Press, 2018), 49–68; Mary Rose D'Angelo, 'The ANHP Question in Luke-Acts: Imperial Masculinity and the Deployment of Women in the Early Second Century', in *A Feminist Companion to Luke*, ed. Amy-Jill Levine (Sheffield: Sheffield Academic Press, 2002), 44–69; John S. Kloppenborg, 'Literate Media in Early Christ Groups: The Creation of a Christian Book Culture', *JECS* 22, no. 1 (2014): 21–59; Shelly Matthews, *Perfect Martyr: The Stoning of Stephen and the Construction of Christian Identity* (Oxford: Oxford University Press, 2010); Christopher Mount, *Pauline Christianity: Luke-Acts and the Legacy of Paul*, NovTSup 104 (Leiden: Brill, 2002); Laura Nasrallah, 'The Acts of the Apostles, Greek Cities, and Hadrian's Panhellenion', *JBL* 127, no. 3 (2008): 533–66; Richard I. Pervo, *Dating Acts: Between the Evangelists and the Apologists* (Santa Rosa, CA: Polebridge Press), 2006; Richard I. Pervo, *Acts: A Commentary*, Hermeneia (Minneapolis, MN: Fortress Press, 2009), 5–7; Joseph B. Tyson, 'The Date of Acts: A Reconsideration', *Forum* 5, no. 1 (2002): 33–51; Joseph B. Tyson, 'Why Dates Matter: The Case of the Acts of the Apostles', *The Fourth R* 18, no. 2 (2005): 8–14; Dennis Smith and Joseph B. Tyson, eds, *Acts and Christian Beginnings: The Acts Seminar Report* (Salem: Polebridge, 2013).

have led the argument for a much later dating of the canonical text of Luke and Acts after a second stage of redaction in the second century. They see Luke's Gospel itself to be a later expansion of Marcion's text, or a reaction to it.[9] They argue that Marcion's gospel could have been substantially the same as an early version of Luke, which was then expanded with elements such as the birth narratives, and to which Acts was added, in an attempt to counter Marcion's Paulinistic claims. This theory presents us with the tantalizing possibility that Marcion's gospel presents us with a Lucan version of the Transfiguration earlier than that found in canonical Luke and that the present Lucan narrative is the fruit of a second redaction in the second century.

I find many of the judgements expressed by D. S. Williams convincing, that so little is known about what *Vorlage* Marcion is working with that neither a position of Lucan or Marcionite priority can be held with huge certainty.[10] It is perfectly possible for Marcion to have relied on an early version of proto-Luke entirely independently from the writing of Acts, whose creation does not automatically need to be shifted to the middle of the second century. This new shift in scholarship also requires the laying aside of an extensive patristic witness that Maricon was, in fact, a redactor of Luke. This near universal ancient consensus needs extensive evidence to overturn. I am minded, therefore, tentatively to assume the traditional view of Marcion as an abridger of Luke. My concern in this study is not to contribute to debate on the origins, redaction or extent of Marcion's text but rather to examine the reception of his Transfiguration narrative and especially to see how it shaped debate about its visionary status. I will follow the methodology adopted by Dieter Roth in simply presenting the 'best attainable text for Marcion's Gospel according to the sources' rather than entering into theorizing about the redaction critical history of the text or assuming that our knowledge of it can ever be exhaustive.

As far as the Marcionite Transfiguration narrative is concerned, evidence for two possible differences between Marcion's text and canonical Luke emerge from Tertullian's treatment of the Transfiguration found in Book 4 of his treatise *Adversus Marcionem*. First, Tertullian implies that Marcion's text did not include mention of Moses and Elijah speaking with Jesus and discussing the exodus

---

9. Ferdinand Christian Baur, *Kritische Untersuchungen über die kanonischen Evangelien* (Tübingen: L.F. Fues, 1847), 397–427, 501–31; Matthias Klinghardt, Markion vs. Lukas: Plädoyer für die Wiederaufnahme eines alten Falles', *NTS* 52, no. 4 (2006): 484–513; 'The Marcionite Gospel and the Synoptic Problem: A New Suggestion', *NT* 50 (2008): 1–27; John Knox, *Marcion and the New Testament: An Essay in the Early History of the Canon* (Chicago: University of Chicago Press, 1942), 77–113; Albrecht Ritschl, *Das Evangelium Marcions und das kanonische Evangelium des Lucas: Eine kritische Untersuchung* (Tuebingen: Ostander, 1846), 276–301; Joseph B. Tyson, *Marcion and Luke-Acts: A Defining Struggle* (Columbia: University of South Carolina Press, 2006), esp. 79–120.

10. D. S. Williams, 'Reconsidering Marcion's Gospel', *Journal of Biblical Literature* 108 (1989): 477–96.

he was about to accomplish, when he states, concerning Moses, 'even though Marcion did not want him to be shown in conversation with the Lord, but just standing there'.[11]

Tertullian accuses Marcion of excising Lk. 9.31 in order to show no figure from the Old Testament having authority over Christ, being glorified or prophesying Christ's future.[12] Roth, in his careful reconstruction of Marcion's gospel judges the second half on 9.31 to have been absent from Marcion's text.[13] Harnack also wonders, though ultimately judges it uncertain, whether Lk. 9.36 and the ending of the Transfiguration was also not present in Marcion's text, as this is not commented on by Tertullian.[14]

In addition to this, a second question concerns whether discrepancy exists between the words uttered from the heavens in canonical Luke and Marcion's text. Epiphanius, in his fourth century list of Marcion's alleged alterations, claims Marcion's version read, 'Out of the cloud, a voice, "This is my beloved Son,"'[15] a reading Roth considers to be 'secure' and likely to be part of Marcion's text.[16] However, it is unclear what Epiphanius judged Marcion's alteration to be. Is it the removal of 'hear him' or the change of 'chosen' to 'beloved'? This question is made more complex by the fact that Tertullian constructs an argument in *Adv Marc* 4.22.1, mocking Marcion's interpretation of the canonical version of Lk. 9.35 that 'hear him' implies that Jesus comes to forbid listening to Moses and Elijah: 'This, you imply, was what he wanted to be understood as the meaning of the voice from heaven, "This is my Son, hear him".'[17] Tertullian's words here would seem to imply that Marcion's did indeed include the words 'hear him'. The situation is rendered even more complicated by the fact that Lk. 9.35 contains a number of textual variants in which the son is 'beloved' rather than 'chosen', as found in A, C*, R, W and *f*13.

According to Roth's nuanced reconstruction, the most significant and noteworthy discrepancy between Marcion's text and canonical Luke is the absence of Lk. 9.31b, with its mention of Jesus speaking with Moses and Elijah about the exodus he was to accomplish in Jerusalem. In addition to this, Roth judges the words uttered by the voice from the cloud describing Jesus as a 'beloved' son rather than 'chosen' as a 'secure' reading of Marcion's likely text. Mention of the vision ending with Jesus being found alone after the heavenly voice and the disciples' silence as they descended the mountain is judged by Roth as 'unattested'. However, this does not mean it was not present but that

---

11. *Adv. Marc.* 4.22.16 (CCSL 1, 604).
12. Moll, *The Arch-Heretic Marcion*, 94.
13. Roth, *The Text of Marcion's Gospel*, 419.
14. Harnack, *Marcion: Das Evangelium vom fremden Gott*, 184.
15. Frank Williams, *The Panarion of Epiphanius of Salamis. Book I (Sections 1–46)*, 2nd edn (Leiden: Brill, 2009), 305.
16. Roth, *The Text of Marcion's Gospel*, 419.
17. *Adv. Marc.* 4.22.1 (CCSL 1, 600).

there is simply no evidence it was. Apart from these discrepancies, the rest of Marcion's Transfiguration text seems to have been the Greek narrative we find in canonical Luke.

'Not knowing what he said': Ecstasy, amentia and prophetic vision

In *Adv. Marc.* 14.22, Tertullian discusses at some length the reference only found in Lk. 9.33 and preserved in Marcion's text[18] that Peter's suggestion concerning tabernacles was made 'not knowing what he said'. Tertullian explores what he sees as the two possible meanings this could have: either Peter was somehow out of his mind or he was mistaken in assuming Jesus to be the Christ of the Old Covenant, represented by Moses and Elijah.[19] It is crucial, therefore, for Tertullian to interpret these words as *not* implying criticism of Peter's verdict. Such an interpretation would play into the hands of his Marcionite opponents and imply that the latter of these two meanings is the more likely. It seems probable from Tertullian's argument here that Lk. 9.33 was used as a key piece of Marcionite evidence showing Peter to have been mistaken in associating Christ with Moses and Elijah. By bestowing on them all equal honour, Marcionite critics may have claimed that Peter failed to see Jesus as the Christ of a different god and a different dispensation than that which Moses and Elijah represent. It is important for Tertullian, therefore, to argue that the ambiguity in Luke's phrase points rather to Peter being in a state of visionary ecstasy. He brings two proofs for this.[20] First, how could Peter recognize Moses and Elijah if not in the spirit, as Jews were not permitted to create any image of what they might have looked like? Second, how could Peter be mistaken concerning what sort of Christ Jesus was, if he had just confessed him a few verses before[21] in a way which did not imply he doubted him to be the Creator's Christ?

Tertullian describes this ecstasy of Peter's as follows:

> How 'not knowing'? Was it the result of a simple mistake? Or was it because of the reason which we, in our argument for the new prophecy claim, that ecstasy or being beside oneself goes hand in hand with grace? For when someone is in the spirit, especially when he glimpses the glory of God, or when God is speaking through him, he must necessarily leave his senses, because he is surely overshadowed by the power of God – a question about which there is debate between us and carnal men.[22]

---

18. Roth categorizes this reading in his second highest category of certainty, 'very likely'. Roth, *The Text of Marcion's Gospel*, 419.
19. *Adv. Marc.* 4.22.4-6 (CCSL 1, 601–2).
20. *Adv. Marc.* 4.22.5-6 (CCSL 1, 601–2).
21. Lk. 9.20.
22. *Adv. Marc.* 4.22.4-5 (CCSL 1, 601).

Tertullian links this ecstasy with Montanist prophetic activity to reject both Marcion and anti-Montanists. He draws a direct parallel between the New Prophecy and Peter's visionary experience in which both cases are a sign of grace, of God's parallel action within the seer. In addition to this, however, they are both seen as part of God's action of 'overshadowing'. If there is ambiguity in the other synoptic accounts concerning who is included in the overshadowing of the cloud, Tertullian here latches onto Luke's assertion that it definitely includes Peter. If God's overshadowing includes Peter, then it may, by extension, include the visionary prophet of Tertullian's day, he argues.

However, this ecstasy results in a paradox. At one and the same time Tertullian argues that it at least partially removes Peter from the realm of sense, yet also somehow transforms his truest sense of sight. Tertullian understands Peter's ecstasy as one in which Peter becomes unaware of what he says and operates as a vessel through which God speaks. He specifically judges that 'because he had spoken in the Spirit, and not in his senses, it was not possible for him to know what he had said'.[23] Peter's ecstasy renders him an unknowing mouthpiece of God's prophetic utterance, for the benefit of others – a scenario not unlike what we can glean was characteristic of prophetic activity in Montanist circles. However, whilst removing him from the realm of sense awareness, Peter's ecstasy retains in him the ability to perceive and imagine visually, as he clearly witnesses the glory scene in front of him. If it weren't for Peter's ecstasy, Tertullian implies that Peter would be unable to recognize Moses and Elijah.[24]

Tertullian also perceives there to be a very grave *danger* inherent in the vision of the Transfiguration. In a brief comment in *Adv. Prax.* 15,[25] Tertullian compares Paul's vision on the Damascus Road with the Transfiguration. He comments that just as the Son's divine glory was harmful to Paul's sight, so Peter, James and John could not experience the Transfiguration's light safely except in a state of mindlessness, 'sine rationis et amentia'. In both incidents, he argues, the Son's glory was apprehended by physical human sight but, in Paul's case, at the dangerous cost of going blind. The Transfiguration, Tertullian asserts, is a similar experience for the three disciples, but their physical vision, by contrast, is protected, or transformed by *amentia* – being out of one's mind. It is not clear whether Tertullian sees the physical faculty of sight as going into a complete abeyance, with the only 'vision' being that of the mind, or whether the vision he refers to is a synthesis of physical sense and the imaginative faculties. It is equally unclear whether the danger Tertullian foresees is simply to physical sight, or whether he imagines some sort of mental derangement as a possibility. Tertullian seems to presume a scenario in which reason has to relinquish some of its controlling function over the interpretation of physical sight as it is overwhelmed by divine glory. Tertullian sees the glory of the Transfiguration as something which can be experienced

---

23. *Adv. Marc.* 4.22.5 (CCSL 1, 602).
24. Ibid.
25. *Adv. Prax.* 15.8 (CCSL 2, 1180).

by mortals but which is so overwhelming that transformed vision bestowed by *amentia* is needed to behold this glory truly and safely.

Prophetic vision and Montanism

Any attempt to understand what Tertullian means by terms such as *amentia* will be closely related to the extent of Montanist influence on Tertullian, who was increasingly influenced by the claims of the sect from 207 onwards. As Christine Trevett's[26] and Laura Nasrallah's[27] work has shown, however, the breadth of beliefs which have since been described under the umbrella term of 'Montanism', not least the sort in Rome and North Africa which influenced Tertullian, was probably much wider and more pluriform than previously suspected. In addition, piecing together a coherent account of the Phrygian Prophecy which lay at the heart of Montanist claims involves a complex evaluation of information preserved exclusively by the group's detractors, frequently many years after the sect's period of greatest popularity. The image of Tertullian, the schismatic heretic, has gradually given way in scholarly discussion to a more nuanced verdict in which his attitude to visionary prophecy can be seen as surprisingly close to views which would later be described as 'orthodox'.[28] Trevett,[29] for example, emphasizes this interest in ecstatic prophecy as a normative characteristic of the sort of Christianity found within Asia Minor, the milieu from which Montanus's prophecy emerged. She rejects any sense in which his teaching represents the intruding of an alien, or pagan, sensibility into Asiatic Christianity. In addition, Cecil Robeck has shown prophetic charismata to be a widespread characteristic of North African 'orthodox' Christian culture through an examination of *The Passion of Perpetua and Felicity*, Tertullian's and Cyprian's writings.[30] Nonetheless, a uniting characteristic of the wide range of people claiming some degree of allegiance to the 'New Prophecy' was an exalting of the importance of prophetic utterance in the teaching and ordering of the

---

26. Christine Trevett, *Montanism: Gender, Authority and the New Prophecy* (Cambridge: Cambridge University Press, 1996), 1–15, 198–223.

27. Laura Salah Nasrallah, *An Ecstasy of Folly: Prophecy and Authority in Early Christianity* (Cambridge, MA: Harvard Theological Studies, Harvard Divinity School, 2003), 95–101, 156–63.

28. See Timothy David Barnes, *Tertullian: A Historical and Literary Study* (Oxford: Clarendon Press, 1985), 130–42; Pierre Champagne de Labriolle, *La crise montaniste* (Paris: Leroux, 1913), 463–4; Eric Francis Osborn, *Tertullian, First Theologian of the West* (Cambridge: Cambridge University Press, 1997), esp. 209–24; Jean Steinmann, *Tertullien*, Collection parole et Tradition (Lyon: Éditions du Chalet, 1967), 245–91, esp. 285–8.

29. Trevett, *Montanism*, 15–26, 46–66.

30. Cecil M. Robeck, *Prophecy in Carthage: Perpetua, Tertullian, and Cyprian* (Cleveland, OH: Pilgrim Press, 1992), 97–145.

Church. The point of highlighting the influence of Montanism on Tertullian is to recognize the way in which his comment on the Transfiguration emerges from a context highly sensitized to ecstatic, visionary and prophetic experience, and its polemic defence within the life of the church.

Ecstasis and amentia

We now turn to the question of what Tertullian meant by *ecstasis* and *amentia*. In *Adv. Marc.* 4.22, Tertullian describes the trance-like state necessary for prophecy, and which gripped Peter at the Transfiguration, as 'ecstasin, id est amentiam',[31] 'ecstasy, which is mindlessness'. He uses almost precisely the same phrase, 'in ecstasi, id est amentia',[32] in Book 5 of *Adversus Marcionem* to refer to the state of mind which produces the sort of inspired visions, psalms and prayers which he claims Marcion lacks but which his Montanist circle possesses. It seems likely that Tertullian may be coining a neologism by using this Greek loanword, *ecstasis*. When Tertullian states, 'ecstasin, id est amentiam',[33] *amentia* operates as the Latin gloss for a foreign-sounding word. *Amentia* is a much more widely used term, having meanings ranging from 'the state of being out of one's mind, madness',[34] through to the more creative sense of 'poetic inspiration',[35] or the negative connotation inherent in 'violent excitement, frenzy' or 'senselessness, extreme folly, infatuation'.[36] *Amentia*, therefore, is a much more general term, referring to a wide range of experiences, both negative and positive, of being out of one's normal mind. In her study of Tertullian's understanding of ecstasy, Nasrallah concludes that Tertullian holds the terms *ecstasis*, *excessus* and *amentia* to be terms equivalent to 'prophecy, the power of the spirit'.[37] However, she also shows he is capable of using the term *amentia* negatively in many contexts, to mean madness in the sense of mental derangement.[38] Nasrallah concludes that Tertullian provocatively uses a term understood in its primary meaning as negative madness and exploits its shock value to emphasize the radical importance of prophetic utterance and its paradoxical reliability. She argues that Tertullian is happy, therefore, with the idea of ecstasy as a form of madness, but one which is normal and natural to humans, especially being comparable to sleep and dreaming.[39]

31. *Adv. Marc.* 4.22.4 (CCSL 1, 601).
32. *Adv. Marc.* 5.8.12 (CCSL 1, 688).
33. *Adv. Marc.* 4.22.4 (CCSL 1, 601).
34. 'amentia', in *Oxford Latin Dictionary*, ed. P. G. W. Glare (Oxford: Oxford University Press, 2012), 129.
35. 'amentia', in *A Latin Dictionary Revised by C. T. Lewis and C. Short* (Oxford: Oxford University Press, 1958), 104.
36. Ibid.
37. Nasrallah, *An Ecstasy of Folly*, 134.
38. Ibid.
39. Ibid., 134–40.

Tertullian's understanding of the soul

It is important, therefore, to establish the character of this 'madness', which Tertullian describes, for, as Nasrallah[40] and Robeck[41] argue, Tertullian does not believe *amentia* and ecstasy to represent a complete leave-taking of reason. Nasrallah points to the importance of Tertullian's more Stoic understanding of the soul.[42] Unlike the Platonic notions found in Philo of a tripartite soul in which *nous* or intellect is the principal faculty evacuated from the soul in ecstasy, to be replaced by the divine mind, Tertullian advocates a created, and unitary, soul. Nasrallah argues that for Tertullian, although one might describe the soul as having different faculties or abilities, it is not made up of separate parts.[43] In addition, he resists Platonic exaltation of the rational soul within the human as the portion most able to apprehend the divine. One of the consequences of this anthropology is Tertullian's ability to describe prophetic insight and vision as a universal charism, open to all Christians,[44] rather than the noetically trained and intellectually superior.

Nasrallah[45] and Robeck[46] show that, although elements of Tertullian's understanding of ecstasy are at times very complex and edge on the seemingly contradictory, it does not for him represent the complete leave-taking of reason, precisely because he does not conceive of the human soul as possessing a separate rational portion, which can either flee (as Philo argued) or be overwhelmed in ecstasy (as Origen argued). For Tertullian, ecstasy represents a state in which the faculty of knowledge becomes dimmed but not completely removed by *amentia*. Tertullian's Stoic conception of the soul prompts him to value the epistemic worth of sense experience and to see ecstasy as never completely able to compromise the rationality of the soul, even though reason may partially retreat and the *amentia* appear like madness.

Ecstasy and sleep

We now explore precisely how Tertullian explains the ecstasy he declares that grips Peter. Whilst *amentia* was a notion known to Tertullian's readers, the meaning of *ecstasis* may have been more uncertain. One of the greatest frustrations in the study of Tertullian's thought in this area is the disappearance of a treatise mentioned by

---

40. Ibid., 139–40.
41. Robeck, *Prophecy in Carthage*, 104–6.
42. Nasrallah, *An Ecstasy of Folly*, 101–11.
43. Ibid., 95–127.
44. Ibid., 140–54; Robeck, *Prophecy in Carthage*, 97–101.
45. Nasrallah, *Ecstasy of Folly*, esp. 111–27.
46. Robeck, *Prophecy in Carthage*, 104–6.

Jerome entitled *De ecstasi*.[47] However, Tertullian explores at some length in *De Anima* 45 what he means by *amentia* and *ecstasis*, which will have to be, *faut de mieux*, our main source of information.

In *De Anima* 45, Tertullian draws an extended comparison between *ecstasis* and sleep, in which he argues they are substantially similar phenomena. In sleep, he explains, the physical body rests, and the physical senses perceiving the world around them go into abeyance. However, the soul does not rest but continues to imagine, perceive and visualize. Because the limbs of the body are resting, the soul uses its own 'limbs', so to speak, to give expression to its activity in dreams. It is like a gladiator without weapons, Tertullian explains, or a charioteer without horses still gesticulating and going through the actions of their sport, unable to stop their combat.[48] 'There is an action, but no real effect,' Tertullian concludes. 'We call this power ecstasy, which is a leaving of the senses, and resembles mindlessness.'[49]

However, dreams can sometimes be vague, inconsistent and ambiguous. Tertullian, therefore, seeks to distinguish between dreams inspired by demons and legitimate experiences in which God speaks. The key in this discernment is memory. It is through memory that God helps us discern his communication, and that *ecstasy* is prevented from becoming a flight from reason. Memory, according to Tertullian, is the 'particular character of *amentia*'.[50] Tertullian suggests that our reasoning faculties frequently seek to suppress what we imagine in dreams. However, when in a state of ecstasy, that controlling action of the intellect is momentarily withdrawn, allowing us to remember the image or message God wishes to communicate to us.[51] For an ecstatic dream or vision to be preserved in our consciousness, therefore, reason needs paradoxically to retreat and cease to act as it usually does, allowing the dream to come to the fore and be visualized; yet reason also need not entirely to disappear, as the dream would not be remembered otherwise.[52]

Ecstasis/amentia: Conclusions

Tertullian sees the terms *ecstasis* and *amentia* as broadly synonymous and as describing the crucial state of mind which is a prerequisite for prophetic vision and utterance. He sees the disciples, and especially Peter, being in just such a state when they witness the Transfiguration. The best analogy he can find to describe the mechanics of this state is a comparison with sleep and dreaming. However,

---

47. See Johannes Quasten, *Patrology*, 4 vols (Westminster, MD: Spectrum, 1950), vol. 2, 317.
48. *De Anima* 45.2 (CCSL 2, 849).
49. *De Anima* 45.3 (CCSL 2, 849).
50. *De Anima* 45.4 (CCSL 2, 850).
51. *De Anima* 45.5 (CCSL 2, 850).
52. *De Anima* 45.6 (CCSL 2, 850).

Tertullian's use of the word *amentia* in contexts where it clearly expresses a simple sense of madness makes me agree with Nasrallah that he uses the phrase provocatively to emphasize the paradox at the heart of his understanding of *ecstasis/amentia*. On the one hand, prophetic utterance is only possible once the everyday control which reason exercises over our imaginations has retreated. Indeed, the state required for prophecy looks like madness, and in this sense, may legitimately be described as such, according to Tertullian, to emphasize the distinct nature of this state. However, at the same time, *ecstasis/amentia* can never represent for Tertullian a complete flight from reason. Without reason, we could never remember our dreams and visions, a conviction his more Stoic anthropology makes it necessary for him to affirm.

Tertullian, the Transfiguration and the New and Old Testaments

Having outlined Tertullian's understanding of *ecstasis* and *amentia*, we now examine how Tertullian's use of the Transfiguration as proof of the prophetic unity of the Old and New Testaments exemplifies the significance of this ecstatic vision. Tertullian points in *Adv. Marc.* 4.22 to a number of ways in which the Transfiguration was prophetically foreseen in the Old Testament. This not only proves the coherence of the scriptural canon he defends against Marcion but also provides legitimizing examples of ecstasy amongst the prophets. Indeed, I will argue that he sees the prophetic vision of the prophets Habakkuk and Zechariah years before Christ's time to be the same sort of prophetic vision experienced by the apostles. We will then examine how the concern of the third-century *Anti-Phrygian Source* employed by Epiphanius to insist that the prophets prophesied *without* any sense of ecstasy confirms and supports this reading of Tertullian's interpretation of the Transfiguration.

Prophetic foreshadowings of the Transfiguration in the Old Testament

Tertullian's first point in *Adv. Marc.* 4.22 concerns the compatibility of the Old Testament with the revelation of Christ. From Tertullian's argument,[53] it would appear Marcion had insisted that when the voice from the cloud tells the disciples to listen to Jesus, this was an instruction to ignore the Law and the Prophets, which Moses and Elijah represented. It seems Marcionites may have preached a Transfiguration which pointed to the eclipsing of the Old Law, and the demiurge which had dictated it, by the greater god revealed by Christ. This probably stood behind the absence of Luke's mention of Jesus being in discourse with Moses and Elijah in Marcion's gospel.[54] Tertullian, by contrast, argues in *Adv. Marc.* 4.22.1

---

53. *Adv. Marc.* 4.22.1-2 (CCSL 1, 600–1); 4.34.15-16 (CCSL 1, 638–9).
54. *Adv. Marc.* 4.22.16 (CCSL 1, 604).

that appearing with someone in glory is a very odd way of signaling that person's demise. He also wonders whether Moses and Elijah are consequently the only prophets Marcion would ban being read. What of Isaiah and Jeremiah who do not appear on the mountain, Tertullian wonders. For him, Christ's companionship with Moses and Elijah in glory reveals Christ as the fulfilment of the prophecy made by the one God through them. Tertullian then describes an extended series of Old Testament motifs, references and incidents which foreshadow the Transfiguration in order further to make his point. I have sorted them below into four broad categories.

Category 1: Reference to the same reality

The first category of Old Testament references involve Tertullian establishing a simple correspondence between the Transfiguration and Old Testament narratives in which both texts are seen as speaking about the same reality. Tertullian's point is to show that the god of the Old and New Testaments is in fact the same, bringing to pass in the New the same saving mystery seen in the Old. Tertullian argues, for example, the voice coming from the cloud declaring Jesus to be God's Son is addressed to the same individual to whom God spoke in Ps. 2.7, 'You are my Son, today I have begotten you.'[55] In a similar way, Tertullian argues that God had asked through Isa. 50.10, 'Who is it that fears God and hears the voice of his Son?'[56] He sees the voice from the overshadowing cloud as commanding the same thing as Isaiah asks about here by virtue of the promise Tertullian sees as implicit in the prophet's words. In these examples, the thing spoken of in Old Testament texts is interpreted as being the same thing spoken of at the Transfiguration.

Category 2: Fulfilment of a prediction

A second category of references is one in which something foretold in the Old Testament comes to pass in time in the Transfiguration. The principal example of this is Moses's prediction at Deut. 18.15 that God would raise up a prophet like himself. Tertullian argues Christ dismisses Moses and Elijah not because they are the prophets of a demiurge but because Moses finally sees his prediction fulfilled.[57] A transfer is made in which the disciples should listen now to Christ as teacher and prophet as a result of a particular stage in salvation history having been reached.[58] This category represents the fulfilment in time at the Transfiguration of a prediction made in the Old Testament.

---

55. *Adv. Marc.* 4.22.8 (CCSL 1, 602).
56. *Adv. Marc.* 4.22.8-9 (CCSL 1, 602).
57. *Adv. Marc.* 4.22.15 (CCSL 1, 604).
58. *Adv. Marc.* 4.22.12 (CCSL 1, 603).

Category 3: Typological connection with Sinai

A third, more complex, category involves Tertullian making what one might describe as a typological connection between the giving of the Law on Sinai and the Transfiguration. He states, 'The creator had first initiated his ancient people in a vision and with his own voice on a mountain. It was necessary that the new covenant should be sealed in just such a raised place as the old covenant had been composed in, and under the same cover of a cloud.'[59] In this link, these two incidents are seen to be parallel both in their function (i.e. to confirm teaching) and in the phenomena that accompanied them (mountain; vision; voice; cloud). However, this typology is made more complex by the comparison Tertullian draws not with Exodus 24 but with Exod. 33.20, in which Moses is *prevented* from seeing fully God's face. Playing on an ambiguity in the Latin translation he uses, Tertullian argues that when God said Moses would see his *later parts* ('Et tunc videbis posterior mea'),[60] he meant not his loins or legs but that Moses would see him in a *later time* ('sed desideraverat gloriam in posteribus temporibus revelandam').[61] In Num. 12.6-8, God promises to Moses that he will see him face to face, in the Tent of Meeting. However, God had also said in Exod. 33.20 that no one can see his face and live. Tertullian holds out the Transfiguration as the point at which both of these seemingly contradictory prophesies are fulfilled. The logic of Tertullian's argument is that the Tabernacle of Meeting which Num. 12.6 really refers to is, in fact, prophetically the Mount of Transfiguration. Here, Moses finally sees the face of God and lives. Tertullian points to Jesus as the embodiment of God's glory and the experience on the mountain as directly comparable with Moses's entry into the Tent of Meeting. Indeed, in just the same way that Moses's appearance was blinding for the Hebrews when Moses left God's presence, so now, Tertullian argues, Moses's appearance upon leaving Christ's presence at the Transfiguration is blinding for Marcion, who fails to recognize the truth.[62]

So, whilst there is here a typological parallel drawn between the Transfiguration and the giving of the Law on Sinai, as broadly parallel incidents, there is a more complex parallel laid over that in which Moses achieves something at the Transfiguration which he didn't manage to in Exodus, which Tertullian interprets the Old Testament as predicting would eventually be fulfilled in the future.

Category 4: Prophetic vision in Zechariah and Habakkuk

A fourth category of Old Testament reference made by Tertullian concerns two texts in Habakkuk and Zechariah. In these, Tertullian seems to argue for a different sort of typological relationship, claiming that Zechariah and Habakkuk

---

59. *Adv. Marc.* 4.22.7 (CCSL 1, 602).
60. *Adv. Marc.* 4.22.15 (CCSL 1, 604).
61. Ibid.
62. *Adv. Marc.* 4.22.16 (CCSL 1, 604).

had some sort of prophetic vision of the Transfiguration, which was to take place in the future. Referring to LXX Hab. 3.1-4, Tertullian argues as follows:

> We have an entire outline of this vision ['habitum visionis'] in Habakkuk as well, where the Spirit, in the person of some of the apostles [says], 'Lord I have heard your speech and was afraid'. What can this be other than the heavenly voice, 'This is my beloved Son, hear him'? 'I considered your works and was astounded.' When can this be other than when Peter saw his brightness, and did not know what he should say?[63]

Tertullian argues that the Spirit spoke in the voice of the apostles who were yet to live through the prophet Habakkuk, and speaks of the ecstatic state Peter was to experience on Tabor.

Much would seem to revolve around precisely what is meant by 'habitum visionis'. 'Habitus' has a wide lexical range, referring to a broad sweep of concepts to do with appearance or outline, especially to do with 'physical make-up, build, form (with emphasis on visual aspect)'.[64] There would seem to be two possible interpretations of Tertullian's phrase 'habitum visionis'. The first could be that when Tertullian speaks of us having an outline of the vision in Habakkuk, he means the person seeing this is the one reading the Old Testament in the light of the Transfiguration. In other words, the 'outline of the vision' is simply a spotting of correspondences by the reader of the New Testament. However, a second interpretation is also possible. This emphasis on 'visual aspect',[65] implied in the word 'habitus', could mean that Tertullian entertains the possibility that Habakkuk had some sort of visual apprehension of the Transfiguration before its time. In this case, the 'outline of the vision' refers to *Habakkuk's* visionary experience.

The distinction between these two sorts of vision is shown by the question of precisely what Tertullian means by 'apud Abacuc'. Does Tertullian mean 'in the *book Habakkuk*', the text, entitled, 'Habakkuk', in which we read *allegorical* correspondences with the Transfiguration? Or does he mean 'with the *prophet Habakkuk*', in the experience of the man who may have undergone some sort of visualization of the Transfiguration as he prophesied, and whose vision establishes a *typological* relationship between his vision and the Transfiguration? If it is the latter case, Tertullian interprets vision to mean not just that which is seen by the physical eyes but also that which is visualized by the prophetic imagination in the spirit, before the physical event takes place in time, even though its prophetic significance may take many years to become clear.

A similar dynamic is evident in Tertullian's comments concerning the prophet's vision of two olive trees in Zechariah 4:

---

63. *Adv. Marc.* 4.22.12 (CCSL 1, 603).
64. 'habitus', in *Oxford Latin Dictionary*, ed. P. G. W. Glare (Oxford: Oxford University Press, 2012), 860.
65. Ibid.

> Zechariah also saw these [i.e. Moses and Elijah] *in the figure* ['vidit in figura'] of the two olive trees and the two olive branches: for these are the ones about whom it was said to him, 'Two noble ones stand by the Lord of the whole earth.'[66]

'Figura' can refer to a general sense of appearance, outline or shape, but can, more specifically, denote things 'seen in dreams, visions etc.; also of the dead'.[67] Tertullian possibly argues that by seeing the Transfiguration in the *figura* of the olive trees, Zechariah had some sort of visual apprehension of the Transfiguration before its time. However, the analogy drawn with the Transfiguration is slightly different than was the case with Habakkuk. There, the prophet spoke prophetically in the person of Peter, and his words and role were shown to be similar to Peter's. In the case of Habakkuk, Tertullian does not say whether he imagines the prophet *seeing* anything. Here, however, Tertullian explicitly understands Zechariah echoing not Peter's words and role but rather his vision. In visualizing the two olive trees, the reality he perceives was the same as that seen by the disciples in the Transfiguration. Although Zechariah saw olive trees, the inspired reader may discern in this a prophetic vision of the same reality seen clearly on the Mount of Transfiguration.

The Anti-Phrygian Source in Epiphanius's Panarion

This reading of Tertullian's reference to Habakkuk and Zechariah appears all the more convincing when seen in the context of the polemical debate concerning Montanist claims, which we witness in the *Anti-Phrygian Source* preserved in Epiphanius's *Panarion*.[68] Although Epiphanius's work dates from the fourth century, the source he uses concerning Montanism is widely seen as contemporaneous with Tertullian's work.[69] Few feel it is possible to prove it was written specifically in reply to any of Tertullian's writings,[70] but it does touch on some very similar issues and appears to participate, in Nasrallah's words, in a 'common discourse with Tertullian'.[71] The fact that one of the *Source's* principal concerns is to deny any notion that the prophets of the Old Testament spoke in ecstasy, makes it highly likely, I would argue, that it was a Montanist commonplace to point to the prophetic vision and writings of the prophets as analogous to the present-day utterance of their Phrygian prophets.

---

66. *Adv. Marc.* 4.22.12, 13 (CCSL 1, 603).

67. 'figura', in *Oxford Latin Dictionary*, ed. P. G. W. Glare (Oxford: Oxford University Press, 2012), 768–9.

68. Frank Williams, *The Panarion of Epiphanius of Salamis Books 2-3 (Sections 47–80)*, trans. Frank Williams, Nag Hammadi Studies (Leiden: E.J. Brill, 1987).

69. See Nasralla, *An Ecstasy of Folly*, 167–71.

70. Ibid., 155.

71. Ibid.

One of the *Source*'s principal assertions is that the sort of ecstasy which Tertullian argues to be epistemically useful is, in fact, a dangerous form of madness and an 'ecstasy of folly',[72] whose peril resides precisely in a decoupling of the soul from reason. The writer marshals a list of Old Testament prophets whom he sees as prophesying *sanely*: Moses, Isaiah, Ezekiel and Daniel.[73] Moses and Isaiah, particularly, are depicted as sane by virtue of the fact that they *saw* God directly.[74] Here, the *Source*'s writer closely links vision with possession of reason. This argument is then extended to the New Testament, as the Anti-Phrygian writer deals with the mention of Peter's ecstasy in Acts 10.10.[75] He argues that ecstasy here simply implies that Peter sees 'other than what men usually see in the everyday world'[76] and, furthermore, does not lead to 'distraction' because 'Peter was rational and not out of his mind'. Indeed, the fact that in Acts 10 Peter sees, but is capable of rationally *refusing* to eat what God urges him to, shows him to be in control of his faculties. Both Tertullian and the *Source* agree that true, inspired prophecy and vision cannot take place without the presence of reason; where they differ is in the *Source*'s accusation that the Montanists' 'ecstasy of folly' represents a madness which takes leave of sanity and therefore cannot be trusted. Tertullian, on the other hand, is happy to use the language of madness, but to assert the paradox that what appears as madness can never represent a complete abandonment of reason.

I suggest the argument deployed in Epiphanius that the prophets saw *sanely* increases the likelihood that Tertullian intends us to see in his interpretation of Habakkuk and Zechariah some sort of prophetic vision of the Transfiguration having taken place before the time of Christ's earthly life. At the very least this is how the *Source*'s writer understood the Phrygian position. Although Nasrallah briefly quotes the portions of *Adversus Marcionem* in which Tertullian refers to the Transfiguration, she does so simply to prove his equating of the term *ecstasis* with *amentia*. I hope that in this chapter we have added to, and strengthened, Nasrallah's thesis and to have shown that the Transfiguration has a very significant role in Tertullian's argument. Through it, the prophetic unity of the Old and New Testaments is established and linked through the disciples' experience at the Transfiguration to the role of ecstatic prophecy which Tertullian hopes to legitimize within the Church. We have shown that Tertullian employs

---

72. *Panarion*, 48.5.6; Williams, *The Panarion of Epiphanius of Salamis Books 2–3 (Sections 47–80)*, 11.

73. *Panarion*, 48.3.3; Williams, *The Panarion of Epiphanius of Salamis Books 2–3 (Sections 47–80)*, 9.

74. *Panarion*, 48.3.4-5; Williams, *The Panarion of Epiphanius of Salamis Books 2–3 (Sections 47–80)*, 9.

75. *Panarion*, 48.7.3-5; Williams, *The Panarion of Epiphanius of Salamis Books 2–3 (Sections 47–80)*, 12.

76. *Panarion*, 48.7.3; Williams, *The Panarion of Epiphanius of Salamis Books 2–3 (Sections 47–80)*.

a sophisticated understanding of prophetic vision, which includes not just the ability of the contemporary reader to notice allegorical correspondences between the Transfiguration and Old Testament incidents but also an understanding of Habakkuk's and Zechariah's writings as constituting prophetic vision. For Tertullian, some visualized apprehension of the same mystery perceived by Peter, James and John is granted to the prophets in their mind's eye before the time of Christ.

It is also important to note that in two of the connections made by Tertullian between the Transfiguration and the Old Testament, temple and tabernacle themes can be detected. Tertullian conceives of the Transfiguration as prophetically embodying the Tabernacle of Meeting. There is also a strong temple and cultic background to the imagery drawn upon in Zechariah 4. Although these temple and tabernacle themes are not as pronounced as will be argued is the case with Origen later in this chapter, it is important to note their presence and that this theme is by no means absent from Tertullian's interpretation.

Ecstasis and Luke's Transfiguration: A possible reconstruction

I will now attempt, in the light of what I have so far established, to piece together as precisely as is possible Tertullian's understanding of the Transfiguration narrative.

Tertullian understands the disciples as having to fall into a state of *ecstasis* in order to be able to witness the Transfiguration. Tertullian's understanding of ecstasy as analogous with sleep coheres closely with the Lucan Transfiguration account. Luke is the only evangelist to describe the disciples' descent into a sleepy state just before their vision. As we have already noted in Chapter 2, it is unclear whether Luke's mention of them becoming alert after being 'weighed down with sleep' – 'βεβαρημένοι ὕπνῳ, διαγρηγορήσαντες' – implies that the disciples fall asleep and then wake up, or are somehow in a drowsy, liminal state, but nonetheless alert. When Tertullian discusses in *Adv. Prax.* 15 the disciples' *amentia*, he points to this being a state characterizing *all three* of the disciples (by contrast with the concentration in *Adv. Marc.* 4.22 on Peter). The logic of his argument in *Adv. Prax.* 15 would seem to open the possibility that Tertullian sees their slipping into a sleepy state marking the beginning of their *amentia*. Their physical senses go into abeyance, as if asleep, and Peter is no longer aware of what he says, even when he speaks to suggest three tabernacles.

A further question is how the disciples see Moses and Elijah. In *De Anima* 9, Tertullian insists that one of the characteristics of *ecstasis* is the ability it affords to see departed souls. He does this with reference to the experience of a Montanist prophetess:[77]

---

77. See Robeck, *Prophecy in Carthage*, 130–4.

We have a sister amongst us at the moment who has been given several gifts of revelation, which she experiences in ecstasy through the Spirit during the liturgy on the Lord's day in church. ... 'Amongst other things,' she says, 'a soul has been shown to me in corporal form and its spirit has been seen by me. It did not have a void and empty quality, but rather such that it gave itself to be touched, tender and bright, of a transparent colour, and its outline was human in all respects.' [78]

For Tertullian, the souls of the departed, though spirit, have a corporeal form, which may be perceived in a state of *ecstasis*.[79] It is unclear whether Tertullian conceives of Moses and Elijah as existing as souls in heaven or, as is frequently asserted in later tradition, as individuals who existed embodied in heaven by virtue of having been assumed. We have here in *De Anima* 9, though, the outline of a model which could be applied to the Transfiguration. The corporeal souls of Elijah and Moses appear before the disciples and are perceived as a result of their *amentia*. The disciples' souls, like the gladiator or charioteer mentioned in *De Anima* 45, continue to 'see' by visualizing the two prophets, even though their physical senses are dulled. It is unclear whether anyone else present on the mountain who was not in an ecstatic state would be able to see Moses and Elijah. The logic of Tertullian's argument from *De Anima* 9 would seem to be that if Moses and Elijah were present as souls, they wouldn't be visible to a person not in ecstasy.

In addition, there is the question of how Christ, who is physically present, is seen and the glory he appears in is perceived. Something about the ecstasy Peter finds himself in makes seeing Christ's glory possible. Again, it is unclear whether someone on the mountain not in ecstasy would be able to see the glory with physical eyes. *Adv. Prax.* 15 implies that if they could, it would be dangerous both to their eyes and to their reasoning faculties. It is unclear whether Tertullian conceives of the disciples seeing Christ's glory only with their mind's eye, or with their physical eyes, or a combination of both.

For Tertullian, *amentia* brings about a dislocation of the usual connection between the physical faculty of sight, and the cognitive faculty of reasoning which interprets what is seen. What emerges is an experience in which things usually invisible to physical sight are seen by the visionary, and in which things usually hidden from the mind by God are understood and communicated. For Tertullian, vision is not just what is physically apprehended by the eye but clearly includes, and maybe principally refers to, what is visualized by the soul.

---

78. *De Anima* 9.4.

79. For an extended examination of Tertullian's understanding of how the souls of the departed can be seen from other visionary experiences he treats, see Robeck, *Prophecy in Carthage*, 128–39.

Tertullian: Conclusions

Several conclusions can be drawn from our survey of Tertullian's interpretation of the Transfiguration. The first is to recognize the importance of his interest in visionary prophecy. This leads him to see the Transfiguration as a key text in the legitimization of ecstatic vision within the Church, by interpreting Peter's experience as ecstatic. Tertullian's polemic interests draw him to see ecstatic elements in the Lucan Transfiguration narrative as key evidence in his anti-Marcionite argument. Tertullian's use of language is of singular importance, especially the word *ecstasis*, which he defines in terms of the more widely understood notion of *amentia*. His varied comments on vision and ecstasy allow us to piece together a reasonably precise summary of Tertullian's understanding of the visionary character of the Transfiguration. He understands this to include, in addition to the physical faculty of sight, the memory and imagination's ability to visualize realities revealed to them in the Spirit, in a way not dissimilar to the processes whereby we dream in sleep. In addition, this interest in ecstatic vision leads Tertullian to interpret the Transfiguration in the light of the Hebrew Scriptures. He views prophetic vision as a crucial part of the way in which the Transfiguration is to be seen as the fulfilment of texts from the Old Testament, inspiring not only the writers of Hebrew prophecy but also those who read the Transfiguration narratives in Tertullian's time. Of great significance is the way in which these interpretive insights are garnered by Tertullian from a reading of Luke's gospel, or the related Marcionite version of Luke's Transfiguration which he commented upon in *Adversus Marcionem*. Tertullian's polemic needs draw him to see visionary and ecstatic elements as a crucial character of Luke's narrative.

Origen

In the second half of this chapter, we explore, by way of contrast, the interpretation of the Transfiguration, which we find in the writings of Origen. Origen writes at almost exactly the same time as Tertullian but came from the very different Greek-speaking context of Alexandria. Origen's considerable literary output makes him one of the most important biblical scholars of the early Christian period, and he comments in a number of places on the Transfiguration.

Origen, like Tertullian, sees in Luke's words evidence of Peter being in ecstasy. However, by contrast with Tertullian, he sees this ecstasy negatively. Origen also draws out a number of tabernacle and priestly themes from our narratives. Origen exploits these themes in a way which enables him to read the Transfiguration side by side with the birth narratives set in the Temple in Luke 2. What unites Tertullian and Origen is their ability to use the Transfiguration's visionary status, as emphasized by Luke, albeit in very different ways, to interpret other parts of the Christian scriptures in their attempts to describe human experience of the vision of God.

We will explore first the significance which Origen sees in Peter's being in a state he judges to be ecstasy and evaluate Origen's ambivalent attitude to ecstatic vision. We then examine Origen's reading of the Transfiguration in the light of a number of motifs appertaining to the High Priesthood and the heavenly tabernacle. Finally, we will compare the comments Origen makes concerning the Temple events of Lk. 2.22-52 and the Transfiguration. There appears to be a connection in Origen's understanding between the Finding in the Temple and his interpretation of the Transfiguration narrative as a temple-like experience. This shows the Transfiguration being used by him as a lens through which to read other portions of Luke's gospel which take place in the Jerusalem Temple.

Transfiguration, vision and ecstasy in Origen

Origen offers a detailed reflection on the Transfiguration in two main contexts: first, in direct commentary on the narratives themselves, particularly in his *Commentary on Matthew's Gospel* and in his *Homilies on Luke*, which will be the principal focus of this chapter; and second, indirectly, in discussion concerning the resurrection and the resurrection body.[80]

Origen underlines the Transfiguration as an incident dependent on the disciples' ability to apprehend the experience. He insists that throughout his earthly life, Jesus had the capacity to appear differently to different people. This took place according to their spiritual maturity and their ability to apprehend the gospel. The Transfiguration is, according to Origen, simply one of many examples in Jesus' life when his appearance changed. He insists that the transfiguration of Jesus' body took place 'whenever he wanted, and for whomever he wanted.'[81] He further argues, 'When people saw him, he did not appear in the same way to everyone, but rather according to the ability of each to receive him.'[82] The evidence he uses to justify this is the fact that he only took three disciples to experience the Transfiguration, as the others did not possess the necessary spiritual maturity.[83]

Origen extends this point concerning the disciples' sight to use the Transfiguration as a broader metaphor pointing to the ability of the soul to ascend to God, or of ordinary believers to apprehend God's presence in the scriptures.[84] He regards the Transfiguration as a paradigm of how God reveals himself to

---

80. Cosmin Pricop offers an excellent resumé and critical examination of Origen's comment on the Transfiguration and its hermeneutic underpinnings as part of his comparison of patristic commentary and modern historical-critical interpretation (*Die Verwandlung Jesu Christi, historisch-kritische und patristische Studien*, Wissenschaftliche Untersuchungen zum Neuen Testament, 2 Reihe (Tübingen: Mohr Siebeck, 2016), esp. 170–225).
81. *Contra Cels*. 2.64 (PG 11, 897, B).
82. *Contra Cels*. 2.64 (PG 11, 896, C).
83. *Contra Cels*. 2.64 (PG 11, 896, C).
84. This point is underlined by Pricop in his examination of Origen's Transfiguration comment and seen by him as one of the most significant differences between the

humankind in which he emphasizes the need for conscious human receptivity to divine revelation and the ascetic preparation that precedes it.[85]

Matthias Eichinger[86] sets this within the context of Origen's broader anthropology. He sees Origen's view of humankind as characterized by a series of dichotomies and paradoxes in which Origen regards fallen man as unable to know God by his own efforts. However, amongst the fallen, he distinguishes between the sinful and the believing. Believing humankind, though fallen, is able to know God through the humanity of the incarnate Word and through having human sight transformed. Unbelieving humanity, however, can only know the human Jesus and see no further. This anthropological conviction, therefore, is typified in the Transfiguration, a mystery visible to believers but not to those who can see no further than Jesus' humanity. Origen extends this analogy by a comparison in *Commentary on Matthew* between the participation of the three disciples in the Transfiguration and the faithful Christian meditating upon scripture. He describes the shining garments of Jesus being like the 'discourses and letters of the gospel'.[87] These sayings become white for those who 'ascend the mountain with him. ... So when you see someone who has not only a profound theological understanding concerning Jesus but can also interpret the sayings of the gospel, do not hesitate to say that for such a person, the garments of Jesus have become as white as light'.[88] The Transfiguration has significance for Origen, therefore, as a visionary experience apprehended by the disciples, and dependent on their spiritual maturity, which may then be used as a broader metaphor for ordinary Christians' encounter with God in the scriptures, which takes place in accordance with their spiritual maturity and level of understanding.

Origen also asserts, however, that the Transfiguration was visible to the disciples not just because of their advanced state of visionary capacity but also because it represented a lesser experience of eschatological glory than that which will be experienced in the Kingdom of Heaven.[89] The body Christ displays at the Transfiguration is not that which he will have in the Age to Come, Origen asserts, as it is not yet a completely spiritual body and had not yet put on incorruption.[90] Indeed, he describes Christ's body at the Transfiguration being 'corruptible garments',[91] even though they are glorious. Origen seems to hold a three-stage

hermeneutic witnessed in Origen and that offered by modern scholarship. See Pricop, *Die Verwandlung Jesu Christi*, 216–24.

85. *Contra Cels.* 4.16 (PG 11, 1047, B); *Hom in Gen.* 1.7 (SC 7, 44).

86. Matthias Eichinger, *Die Verklärung Christi bei Origines: Die Bedeutung des Menschen Jesus in seiner Christologie* (Vienna: Herder, 1969), esp. 26–47.

87. *Com. Mat.* 12.38 (PG 13, 1069, B).

88. Ibid.

89. See Christopher Veniamin, 'The Transfiguration of Christ in Greek Patristic Literature: From Irenaeus of Lyons to Gregory Palamas' (DPhil. diss., University of Oxford, 1991), 52–7.

90. *Frag. Luc.* 140 (GCS 49, 283–4).

91. Ibid.

understanding of Christ's visibility: first, there is the physical body he takes on in the incarnation visible to everyone with physical sense; second, there is a glorified but only semi-spiritualized body shown at the Transfiguration and between the Resurrection and Ascension, visible to those with the spiritual maturity to perceive it, and described by Christopher Veniamin as an 'intermediate state of corporeity';[92] and, third, there is the body he has after the Ascension in heaven which is fully spiritual and can only be seen by those who have put on incorruption and assumed their 'spiritual' bodies. Indeed, Veniamin suspects that Origen holds the body of the ordinary Christian glorified in the Kingdom of Heaven to be more glorious than that shown by Christ at the Transfiguration.[93]

Origen understands the disciples to be able to see the Transfiguration as a result of a number of transformations and stages: first, there is a transformation within Christ himself in which he alters his appearance; second, the disciples who see it need to be of advanced spiritual maturity; and, third, the body of Christ displays eschatological glory, but only so much as it is possible for mortals to see.

Ecstasy and the Lucan narrative

A point of similarity with Tertullian's understanding of the Transfiguration is a shared interpretation of Lk. 9.33 seeing Peter in a state of ecstasy. Remarking that Luke describes Peter as not understanding what he was saying, Origen suggests in *Commentary on Matthew* that Peter may have been in some sort of trance-like state: 'You will consider whether he said this in a trance [κατ'ἔκστασιν], filled with a spirit which prompted him to say these things.'[94] He then points out that the Holy Spirit was not given to the Apostles until after the Resurrection and so comes to the conclusion that Peter must have been possessed by an *evil* spirit. This trance-inducing evil spirit, according to Origen, sought to use Peter to stop Jesus from coming down the mountain in order to be crucified, or else duped Peter into separating Jesus from Moses and Elijah with three tabernacles rather than one.

It is important to note the influence of the Lucan text on Origen's reflection, even in his commentary on Matthew's gospel. He quotes Luke's words, 'he did not know what he was saying,'[95] five times in *Com. Mat.* 40, 41 in order to show Peter was in a state of 'ecstasy'. Origen also employs Luke's mention of the disciples' falling asleep to refer forward to similar demonic possession of Peter at Gethsemane in his inability to keep awake and in his denial of Jesus during his Trial.[96] In addition, in *Com. Mat.* 38, Origen breaks away from Matthew's narrative, and quotes Lk. 9.31's mention of Moses's and Elijah's discussing Jesus' 'exodus' as signifying the compatibility of Jesus' teaching with the prophecy of the Old Covenant. In more

---

92. Veniamin, 'The Transfiguration of Christ in Greek Patristic Literature', 52.
93. Ibid.
94. *Com. Mat.* 12.40 (PG 13, 1074, A).
95. Lk. 9.33.
96. *Com. Mat.* 12.40 (PG 13, 1076).

general terms, the influence of Luke's narrative can also be detected, though not as explicitly, in Origen's language of 'glory'. In *Contra Celsum*, after making a point about the small number of disciples being invited up the mountain, Origen states that it was only Peter, James and John who were capable of 'beholding his glory on that occasion, and of observing Moses and Elijah in glory'.[97] Origen closely echoes here Lk. 9.31 ('οἱ ὀφθέντες ἐν δόξῃ') rather than the Matthean text by referring to Moses and Elijah as 'τους ὀφθεντες ἐν δοξη',[98] and, later in Chapter 6, to Moses as 'ὅς ἐστιν ἐν δόξῃ ὀφθεὶς μετα Ἰησου'.[99]

Origen and ecstasy

We may conclude from Origen's comment on the Transfiguration that his attitude to ecstasy is not as positive as Tertullian's. His comments on ecstatic vision discussed in other works display a similar ambivalence. Although Walther Völker[100] argued ecstasy to be an important part of Origen's understanding of human knowledge, a large number of subsequent commentators has disagreed with his argument and shown Origen not to have seen epistemic value in ecstasy.[101] Henri-Charles Puech[102] shows that Philo used the word 'ecstasy' in two ways: first, as a simple sort of violent astonishment at something unexpected; and, second, as the expulsion of *nous* from the human mind and replacement with the divine spirit, which results in esoteric knowledge and vision. He argues that Origen only ever uses the word in the first sense and not the second. Origen's hesitancy about ecstasy stands as a reaction against Philo's more positive appraisal of it, for whom ecstasy represented an ejection of reason from the human soul, only to be replaced by divine mind, with which it was united and into which it was subsumed.

For Origen, however, the contemplation of God does not require the soul to pass beyond or out of itself, and ecstasy, understood as an ejection of reason,

---

97. *Contra Cels.* 2.64 (PG 11, 896, D).
98. *Contra Cels.* 2.64 (PG 11, 896, D).
99. *Contra Cels.* 6.68 (PG 11, 1401, C).
100. Walther Völker, *Das Vollkommenheitsideal des Origenes: Eine Untersuchung zur Geschichte der Frömmigkeit und zu den Anfängen christlicher Mystik*, Beiträge zur historischen Theologie (Tübingen: J.C.B. Mohr, 1931), 139–44.
101. Jean Daniélou, 'Les Sources bibliques de la mystique d'Origène', *Revue d'ascetique et de la mystique* 23 (1947): 135–6; Irénée Hausherr, 'L'origine de la doctrine occidentale des huit péchés capitaux', *Orientalia Christiana Analecta* 30 (1930): 129; Henri-Charles Puech, 'Un livre recent sur la livre mystique d'Origène', *Revue d'histoire et de philosophie religieuse* 13 (1933): 508–36; Karl Rahner, 'La doctrine des sens spirituels chez Origène', *Revue d'ascetique et de la mystique* (1932): 135; Marcel Viller, 'Aux sources de la spiritualité de S. Maxime le Confesseur: Les ouevres d'Évagre le Pontique', *Revue d'ascetique et de la mystique* 30 (1930): 255.
102. Puech, 'Un livre recent sur la livre mystique d'Origène', 528–33.

dangerously edges towards an abandoning of the very faculty he sees as most important for vision of God. For Origen, ecstasy can be a negative sign of demonic possession as is seen not just in his treatment of Peter at the Transfiguration but also in Origen's criticism of the Pythian seer's ecstasy in *Contra Cels.* 7.3-4.[103] Because Origen asserts the soul's contemplation of the Logos to be a possibility natural to the human condition, he is very suspicious indeed of notions of God's complete unknowability, on the one hand, and of the need for ecstasy to know him, on the other. Indeed, Jean Daniélou, Andrew Louth and Bernard McGinn see Origen's suspicion of ecstasy to be a reaction against Montanist use of the phrase.[104]

Origen does, however, concede that the soul may be possessed by a sort of rapture, or 'sober drunkenness', as a *consequence* of the divine vision. However, as Yochanan Lewy[105] has pointed out, Origen speaks of 'sober drunkenness' in *Joh. Com.*[106] as something which does not involve loss of reason but as a sense of spiritual joy. Indeed, Lewy argues that in *Hom. Lev.* 7[107] Origen's use of the phrase has a more eschatological focus, characterizing *future* vision of God in heaven rather than present-day ecstasy. Origen does use the word ἔκστασις in a positive sense once in *Hom. Nom.* 7, as characterizing the last stages of ascent to the vision of God in an analogy based on the wilderness wanderings. He points out that there is no one Latin word which translates the term ἔκστασις satisfactorily but that his interpretation of the place name Thara, which Rufinus translates as 'contemplatio stuporis',[108] expresses what the Greek term means. For Origen, this 'contemplation of stupefaction' signifies solely 'when the dazed mind is astonished by recognition of wonderful and marvellous things'.[109] Again, he sees the term describing human emotional *response* to revelation rather than a state that prompts it. In none of these instances does Origen state these phrases to involve a Philonic evacuation of human reason. More importantly, at no point does Origen regard ecstasy to be an epistemic prerequisite of divine vision or revelation, as Tertullian does.

---

103. *Contra Cels.* 7.3-4 (PG 11, 1424–5).

104. Jean Daniélou, *Origène* (Paris: La Table Ronde, 1948), 296; Andrew Louth, *The Origins of the Christian Mystical Tradition: From Plato to Denys*, 2nd edn (Oxford: Oxford University Press, 2007), 70; Bernard McGinn, *The Foundations of Mysticism*, The Presence of God: A History of Western Christian Mysticism (London: SCM, 1992), 128.

105. Yochanan Lewy, *Sobria Ebrietas: Untersuchungen zur Geschichte der antiken Mystik*, Beihefte zur Zeitschrift für die neutestamentliche Wissenschaft und die Kunde der älteren Kirche (Giessen: A. Töpelmann, 1929), 119–20.

106. *Joh. Com.* 1, 30 (Die griechischen christlichen Schriftsteller der ersten Jahrhunderte 10, 37).

107. Lewy, *Sobria Ebrietas*, 121–3. See *Hom. Lev.* 7,1 (PG 12, 475–8).

108. *Hom. Nom.* 27.12.7 (PG 12, 796, B).

109. *Hom. Nom.* 27.12.7 (PG 12, 796, C).

Temple and tabernacle motifs

Having examined Origen's understanding of the ecstatic experience Peter undergoes at the Transfiguration, we now turn to how Origen explores a number of High Priestly motifs he sees as present in the Transfiguration, and especially in Luke's version of the narrative. Origen describes on two occasions the transfigured Jesus as a 'High Priest'. Both references are very similar in wording and make, broadly speaking, the same point. In *Frag. Luc.* 140, continuing his analogy between ascending the mountain and human apprehension of the divine, he speaks of the person who metaphorically climbs the mountain with Jesus. If that person is taken up with him, 'he sees the Word transfigured in glory, and sees him as the very Word and as the High Priest who converses with the Father and also prays to him'.[110] Origen makes a similar point in *Commentary on Matthew*, though here it is particularly connected with Jesus' *prayer*. He announces that it is necessary to examine 'the passage given in Mark, "And as he was praying he was transfigured before them"'.[111] In very similar words to the Luke fragment, Origen says if we ascend the mountain with Christ we see 'the Word transfigured before us if we have done the things mentioned above, and have ascended the mountain, and seen the Word himself talking with the Father and praying to him for such things as a true High Priest would pray for to the one true God'.[112] For Origen, Jesus' exalted status points to his being the Eternal Word, but the special fellowship with the Father displayed in the Transfiguration, and his act of praying to the Father, reveals him as a High Priestly figure, something perceived by those who are advanced in the spiritual life. Origen would appear to see a correspondence between the High Priest's role and that of the Eternal Word as both representing mediation of the divine, signalled here by the action of prayer mentioned by Luke.

However, assessment of this second quotation is made problematic by the fact that the reference to Jesus praying is usually seen as a solely Lucan detail, whereas Origen seems to see it present in Mark. It would seem that two explanations for the origin of these unknown Marcan words are possible. One could be that Origen has mistakenly conflated the Lucan and Marcan texts. In favour of this verdict would be the absence of any mention by Origen of Luke also having this detail of prayer. Origen frequently brings in details from Luke elsewhere in his Matthew commentary to strengthen or expand an interpretation, so the absence of a mention here that Luke also mentions prayer might point in the direction of some sort of mistake on Origen's part. Alternatively, Origen could be using a variant of Mk 9.2 similar to that attested in P^{45}, W and f13, which states that it was 'ἐν τω προσευχεσθαι αὐτους' that Jesus was transfigured. However, this variant presumably speaks of all four of those present on the mountain praying, rather than Jesus on his own. A further variant exists in some Q manuscripts from the ninth century that changes 'αὐτους' to 'αὐτον', but this is weakly attested.

---

110. *Frag. Luc.* 140 (GCS Origenes 9/49, 283–4).
111. *Com. Mat.* 12.39 (PG 13, 1072).
112. *Com. Mat.* 12.39 (PG 13, 1072).

It is difficult, therefore, to prove conclusively that Origen sees the mention of prayer as a distinctly Lucan element. However, even if working from a text of Mark that contained a mention of prayer, he certainly comments on its presence in Luke's narrative in *Frag. Luc.* 140. Origen interprets this as showing that Jesus' High Priestly status is something revealed by faithful Christians' reading of the Transfiguration. Those who through ascetic growth and maturity are able to encounter the transfigured Christ in the scriptures see him as a High Priest. Origen does not explicitly say Jesus was revealed as a High Priest at the Transfiguration itself, but rather when this is allegorically experienced by faithful Christians, seeing him as such is a consequence of their understanding.

Cloud as tabernacle

A further interpretation offered by Origen is the significance he gives to the overshadowing cloud as a tabernacle for the presence of God. He notes in *Commentary on Matthew* the inappropriateness of Peter's suggestions and concludes that Peter was fixated with living on the mountain in earthly huts rather than perceiving the experience as a revelation of God's presence: 'He [God], therefore, shows a better tabernacle, a more excelling one, the cloud.'[113] Origen reads the cloud, just as Tertullian and the writer of the *Apocalypse of Peter* do, as a dwelling for the presence of God, concluding that in sending it, God 'made, so to speak, a more divine tabernacle'.[114] In addition to High Priestly motifs, therefore, a significant background to Origen's reading of the Transfiguration is also one in which he sees entry into the overshadowing cloud as comparable with entry into the heavenly dwelling of God. In the light of the presence of these priestly, temple and tabernacle motifs, I attempt in the next section a more speculative examination of ways in which Origen possibly links the Transfiguration with events recounted in the Temple in Lk. 2.22-52.

Temple events in Luke 2 and the Transfiguration

In *Hom. Luc.* 20 Origen makes what seems to be a very simple comparison between the Finding in the Temple and the Transfiguration. He describes being in the Temple as being 'above', whilst living in Nazareth with Mary and Joseph, whose faith had not come to full fruition, as involving a 'going down'.[115] This, he says, is like the Transfiguration, where Peter, James and John could cope with being above on the mountain with Jesus, but the crowds remained below, 'in another place'.[116] The comparison Origen seems to be making is between the spiritual immaturity of the disciples who remained behind – and by extension Mary and Joseph – on the

---

113. *Com. Mat.* 12.42 (PG 13, 1081).
114. *Com. Mat.* 12.42 (PG 13, 1081).
115. *Hom. Luc.* 20.4 (SC 87, 282–4).
116. *Hom. Luc.* 20.4 (SC 87, 284).

one hand, and the maturity of Peter, James and John, who are capable of bearing lofty revelation on the mountain top, on the other. The question I wish to speculate about is whether this forms part of a broader analogy which Origen sees between the temple narratives of Lk. 2.22-52 and the Transfiguration. In such an analogy these two series of events are comparable not just because they involve 'going down' from a place of revelation but also because this descent is seen in both cases to take place after experiences in a temple-like place.

Use of Phil. 2.7

Origen uses Phil. 2.7 to link and explain both Lk. 2.22-52 and the Transfiguration. In *Hom. Luc.* 18, Origen describes the Presentation as the point at which Jesus was filled with what he had lost in the kenosis of the incarnation. He quotes Phil. 2.7 when he points to the moment the two doves are offered for Jesus as the instant at which he is filled with the Wisdom mentioned at Lk. 2.40: 'Scripture was able to say, "He grew, was strengthened, and received the Spirit." But since, "he had emptied himself by taking the form of a slave", as soon as sacrifice was offered for his purification, he recovered in its fullness that which he had been emptied of.'[117] We see here in the sacrifice a corollary to Phil. 2.7, in which the lowly state of Jesus' emptying is reversed. John Anthony McGuckin has pointed to Phil. 2.7 also lying at the heart of Origen's very similar interpretation of the Transfiguration, particularly of his notion of Jesus' changing appearance. McGuckin asserts, 'Origen appears to be the only patristic commentator in the whole tradition of the exegesis of the Transfiguration narrative who connects the metamorphosis of Philippians with the metamorphosis mentioned in the Gospels.'[118] Origen employs Phil. 2.7 as part of a hermeneutic which sees the Presentation and the Transfiguration as an exalting reversal of the kenosis experienced by the divine Word in the incarnation.

The Presentation in the Temple and the Transfiguration

This connection between Origen's interpretation of Lk. 2.22-52 and Lk. 9.28-36, found in *Hom. Luc.* 20, raises questions about a number of other interpretations which Origen brings to Luke 2, which offer tantalizing hints at further connections being made between the two narratives. One such is Origen's conviction that the reason Mary and Joseph searched anxiously for Jesus in the Temple was not because they feared he had perished, because they knew him to be divine, but rather they feared that, being in the Temple, he might have momentarily popped up to heaven. Origen states, 'In just this way, his parents sought Jesus, lest perhaps

---

117. *Hom. Luc.* 18.1 (SC 87, 264).

118. John Anthony McGuckin, 'The Changing Forms of Jesus', in *Origeniana Quarta: die Referate des 4. internationalen Origeneskongress, 1985*, ed. Lothar Lies (Innsbrück: Tyrolia-Verlag, 1987), 217.

he withdraw from them, or leave them and pass over to some other realm, or – what I consider more likely – lest he return to heaven to come down again when it pleased him.'[119] Could it be that Origen sees parallels between the Temple as a natural place for such an event and the way in which the Transfiguration might also represent a momentary entry into heavenly space? *Homily* 19 only exists in Jerome's Latin translation, so it is impossible to know what Origen's original Greek was. However, Jerome's 'recessiset ab eis' certainly echoes the Vulgate's rendering of the Ascension in Lk. 24.51 as '*recessit ab eis* et ferebatur in caelum'. At the very least, Jerome's translation evokes comparison between Luke 2 and Jesus' entry into heaven in Luke 24, something which may have been present in Origen's Greek text. It may be, therefore, that Origen links a series of occasions which he sees as parallel entries into the heavenly presence of God: the possibility of Jesus briefly visiting heaven from the Jerusalem Temple; experience of a 'better tabernacle' at the Transfiguration; and Jesus' final entry into heaven at the Ascension. His seeing a range of priestly, tabernacle and temple motifs present in the Transfiguration forms a crucial part of this comparison.

Origen: Conclusion

Interpreting the Transfiguration in the light of ecstatic, temple, High Priestly and tabernacle motifs forms an important part of Origen's exegesis, which is one particularly focused on Luke's narrative. We have shown where Origen's interpretation hinges on the overshadowing cloud being seen as a tabernacle for God's presence, on those meditating on the narrative experiencing the transfigured Christ as a High Priestly figure and on Peter being seen as experiencing an ecstatic state. Origen sees in Luke's description of Peter evidence of ecstasy but judges it negatively as the result of demonic possession. Origen also draws an analogy in which the Transfiguration becomes a paradigm for God's self-revelation in the words of scripture to the Christian believer, in which Jesus is encountered as a High Priest. For him, the Transfiguration is significant as a model of the participation in Jesus' transfigured presence which the most spiritually and ascetically advanced experience in their meditation upon the New Testament.

We have shown that Origen's interpretation of the Transfiguration prompts him to read Luke 9 in parallel with incidents from Lk. 2.22-52, a reading which turns on a use of Phil. 2.7. Origen uses this interpretation to describe a dynamic of kenosis followed by exaltation present in both narratives. Further possible connections might exist between Luke 2 and Luke 9 through their mutual comparison with entries into heaven. This chapter reveals Origen to be an interpreter whose apprehension of the significance of visionary and ecstatic themes in the Transfiguration, and of Luke's role in emphasizing them, produces a distinct and inventive exegesis of the Transfiguration, which foregrounds its status as a visionary text.

119. *Hom. Luc.* 19.5 (SC 87, 276).

Tertullian and Origen: Conclusion

I have shown through comparison of Tertullian's and Origen's interpretation of the Transfiguration the importance of a series of visionary motifs particularly present in Luke's narrative. This focus on the Transfiguration as a visionary experience leads Origen and Tertullian, in different ways, to see Luke's version as indicating Peter being in a state of ecstasy.

Both Tertullian and Origen see the Transfiguration as an incident dependent on the visionary ability of the disciples to see it. This allows Origen to use the Transfiguration as a broad analogy for human vision of God, and especially for the processes whereby the faithful believer encounters God in the scriptures. This *theoria*, which the Transfiguration exemplifies, is conceived by Origen in noetic terms, as referring to the activity of the intellective faculties, which move human vision beyond the physical to vision of the divine in the rational realm. For Tertullian, by contrast, it is seen as a justifying example of visualization in the prophetic imagination of the revelation God wishes to communicate to his faithful, an experience akin to dreaming.

A further element of the visionary character which Tertullian and Origen recognize in the Transfiguration is their both seeing in Lk. 9.33 evidence of Peter being in ecstasy. Tertullian sees this as a crucial justification for parallel visionary and prophetic phenomena in the Church which he seeks to defend. Indeed, he holds ecstasy to be a moment of great epistemic privilege and an important part of how the mind visualizes the things God wishes to communicate. Origen, by contrast, is more suspicious of ecstasy and judges its presence here in Peter to be a sign of demonic possession. He is more ambivalent in his verdict on the significance of ecstasy. Whilst not necessarily always judging ecstatic states negatively, Origen certainly does not see them as the epistemic prerequisite which Tertullian does.

Both interpreters draw on the kind of temple and tabernacle imagery frequently associated with visionary and apocalyptic texts and their concern for entry into the divine presence. We have shown this to be more pronounced in Origen's interpretation, but that it is not absent from Tertullian's, who sees the Transfiguration as typologically connected to Moses's experience of the Tent of Meeting, and who reads the Transfiguration in the light of the very cultic imagery of Zechariah 4. Origen creates a series of 'cultic' analogies: those who mediate on the Transfiguration, for example, experience Jesus as a High Priest, entering God's presence to pray; he also likens the overshadowing cloud to a tabernacle dwelling for God which the disciples enter.

It is notable that both Tertullian and Origen use their very different understandings of the Transfiguration's visionary and ecstatic motifs as a means for interpreting other parts of the scriptures. Tertullian sees the Transfiguration foreshadowed in the Hebrew Scriptures and uses the Transfiguration to reconcile the Old and New Testaments, particularly to see ecstatic utterance in Habakkuk and Zechariah. Origen exploits the temple motifs we have outlined to read the Transfiguration side by side with Luke 2 in the light of Phil. 2.7.

We see in Tertullian and Origen two readings of the Transfiguration highly sensitized to the consequences of seeing the incident as a visionary experience and to perceiving Luke's version as especially emphasizing this. Although they draw very different conclusions, both their interpretations are rooted in questions appertaining to ecstatic vision and connected analogies concerning how humans see God and understand the divine. For both Tertullian and Origen, the Transfiguration represents an important hermeneutic nexus that raises, through its status as a visionary text, questions concerning human apprehension of God, the prophetic inspiration of the Hebrew Scriptures, the coherence of the Old and New Testaments, and the paradox at the heart of the incarnation concerning the kenotic humbling of God's divine word, as well as his exaltation. We have seen subtly different scopic regimes emerge which prompt Tertullian and Origen to be highly sensitized to visionary elements within the Transfiguration texts. However, they draw very different and intriguing conclusions about what that tells us about the human subject's epistemological capacity to know God and the processes that accompany and enable that knowledge.

Chapter 6

INTERPRETATION OF THE TRANSFIGURATION IN THE GREEK EAST AFTER ORIGEN

In this chapter, I examine interpretation of the Transfiguration narratives after Origen in the Greek-speaking East[1] in order to establish the scopic regimes that informed how writers understood and wrote about the Transfiguration vision. I point to a number of unresolved complexities concerning the way in which commentators understand language used by the New Testament to describe how the disciples 'see' the Transfiguration and how this relates to humankind's ultimate eschatological vision of God. This chapter is not intended, therefore, to be an exhaustive summation of every word written on the Transfiguration in Greek. Others have accomplished that task expertly already.[2] What distinguishes this chapter is its focus on how the New Testament texts were interpreted by Greek-speaking commentators as expressing *vision*, and specifically how motifs present in Luke's narrative have contributed to this.

I point to the significance of two writers, Anastasius of Sinai and John Chrysostom, whose comment stands out as very different from the majority of their contemporaries. Anastasius of Sinai sees Peter as gripped by an ecstasy, which

---

1. All translations of primary texts in this chapter are my own unless otherwise stated.

2. Excellent summaries of Greek patristic comment on the Transfiguration can be found in Michel Coune, *Joie de la Transfiguration d'après les Pères d'Orient*, Spiritualité Orientale no. 39 (Bégrolles-en-Mauges: Abbaye de Bellefontaine, 1985); Brian E. Dailey, S.J., *Light on the Mountain: Greek Patristic and Byzantine Homilies on the Transfiguration of the Lord* (Yonkers, NY: St Vladimir's Seminary Press, 2013); Edouard Divry, *La Transfiguration selon l'orient et l'occident*, Croire et Savoir vol. 54 (Paris: Pierre Tequi, 2009); Georges Habra, *La Transfiguration selon les pères grecs* (Paris: Editions S.O.S, 1974); John Anthony McGuckin, *The Transfiguration of Christ in Scripture and Tradition* (Lewiston, NY: Edwin Mellen Press, 1986); Cosmin Pricop, *Die Verwandlung Jesu Christi, historisch-kritische und patristische Studien*, Wissenschaftliche Untersuchungen zum Neuen Testament, 2 Reihe (Tübingen: Mohr Siebeck, 2016), esp. 225–79 on John Chrysostom; Michael Ramsey, *The Glory of God and the Transfiguration of Christ* (London: Longmans, Green, 1949), 128–39; Kenneth Stevenson, *Liturgy and Interpretation* (London: SCM Press, 2011), 86–102; Christopher N. Veniamin, 'The Transfiguration of Christ in Greek Patristic Literature: From Irenaeus of Lyons to Gregory Palamas' (DPhil. diss., University of Oxford, 1991).

prompts a direct, dreamlike vision of heaven. In addition, I argue that Chrysostom sees the Transfiguration in terms of a version of the imaginative vision similar to that which we have already noted in Chapter 5 in Tertullian. Chrysostom's distinct emphasis on the sensible nature of the Transfiguration sets him apart from much Eastern comment and causes him to see in the Transfiguration a prompt to imaginative visualizing of God's heavenly Kingdom. Elements found solely in the Lucan narrative play an important part in the way both these theologians construct their distinct understandings of the disciples' vision. To make sense particularly of Chrysostom's thought, and to distinguish it from Anastasius's, I use the language and conceptual framework Mary Carruthers[3] has established in her examination of memory in the ancient and medieval period to describe the processes Chrysostom sees at work when the faithful meditate on the Transfiguration.

Transfiguration as vision in the Greek Fathers

We need to explore first one specific aspect which few modern commentators have focused on, namely exactly how Greek-writing commentators understood the vision which the disciples underwent on the Mount of Transfiguration. This will help us to explore later in this chapter the relationship between how the disciples were understood to *see* the Transfiguration and the way in which this effects interpretation of certain elements of the Lucan narrative such as the disciples' sleepiness, their entry into the cloud and Peter's not knowing what he said.

John Anthony McGuckin states that, amongst Greek writers, Basil, Cyril, Andrew of Crete, Anastasius of Antioch, and John of Damascus all propose an interpretation which sees the Transfiguration as a foretaste of the Parousia.[4] However, it strikes me that connections made by ancient writers between the Transfiguration and Christ's return are sometimes more complex than McGuckin asserts. At the heart of this complexity lies the question of how the Transfiguration is understood as *vision* and, therefore, how elements, which one might understand to be connected with the disciples' vision, are interpreted. The interpretation of these elements, in turn, influences how the eschatological gap between seeing now and seeing in the age to come is understood to be overcome.

A recurring assumption at the heart of much Greek patristic comment on the Transfiguration, outlined by Vladimir Lossky,[5] is that one of the characteristics of Resurrection life will be the reconciliation of the intellective faculties of the mind

---

3. Mary J. Carruthers, *The Craft of Thought: Meditation, Rhetoric, and the Making of Images, 400–1200* (Cambridge: Cambridge University Press, 1998); Mary J. Carruthers, *The Book of Memory: A Study of Memory in Medieval Culture*, 2nd edn (Cambridge: Cambridge University Press, 2008).

4. McGuckin, *Transfiguration of Christ*, 120–2.

5. Vladimir Lossky, *The Vision of God*, Library of Orthodox Theology (London: Faith Press, 1963).

with the sensible faculties of physical sight. This will involve a beholding of God which will be embodied but capable of apprehending eternal, immortal realities by virtue of the incorruptibility which will be bestowed on the human subject in the Kingdom of God. The putting on of incorruption not only reconciles the faculties of perception and understanding but also alters them so that the mind is capable of apprehending divine, supernatural realities, in a way which mortal humans are unable to. As the disciples cannot experience that incorruptibility until after the Resurrection of Christ, no matter how similar or close the vision they experience at the Transfiguration is to the eschatological vision of the Kingdom, there will always be ambiguity concerning whether their vision can be wholly identified with that fully integrated, direct vision which will characterize heaven. There will always be a disjuncture between the imperfect vision possible for fallen mortals and the more perfect vision possible in the Kingdom of heaven.

I undertake in this chapter an examination of the several ways which emerge in Greek-speaking commentators of relating the disciples' vision of the Transfiguration to the Parousia. I have divided them into three broad categories. I then show how, in the work of Anastasius of Sinai and John Chrysostom, we see two very different views, one rooted in the need for ecstatic rapture and the other rooted in a mortal, sensible understanding of the disciples' vision.

Category 1: The Transfiguration as an episode in which the disciples' mortal vision is transformed so as not to be overwhelmed

The last figure mentioned by McGuckin as asserting a close connection between the Transfiguration and the Parousia is Anastasius I of Antioch (d. 599). Indeed, McGuckin claims his interpretation 'becomes established exegetical tradition in the Greek Fathers'.[6] Anastasius I of Antioch describes the Transfiguration as an 'enigmatic revelation of the Kingdom of Heaven'[7] and 'a vision that had been called "the Kingdom of Heaven" by the one who was revealed as transfigured with the prophets in front of them'.[8] However, Anastasius throughout his *Homily on the Transfiguration* speaks repeatedly of the disciples' minds and vision being *transformed* so they could witness it: 'The spiritual life is all of one kind. Taking them high up from low down does not mean according to local topography but in divine terms. That is to say, he enables them to receive his exalted illuminations.'[9] He also speaks of the apostles having their souls 'enlightened' and their minds 'formed according to his [Jesus'] divinity'.[10] He seems to hold the glory of the Transfiguration and the Parousia to be substantially the same. As a consequence, however, Anastasius teaches that their vision needed to be transformed so as

---

6. McGuckin, *Transfiguration of Christ*, 122.
7. *Serm.* 1, 9 (PG 89, 1376).
8. *Serm.* 1, 5 (PG 89, 1869).
9. *Serm.* 1, 4 (PG, 1368).
10. Ibid.

not to be overwhelmed, and that this vision's most significant character is that it is a perceiving with the renewed and changed mind.[11] Indeed, he describes it as a pointless question to ask how or why the disciples recognized the physical attributes of Moses and Elijah, emphasizing instead the transformation of their minds and souls as the thing which enabled them to recognize the prophets.[12]

Maximus the Confessor (580–662) and Andrew of Crete (c. 650–712/740) hold similar positions. Maximus argues that the disciples passed from the flesh to the Spirit, which Christopher Veniamin interprets as meaning 'they were transported from the plane of the physical and human to that of the spiritual and divine'.[13] Maximus sees them as experiencing in a moment the purification which the faithful Christian can take years to attain and indeed which is not fully consummated until after death. This transformation meant the Spirit altered their sensible faculties, and the 'veils of the passions were removed from their intellect'.[14] For him, the most important way in which the Transfiguration is 'seen' is by the mind, as the radiance witnessed by the disciples overwhelms the eyes. However, even this is in a way which will only be perfected in the age to come, and the radiance which the disciples see is a mere 'symbol of his divinity, something exceeding all mind or sense or essence or understanding'.[15]

Andrew of Crete also sees the glory revealed in the Transfiguration as overwhelming to human sense but in a positive and transforming way: 'Not being able to bear the magnificence of this irreproachable flesh, a magnificence which emanated through the divinity of the Word hypostatically united with the flesh, they fell upon their faces. What a marvel!'[16] Andrew argues with Cyril of Alexandria (376–444) that the glory of the Transfiguration is the same as that witnessed at the Parousia. Andrew sees this glory as supernatural, and that the disciples, being mortal, were overcome by its immensity and in this life were unable to apprehend it with physical vision. However, Andrew goes beyond Cyril and, as Veniamin has pointed out, interprets the overshadowing cloud and the overwhelming nature of the light as completely *removing* the apostles from the realm of sense perception, leaving them with an entirely noetic vision.[17] For Andrew, the overwhelming of the disciples' sensible sight represents a positive transforming of their perception to behold with the mind. In certain respects, Andrew's view of the Transfiguration emphasizes, through this transformation of 'vision', what the disciples do not see with their eyes more than what they do see.

For most of the commentators who see in the Transfiguration a transformation of the disciples' vision, the Transfiguration is apprehended by virtue of renewal

---

11. Ibid.
12. *Serm. 1*, 5 (PG, 1869).
13. Veniamin, 'The Transfiguration of Christ in Greek Patristic Literature', 189.
14. *Amb. Lib.* (PG 91, 1127).
15. Ibid.
16. *Orat.* 7 (PG 97, 949).
17. Veniamin, 'The Transfiguration of Christ in Greek Patristic Literature', 223.

of the mind, as sensible vision is either overwhelmed or rendered useless. The disciples' perception is altered so as to behold with the mind and not the physical eyes, and is focused on the glorious light revealed in the vision. This increasingly becomes a majority position from the sixth century onwards among Greek-speaking commentators. However, even this intellective vision is still frequently held to be an imperfect version of that which is experienced most perfectly at the Eschaton.

Category 2: Transfiguration glory as eschatological glory which is overwhelming to mortal vision

Although the commentators described above see the disciples' vision as transformed during the Transfiguration, and speak of a change effected in the disciples' noetic 'vision', Cyril chooses to emphasize the way in which that overwhelming of the disciples' mortal vision results in an *inability* to see and perceive.

Cyril sees the glory witnessed in the Transfiguration to be identical to that of the Parousia. However, by contrast with Anastasius, Maximus and Andrew of Crete, he emphasizes the disciples' mortal vision being *overcome* rather than *transformed*. Cyril directly equates the Kingdom Jesus speaks about in Lk. 9.27 with the Parousia when he says, 'The Kingdom of which he spoke was that vision of glory in which he will be seen at that time when he will shine out upon all the earth.'[18] In fact, he explains Peter's suggestion concerning tents by saying he must have thought the 'consummation of the age'[19] was happening and presumably that Jesus, Moses and Elijah needed heavenly dwelling places. In his *Commentary on Luke*, Cyril argues the glory of the Transfiguration also to be that which will be experienced at the Resurrection: 'And so we see that the Transfiguration was an example of that future glory, conferred on the disciples, and revealed in a bodily way to fall under the scope of mortal eyes, even though they were unable to bear the greatness of the splendour.'[20] For Cyril, the role of mortal, sensible, sight is emphasized. Although it is an example of future glory, it is somehow fitted to mortal sense vision, yet also overwhelming to it.

However, Cyril has a distinct understanding of precisely how the Transfiguration glory relates to that of the Resurrection.[21] He asserts in his *Commentary on the Gospel according to John*[22] that the Transfiguration is a vision of Resurrection glory such as was seen by the disciples *after* the Ascension. He argues that the apostles were only capable of seeing Jesus' resurrected glory once they had received the Holy Spirit on the Day of the Resurrection. It is because the disciples have not yet

18. *Hom. Div.* 9 (PG 77, 1011).
19. *Hom. Div.* 9 (PG 77, 1014).
20. *Explan. in Luc.* 9 (PG 72, 655).
21. See also Veniamin, 'The Transfiguration of Christ in Greek Patristic Literature', 125–30.
22. *Com. in Ioh.* 20.19,20 (Pusey 3.1091e-1092c).

received the Holy Spirit, and their vision has *not* yet been transformed, that they are overwhelmed on the day of the Transfiguration by the glory in a way that is not the case at the Ascension or in their encounters with the Resurrected Lord.

For Cyril, the vision witnessed at the Transfiguration is a preview of the glory of the ascended and glorified Jesus, and of the glory humanity will experience in the Resurrection. Although Cyril sees the glory of the Parousia and that of the Transfiguration as closely linked, he is unable to say that the disciples' viewing of that glory operates in the same way at the Transfiguration as it does in the Resurrection. For him the Transfiguration is an experience in which mortal vision is overwhelmed rather than transformed, because the Transfiguration took place before the bestowal of the Spirit. For him, an important motif is the way in which the disciples' sight is overwhelmed, and they are *unable* to see.

Category 3: Transfiguration as a divine vision paradoxically seen by mortal faculties by virtue of being a partial vision of eschatological glory

Cyril argued there was something about the Transfiguration which was fitted to mortal sense in a way that allowed it to be apprehended by human sight. A similar argument can be discerned in Basil of Caeserea's (329–379) view that there was something *partial* about the revelation witnessed at the Transfiguration. Basil states,

> For he who is good is above all human intelligence or power and can be beheld only by the mind. The disciples knew his beauty when he explained the parables to them on their own; but Peter and the Sons of Thunder saw his beauty on the mountain brighter than the splendour of the sun, and they, with their eyes, were found worthy to witness the beginnings of his glorious Parousia.[23]

Basil draws here a distinction between God being contemplated in mind only and the disciples being given the privilege of seeing with their eyes that which in eternity is seen with the mind. He would seem to regard the Transfiguration as apprehended by mortal faculties of sense, something which later at the Eschaton will become principally a viewing of God with the mind. Basil's comments do not exclude the idea that the Transfiguration was perceived, at least in part, by the mind, but he asserts that the vision was entirely susceptible to mortal vision with the eyes. Basil's description of the Transfiguration as the 'beginnings' or 'preliminaries' (τὰ προοίμια) of the Parousia also implies that there is something incomplete about the vision which accounts for why it is visible to mortal sense. It is unclear exactly what Basil means by 'beginnings'. One possibility is that the Transfiguration is a preliminary in a chronological sense, that is, a first glimpse in time of something ushered in by Jesus' life and ministry, which will be revealed more fully later. Alternatively, it could be a beginning in the sense of a reduced

---

23. *Hom. in Ps.* 44, 5 (PG 72, 400).

version, a modified glimpse of something greater. Veniamin argues that Basil sees the Transfiguration as a principally intellective vision, which the disciples were given the ability to see with transformed eyes.[24] It seems to me entirely possible that Basil may imagine some sense in which the disciples' vision is transformed. However, his use of τὰ προοίμια also seems to describe something partial or initial in the Transfiguration which for him also contributes to its being able to be witnessed. It possibly makes better sense to say Basil sees in the Transfiguration a notion of anomaly or paradox: that which should principally be seen with the mind is strangely, and by grace, partially seen by mortal faculties of sense as a preliminary or foretaste.

The writer of the *Commentary on Luke*, often ascribed to Eusebius, seems to hold a similar conception. He argues that the Transfiguration represents a partial revelation of something to be revealed fully at the Eschaton. Comparing the two events, he comments, 'And then [i.e. at the Parousia] his divinity will not shine like the sun but will rather be a light greater than any light which has been created and can be apprehended either by the senses or the intellect.'[25] By contrast with Basil, he sees a distinction between the vision experienced on earth as susceptible to mortal apprehension, be that sensible or intellective, and the vision in heaven as *beyond* mortal human vision of any sort. There seems to be a similar sense of paradox in his thinking concerning the fact that the Transfiguration reveals itself in a form susceptible to mortal vision, which at the Eschaton will be beyond all mortal sense or understanding.

Transfiguration as vision: Conclusion

We see in this initial examination of Greek-writing commentators a wide range of opinion and emphases concerning the way in which the Transfiguration should be understood as vision and how the disciples' experience relates to human vision of the divine in the Kingdom of Heaven. Some see the Transfiguration and the Eschaton as substantially the same phenomenon. However, few regard the disciples' experience of it as exactly the same. Cyril and Andrew of Crete, for example, emphasize the disciples' physical vision as being overwhelmed by the Transfiguration. By contrast with this, Anastasius I of Antioch points to the importance of their vision receiving transformation. Basil, however, sees the Transfiguration's relationship to the Eschaton being that of a mere 'preliminary'. It would appear that many differing emphases can be detected in Greek comment concerning the precise mechanics of the disciples' vision of divine glory.

In the next sections of this chapter, I point to the presence of further complexity in the comment of two theologians who specifically read Luke's narrative as giving particular insight into the nature of the disciples' vision, namely Anastasius of Sinai and John Chrysostom.

---

24. See Veniamin, 'The Transfiguration of Christ in Greek Patristic Literature', 125–30.
25. *Comm. in Luc.* 9 (PG 24, 549).

Anastasius of Sinai: Transfiguration as ecstatic vision of the heavens.

Anastasius of Sinai's (d. post 700) homily on the Transfiguration[26] marks a departure from most of the Greek-speaking comment we have reviewed in this chapter so far, in that he is the only homilist I have encountered, since Origen and Tertullian, unequivocally to see Peter as experiencing a form of ecstasy. This is described as plucking him away from the mountain top and giving him the altered perception necessary to see into heaven. I outline in this section Anastasius's interpretation of the Transfiguration narratives and show how important certain elements of the Lucan narrative are in the argument he offers concerning the disciples' vision. In addition, I also reveal how his reading of the Transfiguration prompts him to see a number of temple and priestly motifs present in the narrative.

His homily begins by seeing the Transfiguration as a model for the transformation of the faithful Christian's vision and understanding. Such renewed faculties place the faithful in the company of the redeemed in heaven, who gaze on Christ perfectly. However, Anastasius then admonishes his hearers to follow the example of Peter and to remove themselves in ecstasy from the physical vision of the Transfiguration and be transported beyond this mortal world:

> Like Peter, be taken up in this vision and divine apparition, and be transformed by this beautiful transformation. Be transported out of this world, and away from the earth, leave mortal flesh, abandon creation, and approach the Creator, to whom Peter says in ecstasy, 'Lord, it is good for us to be here.'[27]

Anastasius encourages his hearers, through ecstatic vision, to join Peter who is in heaven. He sees Peter's experience of the Transfiguration as parallel to the celestial vision of God. In a similar way, for Anastasius, the transformation of the faithful Christian results in a vision of God in this life, in which, like Peter, 'each one of us who possesses God in our hearts and is transfigured into his divine image cries out, "It is good for us to be here".'[28]

Anastasius then embarks on a description of Peter's vision of the Transfiguration. He seems to envisage a Platonic movement from physical sense vision to intellective vision by the mind:

> Peter trembled inside his soul and rejoiced, completely raptured away from the things of this world. He sensed in himself, like a divine illumination, a wonderful power, he sensed a strange and unaccustomed joy, a divine trembling. He saw, to the degree that he could see, forms and natures superior to those which we are

---

26. Edited by André Guillou, 'Le Monastère de la Théotokos au Sinaï: Origènes; Épiclèse; Mosaïque de la Transfiguration; Homélie inédite d'Anastase le Sinaïte sur la Transfiguration (Étude Critique)', *Mélanges d'archéologie et d'histoire* 67 (1955): 215–56.
27. Ibid., 243.
28. Ibid., 243–4.

used to seeing, incorporeal ideas; he saw beauty, incorruptibility, and the absence of passion, the sparkling glory of immortality. Obscurely, as if in a dream, he saw the beauty of incorruptibility, and the absence of passion, the scintillating glory of immortality. Obscurely, as if in a dream, he saw the divine twinklings of future regeneration, and also the kingdoms and cities of the beyond.[29]

Anastasius understands Peter's looking at the Transfiguration to have moved from physical sight of the mountain to an ecstatic vision of the Kingdom of Heaven. It bears a resemblance to seeing, in that it is experienced as an interior visualizing, like a dream. However, this 'seeing' is also intended by Anastasius to be understood as an apprehending of immaterial realities with the mind. Anastasius then proceeds to recount at some length the glories of this future Kingdom of Heaven which Peter sees, with its endless rejoicing, feasting and constant beauty.

However, Anastasius then describes Peter actually entering into heaven as part of this ecstatic dreamlike vision:

> Having been able to open the Kingdom of Heaven up by virtue of possessing the keys of this Kingdom, Peter entered into this vestibule. His spiritual eyes having been opened and illuminated, he saw (to the degree that he could see) heavenly dwellings and tents, carefree nuptial chambers, and the souls espoused to Christ, the unmarriable bridegroom, he saw summons to the incorruptible banquet, thrones of invisible glory, crowns completed with incorruptibility, immortal lights, fountains bubbling with light and unchanging delights. Having touched them as if with his hands, and having tasted, this chief, St Peter, passed with all his soul towards the beyond, his heart being completely transformed.[30]

Anastasius presents this entry into heaven by Peter as the internal dreamlike vision he experiences in ecstasy during the Transfiguration. It is unclear whether Anastasius conceives of this vision being separate from that of the events described in the New Testament, or whether it is simply part of the same vision. Although Anastasius specifically focuses on Peter, in later parts of the homily he understands the other two disciples to experience with Peter his ecstatic vision of heaven.[31] Anastasius describes the Transfiguration in these later sections as prompting a vision of the Eschaton yet to happen. He understands the mountain to provide a temporary opening up of the heavens, allowing those with transformed vision a glimpse of the future Kingdom of Heaven:

> And just as if someone who glanced down from the heights of heaven would see all earthly things, plains, mountains, hills, seas, rivers, the streams, men, cities, villages, farms, animals and reptiles, in sum, the whole of earthly creation; in

---

29. Ibid., 244–5.
30. Ibid., 245.
31. Ibid., 251–2.

the same way, the apostles, who found themselves on the mountain with their spiritual eyes opened saw at a glance (for as much as they were able to see – at least it was a better seeing than they had experienced before), the Kingdom of Heaven to come.[32]

Anastasius says nothing of how the disciples see the events that took place on the mountain of Transfiguration, that is, the arrival of Moses and Elijah. The events described in the gospels either prompt or accompany an ecstatic dreamlike revelation in which Peter's mind, freed from physical passions, experiences eternal, incorporeal realities and gazes into heaven on the future glory in which Jesus will come. Although this involves Peter's mind being transformed, there is something about this experience of Peter's that is akin to mortal seeing and which involves the mind visualizing what it experiences and describing what he observes as if they were physical objects, and his entry into heaven as if it involved physical movement.

Anastasius and Luke

Evidence for Peter's being in ecstasy is nearly all drawn by Anastasius from details only to be found in Luke's narrative. He connects Luke's assertion that Peter did not know what he was saying with his being out of his mind and enraptured. He comments,

> He was completely raptured out of himself, departed towards God, and far from himself. Completely consumed by an intoxication, he was enveloped by glory and revested in truth, and, having forgotten the world and everything in it, he addressed this laudable blessing, crying out in a loud voice, 'It is good, Lord, for us to be here', 'not knowing', it is added, 'what he was saying'.[33]

Anastasius proceeds to see in Luke's description of the disciples' sleepiness evidence of ecstatic rapture. He understands it as a sort of tiredness that came over their exhausted corporeal body as a result of their minds seeing incorporeal realities:

> They were, in effect, seized at the same time by ecstasy and sleep, as the corruptible nature of their body could not contemplate incorruptibility, and their mortal body could not contemplate immortality. Moses and Elijah must have appeared to them in their more exalted bodies. They appeared 'in glory' as it says, and so appeared without fear or trouble on the mountain; whereas, the disciples fell down, seized as if by numbness and ecstasy. Again, Luke says, 'Peter and the disciples were weighed down by sleep'.[34]

32. Ibid.
33. Ibid., 245–6.
34. Ibid., 252–3.

Anastasius sees the disciples' tiredness to be a consequence of their mortal faculties being involved in the seeing of immortal realities. However, because Moses and Elijah return with more exalted bodies, the prophets have no trouble in experiencing God's glory and are capable of standing and seeing the Transfiguration perfectly happily.

It is also intriguing that Anastasius uses very specific language of entry into an *enclosed space* to describe Peter's vision of heaven. He describes it as Peter entering a *vestibule* or *porch*.[35] I have argued in Chapter 2 of this study that Luke exploits the language of movement and distance to create a stronger sense of divine space into which the apostles enter. It must be admitted that Luke does not use the language of vestibules or porches. In addition, Anastasius hardly mentions at all the cloud into which the disciples enter. However, I suggest it might be worth wondering whether this stronger sense of entry into an enclosed space, which Anastasius creates, might be influenced by the feeling of movement and spatial awareness present in the Lucan narrative. It may not be entirely coincidental that Chrysostom, who also finds the Lucan Transfiguration narrative prompts a vision of heaven, speaks of this vision as entry into the enclosed space of a *theatre*, and also a *lawcourt*.

Anastasius and temple readings

A characteristic of Anastasius's ecstatic interpretation of the Transfiguration as an entry into heaven is the re-emergence of temple and priestly motifs. Anastasius addresses a long apostrophe on the part of Moses to Jesus, in which he compares the Transfiguration with a number of Old Testament revelations and theophanies. Indeed, Moses himself is portrayed as a great seer, for whom the Transfiguration marks the culmination of his visionary experience. Speaking in Moses's voice, Anastasius compares the way the Transfiguration reveals the life of heaven with the Feast of Tabernacles and points to Jesus as himself the new Christian temple:

> For you are yourself the Feast of Tabernacles for all people, renewed by immortality and incorruptibility. You are in truth the temple, the son of David and of Solomon, you who have established and made the temple in the heavenly Jerusalem. You are the spotless expiation made to the Father for the sins of the world. You are the true laver and washing basin, and saviour, which the laver prefigured in the law.[36]

In Anastasius's analogy, Jesus himself is the heavenly temple, giving the faithful Christian access to God. However, he is also the sacrifice for sin and, himself, typologically, makes up elements of the temple prefigured in the Law, such as the laver. The view of Jesus as priest, such as we find in the Epistle to the Hebrews,

---

35. Ibid., 242.
36. Ibid., 249.

also informs Anastasius's thinking, for whom access to Jesus, present in heaven, points to him as a priestly figure able to make sacrifice for humanity. Indeed, Anastasius echoes the language of Hebrews 12 and Genesis 28 in his description of the Transfiguration:

> For this is a wonderful place, it is nothing less than the House of God and the gateway to heaven. For we need to hasten to it – I say this boldly – like Jesus, who there and in the heavens is our precursor and guide, who prepares us.[37]

Present in Anastasius's interpretation is a view that the Transfiguration reveals Jesus as a priestly figure and as one who himself constitutes the heavenly temple. The Transfiguration, as an opening of the heavens, echoes for Anastasius the way in which Jesus makes access to God possible, analogous to entry into the earthly temple, or visionary entry into the heavenly temple.

Anastasius: Conclusions

Anastasius's interpretation seems to be a more exaggerated version of that Origenist impulse we have recognized in a number of Greek commentators, which sees the disciples' vision needing to be transformed in order to perceive the Transfiguration, and in which their physical vision is overcome and gives way to a clearer vision provided by the mind in the sphere of immortal realities. However, Anastasius goes far beyond any commentator we have encountered since Origen and Tertullian in insisting that Peter enters into an ecstasy which takes him out of his body and beyond physical reality to give him direct vision of heaven. However, for Anastasius, this ecstasy is not of demonic origin, as Origen had argued. In fact, the way in which he describes this ecstasy as involving a sort of seeing which is dreamlike seems to place his understanding of the disciples' vision remarkably close to the ways, which we explored in Chapter 5, in which Tertullian explains ecstatic vision as involving the same processes of visualizing within the mind as take place during dreaming. Anastasius's interpretation of the Transfiguration also prompts him to see connections with a number of passages from scripture that emphasize entry into God's heavenly presence, such as Genesis 28. In addition, he uses priestly and temple paradigms, echoing the language of Hebrews 12 and Revelation 21 in a way which points to Jesus both as priest and temple.

The question remains, however, whether Anastasius describes here one vision or two. In other words, does he see the appearance of Moses and Elijah on the mountain with Jesus as a first vision, which anyone could see, but which prompts in Peter (and the other two disciples) a second, esoteric experience? Or does Anastasius see the whole experience as one vision, in which he fills in gaps not described by the biblical Transfiguration narratives? It is very difficult to judge. Anastasius's description of Moses and Elijah being present in their 'stronger' or 'more exalted'

---

37. Ibid., 242.

bodies[38] would imply they are corporeally present and would be visible to anyone not in a visionary rapture. However, much in Anastasius's description points to the disciples needing their vision and understanding transformed to see the whole event. For, although Anastasius starts by talking only about Peter's ecstasy, it is clear by the end of the homily that he envisages all three disciples glimpsing into heaven with him. The way in which his additional visions are woven into the text of the New Testament narrative implies that Anastasius probably sees the episode as involving one extended vision. This has all the disciples seeing Jesus in glory, with Moses and Elijah, and then glimpsing into the Kingdom of Heaven. In addition, his description of the disciples hearing 'noetic sounds'[39] as part of their experience might imply that he understood the voice from heaven to be audible only to those in a state of ecstasy with transformed mind. Anastasius sees evidence for his ecstatic interpretation of the Transfiguration in Luke's mention of Peter not knowing what he said and in the disciples' sleepiness.

Anastasius interprets the Transfiguration as a glimpse of the opened heavens by describing ecstatic vision on the part of the disciples and also by alluding to several other biblical texts which speak about access to the heavens and to God's heavenly temple.

John Chrysostom: Transfiguration as mortal vision

In the next section of this chapter we explore Chrysostom's (349–407) interpretation of the visionary character of the Transfiguration, which shares many similarities, but also considerable differences, with Anastasius's reading.[40] By contrast with Anastasius, he emphasizes the Transfiguration as a vision principally seen by mortal eyes and makes little mention of change or alteration to the disciples' vision. However, he, like Anastasius, sees the Transfiguration as capable of prompting vision of the heavens and of the Eschaton. The difference is that for Chrysostom, rather than being the product of an ecstatic state of altered consciousness, this involves the use of the imaginative faculties by those meditating on the Transfiguration as a way of visualizing the reality to which the narrative points.

Chrysostom states in his *Homily on the Transfiguration*, 'Although the disclosure was made in a more *corporeal way* (σωματικώτερον), it contained,

---

38. Ibid., 252–3.
39. Ibid., 254.
40. Cosmin Pricop offers an excellent summary of Chrysostom's wider comment on the Transfiguration as part of his comparison of patristic interpretation with modern historical-critical comment. He sees the tropological turn of Chrysostom's interpretation focused on the actualization of the narrative in the life of the hearer/reader as one of the most significant differences between the two hermeneutic perspectives. See Pricop, *Die Verwandlung Jesu Christi*, 226–79.

nonetheless, much to be desired.'[41] There is in this comment a strong implication that the corporeal faculties of sense play the principal role in apprehending the Transfiguration. One cannot claim Chrysostom sees no role whatsoever for the mind's noetic faculties in perceiving the Transfiguration, but he emphasizes the role played by mortal vision in the disciples' witnessing of the Transfiguration. He sees this 'more corporeal' vision as possible by virtue of insisting, like Basil, that the Transfiguration was only a partial revelation of God's glory. He uses the language of *condescension*[42] (συγκατάβασις) to describe the way in which God reveals only so much of his glory as the disciples' eyes are capable of receiving. In *Ad Theodorum Lapsum*, Chrysostom describes the Transfiguration thus:

> The glory of incorruptible bodies does not give out such light as this corruptible body, nor such as mortal eyes can see. But incorruptible and immortal eyes are what is needed to see that. On the mountain, however, only so much was revealed to those who looked on, as they could see without damage to the eyes. Furthermore, even then they could not bear it and fell on their faces.[43]

We see here the same worry that Tertullian displayed, that the light was dangerous to the disciples' vision. However, by contrast with Tertullian, Chrysostom's concern appears to be with the danger posed to their physical eyes and the peril which overexposure to strong light would bring. He comments in *Homily 21*, 'If he shone like the sun, the disciples would not have fallen down, as they saw the sun every day and did not fall down. But because he shone more than the sun or snow, this is why they could not bear the brightness and fell down.'[44] Although Chrysostom sees the light as very bright indeed, and as overwhelming the disciples, he says nothing to imply that he sees it as anything other than a light which may be apprehended by mortal humans without any alteration to the faculty of sight.

Chrysostom's understanding of the Transfiguration as only a partial revelation of glory makes him emphasize the *dissimilarity* that exists between the Transfiguration and the direct vision of God available in the Kingdom of Heaven. Chrysostom comments, 'He did not show forth [at the Transfiguration] the full splendour of the age to come. The splendour here was a condescension rather than a demonstration of what the true event will be like.'[45] Moreover, in his *Commentary on Matthew's Gospel*, he writes that the vision of God in heaven will be 'not as these [i.e. the disciples] saw him on the mountain, but in a much greater brightness. For he will not come like this in time to come. Whereas, to spare the disciples, he revealed then only so much of his brightness as they could bear, in the future, he will come in the very glory of the Father.'[46] In a further homily, he

---

41. *Hom.* 56 (PG 58, 550).
42. See e.g. *Ad Theo Laps*, 1.11 (PG 47, 292).
43. Ibid.
44. *Hom.* 21 (PG 63, 700).
45. Ibid.
46. *Hom.* 56, 17.4 (PG 58, 554).

explains he understands the word 'transfigured' to mean 'that he opened out a little of the godhead and showed them the indwelling God'.[47] Firmly rooted, therefore, in Chrysostom's understanding is a notion of the Transfiguration as a *partial* revelation of God's divine life, an opening out of only 'a *little* of the godhead', so as to be visible to human sight, and an emphasis on the Transfiguration as a revelation of a lesser glory than that which will be experienced at the Eschaton.

Chrysostom on the disciples' sleepiness

This emphasis on the disciples' mortal vision prompts Chrysostom to interpret in a distinct way the sleepiness of the disciples recounted in Luke. Chrysostom links the sleepiness closely with the mortal nature of the vision experienced at the Transfiguration by describing it as a consequence of the blinding physical light and as a sort of sleepy, stunned state brought about by it:

> He [i.e. Luke] refers to this great torpor which came upon them from the vision as 'sleep'. In the same way that the eyes are darkened by overwhelming light, so it happened to them at that time. It was not, I suppose, night but day, and the greatness of the light pressed down heavily on the weakness of their eyes.[48]

Chrysostom sees the disciples' tiredness not as sleep in the usual sense but as a sort of exhausted, stunned state, almost a momentary case of sunstroke or dazzled disequilibrium brought about by the intense light. Whereas for Anastasius this was because the disciples' corruptible faculties were overcome by incorruptible light, Chrysostom makes no mention of this. There is also a hint that Chrysostom wishes to deny the possibility hinted at solely by Luke[49] that the Transfiguration took place by night. The blinding nature of the light, therefore, is to be found in the fact that it is very strong light indeed and not because it is a momentary example of brightness in an otherwise dark night, or some sort of uncreated light.

He uses here the word κάρος (translated above as 'great torpor') to describe the disciples' sleep, a term which can refer to 'heavy sleep, torpor, unconsciousness'.[50] For Chrysostom, this sleepy, stunned state comes about as an accompaniment to Peter's agonized state of mind, which he sees indicated by Luke's comment that he did not know what he was saying:

> In fact, the other Evangelists, to show this, and to demonstrate that the confusion of his mind with which he spoke these things arose from that terror, said: Mark,

---

47. *Hom.* 21 (PG 63, 700).

48. *Hom.* 56, 17.3 (PG 58, 553).

49. Lk. 9.37 speaks of the disciples descending the mountain of Transfiguration the next morning, as if they had spent the night there.

50. 'κάρος', in *A Patristic Greek Lexicon*, ed. G. W. H. Lampe (Oxford: Oxford University Press, 1962), 703.

'He did not know what to say, for they were afraid'; but Luke added, 'not knowing what he said,' after his comment, 'Let us make three tabernacles.' Then to show that he and the rest were gripped by great fear, he said, 'They were heavy with sleep, but waking, they saw his glory.'[51]

Chrysostom displays here a sensitivity to the consequences of the vision on the state of Peter's mind as described by Luke. By using the language of ἀγωνία to talk here about Peter's fear, he points to him as in a state of considerable mental confusion and intense terror as a consequence of his vision. However, this does not represent any sort of ecstatic altered state of consciousness, such as we find in Origen, Tertullian or Anastasius. This, in turn, results in the stunned state described by Luke as being weighed down by sleep. Chrysostom sees in this detail of Luke's, therefore, confirmation of his understanding of the Transfiguration as a vision seen principally with mortal eyes. Peter is presented in a state of considerable agitation, but one which involves no ecstasy or altered sense of perception.

'An obscure image of things to come'

I now wish to explore the way in which Chrysostom's view of the nature of the disciples' vision results in a very distinct understanding of the way in which it relates to that eschatological vision of God which the faithful Christian can hope for. I wish to explore precisely what Chrysostom means when he describes the Transfiguration in *Ad Theodorum Lapsum*, as 'an obscure image of things to come',[52] and exactly what he understands the link to be between vision of the Transfiguration and that eternal vision of God which will characterize the life of the age to come. For Anastasius, the ecstatic vision the disciples had of heaven and the Eschaton is simply a direct vision of the future. Chrysostom, however, proposes a more complex paradigm for the faithful who wish to meditate on the Transfiguration narratives.

In his letter, *Ad Theodorum Lapsum*, Chrysostom compares the Transfiguration with vision of heaven and argues that vision to be like looking into a theatre:

> On the mountain [of Transfiguration], however, only so much was revealed to those who looked on, as they could see without damage to the eyes. Furthermore, even then they could not bear it and fell on their faces. Tell me then, if someone brought you into a splendid place in which everyone sat adorned with golden clothes, and in the middle of the crowd showed you someone whose clothes and the crown on his head were made solely from precious stones, and then he promised you that you would be enrolled in the number of that people – would you not do all you could to attain such a promise? Open now the eyes of your mind and look into that theatre [Ἀναπέτασον οὖν καὶ νῦν τῷ νῷ τοὺς

---

51. *Hom.* 56, 17.3 (PG 58, 552-3).
52. *Ad Theo. Laps.* 1.11 (PG 47, 292).

ὀφθαλμοὺς καὶ βλέψον εἰς ἐκεῖνο τὸ θέατρον], not that frequented by normal people, but by those who are more worthy in gold, in precious gems, bright sun-rays, and all manner of visible splendour; and not just humans, but those who are far more worthy than they, angels, archangels, thrones, dominions, principalities and powers.[53]

This looking into a theatre which Chrysostom urges is not the vision actually seen by the disciples but rather the eschatological reality which he understands the Transfiguration to signify. A similar comment is made by Chrysostom in the homily on the Transfiguration to be found in his *Commentary on Matthew*. There, he likens the future vision of the Eschaton of which the Transfiguration is a foretaste to a courtroom, in which the curtains before the judge are pulled back:

> So it is with the judges; when they give judgments in public, their assistants drawing back the curtains show them to everyone, so, in a similar way, all people shall see him sitting, and all the human race shall stand around.[54]

Here, the Eschaton is said by Chrysostom to be analogous with the visible revealing of a judge sitting in court. In other words, this comparison with the judge does not give a direct vision of the Last Judgement, but it affords the viewer a vision which is similar to, and somehow comparable with, it. Both the unveiled judge in real life and the transfigured Jesus are mortal visions which may be compared with the Eschaton. Neither is identical with it, but both share similarities, in that they reveal visibly a judging figure who was previously unseen.

It is important to note the nature of the link Chrysostom makes between the Transfiguration and the vision of the 'theatre' of heaven which he urges his audience to imagine. He tells his reader to open the 'eyes of the mind' (Ἀναπέτασον οὖν καὶ νῦν τῷ νῷ τοὺς ὀφθαλμούς) in order to look into this theatre. This vision of heaven as a theatre is an image conjured up by the imagination which the Transfiguration prompts. Chrysostom envisages, therefore, hearing or reading the Transfiguration narrative to cause the imagination to visualize what the Transfiguration *represents*. Hearing the account of Christ appearing with two prophets in glory causes the mind to imagine a greater vision of God's heavenly kingdom, in which there are thousands of angels and saints.

The connection is unlike that which we have seen in any other commentator reviewed so far in this chapter. In the majority of comment we have encountered, the eschatological vision of God relates to the disciples' vision of the Transfiguration in terms of the mind's noetic, transformed 'vision' of God. For Anastasius, this was understood to be made possible by ecstasy. The other commentators we have explored all try to explain how the human subject is enabled to witness essentially the same reality before and after the Eschaton. For Chrysostom, however,

---

53. *Ad Theo. Laps.* 1.11 (PG 47, 292).
54. *Hom.* 56.4 (PG 58, 552, 555).

meditating upon the Transfiguration also triggers an *imaginary* process which causes the mind to *visualize* the reality the Transfiguration represents but is *distinct* from it. In other words, the Transfiguration acts as an imaginative *springboard* which allows the mind to imagine a vision entirely distinct and different from that seen at the Transfiguration.

Indeed, one might interpret Chrysostom as arguing, by contrast with Anastasius, that the faithful Christian meditating on the Transfiguration narrative sees *more* than the disciples did. What they witnessed on the mountain top was apprehended by mortal sense. By contrast, Chrysostom urges the faithful Christian who hears the same narrative with mortal ears to see beyond it by visualizing the heaven it pointed to. For Chrysostom, this imaginative vision is capable of bridging the eschatological divide between the present moment and the life of the age to come. Indeed, it links the contemporary reader backwards in time to the events on the mountain top, and forwards to the Eschaton.

Carruthers and memory

The dynamic Chrysostom suggests here is remarkably close to many of the mechanisms Carruthers has suggested accompany imaginative memory in the ancient world and middle ages, and which were mentioned in Chapter 1. I now wish to use some of her ideas as a tool for ordering and analysing the material we have just examined. Carruthers covers in her works a period which extends later than the scope of my thesis. However, many of the sources she draws from are those of the ancient Greek and Latin world.

Carruthers and Chrysostom

One of the most intriguing of Carruthers's assertions is that for the medieval mind, the image impressed on the *phantasma*, which stores an experience in the memory, does not have to look like the reality it is designed to recall. It simply has to be able to trigger the necessary emotional connections, referred to in medieval discourse as *intentio*,[55] to allow the brain to recall the information. Chrysostom, in the passages quoted above, similarly points to the Transfiguration as an image which is not identical with the reality it prompts. What it helps the mind to visualize is the eschatological vision of Christ in heavenly glory. However, Chrysostom insists that the disciples' vision and their future experience of the Eschaton both evoke a fundamentally similar emotional response, or *intentio*. Speaking of Peter, Chrysostom says,

> If, seeing an obscure image of the things to come, he ejected everything from his soul straight away, because of the delight of what he saw being placed in his soul, then what can be said when the very truth of these things comes to pass;

55. Carruthers, *The Book of Memory*, 27, 65, 85.

when the royal dwellings are opened and the King himself can be seen no longer in enigma, nor through a mirror, but face to face; not by faith any longer, but by direct seeing?[56]

For Chrysostom, Peter's emotional response to the Transfiguration is lesser, but of a similar sort to that which he will experience at the Eschaton.

Carruthers also insists that the mode of visualizing as memory she speaks of was conceived as an important part of how the human subject grows in virtue and maturity. Memory and visualizing, for Carruthers, had an *ethical* character.[57] Chrysostom similarly argues the character of the *intentio* experienced by the faithful who contemplate the transfigured Christ and his return in glory acts as a spur to moral action. Speaking of the attractiveness of the vision conjured up by opening the eyes of the mind and looking into the theatre he spoke of, he asks, 'Tell me, are we going to deprive ourselves of such good things just to avoid a short period of sufferings? Would it not be worth enduring a thousand deaths each day, even Gehenna itself, in order to see Christ coming in his glory, and be reckoned in the assembly of his saints?'[58] Chrysostom's comments cohere closely with the connections Carruthers argues connect vision, memory and emotion. Thinking about the Transfiguration can prompt the faithful Christian to imagine a scene of Christ in glory which evokes a similar emotional response as that experienced by Peter. That response has a significant ethical role in encouraging good action and growth in virtue. This ethical character in turn reveals the *rhetorical* power of Chrysostom's homiletic use of the Transfiguration narrative as hermeneutic reflection designed to prompt action and change in its hearers.

Carruthers discusses the role of memory, rhetoric and visualizing in Chrysostom's writing, though concerning a very different episode. She examines a controversy Chrysostom was involved in at Daphne where Julian the Apostate attempted to resurrect the cult of Apollo and remove the relics of a martyr called Babylas.[59] Chrysostom recognized the importance of the *sight* of the martyrs' relics as able to prompt a visualizing of a greater reality. He comments, 'Because the sight of the coffin, penetrating the soul, affects it and prompts it in such a way that it feels as though it sees the one lying there coming close, and joining in prayer.'[60] Carruthers concludes, 'Here it is important to note that the crucial "power" of the saint lies in the ability of his site/sight to enter the soul, affect it, and so cause one to feel as if one sees the saint himself – both in "the mind's eye" and "heartfully".' I think one could argue that Chrysostom conceives of the power of visualizing the Transfiguration in a very similar way. Meditating on the New Testament narrative evokes in the imagination both the reality to which the Transfiguration points

---

56. *Ad Theo. Laps.* 1.11 (PG 47, 292).
57. Carruthers, *The Book of Memory*, 81–9.
58. *Ad Theo. Laps.* 1.11 (PG 47, 292).
59. See Carruthers, *The Book of Memory*, 65.
60. *Bab.* 65 (SC 362, 174).

forward (i.e the eschatological vision of God) but also triggers the appropriate emotional attitude and sentiment which allows the image to be experienced as if the viewer were there him or herself.

Anastasius and Chrysostom: Conclusions

A significant question remains. Although Chrysostom rejects the kind of ecstatic interpretation Anastasius offers, are they both actually talking about a very similar experience on the part of their hearers? Although they conceive of the processes of vision which the Transfiguration brings about very differently, do they both actually see as their goal an interior visualizing of the Kingdom of Heaven which is remarkably similar? I argue they could be. They are both involved in the rhetorical encouragement of a group of hearers to engage imaginatively with the Transfiguration narratives. Although Anastasius urges his hearers to embrace the same sort of ecstatic vision which Peter had, and describes it in Platonic terms as a 'seeing' of immaterial forms and ideals, he is nonetheless convinced that in certain respects this vision of heaven is experienced as a visualizing of image akin to that brought about in the mind by mortal sense vision. Both commentators have radically divergent understandings of how Peter and the disciples see the events on the mountain, and of what they see. However, when it comes to reflection on the Transfiguration by the faithful, both see room for an overcoming of the eschatological divide which separates them from the life of heaven in a way which involves a visualizing in the mind of a reality different from the Transfiguration. Anastasius talks about this as an esoteric conceiving by the mind in ecstasy of incorporeal realities, yet he describes it in terms of image, movement, colour, light and sense in ways which are comparable to what Chrysostom urges his hearers to imagine. It could be that in terms of what the faithful Christian mediating on this narrative actually experiences, Anastasius and Chrysostom describe an engaging with this text which is very similar, even if they use remarkably different language to describe how it comes about.

Conclusion

Caruthers's work helps tease out a number of the tensions which I have pointed to in the material discussed in this chapter. The basic paradigm many Eastern commentators work with is one which explains the disciples' vision of the Transfiguration in terms of intellective vision and sensible vision. They see the Transfiguration as a direct, unmediated vision of a reality which mortal human beings are incapable of seeing. They have, therefore, to come up with ways of accounting for how the apostles are conceived of witnessing this. The light either overwhelms them, their sight is transformed or both. As part of this, emphasis on divine light becomes a useful metaphor for speaking of the direct apprehension of God by the mind and avoids thinking about the Transfiguration in terms of image.

However, Chrysostom and Anastasius see the Transfiguration as pointing beyond itself in a different way. Anastasius insists that both vision of the Transfiguration and that viewing of heaven which it prompts in the disciples and his sermon's hearers are incorporeal viewings of things beyond sight with a transformed mind. He nonetheless conceives of that as a visualizing, which he describes as dreamlike. As a result of the rapturous ecstasy which Anastasius sees as necessary for this vision, the physical eyes play little role. However, the mind's apprehending of the glory of heaven is described as an internal imaging of a future event, which supplements the otherwise incomplete descriptions of the Transfiguration we have in the New Testament, which, for him, describe only part of the disciples' vision.

Chrysostom represents a different way of dealing with this conundrum altogether. He understands the disciples' vision to be more mortal and sense based. However, he recognizes the Transfiguration texts as rhetorically able to prompt an imaginative visualizing of God's heavenly Kingdom, which allows the faithful to bridge the eschatological gap between now and the Kingdom of heaven. It is also this imaginative viewing which, for Chrysostom, allows the human subject to engage *emotionally* with the reality the Transfiguration represents, an experience with *tropological* consequences. This model seems very close to Augustine's notion of 'spiritual vision' as a prophetic form of vision mediating a way between intellective and sense vision. This Augustinian sense will be seen to exercise a strong influence over much Latin interpretation,to be examined in the next chapter.

Although they understand the processes of vision at work in the disciples very differently, and describe it using very different terminology, both Anastasius and Chrysostom see the Transfiguration narratives as having a rhetorical power capable of bringing about an internal visualizing of heaven which is different and separate from the Transfiguration. They see part of this rhetorical power to stem from elements within Luke's account which describe the disciples' vision, especially its mention of the disciples being sleepy and of Peter not knowing what he said. A significant characteristic of Chrysostom's understanding of the Transfiguration is the way in which he understands it as apprehended principally by the disciples' sensible faculties. For him, the disciples' tiredness is a sign that their sense faculties are overcome with bright light. As a result of this, Peter's not knowing is conceived as a state of considerable confusion, but not ecstatic. Anastasius also sees visionary significance in exactly the same details but interprets their significance very differently. For Anastasius, Peter's not knowing what he says is evidence of rapture and the disciples' sleepiness a sign that their mortal vision was overcome by a vision of immortal realities. It is significant that both these commentators see these distinctly Lucan elements as proof for their argument. Although they often interpret these elements in a very divergent way, they nonetheless see them as able to tell us much about the way in which the disciples 'saw' the events on Mount Tabor.

We have shown in this chapter that there is great complexity in the way in which many Greek-speaking commentators interpret the language used by the New

Testament to express exactly how the disciples 'see' the Transfiguration. I have, in addition, pointed to two very distinct interpretations of the Transfiguration which have frequently been overlooked. It is noticeable that both Chrysostom's 'sensible' reading and Anastasius' 'ecstatic' understanding draw on the Lucan narrative as evidence for their interpretation of the disciples' vision. I hope to have shown that, once again, Luke's version plays a significant, and hitherto undervalued, role in the reception of the Transfiguration narratives as descriptions of visionary experience. We see in this chapter an ancient scopic regime in which the effect of reading or hearing the Transfiguration narrative is increasingly emphasized and shown to prompt a range of imaginative and ecstatic responses in the hearer/reader of the Transfiguration narrative. This participatory and tropological dynamic is largely absent from the concerns of modern historical-critical scholarship but forms a rich seam of important interpretation in ancient comment.

Chapter 7

INTERPRETATION OF THE TRANSFIGURATION IN THE LATIN WEST AFTER TERTULLIAN

We come now to examine interpretation of the Transfiguration among Latin theologians who write after Tertullian,[1] with a continued focus on interpretation of those texts as narratives describing visionary experience. Others have surveyed the broad contours of comment offered by the Latin Fathers in regard to the Transfiguration, and their work does not need repetition here.[2] We will focus in this chapter, therefore, on four specific areas which have received less attention, concerning the disciples' experience as vision. These four areas are as follows: first, the way in which Latin commentators tend to emphasize the disciples' experience of the Transfiguration as involving mortal vision; second, interpretation of Luke's mention of Peter's sleepiness and not knowing what he said; third, extensive comment surrounding the overshadowing cloud; and, finally, a series of hermeneutic connections made between the Transfiguration narratives and other portions of scripture, especially Isaiah 7, Revelation 21 and Hebrews 12, often emphasizing the eschatological vision of God as a *communal* experience.

The influence of much of the interpretation examined here and the scopic regime that undergirds it will be of crucial significance in the next chapter, where we explore how Latin written interpretation is found expressed in the earliest Western depictions of the Transfiguration.

---

1. All translations of primary texts in this chapter are my own unless otherwise stated.

2. E.g. Aaron Canty, *Light and Glory: The Transfiguration of Christ in Early Fransiscan and Dominican Theology* (Washington, DC: Catholic University of America Press, 2011), 11–15; Michel Coune, *Grace de la Transfiguration d'après les Pères d'Occident*, Vie Monastique no. 24 (Bégrolles-en-Mauge: Abbaye de Bellefontaine, 1990); Jean Leclercq, *Regards Monastiques sur le Christ au Moyen Age*, Jésus et Jésus-Christ, no. 56 (Paris: Mame-Desclée, 1993) 89–100; John Anthony McGuckin, *The Transfiguration of Christ in Scripture and Tradition* (Lewiston, NY: Edwin Mellen Press, 1986), 99–125; Cosmin Pricop, *Die Verwandlung Jesu Christi, historisch-kritische und patristische Studien*, Wissenschaftliche Untersuchungen zum Neuen Testament, 2 Reihe (Tübingen: Mohr Siebeck, 2016), esp. 280–326 on Jerome; Kenneth Stevenson, *Rooted in Detachment: Living the Transfiguration* (London: Darton, Longman and Todd, 2007), 25–9.

Latin understandings of vision

One feature of much Latin comment is the way in which it emphasizes the disciples' vision as apprehended by mortal sight. By describing the disciples' vision as *mortal*, I mean to say that their ability to perceive the physical world around them experienced no change that led to any form of altered epistemological state. In other words, it did not result in any form of ecstasy or dream and could be seen by anyone present on the mountain.

The influence of Tertullian's and Origen's view of the disciples' vision

The ecstatic interpretation of the disciples' sight, which Tertullian espoused, exercises little influence over later Latin thought. I have not found any Latin commentator who sees the Transfiguration as an ecstatic dreamlike visualizing of the sort Tertullian advocates, and indeed, as will be shown below, Jerome expressly denies it. However, Origen is widely recognized as exercising influence on Western Transfiguration interpretation, particularly through Ambrose's *Commentary on Luke* and through Jerome who translated Origen. Both Andrew Louth[3] and Jean-Louis Gourdain[4] have shown how aware Ambrose and Jerome were of Origen's Transfiguration exegesis, even if they chose to change or develop it differently. J. N. Hart-Hasler[5] has shown, in turn, Bede's comment to be influenced by that of Ambrose and Jerome. Louth shows that *topoi* such as allegorical interpretation of the mention of 'six days' in Mt. 17.1 and Mk 9.2, for example, or Christ's glorious garments being like the words of scripture are all derived from Origen.[6] However, it is notable how later Latin interpreters also display very different opinions from Origen. The main point of Gourdain's article is to show how Jerome *changes* Origen's comment and reacts *against* it.[7] Both he and Louth wonder, for example, whether Ambrose's and Jerome's more generous verdict on Peter is in reaction *against* Origen's suggestion of demonic possession.[8] Although Orgenist influence is strong in many areas of Transfiguration interpretation in the West, it seems that as far as understanding the precise nature of the disciples' vision is concerned, no Latin writer adopts directly either Origen's understanding of the disciples' vision as ecstatic or Tertullian's view of it as a dreamlike visualizing.

---

3. Andrew Louth, 'St Augustine's Interpretation of the Transfiguration of Christ', *Studia Ephemerides Augustinianum* 68 (2000): 377–9.

4. Jean-Louis Gourdain, 'Jérôme exégète de la Transfiguration', *Revue des Etudes Augustiniennes* 40 (1994) : 365–73.

5. J. N. Hart-Hasler, 'Bede's Use of Patristic Sources: The Transfiguration', in *Papers Presented to the Eleventh International Patristic Conference held in Oxford, 1991* (Leuven: Peeters, 1993), 197–204.

6. Louth, 'St Augustine's Interpretation of the Transfiguration of Christ', 375–7.

7. Gourdain, 'Jérôme exégète de la Transfiguration', 368–73.

8. Ibid., 368; Louth, 'St Augustine's Interpretation of the Transfiguration of Christ', 378.

Hilary on the disciples' vision

In his *Commentary on Matthew*, we see no hint that Hilary of Poiters (300-368) understands the vision experienced by the disciples as anything other than unaltered mortal sight. The first point of hermeneutic importance for Hilary is not comment on the glorious light but rather the assertion that in the episode we find preserved 'ratio et numerus et exemplum'.[9] Jeremy Driscoll renders his words 'a meaning, a number, and an example'.[10] He shows how Hilary finds allegorical significance in the six days mentioned by Matthew, the three taken up the mountain as echoing Noah's three sons and the presence of Moses and Elijah. Driscoll has outlined the significance of the connection between *ratio* and *exemplum* for Hilary.[11] He argues that *ratio* signifies the meaning of an event, which is pointed to by the clue of the *numerus*, whilst *exemplum* has a twofold significance, referring to not only a present-day confirmation or proof but also a future reality. So Hilary sees typological connections reaching back in time to Noah, present confirmation of Christ as mediator of Law and Prophets, and a pointing forward to the Kingdom of God signified by mention of six days.

Janet Sidaway has convincingly shown how important the Transfiguration is for Hilary's theology of human glorification.[12] For Hilary, it reveals what humanity itself hopes to receive at the Resurrection. Moses's *visibility* forms a crucial part of this argument. Hilary asserts, 'At the same time, Moses stands by visibly [*conspicabilis*] so that we might be shown that the glory of the resurrection will be conferred on human bodies.'[13] Both Sidaway and Driscoll assert that the importance of this argument for Hilary lies in the physicality with which Moses received his body for the Transfiguration as a sign of physical resurrection at the end of time. Hilary understands this standing by *conspicabilis* to refer not just to Moses's presence being notable or remarkable but also as signifying the way in which his being visible to mortal sight indicated a corporeal presence. Indeed, Hilary goes on to describe Moses's and Elijah's presence as an 'outline of the future [*ad futuri enim formam*] and proof of the event [*atque ad facti fidem*]'. Driscoll points out that Hilary uses the phrase *forma futuri* five times in his commentary, in a way very similar to the connection outlined above between *exemplum* and a future event. Driscoll sums up *forma futuri* as 'something in the present which develops, which becomes more of itself, as it were, in the future'.[14] As Sidaway has argued, for Hilary it is crucial that Moses is corporeally presented at the Transfiguration and visible

---

9. *Comm. Matt.* 17.2 (PL 9, 1013).

10. Jeremy Driscoll, 'The Transfiguration in Hilary of Poitiers' Commentary on Matthew', *Augustinianum* 29 (1984): 400.

11. Ibid., 400-4.

12. Janet Sidaway, *The Human Factor: 'deification' as Transformation in the Theology of Hilary of Poitiers: 6 (Studia Patristica Supplements)* (Leuven: Peeters, 2016), esp. 115, 124.

13. *Comm. Matt.* 17.2 (PL 9, 1014).

14. Driscoll, 'The Transfiguration in Hilary of Poitiers' Commentary on Matthew', 404.

to mortal sight in a way which required no alteration of the disciples' vision, as a sign of the corporeal nature which his body will have in the kingdom of heaven.

Jerome and Leo on the disciples' vision

This distinctive emphasis on the Transfiguration as able to be received by mortal sight is also present in Jerome (347–420) and Leo the Great (400–461). In what John Anthony McGuckin argues is anti-Origenist rhetoric,[15] Jerome asserts at length that Jesus' Transfiguration does *not* imply any assuming of a body which was either 'spiritual [*vel spirituale*] or ethereal [*vel aereum*]'.[16] Whilst it changes in glory, he argues, it does not cease to be the physical body he has at all other points in his earthly life. However, he uses Mark's mention of an earthly fuller to insist that the glory Jesus appears in is entirely visible to mortal sight, and he explains what he means by 'spiritual and ethereal': 'And what a fuller on the earth can make is corporeal and is subject to touch; it is not spiritual or ethereal, evading the eyes and only being caught sight of in dreams.'[17] Jerome seems expressly to exclude here the notion found in Tertullian that the vision of the Transfiguration is comparable in any way to the imaginary mechanisms that produce dream.

Leo also shares Jerome's emphasis on the Transfiguration being visible to mortal sight, though for Leo it forms part of an emphasis on Christ's *humanity* being revealed. It is precisely through his humanity that divine glory is experienced. He claims that the glory witnessed by the disciples is the radiance 'pertaining particularly to the nature of the assumed humanity. He wanted this to be seen by the three disciples. For the ineffable and inaccessible vision of the divinity itself, which is saved for eternal life for the pure in heart, would not be possible for them to look upon or see while still clothed around in mortal flesh.'[18] For Leo, the Transfiguration is a vision appropriate to mortal sight in its natural state, precisely because the radiance Christ reveals is communicated by his *human* nature.[19]

We also see emerge in Jerome a distinct interpretation concerning the falling down described by Matthew. We have seen that Eastern comment frequently interprets this as evidence of the disciples' *sight* being overwhelmed. This interpretation is not absent from Latin comment, as Ambrose speaks, for example, of Peter not being able to endure the Lord's glory and consequently falling down.[20] However, in both Jerome and Leo, this falling down is interpreted as clear evidence of fear at *hearing* the voice from the cloud, rather than *seeing*

---

15. McGuckin, *Transfiguration of Christ*, 270, footnote 68.
16. *Com. in Ev. Mat.* 3.17.2 (PL 26, 122).
17. Ibid.
18. *Serm.* 51, 2 (PL 54, 310).
19. See Bernard Green, *The Soteriology of Leo the Great* (Oxford: Oxford University Press, 2008), 182–4.
20. *In Ps.* 45, 2 (PL 14, 1133).

Christ's glory. Jerome gives three possible reasons for the falling down: fear at the mistake Peter had made in suggesting three tents; fear of the cloud; or fear of the voice.[21] Leo puts the disciples' falling down to their being overawed by a threefold revelation of the Trinity in the cloud.[22] We see a tendency in Jerome and Leo to disconnect the motif of the disciples falling down from any notion that their sight is overwhelmed by Christ's glory, a reconnecting of it with the advent of the cloud and the hearing of the heavenly voice. The presupposition underlying this would seem to be that their vision of the glorified Christ was neither overcome nor transformed.

Gregory on the disciples' vision

We discover in Gregory the Great's (540–604) writings a similar interpretation of the disciples' falling down, but with a slightly different focus. He asks, 'Why is it that Peter falls down upon hearing the voice resounding with words of such recommendation?'[23] Gregory's verdict is that Peter was

> weak and yet he saw what he was not capable of seeing. He saw, but because of this seeing, he fell down and signified that he could not attain that which he was given the grace to see, 'For nobody can say, Jesus is Lord, except by the Holy Spirit.' Peter had not yet received that fullness of the Spirit and so was not able to preach Jesus because he was weak.

Although many Eastern commentators associate the disciples' need of the Holy Spirit with the transformation of their vision, Gregory associates it here with the courage needed *post eventum* to proclaim the Resurrection. The principal problem is that Peter realizes he cannot attain the wonder he sees without the Holy Spirit and lacks the courage to proclaim what he saw. This is, in fact, an interpretation we encounter first in Hilary, who explains that Christ's ordering of silence concerning the Transfiguration until he was raised was to reward genuine faith rather than the unthinking following of commands such as were heard from the cloud. Hilary argues, 'Christ had sensed the disciples were weak upon hearing the voice, so it would not be until after they were filled with the Holy Spirit that they would be witnesses to spiritual events.'[24] Both Hilary and Gregory assert the paradox that Peter felt overcome because he saw with mortal vision a sight which pointed beyond that mortal vision and which will later require the assistance of the Holy Spirit to attain, understand and proclaim. However, what he saw on the mountain of Transfiguration was nonetheless susceptible to mortal vision.

21. *Comm. in Ev. Matt.* 3.17.6 (PL 26, 123).
22. *Serm.* 51, 6 (PL 54, 312).
23. *Prim. Reg. Expos.* 5.30 (PL 79, 466).
24. *Com. in Mat.* 17.3 (PL 9, 1015).

Bede on the disciples' vision

The Venerable Bede (672–735), with Ambrose, reads the disciples' sight as overcome by the Transfiguration. He comments, 'Since the disciples' eyes were still mortal and corruptible, they could not bear what the whole Church of the saints will be able to look at once it is incorruptible through the resurrection.'[25] Although few Latin commentators see in the vision something the disciples could not bear, Bede seems to understand the vision they experience as involving no alteration of sight, precisely because he contrasts it with the later transformed vision that humans will have in the Resurrection. So whilst he differs from other Latin writers in seeing the disciples as overcome, he is of one mind with the majority of Latin comment in seeing the Transfiguration as perceived with mortal eyes.

Ambrose Autpert on the disciples' vision

Ambrose Autpert (730–784) also understands the disciples' vision as an experience of mortal sight. In offering four explanations as to why Jesus' face is compared with the physical light of the sun, he remarks,

> But it appears to me there may be four reasons why this might be the case. Maybe it was because he was still mortal and the very mortality of the flesh did not permit the glory of his divinity to be shown. Perhaps, in order that the eyes of the beholders would be capable of gazing upon it, he tempered the magnitude of his splendor. Maybe he only put forth that form, which he foreknew would be shown on the Day of Judgment to both the elect and to the cursed. Surely, though, and this is more true and saving, it was because he was displaying in his own glory what kind of form his members would possess when, as has been said, they will shine in the future.[26]

All these remarks presuppose the disciples' vision of Christ's glory to be something under the scope of their mortal vision, requiring no transformation.

Further comments by Autpert cohere closely with the understanding of memory put forward by Carruthers, which we discussed in the last chapter. Autpert talks about the light which was seen on the mountain passing away, but somehow remaining behind in the heart: 'But, brothers, I do not know if they even sensed the night, since they had been granted to see such a great light. For even though it was taken away from their fleshly [*oculis carnis, ut erat corporea*] eyes, which were corporeal, it remained, however, in their hearts where incorporal [*incorporea*] realities do not suffer the shades of sunset.'[27] Autpert envisages a sequence of events in which physical vision prompts the heart to retain the incorporeal reality that vision signified. He draws on the Lucan hint that the Transfiguration may

---

25. *Hom.* 24 (CC 122, 171, lines 57–61).
26. *Hom. In Trans.* 6 (PL 89, 1309).
27. *Hom. In Trans.* 20 (PL 89, 1318-9).

have taken place at night,[28] to argue that the disciples may have retained an inner light after the physical light of the sun had disappeared. This model seems close to that which we outlined in Chrysostom in the last chapter in which the mind envisages and retains a reality prompted by physical vision.

Latin understandings of the disciples' vision: Conclusions

We see a tendency in later Latin comment to emphasize the Transfiguration as an experience visible to natural mortal sight and to require no transformation of the vision, mind or understanding in order to be perceived. One consequence of this in Jerome and Leo is an association of the disciples' falling down with their fear at the hearing of a voice and not as a sign of their sight being overwhelmed. This could be described as a more attentive reading of the Matthean narrative, which makes no connection between the falling down and any mention of vision but rather ascribes it to the disciples being afraid. Others, such as Ambrose and Bede, conceive of a sense in which the disciples' sight is overwhelmed, but they do so presupposing the reason for this to be because it is mortal. Both Gregory and Hilary emphasize the transforming action of the Holy Spirit with Peter's experience but associate it *post eventum* with his proclamation of the gospel and not with any alteration of sight or change in intellective vision.

Having established this general tendency within Latin interpretation, I now wish to explore some of its consequences and particularly the way in which it relates to the reception of Luke's narrative. In the next section of this chapter, therefore, we will look at two motifs within the Lucan narrative which receive a distinct interpretation at the hands of several Latin commentators, namely Peter's not knowing what he said and the sleepiness of the disciples. Elements from the Lucan narratives prove, yet again, to be pivotal to how questions appertaining to the visionary nature of the Transfiguration are explored. Much of the transformation of the intellect and sight, which the East associates with the first moments of the disciples' vision, is often transferred in Latin comment to experience of entry into the overshadowing cloud. For Western commentators, it is the Lucan insistence that the disciples all enter the cloud, and not their vision of light, which often signifies the transformation of their mortal understanding.

Peter's sleepiness and not knowing what he said

We have noted in previous chapters how Luke's distinct assertion that Peter did not know *what he was saying* (as opposed to Mark's insistence that Peter did not know *what to say*) has frequently been the focus of interpretations pointing to his

---

28. Cf. Lk. 9.37. Only Luke speaks of Jesus and the three disciples descending from the mountain early the *next morning*, as if they spent the night on the mountain.

being in some state of ecstasy. Later Latin interpretation, especially Ambrose of Milan's, rejects this understanding and tends to see Peter's not knowing almost exclusively in terms of simple delight rather than an ecstasy which produces a different epistemological state.

Peter's not knowing what he said

A complication in examining Ambrose of Milan on Peter's ignorance is establishing how much the ambiguity in the Greek of Lk. 9.33, indicating that Peter did not know what he was saying, was preserved in Latin translations before the Vulgate. The Vulgate translates Lk. 9.33 as 'nesciens quid diceret', 'not knowing what he should say', which seems to change the verse's meaning and give the Lucan passage more the sense we encounter in Mark. In his comment on Psalm 45, Ambrose echoes the Vulgate translation very closely in his description that Peter 'nesciebat quid diceret'.[29] In his commentary on Luke he also seems to quote the gospel with the words 'Et quamuis nesciret quid diceret'.[30] It is certainly possible, therefore, that this wording may have been in Old Latin versions of Luke known to Ambrose. A further problem is that we cannot say with any certainty whether Ambrose's principal focus of reference was the Greek or an early Latin translation. Although most of his commentary may have started out as homiletic material, it could presumably also have been the fruit of reflection on the Greek text. It is certainly the case that we know Origen's *Homilies on Luke* exercised a significant influence over Ambrose's Luke commentary, as a result of Jerome's unsparing criticism that large amounts of Ambrose's work were plagiarized from Origen.[31] We must consider it likely, therefore, that Origen's understanding of Peter as possessed by a demon will almost certainly have been known to him. It must be wondered, therefore, whether Ambrose's insistence that Peter was experiencing an intense sense of delight rather than ecstasy is, in fact, a reaction against Origen's ecstatic interpretation.

It is also far from clear precisely what 'nesciens' might be intended to mean. 'Not knowing' can imply the sense that Peter was not able consciously to judge what he ought *best* to say, in other words, that he misjudged his speech or, to use modern parlance, that he 'mis-spoke'. However, it could also imply that Peter was gripped by some sense of mental confusion which impeded thought, so that his not knowing was an inability to *understand* the words he uttered. As will be shown below, Ambrose's meaning seems to reside somewhere between these two poles. He sees Peter's not knowing not only in the sense of having got the answer wrong but also as an indication of mental disturbance as a result of intense emotion.

---

29. *In Ps. 45*, 2 (PL 14, 1133).
30. *Expos. in Luc.* 17.18 (PL 15, 1704).
31. See Joseph T. Lienhard, *Homilies on Luke: Fragments on Luke*, Fathers of the Church (Washington, DC: Catholic University of America Press, 1996), xxxii–xxxiv.

Ambrose of Milan on Peter's not knowing

In Ambrose of Milan's *Commentary on Luke's Gospel*, we see a more extended exploration of the state of Peter's mind described by the third evangelist. Ambrose describes Peter as being somehow beside himself at the sight of the Transfiguration, when he says, 'Peter was enraptured. The grace of the resurrection captured him rather than the charms of the present age [**delectatus** est Petrus, et quem saeculi huius illecebrosa non caperent, gratia resurrectionis illexit].'[32]

A key question would seem to be precisely what Ambrose means by *delectatus*. Does it refer to delight, in the simple sense of emotional excitement or enjoyment, or does it imply some sort of ecstatic state in which Peter is transported to a very different state of awareness or vision? It strikes me that the former is more likely in the light of further remarks made by Ambrose in this commentary. Ambrose's principal criticism of Peter's comment is that it was made as the result of a mistaken wanting to remain on the mountain and that he, with corruptible body, was unable to remain there or build a tabernacle for Moses, Elijah and Jesus. He comments, 'Even though he did not know what to say, he offered this service. It was not a rash petulance, but rather a premature devotion, to multiply the fruit of his piety. His not knowing was the result of his condition; his promise sprang from devotion.'[33]

Ambrose sees here in Peter's being 'delectatus', rather than any hint at visionary ecstasy, a premature delight in witnessing moments of the life of heaven which he, as a mortal, can only experience in the Age to Come. Although not ecstatic, it is nonetheless such an intense sense of joy that this 'condition' confuses Peter's mind and prompts him to speak inappropriately.

This rapturous 'condition', however, is linked by Ambrose to the disciples' sleepiness. He sees the Lucan motif of sleepiness as a sort of physical exhaustion brought about by beholding divine splendour with mortal senses, when he observes, 'Peter saw this grace; those with him also saw it, even though they were burdened by sleep. This was because the incomprehensible splendour of divinity weighs down the senses of our body.'[34] The exhausted sleepiness would seem to be the consequence of both the extraordinary glory of the vision and a concomitant of Peter's being *delectatus*. Ambrose points quite consistently, therefore, to both of these things as the consequence of strained, but nonetheless mortal, vision. It would seem, from both the thread of Ambrose's surrounding argument in his *Commentary on Luke* and his understanding of the disciples' sight as mortal, that we should interpret Peter's being *delectatus* as not knowing what he says in terms of simple delight and joy. If this is an attempt on his part to counter Origen's teaching concerning Peter being possessed by a demon, then Ambrose may be trying to say two things about Peter: first, he seems to be aware of an ambiguity in Lk. 9.33's description that Peter did not know what he was saying, which points to his being in a state of such considerable mental disorientation and emotional disturbance;

---

32. *Expos. in Luc.* 7.17 (PL 15, 1704).
33. *Expos. in Luc.* 7.18 (PL 15, 1704).
34. *Expos. in Luc.* 7.17 (PL 15, 1703-4).

second, he wants, at the same time, to resist the idea that the disciples' vision was anything other than mortal and counter Origen by insisting that Peter was neither in an ecstatic state nor possessed by a demon. He wants to push the meaning of Peter's not knowing what he said to indicate the highest degree of mental agitation, without implying any sort of ecstasy, altered vision or heightened consciousness.

Leo on Peter's not knowing

This interpretation of Peter's not knowing what he said as a form of delight which borders on the ecstatic, but which does not brim over into an altered state of consciousness or vision, is found in Latin writers after Ambrose. Leo echoes Ambrose in describing Peter in such a state of joy that he experiences a sort of forgetful lack of awareness of earthly realities.

> So moved by these revelations of mysteries and wishing to scorn worldly things, Peter the Apostle's mind was seized by a kind of elated distraction in his desire for eternal things [in aeternorum desiderium quodam mentis rapiebatur excessu]. He was filled with the joy of this whole vision [gaudio totius visionis impletus] so that he wanted to remain with Jesus in this place where his manifested glory made him joyful.[35]

Some have translated Leo's use of *excessus* as 'ecstasy'.[36] However, I have rendered it here as 'elated distraction' because Leo defines it solely in the emotional terms of an intense desire to remain on the mountain which consumes Peter and prompts him to say the wrong thing. There is no mention here of altered vision or a change in the ability of his mortal sight to apprehend the vision before him. Leo appears, like Ambrose, to point at a strong sense of emotional disturbance, which may *appear* to border on some sort of ecstasy but which neither affects Peter's vision nor is the result of any kind of dream or demonic possession.

Bede on Peter's not knowing

Bede also sees Peter is a state of intense joy. Following Leo's insistence on the Transfiguration as a revelation of Christ's humanity, he comments on Peter's suggestion concerning three tabernacles thus:

> But if, when blessed Peter had contemplated the glorified humanity of Christ, he was overcome with such great joy that he never wants to be parted from the sight

---

35. *Serm.* 51, 5 (PL 54, 311).
36. Translated as 'seized by some sort of ecstasy' in Jane Patricia Freeland and Agnes Josephine Conway, *Sermons*, Fathers of the Church (Washington, DC: Catholic University of America Press, 1996), 221; translated as 'ravi en exstase' in Jean Leclercq and Rene Dolle, *Sermons*, 4 vols, Sources Chretiennes (Paris: Editions du Cerf, 1949), 18.

of this vision, then what should we imagine, my dear brothers, is the happiness of those who have been found worthy to see the immensity of his divinity?[37]

Bede does not use here the language of ecstasy or *excessus* but conceives of Peter's being overcome simply in terms of intense joy. He draws on Leo's interpretation by describing it as a joy which prompts a certain forgetfulness:

> The more one tastes the sweetness of heavenly life, the more one will loathe the base things that used to please. Peter immediately rightly forgets all the earthly things that he knew once he has seen the majesty of the Lord and his saints, and he rejoices in focussing uninterruptedly only on those things which he sees...[38]

Bede, following Leo, sees Peter's state of mind dictated by an intense emotion of joy which, although it causes forgetfulness, and Peter's inappropriate comments, does not effect a change in his vision.

Augustine and Ambrose Autpert on Peter's not knowing

It is important not to underestimate the importance of this distinct Western interpretation of Peter's state of mind. I wish to suggest that it lies, at least in part, behind the Latin interpretative tradition which directs a prolonged address to Peter, criticizing him for wanting to dwell too long on the mountain as a result of his being in an elated mood of joy and, therefore, preventing Jesus from descending to suffer the Passion. A notable first example is to be found twice in Augustine's comment on the Transfiguration, where he upbraids Peter for wanting to keep Christ on the mountain and prevent the revelation of his light being taken into the world.[39] The most elaborate example of this Latin tendency is to be found in Autpert's Transfiguration homily. He similarly chides Peter but starts making up suggestions concerning what Peter should have said as part of an imagined alternative conversation. Autpert, however, also connects Peter's state of mind with the sleepiness mentioned by Luke and offers this as a mitigating consideration as he addresses him:

> You are allowed indulgence, since you experience sleep when you say these things. The evangelist says the following about you and those with you: 'But Peter and those who were with him were weighed down with sleep.' It was a sleep, evidently, of the mind, rather than of the flesh [*somno videlicet, non carnis, sed mentis*].[40]

---

37. *Hom.* 24 (CC 122, 175, lines 187–91).
38. *Hom.* 24 (CC 122, 174, lines 166–71).
39. *Hom.* 78.3 (PL 38, 401).
40. *Hom. in Trans.* 16 (PL 89, 1316).

This rather curious notion of sleepiness of the *mind* is described by Autpert as involving a sort of forgetfulness, when he comments, 'From this it comes that your companions forgot the Lord and were more concerned with Moses and Elijah saying, "Let us make three tabernacles ... ".'[41] Autpert would seem to be describing a sort of forgetful befuddlement which befell Peter's mind as a result of his delight at the Transfiguration vision. The forgetful befuddlement prompts him to think too much about Elijah and Moses, rather than Jesus.

Peter's not knowing: Conclusions

We see in Autpert a bringing together of a number of interpretations which we have encountered in Ambrose, Leo and Bede, all focused on Peter's state of mind. Although Peter's mind may be gripped by considerable confusion, befuddlement and overwhelming joy, all seem to reject the idea that Peter experiences an ecstasy in the sense that he is sent mad, out of his mind, possessed by a demon, enters a dream world or has his sight altered. However, they do detect some degree of significance both in Luke's description of his not knowing what he said and also his description of the disciples' being sleepy. Peter's joyful state of mind is described as having a distracted inability to focus on earthly things in Ambrose and Leo, and as lapsing into forgetfulness by Bede. Two writers connect this joyful forgetfulness with Luke's mention of sleepiness: Ambrose sees it as an exhaustion of the senses, whilst Autpert interprets it as a sleepiness of the mind. It is important to note here a number of the ways in which the Latin understanding of the Transfiguration as a mortally apprehended vision prompts a focus on a number of Lucan details in order to describe Peter's state of mind and the way he sees the vision.

Interpretation of the cloud

The next section of this chapter focuses on ways in which interest in the overshadowing cloud present at the Transfiguration becomes a particular interest of Latin interpretation. Much of this comment draws heavily on elements only present in Luke's narrative or emphasized by him.

Cloud as revelation of the Spirit

Many Latin commentators associate the overshadowing cloud with the Holy Spirit and describe the cloud as a place of revelation, especially of the Trinity. In the Greek interpretation we examined in the last chapter, the experience of divine light is often seen as the principal revelation of God's presence. In Latin comment, however, a parallel status is sometimes afforded to the cloud, with an emphasis on the disciples' entry into it.

---

41. Ibid.

The association of the cloud with the Holy Spirit is one which begins in Hilary and Ambrose. Hilary comments, 'But whilst he was still talking, white clouds overshadowed them and they were enveloped by the Spirit of divine power.'[42] The principal character of the revelation made to them is, for Hilary, the voice of the Father pointing to Jesus as Son and Beloved. Ambrose also takes up this theme. He remarks of the cloud, 'It is from the Holy Spirit that this cloud comes, which does not obscure the heart, but reveals to it hidden things.'[43] Ambrose, however, brings an intriguing interpretation to bear on the cloud by then describing it as being made up, not of vapours or smoke, but of light itself: 'It is a luminous cloud. It does not wet us with downpours of rain, or flooding storms, but like the dew of faith sent out by the voice of God almighty, it speaks to the minds of men.' For Ambrose, it is *in the cloud* itself that the mind is transformed so that mysteries otherwise unknowable are revealed to the human mind through faith. It must be noted that this interpretation requires an assumption that all the disciples enter the cloud as Luke asserts, which is the text Ambrose is commenting on.

Cloud as heavenly tabernacle

We also see interpretation emerge amongst Latin writers concerning the cloud as a tabernacle for God's presence. Jerome, for example, points to the cloud being a *single* tabernacle dwelling for God in response to Peter's suggestion of *three* tabernacles. Jerome comments,

> Because [Peter's] request was an imprudent one, he did not deserve an answer from the Lord. So the Father replied on behalf of the Son ... The cloud appears bright and overshadows them so that those who were looking for a material tabernacle of leaves, or a tent, might instead be enveloped in the shelter of a bright cloud.[44]

Jerome seems to draw a contrast here between the physical shelter offered by the earthly tabernacles Peter could build and the heavenly shelter afforded by the cloud.

Augustine continues this theme and also holds the cloud to be akin to a *single* tabernacle:

> Peter wanted three tabernacles but the heavenly reply showed him that we have just one, which human thinking desired to divide ... As the cloud overshadowed them, and in this manner made one single tabernacle for them, 'a voice came from the cloud saying, "This is my beloved Son."'[45]

---

42. *Comm. Matt.* 17.3 (PL 9, 1014).
43. *Expos. in Luc.* 7.19 (PL 9, 1704).
44. *Com. in Ev. Mat.* 3.17.5 (PL 26, 122–3).
45. *Serm. 78*, 3 (PL 38, 401).

Augustine's emphasis here is on the singleness of the tabernacle represented by the cloud, as a reproof to Peter for suggesting three shelters. For him, out of the multiplicity represented by Moses and Elijah, the gospel represented by the single tabernacle presents us with a unity of revelation in Christ.

Bede sees the cloud as a heavenly tabernacle and as a criticism of Peter's suggestion:

> Because they wanted to make tents, a covering of bright cloud admonished them that houses are not necessary in the habitation of the life of heaven, where, under the eternal shade of his light, the Lord protects everything. Whilst the people journeyed through the desert, he spread a cloud out for their protection for forty years, in case the sun might scorch them by day or the moon by night.[46]

Bede points to the difference between the earthly dwellings the disciples would have constructed and the heavenly nature of the overshadowing cloud. Earthly dwellings are inappropriate precisely because the cloud embodies entry into a space signifying the 'habitation of the life of heaven'. Bede sees this experience of 'the life of heaven' as a sort of *protection* parallel to that enjoyed by the people of Israel as they were journeying to the Promised Land.

We find a version of this emphasis in Autpert's comment. However, he is the only Latin commentator I have encountered who does *not* see the disciples as included in the cloud. He sees the singleness of the overshadowing cloud as a correction of Peter's suggestion. However, he points to the way in which the bright cloud also *hides* or *removes* Moses and Elijah, so that only the voice of the Father is the focus of attention:

> We also note how this bright cloud takes and cloaks Moses and Elijah, snatches them away and conceals them. And once it takes Moses and Elijah and conceals them, it is not Moses and Elijah who call out from the cloud in which they are concealed, but rather only the Father speaks through the cloud.[47]

Autpert sees Moses and Elijah as removed or taken away from the scene by the cloud so there is no confusion as to whose the voice is. His comment presumes the disciples are not in the cloud, when he states, 'Think upon this, blessed Peter, your concern to construct tabernacles is taken away from you. Moses has departed, Elijah has withdrawn, for whom you wanted to make tabernacles … he who remains alone is Lord.'[48] It is crucial to his argument that the disciples are not included in the cloud. Autpert does not say where the prophets are snatched away

---

46. *Hom.* 24 (CCSL 122, 175).
47. *Hom. in Trans.* 18 (PL 89, 1317).
48. *Hom. in Trans.* 18 (PL 89, 1317).

to, though the fact that Moses and Elijah are not seen again would seem to imply this snatching away involves their return to heaven. This interpretation may be based on the Vulgate's rendering of Lk. 9.33. I have already pointed in Chapter 2 to the ambiguity present in the Greek of Lk. 9.33. However, the Vulgate interprets the verse with a definite sense that Moses and Elijah are beginning to depart when Peter spoke, 'et factum est cum discederent ab illo.' Although Autpert takes a view very different from the reading we find in many Latin commentators and sees the disciples as excluded from the cloud, his conviction that only Moses and Elijah were covered by it is dependent on a reading of Luke's version in the Vulgate in which they are described as on the verge of departing. For Autpert, therefore, the cloud is a place of revelation, but it also reveals Christ as attested by the Father's voice by hiding Moses and Elijah, and could be the means through which they return to heaven.

We see that much Latin patristic interpretation displays interest in the idea that the cloud represents some sort of single tabernacle dwelling for God's divine presence. The cloud either places the disciples in God's presence, protects them with it, is a place of divine revelation or, in the case of Autpert, is a means of hiding Moses and Elijah, and possibly returning them to heaven.

Who enters the cloud?

In the light of the Latin emphasis we have noted on the cloud being not just a single tabernacle space but also a place of revelation and protection, one finds a greater degree of agreement amongst Latin commentators concerning the question of who is found within the cloud and a more pronounced fidelity to Luke's insistence on this detail.

No Latin commentator explicitly states the disciples enter into the overshadowing cloud. Gregory comes closest when he remarks upon Peter's being enveloped with cloud when he asserts, 'The apostle Peter, not just prophet but also supreme patriarch, also saw the indescribable light pouring down from above as the cloud overshadowed him and the Father's voice resounded, "This is my beloved Son in whom I am well pleased."'[49] However, an *implicit* understanding of the disciples as being found within the cloud is to be found in a wide range of Latin writers. Hilary seems to assume this reading. He speaks of 'them' being overshadowed by the cloud in a passage in which every other third-person plural verb clearly refers to Peter, James and John.[50] Ambrose is one of the few specifically to be writing on Luke's gospel, and although he doesn't actually comment on the distinctly Lucan wording of the disciples' entry, his discussion of the cloud as a place where the Spirit is encountered in order that 'hidden things'[51] might be revealed to the disciples assumes that they entered the cloud. Jerome, too, presupposes a Lucan

---

49. *Prim. Reg. Expos.* 5.30 (PL 97, 466).
50. *Com. in Mat.* 17.2 (PL 9, 1013-4).
51. *Expos. in Luc.* 7.19 (PL 15, 1704).

understanding of the scene when, commenting on Matthew's text, he points to those who had wanted to build earthly tabernacles, presumably the disciples, being 'enveloped in the shelter of a bright cloud'.[52]

A number of writers retain a certain ambiguity concerning whether the disciples are to be found within the cloud. Augustine emphasizes the singleness of the cloud-tabernacle as a sign of the Kingdom and the Church.[53] He never clearly states that the disciples enter the cloud, and his language retains the ambiguity found in the New Testament narratives. The logic of his argument, however, points in the direction of the disciples being included, if they are seen as fit to enjoy the Kingdom with God's saints and are part of his Church.

A fifth-century Pseudo-Augustinian source, *Tractatum Contra Quinque Haereses*, also seems to presuppose that the disciples are found within the cloud, by continuing the Latin tradition of seeing it as the place of revelation and learning. The author uses language appertaining to entry and being inside and outside in the analogy he draws. In a passage commenting on hearing the heavenly voice, he remarks, 'Why are you standing outside murmuring, you heathen? Enter into the school of God here, open the ears of your hearts, hear the voice of the Lord, and learn to know the Son of God.'[54] Again, it is never explicitly stated that the disciples enter into the cloud, but this author clearly sees entry by his readers into the analogous metaphorical cloud of the 'school of God' as a desirable thing.

It is also probable that Bede sees the disciples within the cloud from the logic of his argument. The comparison he makes, outlined above, between the Transfiguration cloud and the *protecting* cloud that covered the Israelites in their wilderness wanderings, mentioned in Ps. 105.39, would seem to assume the disciples were included as the heavenly figures of Moses and Elijah wouldn't need protection of any sort.

It would seem a consensus exists across a range of Latin comment on the Transfiguration concerning the entry of the disciples into the overshadowing cloud. Although few make this explicitly clear, a majority seem to presuppose this more Lucan reading. Only Autpert espouses a radically different understanding and appears to countenance the possibility of only Moses and Elijah being overshadowed, as a way of hiding them or snatching them away. This emphasis on the disciples' entry into the cloud seems to go hand in hand with a more pronounced interest in Latin thought in the cloud being a single tabernacle and a place of revelation or of transformation of the mind, which requires the disciples to be *inside* it to experience the presence of the Holy Spirit. In this respect, the influence of the Lucan narrative on Western comment is more pronounced.

---

52. *Com. in Ev. Mat.* 17.3.5 (PL 26, 123).
53. *Serm.* 78 3 (PL 38, 401).
54. *Tract. Adv. 5 Haer.* 7 (PL 42, 1114).

Cloud interpretation: Conclusions

Latin commentators frequently display interest in the overshadowing cloud and associate it with some sort of encounter with the divine. In Hilary and Ambrose, the cloud is associated with the Holy Spirit and with the revelation of 'hidden things' to the disciples' transformed minds. Jerome and Augustine emphasize the cloud as a single tabernacle, which is entered by the disciples, whilst Bede associates it with the divine protection afforded by the pillar of cloud during the wilderness wanderings. Autpert sees it as a mechanism which hides Moses and Elijah and snatches them away to heaven. Luke's narrative exerts a strong influence over all this speculation, as Gregory, Augustine and Bede all assume with Luke that the disciples enter the cloud. Although Autpert reads Luke differently and decides that the disciples do not enter the cloud, his reading of the cloud as a vehicle of separation draws strongly on different elements, which are nonetheless solely present in Luke's version of the narrative in the Vulgate. Although we see a range of differing interpretation, most of the commentators we have examined see the cloud in some way as a single tabernacle or place of encounter with the divine. These tabernacle interpretations form a crucial foundation of many of the more ecclesial and corporate descriptions of the vision of God which we see in interpretation, which compares the Transfiguration with Hebrews 12 and Revelation 21, and which will be explored in the next sections of this chapter. This will then be shown in Chapter 8 to play a particularly important role in early visual depiction of the Transfiguration in the West.

Latin hermeneutic connections

A further characteristic of Western Latin comment on the Transfiguration is a tendency to use the narrative to make hermeneutic connections with other scriptural passages. The rest of this chapter explores examples of this.

Interpretations connected with Isaiah 7 and the Annunciation

We see emerge in a number of Latin Commentators a range of intriguing connections made with Isaiah 7 and the Annunciation. Referring to Luke, Ambrose, for example, comments,

> And then Moses and Elijah appeared. That is, Law and Prophecy with the Word, for Law cannot exist without the Word, and one is not a prophet except by prophesying about the Son of God. Indeed, the Sons of Thunder gazed on Moses and Elijah in bodily glory, but we also see Moses every day with the Son of God because we see the Law in the Gospel when we read: 'Love the Lord your God.' We see Elijah with the Word of God when we read: 'Behold a virgin shall

conceive in her womb.' Luke adds to this appropriately that, 'they were talking about his departure that he was to accomplish in Jerusalem.'[55]

Ambrose's comment has usually been interpreted as meaning that in the same way that Moses represents the Law, which finds its fulfilment in the love command of Mt. 22.37, so Elijah represents prophecy, signalled by the way in which Isa. 7.14 finds its fulfilment in the incarnation.[56] Despite the fact that Elijah is not the writer of a body of prophetic text, in the way that is attributed to a prophet like Isaiah, he is held to embody the reconciliation of prophecy in Christ, and the prophecy which exemplifies this *par excellence* is held by Ambrose to be Isa. 7.14. So in this comparison, Moses and Elijah stand as representative figures in a metaphorical encounter between the faithful Christian and Christ, in which they embody the Law and the Prophets. However, Ambrose also goes on to make a very different connection with the Annunciation. He comments,

'And while he was speaking a cloud came and overshadowed them.' It is from the Holy Spirit that this cloud comes, which does not obscure the heart, but reveals to it hidden things. This is also found in another place when the angel says, 'And the power of the Most High shall overshadow you.' Its result is shown in the voice of God which says, 'This is my beloved son; listen to him.'[57]

Here, Ambrose would seem to be making a simple connection with Luke's Annunciation narrative through the shared use of the verb *overshadow*. He also sees a parallel action by the Holy Spirit, which enlightens the heart of the disciples at the Transfiguration and in some sense also reveals 'secret things' to Mary at the Annunciation. It could be that both are revelations of Jesus' divine sonship: here through the words of the Father's voice; and in Nazareth through Gabriel's word that Mary's son will be 'called Son of the Most High'.[58]

This connection to Isaiah and the birth narratives is then developed by Jerome, but in a more complex way. He, too, uses Isaiah 7 to explain the presence of Moses and Elijah, but using the Lord's instruction to Ahaz:

When the scribes and Pharisees wanted to tempt him by demanding signs from heaven, he would not give them any. But he frustrated their wicked request with his wise response. But by contrast, in order to increase the faith of his apostles, he gives here a sign from heaven. So Elijah comes down from whence he had ascended, and Moses rises up from Hades. This was anticipated through Isaiah

---

55. *Expos. in Luc.* 7.10 (PL 15, 1702).
56. See McGuckin, *Transfiguration of Christ*, 319, footnote 54; see also Ide M. Ni Riain, *Commentary of Saint Ambrose on the Gospel According to Saint Luke* (Dublin: Halcyon Press, 2001), 195, footnote to section 10.
57. *Expos. in Luc.* 7.19 (PL 15, 1704).
58. Lk. 1.32.

when Ahaz asked for a sign for himself either from the heights or from hell. It is written, 'There appeared to them Moses and Elijah speaking with him.' In another gospel it is reported that they recounted to him all that he would suffer in Jerusalem. The Law and the prophets are shown, therefore, whose words so frequently announced the Lord's Passion and Resurrection.[59]

In essence, Jerome makes the same point as Ambrose, namely that the Law and Prophets point to Christ. However, Jerome sees here in the Transfiguration a very particular embodiment of the Lord's word to Ahaz at Isa. 7.14. Elijah is the sign as high as heaven, corresponding to his having been assumed into heaven, and Moses is the sign as low as Sheol, he having died and come up from Hades. Isaiah 7 is not just an example of the *sort* of fulfilment which Elijah represents, as Ambrose taught, but rather, for Jerome, the Transfiguration is itself a fulfilment of Isaiah's prophecy, in which the Lord gives the sign which Ahaz refused to ask for.

It is unclear whether these three references have some common origin or inspiration. They do, however, bear some comparison with the description of Jesus' birth found in the *Protevangelium of James*, and it has to be wondered whether this apocryphal text might, in part, be the source of connections made between the Transfiguration and the Lucan birth narratives.

Possible connections through the Protoevangelium of James and the Ascension of Isaiah

The *Protoevangelium of James* describes Jesus' birth in a way which clearly echoes elements from the New Testament Transfiguration narratives:

> And they stood at the entry to the cave. A bright cloud overshadowed the cave. And the midwife said, 'My soul has been magnified today, for my eyes have seen marvellous things, for salvation has been born to Israel.' And immediately the cloud started to withdraw from the cave and a great light appeared in the cave, so that it was not bearable for the eyes. After a little, that light began to withdraw until a new born child appeared and it came and took the breast of Mary, its mother.[60]

In addition to clear connections with the Transfiguration through the motif of light and overshadowing clouds, we also see here the splicing together of a number of scriptural echoes from the Lucan birth narratives, including the Presentation and the Magnificat. The writer uses the Transfiguration in two ways. First, he

---

59. *Com. in Ev. Mat.* 3.17.3 (PL 26, 122).
60. *Prot. Jas.* 19.2, J. K. Elliott and M. R. James, *The Apocryphal New Testament: A Collection of Apocryphal Christian Literature in an English Translation* (Oxford: Clarendon Press, 1993), 64.

employs it to occlude any vision of the miraculous birth. The light appears and prevents those watching from seeing how Jesus is born, precisely to draw a veil over the tricky biological conundrum of Mary's virginity *in partu*, an idea this text has frequently been connected with. Once the light has withdrawn, the baby has already been born, but the mechanics of how have been kept from our sight. Second, we hear echoes of the filling of Solomon's temple with God's glory recounted in 2 Chronicles 5. Christ emerges into the world as the embodiment of God's glory as the cave in which this takes place is turned into a temple space, and Joseph and the midwife wait outside, like the priests who could not enter the Temple in 2 Chronicles 5. We see in this passage a connecting of the Transfiguration with the Lucan Nativity narratives along with the presence of temple ideas as a way of interpreting them both. There does seem to be some overlap with the ideas we encountered in Origen, concerning his comparison of the Presentation and the Transfiguration. In both the *Protevangelium of James* and Origen, the glory which Christ embodies is not usually seen during his earthly life, apart from a small number of special revelations, which are described as temple-like scenes, or are compared with episodes set in the temple.

Is it possible that the influence of the *Protevangelium of James*'s account of the Nativity can be found in these comments of Ambrose's and Jerome's which emerge in the fourth and fifth centuries? Indeed, might the *Protevangelium of James* in part be the source of Origen's connecting of the Transfiguration with Luke's infancy narratives?

The reception of the *Protevangelium of James* in the Latin West is a complicated question, principally because of the complete lack of any early Latin translations of it. Jerome wrote strongly against the authenticity of the *Protevangelium of James* because of its assertion that the gospels' mention of Jesus' 'brothers' refers to children Joseph had by a first marriage.[61] This essentially led to its prohibition in the West. We can be sure, therefore, that Jerome knew the *Protevangelium of James* because of his documented hostility to it. Origen also knew the *Protevangelium of James*, as there is reference to it in his *Commentary on Matthew* in the discussion of the idea of Joseph having a first marriage.[62] Origen also makes clear in *Against Celsus*, that he is aware of the notion that Jesus was born in a cave.[63] Origen is widely held to be a significant influence on Ambrose's *Commentary on Luke* because of Jerome's accusation that large portions of it were cribbed from Origen,[64] and it is from his *Commentary on Luke* that Ambrose's comments concerning Isaiah 7 come.

Although there seem here to be a series of allusive similarities, it is very difficult indeed conclusively to prove documentary reliance by Ambrose and Jerome on the *Protevangelium of James*. In the first place, the points being made by Ambrose

---

61. Ibid., 48–9.
62. *Com. Mat.* 10.17 (PG 13, 876-877).
63. *Contra Cels.* 1.51 (PG 11, 756).
64. See, Lienhard, *Homilies on Luke*, xxxii–xxxiv.

and Jerome are quite distinct and different from each other. One sees Elijah as a representative of prophecy which is exemplified by Isa. 7.14. Another is highlighting shared use of the verb 'overshadow', and a third sees the Transfiguration as a fulfilment of Isa. 7.14. Although all three are closely connected with the broad theme of the Nativity, they are not specifically focused on the birth and do not describe it as a small Transfiguration in itself, as the *Protevangelium of James* seems to. It is far from clear that we can prove any connection between Ambrose and Jerome's comments and the *Protevangelium of James* other than to say we know Jerome knew the *Protevangelium of James* and that we see here a coming together of three interpretations of the Transfiguration loosely connected by their use of Isa. 7.14 and Luke's Annunciation. There does seem to be a closer connection between Origen's ideas concerning the Presentation and Finding in the Temple and the Nativity account we read in the *Protevangelium of James,* in that both draw on temple and transfiguration motifs. However, that doesn't really seem to be the point Ambrose and Jerome are making.

It must also be wondered if Ambrose and Jerome's comments can be illuminated by reference to the *Ascension of Isaiah*, as this text is itself frequently held to be influenced by the *Protevangelium of James*. In *Asc. Isa.* 11, Isaiah has a vision in which Christ's life, which he will prophecy, is revealed to him. The principal influence of the *Protevangelium of James* on this portion of the *Ascension of Isaiah* most clearly resides in the fact that here too, Mary does not undergo a real human childbirth. Christ miraculously appears in the house Mary is living in with Joseph as her pregnant womb deflates, and her virginity *in partu* is preserved. Faint echoes of the Transfiguration are present, as a voice instructs them to tell nobody of the vision in a way reminiscent of Mt. 17.9. Later on in the same chapter, Jesus' ascension is described in terms of an ascension through seven heavens which results in a glorification at his session at the right hand of the 'Great Glory'. Although there still seems to be a latent connecting of elements of the Transfiguration narrative with Christ's birth, there is no connection made with Elijah through Isaiah 7, nor through the Annunciation.

It seems we cannot claim there is here anything like a coherent, systematic or frequent connecting of the Transfiguration with Isaiah 7 and Luke's birth narratives, which can be pinned down to one particular source, or in which an identical hermeneutic can be discerned. However, we have outlined a series of sporadic, unpredictable, but nonetheless persistent connections made in different ways between the Transfiguration and the Nativity accounts. These are found in Origen, Ambrose, Jerome and the *Protevangelium of James*, along with the *Ascension of Isaiah*. It is difficult to argue these are entirely coincidental and take place in complete isolation from each other. It is equally difficult, however, to establish where Ambrose's and Jerome's interpretation comes from. It could be original to them, or be influenced by earlier thought stemming from Origen and the *Protevangelium of James*. However, it would be foolhardy to dismiss their comment as insignificant or inconsequentially random, especially as I show in the next chapter the continuing persistence of their ideas in the Transfiguration mosaic found at Santi Nereo e Achilleo in Rome, the earliest surviving depiction in that city. In that mosaic, dating from the ninth century, an image of the Transfiguration is placed side by side with depictions of the Annunciation and of the Virgin Mary sitting with her divine child. Comparing the Transfiguration with Luke's birth and infancy narratives, though not particularly common, is nonetheless a repeated hermeneutic strategy deployed by a number of commentators in the reception history of the Transfiguration.

Communal, ecclesial and corporate readings: Revelation 21 and Hebrews 12

I now wish to point to the way in which the disciples' vision is frequently interpreted in Latin thought in more communal, or ecclesial, terms than is seen in Greek reflection. I wish to conjecture that the way in which the Transfiguration is seen as pointing forward to *corporate* eschatological vision of God is a very important factor which contributes to the way in which Latin commentators and artists more frequently seek to interpret the Transfiguration in terms of the corporate vision of the heavenly Jerusalem described in Revelation 21 and Hebrews 12. This is a dynamic which I explore further in the next chapter in artistic depiction of the Transfiguration, especially in the Church of Santa Prassede in Rome.

Corporate interpretations: Augustine

We see a distinct ecclesial character to much of the interpretation given by Augustine, the importance and originality of which Louth[65] has pointed to. Augustine is the first, for example, to describe Jesus' shining garments not as representing the words of scripture, following the widespread Origenist interpretation, but rather the Church.[66] He argues that just as garments only hold together and stand up when someone is wearing them, so the Church must have Christ at its centre.[67] However, Augustine also develops a further argument through his *Homily on the Transfiguration* concerning the location of the Kingdom of God. At the beginning he seeks to establish how the mountain-top vision could be that seeing of the Son of Man in his Kingdom which Jesus predicts.[68] 'This is not an insignificant question, however, for that mountain does not take in the whole of his kingdom.'[69] In answer to this conundrum, Augustine concludes, 'In numerous places, he calls "his kingdom" what he describes as "the kingdom of heaven". Moreover, the kingdom of heaven is the kingdom of the saints.'[70] So, for

---

65. Louth, 'St Augustine's Interpretation of the Transfiguration of Christ', 379–82.
66. *Serm.* 78, 2 (PL 38, 490).
67. Ibid.
68. Mt. 16.28; Mk 9.1; Lk. 9.27.
69. *Serm.* 78, 1 (PL 38, 490).
70. Ibid.

Augustine, the Transfiguration is a revelation of the Son of Man's Kingdom by being a revelation of 'the Kingdom of the saints', a place where God reigns with the 'apostles and all the faithful preachers of the Word of God'.[71] In a later section of the same homily, Augustine concludes that, because a single tabernacle cloud overshadowed Jesus, Moses and Elijah, 'the Kingdom of God, is revealed to us in the Church'.[72] Augustine sees in the Transfiguration both a revelation of the life of the Kingdom of the saints and also an image of the Church, which is the place where, for his hearers, that Kingdom is to be found. The vision of God that it reveals is one in which God is to be found in the company of his saints, and which speaks of the mystery of the Church as the embodiment of God's Kingdom.

Ecclesial interpretations: Bede and Ambrose Autpert

Further 'ecclesial' readings have been pointed to in Bede and Autpert. Bede, for example, emphasizes the Transfiguration as displaying what the Resurrection will be like, with an Augustinian emphasis on Christ's garments signifying the Church.[73] However, Bede is the first Latin writer explicitly to connect the Transfiguration with the heavenly Jerusalem of Rev. 21.22 and does this through using Luke's detail that Peter did not know what he was saying. He explains Peter's not knowing in terms of his having mistaken the need for three tabernacles:

> A house will not be necessary in the glory of the life of heaven, where the light of divine contemplation, pacifying everything, leaves no fearful wind of adversity. This was testified by the Apostle John, who, describing the brightness of that lofty city, says, among other things, 'And I saw no temple in it. For the almighty Lord and the Lamb are its temple.'[74]

In addition to this, Bede also draws an analogy with Heb. 12.22. Following Leo's interpretation, he argues that if merely seeing the glorified humanity of Christ on the mountain makes Peter not want to be separated from the sight of Christ, how much more alluring will be the final vision of God:

> What kind of discussion is capable of explaining, or what sense can understand what will be the joys of the just when they come to, 'Mount Zion, and to the city of the living God, Jerusalem, and to the throng of many thousands of angels,' and when they gaze upon God, the builder and founder of this very city, not through a glass darkly now, but face to face?[75]

71. Ibid.
72. *Serm.* 78, 4 (PL 38, 491).
73. *Hom.* 24 (CC 122, lines 100, 173).
74. *Hom.* 24 (CC 122, 175, lines 176–80).
75. *Hom.* 24 (CC 122, 175, lines 191–9).

For Bede, the Transfiguration is a mortal vision of three people on a mountain, which prefigures the greater vision of God surrounded by all his saints which the faithful Christian will experience in the future, and which he sees described in Rev. 21.22 and Heb. 12.22. Although the vision the disciples experience is one in which only six people are present, when the faithful Christian experiences it in the Kingdom of Heaven, it will be a corporate and communal vision of God which is shared with many angels and saints.

Autpert also brings a similar ecclesial reading to bear on the Transfiguration, seeing the narrative pointing to the future corporate life of the Church in heaven, when he comments, 'But in this transformation, there is also shown what the future of the Church in its heavenly homeland will be like for the saints.'[76]

He later picks up Augustine's interpretation, just as Bede does, seeing Christ's garments signifying the Church, but argues this is the Church of the future, purified and free from sin in heaven: 'It is like this with God's elect, for when they reach this and obtain the glory of God, they shall attain the splendour of purity.'[77] He also criticizes Peter's instinct for wanting to build three tabernacles as too isolationist, saying, 'Say, therefore, I ask you, were you brought up the mountain just to build tabernacles and have the Lord to yourself, with just a few others?'[78] The Transfiguration points, for Autpert, away from isolated, individual experience of the Lord's presence and towards corporate enjoying of the divine vision with the whole company of heaven.

Priestly motifs in Ambrose Autpert

In addition to Revelation 21 and Hebrews 12 being used in conjunction with communal understandings of the Transfiguration, it is notable that Hebrews is also used as a way of bringing priestly understandings of Jesus' role to interpretation of the Transfiguration. In Autpert's *Homily on the Transfiguration*, for example, we see a series of priestly interpretations drawn from the Epistle to the Hebrews woven around the Lucan motifs of the disciples' sleepiness and Jesus' going up the mountain to pray. He uses Luke's mention of sleep to begin a section commenting on the importance of perseverance in prayer and the number of times Jesus sought out a private place to pray. He then contrasts this spending of nights in prayer with the Lucan sleepiness of the disciples on the Mount of Transfiguration. For Autpert, this is simply an exemplary lesson in which Jesus displays how to pray well, persevering against tiredness. However, this then leads to a prolonged description of Jesus as a priestly figure, in a passage which draws on the language of the Epistle to the Hebrews. As part of his exposition of the Transfiguration, Autpert points to Jesus as a figure who ceaselessly prays on humankind's behalf:

---

76. *Hom. in Trans.* 2 (PL 89, 1306).
77. *Hom. in Trans.* 8 (PL 89, 1310).
78. *Hom. in Trans.* 16 (PL 89, 1313).

With frequent lamentation, full of tears, and on bowed knee, he often spent the night as if he were guilty of mortal vices, though it should not surprise us that he might be subject to human frailty, for he did all this and approached death for our sakes. It was our sins he carried, and interceded for us with the Father, even as if he himself were a sinner. In doing this, he offered himself as an example for us to learn from, for he intercedes with the Father on our behalf, and never ceases from prayer. For he himself, now present before the face of God, intercedes continuously for us all. Let us therefore, cast aside laziness and torpor, and let us follow the example of the Lord. As his blessed Passion approached, as we have said, completely innocent as he was, he prayed all the more often and at length and struggled so that instead of bodily sweat, there flowed forth drops of blood.[79]

We hear in this passage echoes of Heb. 5.7, with its mention of Jesus offering up prayers and supplications in the day of his flesh, and also of Heb. 12.1, with its encouragement to lay aside what holds us back and run the race set before us. Autpert also, however, employs here a second argument from Hebrews, namely that Jesus' priestly status is revealed by his being innocent of all sin and therefore able to offer the perfect sacrifice of himself, which is also made continuously effectual by the fact that he is now in his Father's presence. All these connections concerning Jesus' priestly office drawn from Hebrews are connected with the Transfiguration narratives through the solely Lucan details of Jesus going up the mountain to pray and the disciples falling asleep.

Conclusion

Although many common threads of interpretation are shared between the West and East, especially in their shared reliance on Origen, I have outlined in this chapter a number of ways in which distinct hermeneutic traditions evolve in Latin comment which display a considerable degree of creativity and originality, especially in its understanding of the Transfiguration as a visionary text. I hope the significance of much of this Latin interpretation will be shown in the next chapter, when I come to demonstrate how it influenced the earliest examples of depiction of the Transfiguration in Rome, Ravenna and France.

Latin writers tend to see the Transfiguration as a vision solely apprehended by the mortal faculty of sight in an unaltered state. Indeed, this conception is made clear in the way in which many Latin commentators interpret elements of the Lucan narrative, such as Peter's not knowing what he said as a form of joy and the disciples' sleepiness as the physical symptom of overwhelmed mortal vision.

Latin comment also displays interest in the overshadowing cloud, which is frequently associated with the presence of the Holy Spirit. Indeed, the

---

79. *Hom. in Trans.* 5 (PL 89, 1308).

transformation of the mind and senses, which Eastern comment tends to associate with the seeing of divine light, is frequently associated in Latin comment with the entry into the cloud, which is so emphasized by Luke. This is frequently interpreted as an entry into a single tabernacle dwelling in which God is found and in which hidden mysteries are revealed.

A more ecclesial, communal and temple-influenced interpretative lens is also brought to bear on our texts by Augustine, Bede and Autpert, especially in connection with Revelation 21 and Hebrews 12. We have also noted priestly interpretations emerge in connection with Luke's mention of sleep and prayer in Autpert. In the next chapter I draw on these priestly interpretations in connection with the depiction of the Transfiguration in Sant'Apollinare in Classe, Ravenna. I also hope to show the influence Revelation 21 and Hebrews 12 continued to have on the depiction of the Transfiguration we see in the Basilica of Santa Prassede in Rome.

I have also shown a number of distinguishing hermeneutic traditions in which the Transfiguration is interpreted in the light of other passages from scripture, such as interpretation found in Jerome and Ambrose concerning the birth narratives, and Isaiah 7. These traditions will play an important role in our examination of Transfiguration images in the church of Santi Nereo e Achilleo in Rome. I hope this and the following chapter reveal Latin reception of the Transfiguration narratives to be capable of significant creativity and display an appreciation of the distinct character of Luke's version, and of the Transfiguration narratives' status as accounts of visionary experience.

Chapter 8

THE EARLIEST DEPICTION OF THE TRANSFIGURATION

We change gear in this chapter dedicated to artistic depiction of the Transfiguration and examine a series of different idioms in which the Transfiguration narratives are interpreted, presented and experienced in the earliest depiction from the sixth century onwards. It is in this chapter that conversation partners such as Jas Elsner, Judith Kovacs, Christopher Rowland and Natasha O'Hear, whose thought I have outlined in Chapter 1, become particularly important. Having surveyed written commentary on the Transfiguration, I aim to show that many elements of that interpretation can be found expressed in a number of depictions of the Transfiguration. Many of the earliest images of the Transfiguration attempt to express the ambiguities and complexities which we have shown exist in the New Testament narratives concerning vision, they bring it into conversation with other scriptural narratives, they evoke priestly and temple themes, and are frequently influenced by the distinctive characteristics of the Lucan version. This chapter focuses on the ways in which many of the visionary motifs we have examined come to be expressed by artists, especially in Western depictions, and the influence of the Lucan narrative on them. This is crucial evidence in building up a picture of the scopic regime within which early reception of the Transfiguration took place.

I seek to show in this chapter how visual depiction of the Transfiguration allows new facets of its character as a visionary incident to be expressed and how important elements within Luke's narrative become for artists. I suggest, in line with the approach proposed by O'Hear and outlined in Chapter 1, that there may be something characterizing artistic depiction which is particularly suited to the exploration of an incident which claims to be visionary in nature. This dynamic allows artists to draw out different understandings of what it might mean to see God. The fact that many of these depictions are to be found in churches points to the liturgical context in which they were seen, and to the way in which what they depict was frequently held to be enacted through the liturgy of the Church.

This chapter will also reappraise the sometimes underrated iconographic tradition of Latin Christianity concerning the Transfiguration in our period. My concern in this chapter is not principally a linear description of various images' history, though that will sometimes be necessary. Rather, it is an attempt to show how different images may have been read, interpreted and used by those who saw them. In other words, our principal concern is hermeneutic and an attempt to show how visual depiction was used as a way of interpreting the synoptic Transfiguration narratives, and especially how important Luke's narrative is within these processes.

Scope and choice of material

This chapter is able to touch on all the most significant early Transfiguration images created in the period up to 900 AD for the simple fact that very few images of the incident survive from this period. Eastern Christendom experienced periods of iconoclasm from the sixth century onwards, during which many images were destroyed and the creation of new ones hampered. The earliest two monumental images unequivocally held by a majority of historians to be of the Transfiguration are those found in Sinai and Classe, which will be examined in this chapter. We then see a gap of three hundred years or so before evidence of a second proliferation in the West of Transfiguration images in the ninth century, principally those created in Rome under the reign of Pope Paschal I, also to be examined in this chapter. In the East, widespread production of Transfiguration images only recommences from the tenth century onwards, with the decline of iconoclasm.

Three highly contested images which, some have argued, might be Transfigurations predate the great apses of Sinai and Classe. One of these images is found on the third-century doors of Santa Sabina in Rome, a second is on a fourth-century ivory container frequently referred to as the 'Brescia Casket' and the other possible image of the Transfiguration dates from 580 and is to be found in the Syriac Rabbula Gospels.[1]

Whilst Andreas Andreopoulos identifies the Santa Sabina image as a Transfiguration,[2] it bears a number of curious characteristics which point in other directions, such as the strange rugby ball-shaped object being held by the 'transfigured' Christ and the debated identity of the two figures standing with him. J. Wiegand,[3] for example, argued that it might depict the Emmaus encounter. Gisela Jeremias[4] and Jean-Michel Spieser[5] held it to be a depiction of the *tradito legis*,

---

1. For illustration, and further discussion of the three images, see Andreas Andreopoulos, *Metamorphosis: The Transfiguration in Byzantine Theology and Iconography* (Crestwood, NY: St Vladimir's Seminary Press, 2005), 102–11.

2. Ibid., 102–6.

3. J. Wiegand, *Das altchristliche Hauptportal und der Kirche der Hl. Sabina* (Trier: Paulinus Druckerei, 1900), 77.

4. Gisela Jeremias, *Die Holztür der Basilika S. Sabina in Rom* (Tübingen: E. Wasmut, 1980), 77–80.

5. Jean-Michel Spieser, 'Le programme iconographique des portes de Sainte-Sabine', *Journal des Savants* 1 (1991): 63–9.

whilst Richard Delbrück[6] and Erich Dinkler[7] see it as representing a conflation of imagery from Christ's saying concerning the Pearl of Great Price[8] with *traditio legis* imagery.

Although many commentators identify an image on the Brescia Casket image as a Transfiguration,[9] a considerable number have different suggestions including that it depicts Christ with Peter and Andrew,[10] or, indeed, the calling of Peter and Andrew,[11] a glorification of Christ before Matthew and Philip,[12] some form of resurrection appearance, be that apocryphal[13] or on the sea of Tiberias echoing John 21,[14] or a representation of Christ at a water's edge of some sort.[15]

The problem with the Rabbula image of a gathering of three men is that it appears on one side of a canon table, with a scratched-out image in the other margin. Opinion is divided as to whether the image of the three men might be Moses, Elijah and Jesus,[16] whether it simply depicts three

---

6. Richard Delbrück, 'Notes on the Wooden Doors of Santa Sabina", *Art Bulletin* 34 (1952): 139–45.

7. Erich Dinkler, *Das Apsismosaik von S. Apollinare in Classe*, Wissenschaftliche Abhandlungen der Arbeitsgemeinschaft für Forschung des Landes Nordrhein-Westfalen (Köln: Westdeutscher Verlag, 1964), 32–4.

8. Mt. 13.45-46.

9. Carl Maria Kaufmann, *Handbuch der christlichen Archäologie* (Paderborn: F. Schoningh, 1913), 555; J. Kollwitz, *Die Lisanothek von Brescia* (Berlin: de Gruyter, 1933), 28–9; Gaetano Panazza, *I musei e la Pinacotecca di Brescia* (Bergamo: Instituto Italiano d'Arti Grafiche, 1959), 57; A. C. Soper, 'The Italo-Gallic School of Early Christian Art', *Art Bulletin* 20 (1938): 177; H. G. Stuhlfauth, *Die altchristliche Elfenbeinplastik* (Freiburg-Leipzig: Mohr, 1894), 41; Ludwig von Sybel, *Christliche Antike: Einführung in die altchristliche Kunst* (Marburg: N.G. Elwert, 1909), vol. 2, 247; John Obadiah Westwood, *A Descriptive Catalogue of the Fictive Ivories in the South Kensington Museum. With an Account of the Continental Collections of Classical and Medieval Ivories* (London: Eyre and Spottiswoode, 1876), 37.

10. Franz Kraus, *Geschichte der christlichen Kunst* (Freiburg in Breisgau: Herder, 1896), 503; Frederico Odorici, *Antichita cristiane di Brescia* (Brescia: Pio Instituto in S. Barnaba, 1845), 67, 76–8.

11. Carolyn Watson, 'The Program of the Brescia Casket', *Gesta* 20 (1981): 286, 295.

12. Adolfo Venturi, *Storia dell'arte italiana* (Milan: Ulrico Hoepli, 1901), vol. 1, 460.

13. Richard Delbrück, *Probleme der Lipsanothek in Brescia* (Bonn: Peter Hanstein Verlag, 1952), 24, 32–4.

14. J. M. C. Toynbee, 'Review of Delbrück, *Probleme der Lipsanothek in Brescia*', *The Antiquaries Journal* 35 (1955): 238–40; Watson, 'The Program of the Brescia Casket', 286, 295.

15. Pierre du Bourget, *Early Christian Art* (London: Weidenfeld and Nicholson, 1972), 178; W. Volbach, *Early Christian Art* (New York: h. Abrams, 1962), 328.

16. Gertrud Schiller, *Iconography of Christian Art* (London: Lund Humphries, 1971), vol. 1, 147.

disciples[17] or whether it might be part of a split scene, with the scrubbed-out patch on the other page showing the other half of a Transfiguration scene.[18]

The highly contested nature of these three early fragmentary images means that it is difficult to rely on them unequivocally as evidence in the history of Transfiguration depiction. The degree of uncertainty amongst scholars in categorizing them as images of the Transfiguration prompts me simply to acknowledge their presence and contested status, but to focus on the emergence of the monumental mosaics in Sinai and Classe in the sixth century as our principal starting point in the exploration of the history of the depiction of the Transfiguration.

Apse Mosaics: Sinai and Ravenna

In the next two sections, we explore the interpretation of the Transfiguration found in the great monumental apse mosaics found in the monastic church at St Catherine's Monastery on Mt Sinai and in the Basilica of Sant'Apollinare in Classe, Ravenna, both of which were built under Emperor Justinian's patronage at about the same time in the sixth century. The significance of these two mosaics resides in the fact that they are the earliest unequivocal depictions of the Transfiguration to survive from the first millennium and yet are so extraordinarily different.

The apse mosaic of St Catherine's Monastery, Sinai

The mosaic in the sanctuary apse of the monastery church on Mt Sinai dates from between 548 and 565. It is regarded by many commentators as exercising considerable influence over later Eastern depiction of the Transfiguration and as providing a template for the presentation of the Transfiguration within later Orthodox iconography.[19] The apse itself is located in the place traditionally held to have been where Moses encountered the Burning Bush, and for many years until the medieval period, a shrub grew on the other side of the apse wall believed to be that very bush. The Transfiguration mosaic is surmounted by two further images of Moses receiving the Law on Sinai and his discovery of the Burning Bush.

---

17. Dinkler, *Das Apsismosaik von S. Apollinare in Classe*, 34–6; Gabriel Millet, *Recherches sur l'iconographie de l'évangile aux xiv, xv, Et xvi siècles: D'après les monuments de Mistra, de la Macédoine et du Mont-Athos* (Paris: E. de Boccard, 1960), 219.

18. Carlo Cecchelli, *The Rabbula Gospels, Facsimile Edition of the Minatures of the Syriac Manuscript Plut. 56 in the Medicaean-Laurentian Library* (Olten: Urs Graf Verlag, 1959), 58.

19. E.g. Andreopoulos, *Metamorphosis*, 127; Christa Ihm, *Die Programme der christlichen Apsismalerei vom vierten Jahrhundert bis zur Mitte des achten Jahrhunderts*, Forschungen Zur Kunstgeschichte Und Christlichen Archäologie (Wiesbaden: Steiner, 1960), 69.

Figure 1 Saint Catherine's monastery in Sinai, Egypt – Mosaic of the Transfiguration (sixth century).
Source: Photo by Jean-Luc MANAUD/Gamma-Rapho via Getty Images.

Elsner's[20] interpretation of the mosaic has been of particular importance in integrating the particularity of its location, the surrounding images of Moses's experiences on Sinai and the liturgical space in which the apse is found. He sees the apse mosaics as a meditation on what it means to see and encounter God, through the processes of what he calls 'mystic viewing'. He understands this to refer to a pre-modern way of viewing art and image, in which the distance between viewer and viewed is broken down, in an experience which involves union with the reality depicted in a way that overcomes the duality of the object and subject of viewing. For Elsner, the artist's choosing of the Transfiguration as the subject of this mosaic exemplified the way in which an image can lead to experience of the reality it depicts through this process of mystic viewing.

Sinai and tabernacle themes

I want to elaborate on Elsner's ideas and to make two further points. The first is to underline the importance of the way in which this mosaic's reading of the Transfiguration through the lens of the Moses narratives shows its creator to be

---

20. Jas Elsner, *Art and the Roman Viewer: The Transformation of Art from the Pagan World to Christianity* (Cambridge: Cambridge University Press, 1995), 99–124.

bringing a series of ideas connected with God's heavenly tabernacle and earthly temple to bear on his interpretation of the Transfiguration.

Elsner argues that the mystic viewing he speaks of was also connected in the ancient world with a number of analogies linked to earthly temples. He points to a comparison drawn by Plotinus in his sixth *Ennead* in which the processes of human contemplation are compared with a man entering into a temple and walking past earthly statues and images in the outer precincts until he comes face to face with the true divinity residing in the sanctuary.[21] Elsner points to ways in which the Sinai image could be evoking not just entry into an earthly sanctuary but also entry into its celestial counterpart, God's heavenly tabernacle. Elsner[22] reads the whole mosaic as a series of revelations of God's presence, leading from the summit of mystical vision in the Old Testament to a new and ultimate summit in the New Testament in which God is seen face to face. He does this by interpreting the images against the background of Gregory of Nyssa's *Life of Moses*. Gregory points to these theophanies as a paradigm for the processes of human reception of revelation and speaks of Moses's reception of the Tablets of the Law as like entry into a Holy of Holies, or a heavenly tabernacle.[23] Elsner's work shows that the Moses imagery used to surround the apse was capable of evoking a range of analogies which pointed to Moses's experience, and that of the disciples, as being akin to entry into the heavenly tabernacle of God.

When Elsner's conclusions are placed in the context of the wider survey of reception we have undertaken in this study, in which I have shown the recurrence of interpretation associated with temple and priestly themes, these temple echoes which Elsner sees take on greater significance and are seen to be far from isolated phenomena.

The second point I want to make concerning the Sinai image touches the largely overlooked debt the apse mosaic owes to the Lucan narrative. One notable feature is the lack of any other features such as the landscape of the mountain, the approaching cloud or a hand symbolizing the Father's voice.[24] The mosaic makes more sense if seen as depicting the series of events as recounted in Luke's gospel. It is possible we see in this mosaic the six figures *in the midst of the cloud* as Luke describes at Lk. 9.34. The gold background could represent the divine glory perceived from *within* the overshadowing cloud, making this a depiction of that moment of entry which Luke describes. This would seem to be confirmed by the fact that the disciples are depicted in and amongst the heavenly three, between Jesus and the two prophets, sharing the same space. This is in contrast to the later Eastern artistic tradition of presenting them as Matthew recounts, prostrate on a lower level than the three who appear in glory, and outside the immediate mandorla with the surrounding countryside visible. A further detail indicating

---

21. Ibid., 91.
22. Ibid., 88–124.
23. Ibid., 108–9.
24. See Andreopoulos, *Metamorphosis*, 138–9.

reliance on the Lucan text is the fact that the disciples are looking up, and waking from sleep as described by Luke, rather than falling 'on their faces', as described by Matthew, which becomes the mainstay of later Eastern depictions.[25]

It would seem reasonable, therefore, to point to the Lucan narrative as a significant influence in this image. If this is so, then the Sinai image is possibly less of the direct template for later Orthodox images of the Transfiguration than so many have asserted.[26] It presents a distinct moment from the Lucan narrative and argues the disciples to have entered into the cloud and to be encircled by divine glory. This is different from the assertion of later Orthodox iconographic tradition which places the apostles falling on their faces as Matthew recounts, *outside* the mandorla of glory and at the *end* of the incident.[27] If the image presents a view from within the cloud, then the viewer is being afforded a perspective on the incident which is identical to that of the disciples who were present. Several elements of Luke's narrative are crucial to the way in which this mosaic's viewers are drawn in to the incident and invited to see the same thing that the disciples see.

Sinai: Conclusions

A number of Elsner's conclusions take on new weight and importance in the light of evidence I have marshalled in previous chapters, especially concerning the Transfiguration as an entry into a temple or tabernacle space. In addition to this, I have conjectured that the Lucan narrative exercises more influence over this image than many commentators have noticed, and that it is not the simple template for later Orthodox iconographic depiction that so many have argued. I contend that we see here in Sinai a depiction of the Transfiguration which focuses on the Lucan moment of entry into the cloud, showing the three disciples actually within the cloud sharing in Jesus' heavenly glory. If these two conclusions are correct, then we see Luke's narrative being paired with an interpretation of the Transfiguration that emphasizes the episode as an entry into the divine presence in heaven.

25. Elsner interprets Peter to be waking from sleep in the Sinai image, as described by the Lucan narrative: Elsner, *Art and the Roman Viewer*, 114–15.

26. Andreopoulos, *Metamorphosis*, 127; Ihm, *Die Programme der christlichen Apsismalerei*, 69.

27. Examination of the only two Eastern manuscript images which remain from the ninth century shows a median position emerging between the sixth-century conception proposed in the Sinai image and the later standard Eastern arrangement which emerges from the middle ages onwards. In both of the ninth-century Transfiguration images found in the Chludov Psalter and in the works of Gregory Nazianzen found in the Paris Bibliotheque Nationale Cod. Gr. 510, the distinctly Lucan arrangement of the apostles emerging from sleep with Peter standing and speaking persists. In both these images, however, the typography of the mountain is beginning to emerge and the apostles are now distinctly outside the mandorla, which only takes in Moses and Elijah, in counter distinction to Sinai. See Andreopoulos, *Metamorphosis*, 171, 179–97; Dinkler, *Das Apsismosaik von S. Apollinare in Classe*, 44.

Figure 2 Transfiguration apse over high altar, St Apollinare in Classe, Ravenna. Source: © Peter Anthony.

The apse mosaic in Sant'Apollinare in Classe, Ravenna

Built in 549, around the same time as the monastery on Sinai, Sant'Apollinare in Classe also contains an apse depiction of the Transfiguration but which, in certain respects, could hardly be more different from Sinai. Classe presents the scene in a much more allusive symbolic idiom, with Christ represented by a huge cross on a background of blue stars with a small medallion of his face in the centre. In many ways this image has remained an enigma to commentators. They have found it difficult to explain the origins of the imagery it uses and have been uncertain about its later influence. I wish to make three broad points about it. First, I want to make a renewed argument for the influence of the *Apocalypse of Peter* and of the Lucan version of the Transfiguration on this mosaic. Second, I aim to prove that a number of temple and priestly motifs are present in this image. Third, I aim to show that the Classe image has had a significant impact on later Transfiguration images in Rome.

Modern interpretation of the Classe image

A clear tendency on the part of many who have commented on this image is to interpret it in eschatological terms, as a fulfillment of the words concerning the return of the Son of Man which precede each Transfiguration narrative[28] and as a

---

28. Mt. 16.28; Mk 9.1; Lk. 9.27.

depiction of the Transfiguration revealing the Parousia of Christ.[29] However, many have also argued the mosaic, especially the Cross, operates as a multivalent symbol, capable of communicating several theological themes, motifs and events at once in one image, such as the Passion, the exaltation of the Cross, the Ascension and the Second Coming.[30] Andreopoulos sees the image as so complex, and interprets it in such resolutely eschatological terms, that he denies Classe ought properly to be classified as a Transfiguration scene at all.[31] Others, such as Julius Kurth[32] and Alberto Pincherle,[33] seek explanation for the mosaic's allusive imagery in local legend by suggesting unconvincingly[34] that it might be the depiction of a vision which Apollinaris himself may have had whilst strolling in a nearby wood. It must be suspected that the lack of consensus concerning so many of the mosaic's elements has contributed to the notion, voiced by Andreopoulos[35] and Manfred Krüger,[36] that the Classe apse has had little influence on later depictions of the Transfiguration and that it stands almost as an isolated fossil with, in artistic and theological terms, no progeny at all. Andreopoulos's sense of baffled puzzlement in the face of this image is evident when he states, 'Although impossible to ignore because of its beauty, magnitude, and bold visual experimentation, it did not set a pattern for subsequent images, and even if this majestic work had never been made, the history of the Transfiguration iconography would not have been different.'[37]

29. Andreopoulos, *Metamorphosis*, 119-21; Dinkler, *Das Apsismosaik von S. Apollinare in Classe*, 106-17; André Grabar, *Martyrium: recherches sur le culte des reliques et l'art chrétien antique* (Paris: Collège de France, 1946), vol. 2, 193-5; Manfred Krüger, *Die Verklärung auf dem Berge: Erkenntnis und Kunst* (Hildesheim: Georg Olms Verlag, 2003), 95-9; Solrunn Nes and Arlyne Moi, *The Uncreated Light: An Iconographical Study of the Transfiguration in the Eastern Church* (Grand Rapids, MI: Eerdmans, 2007), 74-84; Carl Otto Nordström, *Ravennastudien; Ideengeschichtliche und Ikonographische Untersuchungen über die Mosaiken von Ravenna* (Stockholm: Almqvist & Wiksell, 1953), 129-32; Erik Peterson, *Frühkirche, Judentum und Gnosis; Studien und Untersuchungen* (Rom: Herder, 1959), 15-35.

30. Friedrich Wilhelm Deichmann, *Ravenna: Hauptstadt des spätantiken Abendlandes* (Stuttgart: Franz Steiner, 1958), vol. 2, esp., 251-4; Claudia Müller, 'Das Apsismosaik von Sant'Apollinare in Classe: eine Strukturanalyse', *Römische Quartalschrift* 75 (1980): esp. 49-50.

31. Andreopoulos, *Metamorphosis*, 118.

32. Julius Kurth, *Die Mosaiken der christlichen Ära* (Leipzig: Deutsche Bibelgesellschaft, 1902), 210-11.

33. Alberto Pincherle, 'Intorno a un celebre mosaico Ravennate', *Byzantion* 36 (1966): 491-534.

34. Deichmann shows how unlikely this theory is by pointing to the fact that no record or legend exists of Apollinaris having a vision in any of the extensive hagiography written about him. See Deichmann, *Ravenna*, 247.

35. Andreopoulos, *Metamorphosis*, 117.

36. Krüger, *Die Verklärung auf dem Berge*, 100.

37. Andreopoulos, *Metamorphosis*, 117.

I aim to challenge this verdict and demonstrate that Classe exercised considerable theological influence over later depictions of the Transfiguration.

Possible connections between Classe and the Apocalypse of Peter

The first point to be made is a renewed argument for the influence of the *Apocalypse of Peter* upon the apse mosaic in Classe. Andreopoulos,[38] Dinkler,[39] Krüger,[40] and Solrunn Nes[41] countenance the possibility of some degree of influence, though several commentators, such as Giuseppe Bovini,[42] Vanda Gaddoni,[43] Otto von Simson,[44] Christa Ihm,[45] Ernst Uehli,[46] and Carl Nordström[47] do not mention the *Apocalypse of Peter* at all in their extensive treatments of the basilica at Classe. Indeed, Pincherle and Friedrich Deichmann explicitly reject the idea that the *Apocalypse of Peter* has any influence on the Classe image.[48] Although the *Apocalypse of Peter* does not resolve all of the conundrums present in this remarkable mosaic, I argue that it makes at least slightly more coherent sense when read in connection with that text.

I have shown in Chapter 4 the reception history of the *Apocalypse of Peter* to be a complex question made very difficult to assess by a paucity of evidence. The hesitancy which Dinkler displays in asserting that the *Apocalypse of Peter* was undoubtedly known in Ravenna in the sixth century is probably well placed. He rightly raises a range of questions concerning uncertainties in making a connection between the *Apocalypse of Peter* and Classe, such as the possibility of influence from other texts or the lack of clarity concerning which version of the *Apocalypse of Peter* was available to the artists.[49] However, even taking these caveats into account, he rightly concludes that some influence by the *Apocalypse of Peter* is very

---

38. Ibid., 119.
39. Dinkler, *Das Apsismosaik von S. Apollinare in Classe*, 90–5.
40. Krüger, *Die Verklärung auf dem Berge*, 95.
41. Nes and Moi, *The Uncreated Light*, 78–81.
42. Giuseppe Bovini, *Ravenna, Art and History* (Ravenna: Longo Publisher, 1991), 94–106.
43. Vanda Frattini Gaddoni, *The Basilica of St Apollinare in Classe, an Illustrated Art Guide*, trans. Annie Vancini (The Vallombrosian Benedictine monks of the monastery of St Apollinare in Classe).
44. Otto Georg von Simson, *Sacred Fortress: Byzantine Art and Statecraft in Ravenna* (Chicago: University of Chicago Press, 1948), 40–61.
45. Ihm, *Die Programme der christlichen Apsismalerei*, 70–4.
46. Ernst Uehli, *Die Mosaiken von Ravenna: Mit 45 Abbildungen* (Basel: B. Schwabe, 1954), 70–3.
47. Nordström, *Ravennastudien*, 120–32.
48. Deichmann, *Ravenna*, 252; Pincherle, 'Intorno a un celebre mosaico Ravennate', 508, 515.
49. Dinkler, *Das Apsismosaik von S. Apollinare in Classe*, 90–5.

difficult entirely to discount and could be quite likely. The only evidence, however, we have to judge by is a comparison of the text with the mosaic itself. This cannot, in itself, prove my argument, but it can at least offer a possible hypothesis, which I argue explains much which commentators find perplexing about this mosaic.

The similarities between the Classe image and the *Apocalypse of Peter* are striking. The most frequently remarked-upon connection is the similarity between the background scene in Classe of plants, flowers and birds, and the paradisal garden revealed in the *Apocalypse of Peter*. Both the Ethiopic and Akhmim versions make mention of lush vegetation in the vision of heaven revealed to the apostles:

> And he showed us a great garden, open, full of fair trees and blessed fruits and of the odour of perfumes. The fragrance was pleasant and reached us. And of that tree ... I saw many fruits.[50] (*Ethiopic, Ap. Pet* 16)

> And the Lord showed me a very great region outside this world exceedingly bright with light, and the air of that place illuminated with the rays of the sun, and the earth itself flowering with blossoms that do not fade, and full of spices and plants, fair-flowering and incorruptible, and bearing blessed fruit.[51] (*Akhmim Ap. Pet.* 15)

Andreopoulos,[52] Dinkler[53] and Nes[54] all see distinct similarities with the Classe image. This paradisal garden stands out in contrast to the later Eastern tradition in which the mountain is portrayed as a bleak, craggy place bereft of vegetation. This later tradition would seem to infer from Mark's and Matthew's description of the mountain as 'high', that the summit was characterized by the arid, rocky vista one finds at higher altitudes. It has to be wondered whether there is any connection between Luke's removal of the adjective 'high' from his description of the mountain and the conception of the mountain as verdant here in Classe. If the paradisal garden is evidence of influence by the *Apocalypse of Peter*, then the Classe image is not just presenting the Transfiguration as a foretaste of the Eschaton but could also be specifically evoking the heavenly journey which Peter experiences in the *Apocalypse of Peter* and the vision of Paradise he has there.

A second point of possible contact between the *Apocalypse of Peter* and the Classe image concerns the large cross depicted in the centre of the apse. This bejeweled cross has been explained variously. Art historians have compared it with an extraordinarily wide range of other jeweled and glorious crosses depicted in mosaics and apses elsewhere.[55] Some commentators see it simply as

---

50. J. K. Elliott and M. R. James, *The Apocryphal New Testament: A Collection of Apocryphal Christian Literature in an English Translation* (Oxford: Clarendon Press, 1993), 610–11.

51. Ibid.

52. Andreopoulos, *Metamorphosis*, 119–20.

53. Dinkler, *Das Apsismosaik von S. Apollinare in Classe*, 95.

54. Nes and Moi, *The Uncreated Light*, 78–81.

55. See especially Dinkler, *Das Apsismosaik von S. Apollinare in Classe*, 50–72.

a figurative symbolizing of Jesus.[56] Others have read it as evoking the triumphal cross Constantine saw in the heavens[57] or as reference to the Cross as a gateway to Paradise.[58] However, others have also seen it as an eschatological reference to the sign of the Son of Man[59] mentioned at Mt. 24.30. The *Apocalypse of Peter* appears to interpret this as the Cross of Christ when it describes Jesus asserting, 'So I will come upon the clouds of heaven with a great host in my majesty; with my cross going before my face will I come in my majesty; shining seven times brighter than the sun will I come in my majesty with all my saints and angels.'[60] Whilst all three synoptic gospels precede the Transfiguration with prediction of his eschatological return by Jesus,[61] none so explicitly connects it with the image of a cross, as does the *Apocalypse of Peter*. It seems more than possible that this enigmatic cross with a small image of Christ's face at the centre could be an attempt to evoke the *Apocalypse of Peter*'s description of Jesus' Cross going 'before my face' at the Eschaton.

A third connection between the *Apocalypse of Peter* and the Classe mosaic concerns the evocation of Christ's Ascension. Some commentators have seen hints at various heavenly ascents in Classe's depiction of the Transfiguration. Both André Grabar[62] and Nordström[63] do not mention the *Apocalypse of Peter* at all, yet they see Apollinaris's place modelled on the traditional role taken by the Blessed Virgin Mary in Assumption scenes. They suggest that the image's origins are to be found in Palestinian depictions of heavenly ascents. Nordström also wonders whether the depiction of Moses and Elijah might be influenced by images showing the two angels who escort Jesus into heaven in Acts 1.[64] It is noteworthy that these two commentators, who seem otherwise to be unaware of the *Apocalypse of Peter*, see the Classe mosaic as evoking precisely the sort of ascension which the *Apocalypse of Peter* elaborates in detail.

A fourth similarity between the *Apocalypse of Peter* and the apse mosaic in Classe is the presence of twelve lambs at the bottom of the hill. It could be that this detail echoes the *Apocalypse of Peter*'s insistence that all the Twelve were present at the Transfiguration/Ascension scene it describes. Little consensus exists surrounding the exact significance of the sheep depicted in the image. Some commentators

---

56. Nordström, *Ravennastudien*, 122; Uehli, *Die Mosaiken von Ravenna*, 71–2; A. de Waal, 'Zur Ikonographie der Transfiguratio in der älteren Kunst', *Romische Quartalschrift* 16 (1902): 27.

57. Nes and Moi, *The Uncreated Light*, 75–6; Simson, *Sacred Fortress*, 43.

58. Ihm, *Die Programme der christlichen Apsismalerei*, 72.

59. Andreopoulos, *Metamorphosis*, 120–2; Dinkler, *Das Apsismosaik von S. Apollinare in Classe*, 75–87; Krüger, *Die Verklärung auf dem Berge*, 98.

60. Elliott and James, *The Apocryphal New Testament*, 600.

61. Mt. 16.28; Mk 9.1; Lk. 9.27.

62. Grabar, *Martyrium*, esp. 193–6.

63. Nordström, *Ravennastudien*, 125–30.

64. Ibid., 127.

hold them to represent the Twelve,[65] whilst others see them standing for the whole Christian community, petitioning Apollinaris for intercession.[66] Dinkler compares them with a wide range of other ancient depictions of lambs and finds it difficult to come to any unambiguous conclusion as to the identity of the Classe ones.[67] An obvious complexity associated with seeing these lambs as the Twelve is the presence of lambs representing Peter, James and John higher up in the apse, though those who see them as the Twelve tend simply to view them as being depicted twice. I have been unable to find any commentator refer to the *Apocalypse of Peter* in an attempt to identify these twelve lambs. Is it possible their presence is further evidence of an attempt to depict the Transfiguration in the light of Christ's Ascension into heaven akin to the way in which the *Apocalypse of Peter*'s vision of Paradise is followed by the disciples' witnessing of Christ's Ascension? The three lambs around Christ clearly represent Peter, James and John, but the twelve at the bottom of the apse could represent the Apostles witnessing his Ascension as described in the *Apocalypse of Peter*. Only the *Apocalypse of Peter* asserts *twelve* apostles to be present at the Ascension. The Luke/Acts Ascension presents *eleven*, with Judas not part of the group of eleven who witness it in Acts and Matthias not having been selected as an apostle yet.

The question remains how we are to evaluate these four connections which I have drawn between the Classe image and the *Apocalypse of Peter*. In all four cases, the only evidence available is that offered by a simple comparison of the mosaic with the *Apocalypse of Peter*. By no stretch of the imagination has this decisively proven a documentary link between the two. However, there is some weight in the cumulative argument I have made, showing how not just one, but several elements, of this mosaic might be more satisfactorily explained by reference to the *Apocalypse of Peter*. Even so, there remain distinct problems in working out the precise nature of any possible link with the *Apocalypse of Peter*. First, did the artists who designed this apse actually have access to a copy of the text of the *Apocalypse of Peter*, or was their knowledge of its narrative mediated by some other source or tradition? This is almost impossible to establish. Second, is the apse image intended as a simple presentation of one theological idea or text, which we can definitely identify, or is it intended as an evocation of a whole series of narratives, allusions, and motifs, of which the *Apocalypse of Peter* is but one?

At the very least, we may conclude that those who made the Classe image did not see the synoptic Transfiguration narratives and the sort of apocalyptic theological outlook embodied by the *Apocalypse of Peter* as mutually exclusive. Indeed, they saw them as complementary to each other and that this complementarity frequently revolved around the Lucan narrative. It is noteworthy how frequently both the Classe image and the *Apocalypse of Peter* draw upon details from the Lucan narrative. Reading the Lucan narrative as embodying the kind of apocalyptic interpretation

---

65. Andreopoulos, *Metamorphosis*, 123; Nes and Moi, *The Uncreated Light*, 76.
66. Grabar, *Martyrium*, 194; Nordström, *Ravennastudien*, 127–8.
67. Dinkler, *Das Apsismosaik von S. Apollinare in Classe*, 72–5.

which we find in the *Apocalypse of Peter* was possibly a far more frequent occurrence in the sixth century than some have realized. This coheres not just with many examples I have pointed to in the survey of patristic comment in previous chapters but also with the sort of argument Deichmann has offered.[68] He argues that the mosaic presents at once, in one image, a range of theological ideas and motifs which the artist understands the Transfiguration to touch upon and represent. In the light of that kind of interpretation, I argue that Classe presents Christ's Transfiguration as an entry into heavenly glory, embodying the 'exodus' Luke says Jesus was to accomplish in Jerusalem. In other words, the glorious cross evokes not just the Transfiguration and Christ's return but also the 'exodus' which enabled that, his death, Resurrection and Ascension, through which he leaves his disciples and returns to the Father.

Priestly motifs

Having made a renewed argument for the influence of the sort of thinking expressed in the *Apocalypse of Peter* on the Classe Transfiguration, we now explore a series of priestly and temple connected themes which it appears to embody. These priestly and temple themes become more pronounced when the role of St Apollinaris within the mosaic is taken into account.

A number of commentators have seen the figure of Apollinaris as the key to interpretation of the whole mosaic. Grabar, for example, places Classe within the context of a number of other Palestinian locations where the presence of martyrs' remains is connected with theophanies of Christ.[69] Nordström develops some of Grabar's ideas and sees the central figure of Apollinaris pointing forward echatologically to the Last Day.[70] Claudia Müller similarly sees the composition's presentation of the Transfiguration as a meditation on the Last Judgement, with Apollinaris as the pivotal interceding figure.[71] One of the most convincing and sustained arguments focusing on the importance of Apollinaris, however, has been offered by Simson.[72] He sees Apollinaris, whose relics were found below the altar under the mosaic, as the key figure in the whole composition, a figure who links the Transfiguration with the notion of martyrdom, sacrifice and priesthood. Simson argues that it is through martyrdom that Apollinaris comes to participate both in Christ's self-sacrifice and also his glory, from which position the bishop saint is able to offer intercession. Simson also recognizes the importance of the mosaic's eucharistic setting. He sees this as the liturgical context in which the miracle of transfiguration is experienced in the life of the faithful, as bread and wine, along with the lives of those participating in worship, are transformed. For Simson, the Mass links the idea of transfiguration with notions of sacrifice. He argues that

---

68. Deichmann, *Ravenna*, 253.
69. Grabar, *Martyrium*, esp. 193–6.
70. Nordström, *Ravennastudien*, 127–32.
71. Müller, 'Das Apsismosaik von S. Apollinare in Classe', esp. 43–50.
72. Simson, *Sacred Fortress*, 45–7, 53.

the place where this is seen particularly clearly is in the life of the martyrs, and in Apollinaris's life in particular. Apollinaris as a bishop and high priest mirrors the transfigured Christ. They are both priestly figures who attain glory through self-sacrifice, according to Simson.[73] It should be noted that reflection on the apse in the light of eucharistic and sacrificial ideas continues to be a characteristic of the way in which the apse is decorated in later years. An image of the three archetypal sacrificing figures of Melchizedek, Abel and Abraham mentioned in the Roman Canon, for example, is placed below the image in the seventh century.

Simson's reading of the apse mosaic in Classe is highly convincing. However, I wish to add to Simson's ideas by suggesting that recognition of the influence of ideas such as what we see in the *Apocalypse of Peter* strengthens his argument. He does not mention the *Apocalypse of Peter* at all in his treatment of the basilica. However, I have shown in Chapter 4 of this study a number of tabernacle and priestly motifs to be present in the *Apocalpse of Peter*'s presentation of the Transfiguration. It strikes me that the priestly motifs Simson sees emerge from the liturgical context of the mosaic's setting draw on and develop a conceptual background of priestly and temple themes associated with the Transfiguration, which were already present in the tradition of interpretation. These themes are embodied in the *Apocalypse of Peter* and frequently draw on details from Luke's version of the Transfiguration narrative.

Influence of the Sant'Apollinare in Classe mosaic

It is important to challenge the opinion voiced by Andreopoulos[74] and implicitly present in much comment on the apse mosaic in Sant'Apollinare in Classe that it stands isolated from the main traditions of Transfiguration interpretation. Our discussion of the apse mosaic has shown that many ancient traditions of Transfiguration interpretation can be detected in this image, especially the sort of priestly and temple motifs embodied in the *Apocalypse of Peter* and in other commentators whom we have surveyed in previous chapters. The image is far from disconnected from the traditions of interpretation which precede it. In the later sections of this chapter, it will be shown that it continues to influence depictions of the Transfiguration long after its creation in ways that many art historians have overlooked. It is far from being the case that the Classe apse is an orphaned image with no parents, and no progeny.

Santa Stephania, Naples

No unequivocal images of the Transfiguration survive in the West from the period between the construction of the basilica in Classe and the renaissance in Carolingian

---

73. Ibid., 45–7.
74. Andreopoulos, *Metamorphosis*, 117.

artistic creation at the beginning of the ninth century.[75] A characteristic of this ninth-century spate of mosaic construction is the frequent presentation of the Transfiguration narratives in the light of other portions of scripture, especially the book of Revelation. It is possible, however, that artistic interpretation in the light of Revelation 21 may have characterized the first images of the Transfiguration, which emerged earlier in the sixth century. In addition to the great mosaics found in Sinai and Classe we know of two other apse images of the Transfiguration, created in the sixth century in Naples and Constantinople, both now lost, but one of which, Santa Stephania in Naples, may have contained imagery from the book of Revelation.[76]

Between 535 and 555, Bishop John of Naples rebuilt his Cathedral of the Saviour after a fire, and there is inscription evidence[77] that the new cathedral contained an image of the Transfiguration, which has now been either lost or covered. Ihm is convinced it was probably modelled on that found at Sinai.[78] However, it is also likely that the image was somehow married with images from the book of Revelation. She points out that comments made by a seventeenth-century observer, Cesare Carraciolo, indicate the reason that the Cathedral of the Saviour was known as Santa Stephania was because of the images found in it of the Twenty-Four Elders casting their crowns before the Lord.[79] A neighbouring church of Santa Restituta was built onto Santa Stephania as part of an extension, replacing it as the cathedral in the thirteenth century. We know Santa Restituta definitely contained imagery of the Twenty-Four Elders and lampstands of Revelation 1 and 4. This has prompted Ihm to wonder whether Carraciolo is, in fact, confusing the two physically connected churches. Ihm's theory, although perfectly plausible, by no means represents conclusive evidence that Santa Stephania definitely did not contain such imagery. One might argue it to be equally plausible that the newer church of S. Restituta might have been echoing the internal decoration, already

---

75. Schiller, *Iconography of Christian Art*, 150, lists only two other known Transfiguration images apart from those discussed in this chapter dating from the ninth century: a largely destroyed depiction in the church of St Johann, Mustair, dating from the early ninth century and an image which is supposed to have formed part of the mosaic cycle in Old St Peter's, Rome, now lost.

76. One was in the Church of the Holy Apostles in Constantinople. Literary evidence from the twelfth-century writer Nicolaos Mesarites describes what seems to be a Transfiguration image in the north dome of the Church, which was built in Justinian's time. All that can be gleaned from this description is that the disicples all had a different pose, that Moses was distinguished by holding the Law, and Elijah by his camel skin mantle, and that John was shown asleep. It is difficult to draw any firm conclusions from Mesarites's devotional meditation concerning precisely what the image may have looked like. See ibid., 147.

77. For original text, with German translation see, August E. K. Heisenberg, *Grabeskirche und Apostelkirche, zwei Basiliken Konstantins* (Leipzig: J.C. Hinrichs,1908), 32–7.

78. Ihm, *Die Programme der christlichen Apsismalerei*, 70.

79. This is because Greek for 'crown' is 'stephanos'. See ibid., 177.

established, of the older Santa Stephania. It is unclear, therefore, exactly how these two sets of images are related to one another. All we know for sure is that Santa Stephania contained a monumental image of the Transfiguration and that Santa Restituta contained imagery from Revelation 1 and 4 of unknown date. It is possible, though not certain, that the now lost Transfiguration image in Santa Stephania was also surrounded by, or connected to, images from Revelation 4.

We see in these tantalizing hints at what the original Transfiguration image in Santa Stephania was like, possible evidence of the sort of Transfiguration interpretation focused on comparison with portions of the book of Revelation, which we noted in Chapter 7 as particularly characteristic of more 'corporate' Latin interpretation. It is far from easy to draw any definite conclusions from the fragmentary evidence that exists concerning Santa Stephania. However, we can say it is possible there existed a sixth-century monumental Transfiguration mosaic in Naples which also drew on imagery from the book of Revelation.

One of the first comparisons in the West between the Transfiguration and the book of Revelation, which still survives, is the decoration added to the apse mosaic in Classe some time after 804, by Leo III, after he visited the Basilica.[80] Over the apse image, he added in the archway a medallion depicting the face of Christ surrounded by the Four Creatures of Revelation 4. This frieze surmounted an image of two walled cities, out of which stream lambs ascending a hill to Christ. These images have been the focus of much discussion and debate, especially concerning the identity of the lambs, their dating and the relationship they have to the image of Christ and the Four Creatures above them.[81] However, the most important element for the purposes of the argument put forward by this study is the evidence the upper frieze offers concerning association of the Transfiguration with the description of the heavenly throne room in Revelation 4. Rotraut Wisskirchen convincingly shows that this addition by Leo III is intended to echo the depiction above the apse of St Paul's Outside the Walls in Rome of Revelation 4, in which Christ is surrounded by the Four Creatures and the Twenty-Four Elders.[82] She sees this as an attempt by Leo III to show the relationship of the see of Ravenna to Rome to be sisterly, but subordinate, by imposing imagery from one of Rome's greatest churches on the basilica in Classe. The creatures depicted here in Classe are not directly identical with the scene described in Revelation, and the fact that they each carry a book points to them also being depicted representing the four evangelists. The frieze in Classe also lacks any depiction of the Twenty-Four Elders. However, at least some evocation of Revelation 4 seems likely, especially in the light of the well-argued case proposed by Wisskirchen.

---

80. For further details of Leo's visits, see Rotraut Wisskirchen, 'Leo III und die Mosaikprogramme von S. Apollinaris in Classe in Ravenna und Santi Nereo e Achilleo in Rom', *Jahrbuch für Antike und Christentum* 34 (1991): 139–41.

81. For a good summary of this debate, see Deichmann, *Ravenna*, 279.

82. Wisskirchen, 'Leo III und die Mosaikprogramme', 141.

Figure 3 Ss. Nereo ed Achilleo, Rome.
Source: © Lawrence Lew, O.P.

If evocation of Revelation 4 can be detected in this frieze, then Leo III could be making a comparison between the Apostle John's experience of the Transfiguration and his being taken up in the Spirit through a heavenly door into heaven to witness the heavenly throne room of God in Revelation 4.

Santi Nereo e Achilleo, Rome

The placing by Leo III of this Revelation 4 archway scene over the apse mosaic is also linked with a proliferation of Transfiguration images which takes place in early-ninth-century Rome. Wisskirchen has pointed convincingly to connections between the mosaic programmes in Classe and those found in the Church of Santi Nereo e Achilleo, Rome.[83] Ten years after his adorning of the basilica in Classe, the earliest known depiction of the Transfiguration in Rome was created in 814 at Leo III's behest, during his rebuilding of the church entitled the *Titulus Fasciolae*, which had also been known as Santi Nereo e Achilleo. All that is left of Leo III's decoration of the apse of Santi Nereo e Achilleo is the arch mosaic of the Transfiguration over the apse. The apse mosaic was replaced by Cardinal Baronio in the sixteenth century with the fresco we see there today, but a sixteenth-century

---

83. Ibid., 139–41.

Figure 4 Close up of Transfiguration image, Ss. Nereo ed Achilleo, Rome.
Source: © Lawrence Lew, O.P.

image by Pompeo Ugonio found by Giovanni Battista de Rossi[84] still exists of the original apse, giving some idea of what it looked like before Baronio's alterations.[85] Wisskirchen[86] has shown the considerable number of similarities between Leo III's new Roman image and that which he had seen and further adorned in Classe. It appears Leo III's apse displayed a large cross against the background of a huge veil being approached by lambs on both sides. Wisskirchen[87] also points to the way in which Leo III's assembling of the relics of various martyrs under that image replicates the presence of Apollinaris's remains in Classe, and he argues that this creates a similar dynamic to that found in Classe, in which the martyrs are seen sharing the victory of Christ through their martyrdom.[88]

84. See, Giovanni Battista de Rossi, *Mosaici cristiani e saggi dei parimenti delle chiese di Roma anteriori al secolo xv., tavole cromo-litografiche con cenni storici et critici, con tr. francese* (Rome: Libreria Spithöver di Guglielmo Haass, 1872), vol. 1, 'Mosaico dell'arco della basilica urbana dei Santi Nereo e Achilleo'.

85. Pompeo Ugonio's image is reproduced in Richard Krautheimer, Spencer Corbett and Volfango Frankl, *Corpus Basilicarum Christianarum Romae: le basiliche cristiane antiche di Roma (Sec. IV-IX)* (Città del Vaticano; New York: Pontificio istituto di archeologia cristiana; Institute of Fine Arts, 1937), vol. 3, 149; drawing on Rossi's evidence, Wisskirchen, 'Leo III und die Mosaikprogramme', 142, also contains a sketched impression of what the sanctuary apse probably looked like after Leo's decoration.

86. Wisskirchen, 'Leo III und die Mosaikprogramme', 141–4.

87. Ibid., 143–4.

88. It was not, however, until Baronio's restoration of the church in the sixteenth century that the relics of Nereus and Achileus themselves finally made their way to the church which bore their name by the Baths of Caracalla, from the earlier basilica which bore their patronage by the Catacomb of Domitilla. See Umberto M. Fasola, *The Catacomb of Domitilla and the Basilica of Saints Nereus and Achilleus*, The Churches of Rome Illustrated (Rome: Marietti), 19–20.

However, there are also some considerable differences between this mosaic and that found in Classe. The image in Santi Nereo e Achilleo adopts a 'naturalistic' mode of depiction, unlike that found in Classe, and was separate from the apse cross. Whereas the image in Classe proposes the apse cross itself as representing the transfigured Christ, the incident here is presented over the apse. The Classe mosaic evokes a series of events and theological motifs as well at the Transfiguration. This contrasts with the arch image found in Santi Nereo e Achilleo which unequivocally presents solely the Transfiguration of Jesus. The connection between these two churches' apses is complex and possibly impossible to establish precisely, because the apse mosaic in Santi Nereo e Achilleo has been destroyed. At the very least, the iconographic and theological parallels pointed to between Classe and Santi Nereo e Achilleo by Wisskirchen significantly undermine the overly simplified view of Classe as an image exerting no influence at all on later Transfiguration imagery.

The Transfiguration is depicted under the same overshadowing cloud as two other images on either side, one of the Annunciation to the left and a second image of the Virgin and child on the right. These two marian images have experienced considerable scholarly neglect amongst art historians. Many studies of Santi Nereo e Achilleo make only the most cursory and fleeting mention of their presence. Some studies of the church do not even describe the marian images at all.[89] What little comment there is simply puts the presence of the surrounding images of the Virgin down to marian piety without offering much theological explanation as to how these three images might be connected, or indeed with the assertion that the three images are not related at all.[90] Amongst those who do comment on the two marian images, there tends to be a focus on the left-hand side Annunciation scene, with the right-hand scene left a largely unexplained mystery.[91] D. Giunta[92] has offered a reading based on seventh-century Roman opposition to Spanish adoptionism by showing Christ's divine birth and conception. Gaetano Curzi, by contrast, sees the images as Roman propaganda against Byzantine iconoclasm.[93]

---

89. No mention of the images of the Virgin are mentioned in discussion of Santi Nereo e Achilleo in Richard Krautheimer, *Rome: Profile of a City, 312–1308* (Princeton, NJ: Princeton University Press, 2000), 127–30; and Emile Mâle, *The Early Churches of Rome* (London: Ernest Benn, 1960), 152.

90. R. Garruchi, *Storia dell'arte Cristiana* (Prato: Guasti, 1877), vol. 4, 110; Marguerite van Berchem and Étienne Clouzot, *Mosaïques chrétiennes du IVme au Xme siècle* (Genève: Les presses de l'imprimerie du "Journal de Genève," 1924), 221; Guglielmo Matthiae, *Mosaici medioevali delle chiese di Roma* (Rome: Istituto Poligrafico dello Stato, Libreria dello Stato, 1967), 231; P. Toesca, *Il Medioevo* (Turin: Unione Typographico-Editrice Torinese, 1927), vol. 1, 394.

91. Krautheimer, Corbett and Frankl, *Corpus Basilicarum Christianarum*, 149.

92. D. Giunta, 'I mosaici dell'arco absidale della basilica dei Santi Nereo e Achilleo e l'erresia adozionista del sec. VII', in *Roma e l'eta carolingia* (Rome, 1976), 195–200.

93. Gaetano Curzi, 'La decorazione musiva della basilica dei Santi Nereo e Achilleo in Roma: materiali e ipotesi', *Arte Medievale* 7, no. 2 (1993): 145–235.

Little theological consensus exists, therefore, concerning an appropriate theological reading of these images.

In addition, many art historians hold the proportions of the Transfiguration mosaic to be infelicitous by virtue of it having been squeezed into the space at the apogee of the arch.[94] Agnese Guerrieri describes the archway mosaic as *rozzo*,[95] 'rough', and characterized by a certain *barbarie*,[96] or 'barbarousness', of style. Indeed, Walter Oakeshott, after describing the Transfiguration image as 'awkward', sees the whole composition as displaying iconoclastic tendencies and to be the second-rate work of incompetents, which, for him, explains why Baronio got rid of the mosaic in the sixteenth century.[97] I want to show these negative views to be misjudged and to conjecture that these three images are, in fact, intimately related to each other and are the product of complex theological reflection.

One obvious connection which the artist would seem to be making through the Annunciation scene on the left-hand side of the arch is with the overshadowing which Mary receives by the power of the Holy Spirit. We have seen in Chapter 7 that a recurrent theme in Western comment, and especially in Ambrose's *Commentary of the Gospel According to Luke*, was to associate the overshadowing cloud with the activity of the Holy Spirit. It could be that we see here a visual presentation of the connection he made between Lk. 9.34 and Lk. 1.35,[98] a depiction of two parallel overshadowings under the same cloud. In both, the Spirit reveals Jesus' sonship, one through Gabriel's words that Mary's baby will be 'called Son of God'[99] and in the other through a voice from heaven proclaiming him to be 'my son, my chosen'.[100]

It has to be admitted the imagery on the right-hand side of the apse is more difficult to explain. Perhaps when set in the light of the evidence we have surveyed in Chapter 7 we see here a more extended meditation on the incarnation as a fulfilment of Isaiah 7 and possible influence from the *Protoevangelium of James*. We explored in Chapter 7 Ambrose's and Jerome's discussion of the Transfiguration as the fulfilment of Isa. 7.11. Could it be that we see here the depiction of their discussion? In the middle of the arch we see the sign Ahaz would not ask for (cf. Isa. 7.11), as high as heaven (Elijah, who ascended there) and low as Sheol (Moses,

---

94. Guglielmo Matthiae, *Le chiese di Roma dal IV al X Secolo*, Roma Christiana (Bologna: Cappelli, 1962), 271.

95. Agnese Guerrieri, *La chiesa dei Santi Nereo e Achilleo* (Città del Vaticano: Società Amici Catacombe presso Pontificio Istituto di Archeologia Cristiana, 1951), 121–2; Matthiae, *Le chiese di Roma*, 271.

96. Guerrieri, *La chiesa dei Santi Nereo e Achilleo*, 121–2; Ihm, *Die Programme der christlichen Apsismalerei*, 74–5.

97. Walter Oakeshott, *The Mosaics of Rome from the Third to the Fourteenth Centuries* (London: Thames & Hudson, 1967), 200.

98. *Expos in Lucam* 7.19.

99. Lk. 1.35.

100. Lk. 9.35.

Figure 5 Close up of Annunciation scene, Ss. Nereo ed Achilleo, Rome.
Source: © Lawrence Lew, O.P.

The Earliest Depiction of the Transfiguration 173

Figure 6 Close up of virgin and child, Ss. Nereo ed Achilleo, Rome.
Source: © Lawrence Lew, O.P.

who died and whose grave nobody can locate). On either side, however, is the sign the Lord announced he would give instead (cf. Isa. 7.14), a virgin, on the left, conceiving, by the overshadowing of the Spirit, and on the right, sitting, having borne her son.

Chapter 7 of this study showed a number of connections to have been made in the *Protevangelium Of James*, between the Transfiguration and the place of Christ's birth as a temple space overshadowed by God's glory, which may have influenced Origen's, Jerome's and Ambrose's thinking. Traditions similar to those found in the *Protevangelium of James* may be present in the presentation of the Annunciation here. If one examines carefully the Annunciation scene on the left, Mary holds two spindles. The idea that she was spinning the veil of the Temple when Gabriel visited her is one we see described for the first time in the *Protevangelium of James*. In chs 10 and 11[101] of the *Protevangelium of James*, Gabriel appears between her putting down the red yarn, drawing a jug of water and then taking up the purple yarn. This spinning tradition found in the *Protevangelium of James* seems to be exerting a strong influence on this depiction of the Annunciation. If there is evidence of influence from the *Protevangelium of James* on the image on the left, could it be that the seated virgin on the right is also influenced by that text? The *Protevangelium of James* recounts the appearance of a blinding light under an overshadowing cloud at Jesus' nativity, which prevents the narrator from seeing Christ's actual birth but reveals a baby on his mother's knee, feeding.[102] Does the depiction on the right of this apse display the same hesitancy at describing the actual birth, which we explored in Chapter 7 and is seen in the *Protevangelium of James*, and simply presents the baby having been born?

The more puzzling elements within this series of images make some sense when read in the light of the portions of Ambrose, Jerome and the *Protevangelium of James* which I examined in Chapter 7. I am aware that much of the theory propounded here can be no more than hypothesis. The weakest part of this argument is the status of the image on the right of the arch. I am also unable to explain satisfactorily the presence of the angel figure who looks like Gabriel. The exact nature of any influence from the *Protevangelium of James* is also a remarkably complicated issue. It may be more than possible that elements from the *Protevangelium of James*, such as the association of the Annunciation with spinning, remained part of iconographic tradition long after the text itself ceased to circulate in a complete form. However, even with all these caveats made, I hope to have shown at the very least that it is possible that the Transfiguration is being used here to make a series of hermeneutic connections with texts associated with the incarnation. It is certainly the case that the neglect this earliest depiction of the Transfiguration in Rome has suffered is short-sighted, and that the scholarly consensus that it is of little note and limited sophistication is misjudged. An examination of the reception history of the Transfiguration in both commentary and artistic depiction has revealed the

---

101. Guerrieri, *La chiesa dei Santi Nereo e Achilleo*, 111.
102. *Prot. Jas.* 19.2; Elliott and James, *The Apocryphal New Testament*, 64.

possibility of a fascinating seam of interpretation, which otherwise could have gone almost entirely unnoticed.

Paschal I and depictions of the Transfiguration in ninth-century Rome

In the next section of this chapter, we examine a number of depictions of the Transfiguration which emerge in Rome under the papacy of Paschal I, a few years after Leo III constructed the first Roman image of the Transfiguration, which we have just examined. We see in them readings of the Transfiguration which compare it with portions of the book of Revelation and which present the episode as a visionary entry into God's heavenly paradise.

Paschal I's building project

One fruit of the Carolingian Renaissance in Rome was an extensive rebuilding project undertaken by Pope Paschal I, who reigned from 817 to 24, to renew and extend a number of the city's basilicas, often as a preparation for the translation of saints' relics to new and more imposing shrines. He undertook the reconstruction of three basilicas in the years 818–22: Santa Prassede, Santa Maria in Domnica and Santa Cecilia.[103] Caroline Goodson[104] and Thomas Noble[105] have pointed to the significance of these three churches' location in highly populated parts of Rome and the political importance of the papal stational liturgies that took place in them. The significance of this period for our study, however, lies in the sudden and frequent appearance in Rome of depictions of the Transfiguration in these restored or rebuilt churches.

The heavenly Jerusalem scene in Santa Prassede, Rome

The Basilica of Santa Prassede was originally built in 780 by Hadrian I on top of a fifth-century structure, the traditional burial site of the sister martyrs Praxedes and Pudentiana. The church was substantially rebuilt by Paschal I in 822 in order to rehouse the remains of over two thousand saints brought into the city from the

---

103. The two titular churches of S. Prassede on the Esquiline Hill, S. Cecilia in Trastevere and the diaconia church of S. Maria in Domnica.

104. Caroline Goodson, *The Rome of Paschal I: Papal Power, Urban Renovation, Church Building, and Relic Translation 817–824* (Cambridge: Cambridge University Press, 2010), esp. 81–159.

105. Thomas Noble, 'Topography, Celebration, and Power: The Making of a Papal Rome in the Eighth and Ninth Centuries', in *Topographies of Power in the Early Middle Ages*, ed. Mayke De Jong (Leiden: Brill, 2001), 45–91, esp. 83–91.

Figure 7 S. Prassede, Rome.
Source: © Peter Anthony.

Figure 8 Close up of heavenly Jerusalem, S. Prassede, Rome.
Source: © Peter Anthony.

Figure 9 Moses figure in the heavenly Jerusalem scene, S. Prassede, Rome. Source: © Peter Anthony.

catacombs.[106] This restoration included the addition of an extensive series of apse mosaics over the altar depicting scenes from Revelation 1, 4 and 21.

The reason these images are significant for the purposes of this study is the presence of two figures who resemble the prophet witnesses of the Transfiguration within a walled city depicting the heavenly Jerusalem of Revelation 21. A broad majority of commentators identify these two men as Moses and Elijah,[107] though a small minority has questioned this.[108] This identification rests principally on the

---

106. The Liber Pontificalis (LP 100:9) claims 2,000 saints were transferred to S. Prassede. A marble inscription in the church itself records 86 saints by name and then lists the total number reinterred by Paschal at S. Prassede as 2,300: 'fiunt etiam in simul omnes s(an)c(t) I duomilla CCC' (see Goodson, *The Rome of Paschal I*, 167 and 228).

107. Wolfgang Braunfels and Engelbert Kirschbaum, *Lexikon der christlichen Ikonographie*, 8 vols (Rom: Herder, 1968), vol. 3, 293; Dinkler, *Das Apsismosaik von S. Apollinare in Classe*, 25–50; Mâle, *The Early Churches of Rome*, 90; Matthiae, *Mosaici medioevali delle chiese di Roma*, 238; van Berchem and Clouzot, *Mosaïques chrétiennes du IVme au Xme siècle*; Rotraut Wisskirchen, *Das Mosaikprogramm von S. Prassede in Rom: Ikonographie und Ikonologie*, Jahrbuch für Antike und Christentum Ergänzungsband (Münster: Aschendorff, 1990), 91.

108. Oakeshott sees the figure on the right, because of his long hair, as John the Baptist, and the left-hand one, because of his youth, as John the Evangelist. Wisskirchen points out that although John the Baptist is frequently depicted with long hair, it is hardly ever white,

Figure 10 Close up of Elijah figure in heavenly Jerusalem scene, S. Prassede, Rome. Source: © Peter Anthony.

presence of a tablet or scroll in the hands of the young man to the left, bearing the word 'Lege'. This could point to the Law through the instruction, 'read', or, alternatively, the young man's hand could be seen as covering the last letter of the word 'Leges', rendering it a tablet of the 'laws' given to Moses on Mount Sinai. In addition, many point out the close correlation between these two figures and depictions of Moses and Elijah elsewhere in the guise of a younger and an older man, especially in the Church of Santi Nereo and Achilleo built only a few years before by Paschal I's predecessor but one, Leo III.[109] This identification is also strengthened by the fact that two further portrayals of the Transfiguration are to be found in other churches beautified by Paschal: another depiction in the St Zeno Chapel of Santa Prassede and a further image of Moses and Elijah in the apse arch of Santa Maria in Domnica pointing to it as a biblical subject favoured by Paschal.

---

as here in S. Prassede. It is also unclear what the connection would be between the concept of 'Law' or 'reading' displayed in the left-hand figure's scroll and John the Evangelist. Van Berchem and Clouzot also discuss the possibility of these two figures being Isaiah and Jeremiah but judge it to be unlikely by virtue of the fact that the prophets of the exile both tended to be portrayed as older men. See Oakeshott, *The Mosaics of Rome*, 207; van Berchem and Clouzot, *Mosaïques chrétiennes du IVme au Xme siècle*, 233; Wisskirchen, *Das Mosaikprogramm von S. Prassede in Rom*, 88.

109. Wisskirchen, *Das Mosaikprogramm von S. Prassede in Rom*, 89.

Two significant interpretations of this arch have been offered by Wisskirchen and Marchita Mauck. Wisskirchen[110] reads the triumphal arch as having a fundamentally eschatological orientation, pointing forward to the Parousia. She sees the presence of Transfiguration elements as an allusion to the light of the city mentioned at Rev. 21.24 and as an evocation of Isa. 60.19. She interprets the presence of Moses and Elijah simply as confirmation of her eschatological reading of the whole arch. Mauck[111] offers a very different interpretation. She points to the ways in which the arch shows the many ranks of people who enter the heavenly Jerusalem described in the funeral antiphons *In Paradisum* and *In Regnum Dei*. She argues that the Roman liturgy used for the reinterring of saints' relics was essentially a funeral rite, which would have used these texts. She concludes that what we see here in the arch is a depiction of the liturgical texts which were used on the day the church was dedicated by Paschal I, situating his assiduous care for the remains of Rome's saints, and the papal liturgy which inaugurated this new church, within the timeless worship of heaven.

Whilst Mauck and Wisskirchen offer insightful and useful interpretations, neither really sees just how novel and innovative the presence of Moses and Elijah in this Revelation 21 scene is. Mauck's theory concerning the influence of texts such as *In Paradisum* is by no means implausible. However, it offers no explanation as to why Moses and Elijah should be present within this image. She essentially ignores their 'mysterious'[112] presence, dismissing them as 'idiosyncratic with the context of the program'.[113] Very few people have attempted to explain the significance of Moses's and Elijah's depiction in this heavenly Jerusalem scene, and no satisfactory account for their presence has emerged. I outline here six parallels between the Transfiguration narratives and Revelation 21 which may explain their being read in the light of each other and the connections drawn by Paschal between these two texts, by depicting them together in one image.

Mountain-top visions

The first parallel possibly being drawn is the way in which the Transfiguration and John's vision of the heavenly Jerusalem could both be seen as mountain-top visions. Rev. 21.10 explicitly uses the language of ecstatic vision in connection with a mountain top, speaking of John being taken 'in the spirit' to a high mountain. Mention of a 'high mountain' is also a feature found in both Mark's and Matthew's Transfiguration narrative. This mosaic could be pointing to a parallel in the experience of John on Patmos and John (and the other two disciples) on Mount Tabor, whose visionary experience takes place 'in the spirit' and is preceded by

110. Ibid., 63–99, 119–23.
111. Marchita Mauck, 'The Mosaic of the Triumphal Arch of S. Prassede: A Liturgical Interpretation', *Speculum* 62, no. 4 (1987): 813–28.
112. Ibid., 814.
113. Ibid.

being led up a mountain.[114] The presence of an angel holding a measuring stick close to Elijah underlines this parallel further.[115] If this represents the angel of Rev. 21.15, then Elijah's experience of the Transfiguration is also compared with John's ascent to view the holy city in Rev. 21.9.

Glory

A second parallel concerns vision of God's glory. Revelation 21.11 describes the Holy City as possessing the 'glory of God'. At Rev. 21.23, this is interpreted in terms of light: God's glory is the city's light; its presence is also the reason why the city does not need sun or moon; and the source of that glory, the city's lamp, is the Lamb. The Transfiguration narratives also describe an experience involving light, something particularly emphasized in Luke's version by the addition of the word *glory* to his narrative. The frequent connection of *glory* with the cultic presence of God in the tabernacle and temple allows the mosaicist to point to both Revelation 21 and the Transfiguration as comparable mountain-top visions involving an experience of God's presence seen as glory within his heavenly temple dwelling.[116]

Cloud

A third parallel which could point to a connection between the Transfiguration and this depiction of Revelation 21 is the presence of a cloud over the Holy City. There is no mention of any clouds in Revelation 21. This detail could, therefore, be seen as a direct importing of the overshadowing cloud from the Transfiguration narratives. However, the City is described as descending from heaven (Rev. 21.2, 10), and so its emergence out of clouds could simply be a way of portraying the city's descent. It is more than possible these clouds are intended to evoke both those points; it would seem difficult to exclude entirely the idea that at least some reference to the cloud of the Transfiguration is being made. If this is so, the artist could be suggesting that the space overshadowed by the Transfiguration cloud is comparable with the heavenly Jerusalem depicted here.

---

114. The traditional ascription of Revelation to the Apostle John would, of course, also make him the subject of both visions, though the figure of John does not seem to be emphasized here in S. Prassede.

115. Wisskirchen wonders if this might be the angel of Revelation 10. In the end she concludes that he points to Elijah as some sort of generic precursor or forerunner figure. See Wisskirchen, *Die Mosaikprogramm von S. Prassede in Rom*, 91–3.

116. Schiller points to another instance of the Transfiguration being compared with other scriptural passages involving the word *doxa* in the Pala D'Oro, a Milanese golden altar frontal created not more than twenty years after the S. Prassede images, in which the Transfiguration is placed between depictions of the Presentation in the Temple and the Wedding in Cana of Galilee. A similar process of connection through the notion of glory

Figure 11 Close up of Christ in the heavenly Jerusalem, S. Prassede, Rome. Source: © Peter Anthony.

Exodus

A fourth parallel which might be drawn between the Transfiguration narratives and Revelation 21 is one which focuses on an element present solely in Luke's gospel, namely the mention of the topic of conversation on the mountain top being the 'exodus' Jesus was to accomplish in Jerusalem.[117] It could be, as I have argued is the case in Classe, that this mosaic scene is intended as a depiction of the exodus discussed on the Mount of Transfiguration, an exodus in which Jesus leaves the earthly Jerusalem and enters the heavenly one. This parallel could explain the presence of two angels on either side of Jesus in the middle of the mosaic as a reference to the two men in bright clothing present at Jesus' Ascension in Acts. It may be that this mosaic seeks to present the connection already made between the Transfiguration and the Ascension through Luke's phrase 'behold two men'. If this is the case, the mosaic reads the Transfiguration as a similar entry by Jesus into the dwelling place of God in heaven. It could be that we see here the 'exodus' in Jerusalem discussed by Jesus, Moses and Elijah being realized before them: Jesus, after accomplishing his work in the earthly Jerusalem, is depicted reigning in the

---

seems to be at work here but, in this case, linking the Transfiguration with very different passages (Lk. 9.31/Jn 2.11/Lk. 2.32). See Schiller, *Iconography of Christian Art*, 150.

117. Lk. 9.31.

celestial Jerusalem, having entered the heavenly tabernacle accompanied by the two angelic men of Acts 1.10.

Revelation 11

A fifth parallel between the Transfiguration narratives and this heavenly Jerusalem scene revolves around Rev. 11.1-13. In Revelation 11, there is a description of two enigmatic prophet figures, several features of which seem to cohere with elements of the Transfiguration narratives. These two figures both have the characteristics of Moses and Elijah, being able to close the heavens[118] and to turn water into blood,[119] though they are never explicitly named as such. However, other elements of Revelation 11 have no parallel with the Transfiguration narratives, such as the prophets killing their enemies with fire, their dying at the hands of the Beast, being raised in the earthly Jerusalem and subsequently transported to heaven on a cloud. Further complexity is added by the fact that Revelation 11 points to Moses more as an eschatological figure than the lawgiver he is presented as here. In addition, the two figures of Revelation 11 *both* share the characteristics of Moses and Elijah, rather than each being separate embodiments of the two prophets as presented in the synoptic narratives. It is also the case that the prophets' prophesying takes place *outside* the temple in Rev. 11.2-3 rather than inside the walls as Moses and Elijah are depicted here. It is important to note that the angel holding the measuring rod next to Elijah is far more likely to be a reference to Rev. 21.15 than to Rev. 11.1, as the measuring rod of 11.1 is given to John the seer and is not held by an angel. Although Revelation 11 may be a strong influence, it can't *on its own* account exhaustively for the depiction of Moses and Elijah in this scene. Revelation 11 does, however, point to one other context in which two mosaic and Elijan figures are closely linked with God's temple in Jerusalem (Rev. 11.1, 8), with standing in the presence of God (Rev. 11.4) and in which they are perceived as figures who experience an ascent into heaven (Rev. 11.12). As such, this could point to Revelation 11 operating as an intertext, allowing the synoptic Transfiguration narratives to be read side by side with Revelation 21.

Temple connections

One of the characteristics of Revelation 21's description of the New Jerusalem is that it is a temple space, in which God's presence is freely available to all who dwell there. Revelation 21.22 does not state that there is no temple in the city but that John did not *see* one, for 'the Lord God the Almighty and the Lamb' constitute its temple. The vision recounted by Revelation 21, therefore, is one in which the whole space of the city is a temple. This is particularly pointed to in Rev. 21.16 where the city is described as four square, with equal height, width and

---

118. Cf. Elijah in 1 Kgs 17.1 and 18.1.
119. Cf. Moses in Exod. 7.14-19.

length, echoing the cubic proportions of the Holy of Holies[120] in the Jerusalem Temple.[121] A further allusion to the whole of the holy city being a temple space is the language used at Rev. 21.3, describing God's dwelling in that city in terms of a 'tabernacle' (σκηνὴ), echoing the language of the wilderness tradition concerning Moses's earthly tabernacle. If Paschal I is drawing a comparison between the Transfiguration narratives and Revelation 21's account of the New Jerusalem, then one of the parallels being presented here in Santa Prassede could be the Transfiguration as a visionary experience of God's presence conceived of as a temple dwelling.

Santa Prassede: Conclusion

The presence of imagery from the Transfiguration within this depiction of Revelation 21 reveals a series of important points being made by Paschal I about the Transfiguration. One of the most significant of these must be the shared status of Revelation 21 and the Transfiguration as texts claiming to be the fruit of visionary experience. Paschal I's mosaic shares the Western tendency which we detected in Chapter 7 of interpreting the Transfiguration in terms of a corporate vision of the life of heaven and of understanding it as an experience akin to seeing the heavenly temple dwelling of God which is revealed in Revelation 21. In addition to this, it is possible that several key elements only found in Luke's narrative are important in many of the connections Paschal I makes, such as those revolving around the *exodus* Jesus was to accomplish in Jerusalem and the notion of *glory*. It is clear that the significance of this mosaic as, in part, an interpretation of the Transfiguration has been largely neglected in the reception history of the Transfiguration, and that few have noticed the striking points that could be being made by Paschal I through his comparison of the Transfiguration with John of Patmos's vision of the heavenly Jerusalem.

I want to suggest that the presence of the saints' relics within Santa Prassede makes the reading I have outlined more convincing. Paschal's transferring of relics to Santa Prassede enables him to articulate a broader notion of sacred space. Goodson[122] has written extensively on the way in which Paschal I's building programme was designed to emphasize and aggrandize the political power of the papal court. Indeed, she argues that Paschal I's reinterring programme was designed to emphasize the whole of the city of Rome, the Pope's seat, as, in some sense, 'sacred space'. She points to the heavenly city depicted in the triumphal arch in Santa Prassede as, in part, a depiction of Rome, a dwelling place of the saints, whose gates are guarded by the city's apostolic patrons Peter and Paul. It

---

120. 1Kgs 6.20.

121. Wisskirchen, in fact, argues that the city presented here in the triumphal arch is indeed square but that the perspective of the space it is placed in makes it seem wider. See Wisskirchen, *Das Mosaikprogramm von S. Prassede in Rom*, 87–93.

122. Goodson, *The Rome of Paschal I*, esp. 197–256.

Figure 12 Transfiguration image, St Zeno Chapel, S. Prassede, Rome.
Source: © Peter Anthony.

is almost impossible not to see a connection between the scenes depicted in the Santa Prassede mosaics and their being situated in a liturgical space in which are enshrined the physical remains of many of those same saints. Finding motifs from the Transfiguration amongst such a theological scheme points to the very great likelihood of the Transfiguration being interpreted in this context as a similar entry into the heavenly Jerusalem which the saints share with God, and of worship in that church being seen as experience of a similar reality.

St Zeno Chapel in Santa Prassede, Rome

As a way of contextualizing the mosaics we have examined in Santa Prassede, we next examine other depictions of the Transfiguration in structures erected by Paschal I, in which I argue that one can detect a series of theological motifs which support the reading we have brought to bear on the Transfiguration elements in the sanctuary mosaics of Santa Prassede.

Two other Transfiguration images exist: one in the St Zeno Chapel of Santa Prassede and one in the apse of the church of Santa Maria in Domnica, both created at Paschal I's behest. The image in the St Zeno Chapel is undoubtedly of the Transfiguration, but largely destroyed; the image in Santa Maria in Domnica is in excellent condition, but its designation as a Transfiguration scene is debated. The first point to be made about both of these images must be the simple fact that their presence in two of the three churches Paschal I rebuilt points to the

Transfiguration as having been a clear focus of some theological interest to him. However, the fact that all three depictions are significantly different from each other shows this fascination not to be with the Transfiguration as a static image or fixed narrative but rather as a flexible theological lens through which other narratives and theological motifs can be explored and depicted.

The St Zeno Chapel was substantially rebuilt and adorned by Paschal I as a mausoleum for his mother and, though very small indeed (3.5 square metres), is completely filled with an extraordinary array of mosaics.[123] As one enters the chapel, on the wall directly facing the visitor are the remains of a Transfiguration image, about two-thirds of which have been destroyed to make way for a thirteenth-century icon of the Blessed Virgin, housed in a seventeenth-century altarpiece. All that one can see are the heads of five figures: Christ in the middle; Moses and Elijah on each side; and just visible, two of the three apostles, probably Peter on the left and John on the right; and on the far right is a disembodied hand and a hint at what could be the outline of the head of a third apostle. This appears to be a very different evocation of the Transfiguration from that seen over the high altar, and to be more in keeping with the sort of naturalistic depiction seen in Santi Nereo e Achilleo, which will have been created only ten to fifteen years earlier. Three small, but significant, points need to be made about this mosaic.

First, it is notable just how closely the figures of Moses and Elijah here mirror the two figures I have pointed to in the triumphal heavenly Jerusalem scene over the altar of Santa Prassede. Although Moses and Elijah are on opposite sides of Christ here from the arch scene, and although Moses does not hold a tablet of the Law, they replicate the depiction there of Elijah as an older, grey-headed man and Moses as a younger man with short, dark hair. This image offers considerable resolution to the question of the identity of the figures in the triumphal arch against those who claim there is no evocation at all of Moses and Elijah in the Revelation 21 scene.

Second, there is ambiguity concerning the mandorla of glory, which appears to encompass Peter but not John. The inclusion of Moses and Elijah within the mandorla of glory sets this image apart from that seen at Santi Nereo e Achilleo, where only Christ is in the central nimbus. There is disagreement amongst commentators as to what the dark line which seems to delineate the mandorla represents and whether it includes the disciples or not. Wisskirchen has argued that it outlines not the mandorla of glory but the mountain.[124] However, this would

---

123. For illustrations and brief descriptions of the chapel's history, see, Paola Gallio, *The Basilica of Saint Praxedes* (Rome: Monaci Benedictini Vallombrosani, 2009), 25-37; Krautheimer, Corbett and Frankl, *Corpus Basilicarum Christianarum Romae*, 252-5; Matthiae, *Le chiese di Roma*, 233-42; *Mosaici medioevali delle chiese di Roma*, 239; Rotraut Wisskirchen, *Die Mosaiken der Kirche Santa Prassede in Rom* (Mainz am Rhein: Verlag Philipp von Zabern, 1992), 54-65.

124. Wisskirchen, *Die Mosaiken der Kirche Santa Prassede in Rom*, 57.

Figure 13 Close up of the Transfiguration image, St Zeno Chapel, S. Prassede, Rome. Source: © Peter Anthony.

seem not to include the figure on the right, and leave the mountain an odd, lopsided shape. Most hold it to show the extent of the glory in which Jesus, Elijah and Moses appear.[125] However, on the left of the image, this green line appears to have been extended out to include Peter in the glory. A number of different explanations have been offered, not least that this shows recognition of the ambiguity concerning whether the disciples enter the cloud with Jesus. Some have wondered whether this line was added later as some sort of theological correction[126] or as an attempt to include the disciples as recognition of the more explicit description in Luke's gospel of his entry.[127] If that is the case, perhaps agreement was unable to be found amongst the mosaic's creators concerning whether Peter was to be included within the glory or not. It is equally possible that the confused image might simply be a sign of artistic incompetence or mistake.

Third, it is important to note a number of local traditions concerning the chapel, which point to it being seen as a paradise and as a Holy of Holies, and to associations of the chapel with visionary activity. The St Zeno Chapel itself is

---

125. Goodson, *The Rome of Paschal I*, 169; Josef Wilpert and Walter Nikolaus Schumacher, *Die römischen Mosaiken der kirchlichen Bauten vom iv.-xiii. Jahrhundert* (Freiburg im Breisgau: Herder, 1976), 335.

126. Dinkler, *Das Apsismosaik von S. Apollinare in Classe*, 31.

127. Nordström sees evidence of strong influence on this image by the Lucan narrative (*Ravennastudien*, 123).

square in shape, with every inch covered in gold mosaics. Some suspect Paschal I rebuilt the chapel using at least one partially pre-existing wall, and that it may have inherited its shape from the previous building.[128] Even though the chapel is actually taller than it is wide, upon entering the chapel, one is immediately struck by the cubic feel of the space. It may be that some sort of cubic Holy of Holies is being evoked. Indeed, both Paola Gallio and Emile Mâle point to a Roman tradition of uncertain age, but possibly ancient, in which this chapel is referred to by locals as the 'Hortus Paradisi'.[129] Many of the arches in the chapel are decorated with lush flowers and plants. This local name could simply be a reference to that. However, may we perhaps wonder whether this local tradition stems from a deeper theological statement being made about the Transfiguration, the first image one sees upon entry into the chapel, as the revelation of a paradisal place of God's dwelling, such as we saw in Classe? Could this chapel also evoke, through its square proportions, the Holy of Holies, so often portrayed in Old Testament tradition as a new Eden and described as having been decorated with flowers and palm trees?[130] Gallio also points to another name which the chapel has traditionally had, being also dedicated to Our Lady under the title *Sancta Maria, Libera nos a Poenis Inferni*. She states this stems from a vision Paschal I himself is supposed to have had, whilst saying Mass in the chapel, of the soul of his nephew being released from Purgatory and taken to heaven.[131] Could it be more than simple coincidence that a place known as a paradisal garden, and which echoes the proportions of the Holy of Holies, became known in local tradition as the place in which Paschal I, the church's saintly rebuilder, was supposed to have had a vision of heaven? Many of these questions cannot be answered definitively but do point to intriguing possibilities concerning the way in which Paschal I's image of the Transfiguration may have prompted local tradition to see the chapel as a Holy of Holies and as a place where vision of heaven took place.

Santa Maria in Domnica

The church of Santa Maria in Domnica was also rebuilt and substantially adorned by Paschal I. The mosaic figures of greatest interest for our discussion here are those on either side of the apse over the altar, pointing up to a frieze containing Christ flanked by the two angels and the Twelve Apostles in a paradisal garden.

---

128. G. Baldracco, 'La cripta della chiesa di Santa Prassede', *Revista di Archeologia Cristiana* 18 (1941): 277–96.
    129. Gallio, *The Basilica of Saint Praxedes*, 25; Mâle, *The Early Churches of Rome*, 91.
    130. See 1 Kings 6.
    131. Gallio, *The Basilica of Saint Praxedes*, 25.

Figure 14 S. Maria in Domnica, Rome.
Source: © Peter Anthony.

The identification of these two figures is contested. Some see them as Moses and Elijah,[132] whilst others have suggested they could be John the Baptist and John the Evangelist,[133] or even Isaiah and Jeremiah.[134] The figure on the right is presented in a manner very similar to the Moses images in Santa Prassede, as a younger, clean shaven man with short hair. The only difference with the other images is that here Moses is dressed in a red toga and carries a scroll rather than a tablet depicting the Law. The other figure is very unlike all the Elijan figures we have examined in this chapter. Here he is presented as a younger but mature man with long hair and a full, dark beard. He wears a yellow tunic with a brown mantle, which has prompted some to see him as a John the Baptist figure. He resembles very strongly the individual widely identified as the Baptist in the heavenly Jerusalem scene in Santa Prassede,[135] particularly as a result of his brown and yellow clothing, a frequent artistic convention associated with the forerunner. It strikes me, however,

---

132. Guglielmo Matthiae, *S. Maria in Domnica*, Chiese di Roma Illustrate (Roma: Marietta, 1960), 42; *Le chiese di Roma dal IV al X secolo*, 274; *Mosaici medioevali delle chiese di Roma*, 237; Floriana Svizzereto, 'Il mosaico absidale, manifesto iconoduluo: proposta di interpretazione', in *Caulius I: Santa Maria in Domnica, San Tommaso in Formis e il Clivus Scauri*, ed. Alia Englen (Rome: Palensesti Romani, 2003), 249.

133. Goodson, *The Rome of Paschal I*, 153; Oakeshott, *The Mosaics of Rome*, 241.

134. van Berchem and Clouzot, *Mosaïques chrétiennes*, 241.

135. Wisskirchen, *Das Mosaikprogramm von S. Prassede in Rom*, 94.

Figure 15 John the Baptist/Elijah figure close up in S. Maria Domnica, Rome.
Source: © Peter Anthony.

Figure 16 S. Maria in Domnica, Moses figure close up.
Source: © Peter Anthony.

Figure 17 Close up of chancel arch, S. Maria in Domnica.
Source: © Peter Anthony.

that much of this debate takes place in apparent ignorance of the notion that it may not be problematic that the Elijan figure in this arrangement looks like John the Baptist. John is frequently portrayed as an Elijah figure in the synoptic gospels.[136] In fact, this question is closely linked with the discussion which takes place directly after the Transfiguration in Matthew and Mark in which Jesus explicitly describes John as Elijah.[137] We might see here interpretation of the Transfiguration in which that conversation is evoked through presentation of Elijah as John the Baptist.

A further question is precisely what is being presented in this series of images over the sanctuary arch. In the light of our discussion of the images in Santa Prassede, it could be the case that we see here a very similar combining of the Transfiguration with imagery of Christ seated in heavenly glory presented in paradisal terms. Here heaven is not presented as a heavenly Jerusalem but rather as a paradise garden in a way reminiscent of the image we saw in Classe and in the St Zeno Chapel of Santa Prassede. However, Christ is accompanied here on either side by two angels, just as he is in Santa Prassede, implying we see a depiction of him entering heaven in glory accompanied by the two angelic men of Acts 1.10. It could be that we see here a very similar conception to that expressed in Santa Prassede but with the significant difference that heaven is presented as a garden rather than the city of Revelation 21.

---

136. John's wearing camel skin is often seen as evoking Elijah's appearance described in 2 Kgs 1.8, whilst Lk. 1.17 explicitly speaks of John inheriting the spirit of Elijah, and Jesus speaks of John as Elijah in Mt. 11.13-14.

137. Mt. 17.10-13; Mk 9.10-13.

Moses and Elijah point to Christ showing his ascension and glorification in heaven to be the same thing they witnessed on the Mount of Transfiguration.

St Zeno Chapel and Santa Maria in Domnica: Conclusion

Examination of the two other Transfiguration images created by Pope Paschal I reveals, first, that they make the identification of the two figures as Moses and Elijah in the St Prassede apse mosaic more likely to be correct. The St Zeno Chapel image prompts tantalizing questions concerning connections in local tradition between the location of this Transfiguration image as a place associated with vision of heaven and understood to be like a Holy of Holies. In addition to this, the image in Santa Maria in Domnica depicts the Transfiguration as like entering a paradisal garden. It also repeats the connection particularly emphasized by Luke between the Transfiguration and the Ascension, which we see in Santa Prassede. A distinct character of the images in Santa Maria in Domnica is meditation on the Elijan character of John the Baptist's identity.

We have noted that a number of distinctive Transfiguration interpretations emerge in ninth-century Roman depictions and that they frequently pick up ideas which we have explored in written comment. This raises the question whether these perspectives are solely the fruit of one man's mind in one particular place, namely Paschal I, or whether these themes come to be repeated in other contexts. One problem in answering that question is the significant scarcity of Transfiguration images from the ninth century. However, in the next section of this chapter we examine further examples of Transfiguration depictions from different Western locations, and in different media, but from the same period, which display a great degree of artistic and theological creativity in the ways in which they present the Transfiguration.

The Utrecht Psalter

The first is an image found within the Utrecht Psalter.[138] Probably produced somewhere around Rheims, this manuscript is dated by scholars to some time in the ninth century, usually between 816 and 835,[139] at almost exactly the same time as Paschal I's reign as pope (817–24).

Each Psalm is illustrated by a series of line drawings. These images range across a wide selection of typologies, personifications, allusions and literal illustrations

---

138. A full facsimile of the manuscript can be found in Ernest T. DeWald, *The Illustrations of the Utrecht Psalter*, Illuminated Manuscripts of the Middle Ages (Princeton, NJ: Princeton University Press, 1932).

139. See K. van der Horst, William Noel and Wilhelmina C. M. Wüstefeld, *The Utrecht Psalter in Medieval Art: Picturing the Psalms of David* (Utrecht: HES in conjunction with Harvey Miller, 1996), 23–9.

Figure 18 Utrecht Psalter, Ms. 32, for 1 83v, reverse.
Source: © Utrecht University Library.

Figure 19 Close up of Transfiguration scene in Utrecht Psalter, Ms. 32, for 1 83v, reverse. Source: © Utrecht University Library.

of phrases and incidents mentioned in the Psalms.[140] There is much discussion concerning the genesis and original purpose of the book.[141] It is not large enough to have been a text read from in choir, and the Psalms are laid out in canonical rather than liturgical order. In addition, the fact that the illustrations are not coloured implies it may not have been a luxury item made for an aristocratic patron. Both these considerations have led K. van der Horst, F. A. Bischof and Ingo Walther[142] to suggest that it may have been intended as a tool for young monks learning the Psalms by heart, and that the extensive illustrations at the head of each text operate as aide-mémoire.[143]

---

140. For further examples, see ibid., 56–70.

141. For an exhaustive survey of this scholarly debate, see ibid., 73–81.

142. F. A. Bischof, 'Zur Function and zur Datierung des Utrecht Psalters', *Idea: Jahrbuch der Hamburger Kunsthalle* 4 (1985): 43–51; Horst, Noel and Wüstefeld, *The Utrecht Psalter in Medieval Art*, 81–3; Ingo Walther, *Codices Illustres: The World's Most Famous Illuminated Manuscripts 400–1600* (Köln: Taschen, 2001), 90–1.

143. Lawrence Nees makes a tantalizing suggestion that one of the illustrators of the Utrecht Psalter may in fact be the creator of the extraordinary image of the Transfiguration found in the Ottobani Gospels. However, Nees's theory depends on an earlier dating of the Ottobani Transfiguration image, which is more convincingly identified by Judith Bierbrauer as a later tenth- or eleventh-century addition to the gospels. See Lawrence Nees, 'On Carolingian Book Painters: The Ottobani Gospels and Its Transfiguration Master', *Art*

There is within this Psalter what seems to be a depiction of the Transfiguration placed between Psalm 150 and the canticle of Isaiah 12. Between these two texts, we see a transfigured Jesus on a mountain, surrounded by Moses, Elijah and the three disciples. Two of the disciples are lying on the ground and one is standing up. However, this mountain itself is placed within what appears to be a city wall and is surrounded by two large crowds of people. Within the walled area is a fountain from which two individuals are drinking. Water from the fountain flows from the well out of the walled space and reaches those outside the walls, who also drink from it.

The image is an illustration of the canticle from Isaiah 12 set below it. We see a depiction of the drawing of water from the wells of salvation mentioned in Isa. 12.3, with the Transfiguration probably illustrating the final verse of the canticle, 'Exsulta et lauda, habitatio Sion, quia magnus in medio tui Sanctus Israel.' The walled city is the dwelling of Sion, rejoicing in the presence of the Holy One of Israel. The few scholars who comment on this Transfiguration image simply recognize it as such and have not offered any explanation as to why the Transfiguration should be connected with Isaiah 12,[144] and, indeed, they often seem slightly puzzled by it.

In the light of our exploration of the mosaics of Santa Prassede, and of the importance of Revelation 21 and 22 in its interpretation of the Transfiguration, however, this image becomes easier to explain. Revelation 21 and 22 play a key role in linking this Transfiguration scene with Isaiah 12. I want to argue that the artist who created this image interpreted Isaiah 12 as pointing forward to Revelation 21 and 22. Both passages describe Jerusalem: Revelation 21 and 22 take place in the heavenly Jerusalem; and Isaiah 12 urges the people of the dwelling of Sion to rejoice. Both passages describe life-giving water: Revelation 22 speaks of the river of the water of life flowing through the heavenly Jerusalem, with the Tree of Life on either side of it; whilst Isaiah 12 speaks of drawing water from the wells of salvation. Both passages speak of God being in the midst of his people: Rev. 22.3 asserts God tabernacles with his people; and Isaiah 12 urges exultation in the Holy One of Israel being in the midst of the dwelling of Sion. The artist assumes there was so close and obvious a connection between the Transfiguration and Revelation 21 and 22 that he uses it as a way of connecting Isaiah 12 and Revelation 21. Seeing an image of the Transfiguration enables the reader to remember Revelation 21 and 22, which, in turn, enables that reader to remember Isaiah 12. It seems the artist, like those who created the image in Santa Prassede, saw both the Transfiguration and Revelation 21 as parallel mountain-top visions in which Christ appears in glory in his heavenly temple dwelling. An intriguing character of the image we see in the Utrecht Psalter is that it comes from a very different cultural milieu, in

---

Bulletin 83 (June 2001): 231; and Judith Bierbrauer, in, Joachim Plotzek and Ulrika Surmann, *Biblioteca Apostolica Vaticana: Liturgie und Andacht im Mittelalter* (Stuttgart: Belser, 1992), entry no. 7.

144. DeWald, *The Illustrations of the Utrecht Psalter*, 65–6; e.g. Suzy Dufrenne, *Les illustrations du psautier d'Utrecht: Sources et apport carolingien*, Association des publications près les universités de Strasbourg (Paris: Ophrys, 1978), 142, footnote 466.

Northern France, from the images we see in Santa Prassede, but that both were created at most ten years apart from each other. There is no way of proving any connection between the two images, but they both display a very similar interest in linking the Transfiguration with Revelation 21 and 22.

However, even though the two images express a similar interpretation, they were clearly used very differently. The notion that the Utrecht image of the Transfiguration could be a mnemonic device for memorizing Isaiah 12 connects us once again with Mary Carruthers and her theory of ancient memory.[145] If the theory is correct that the Psalter's images are mnemonic devices, it shows that the strength of the connection between the Transfiguration and Revelation 21 and 22 was so pronounced that it could be used to prompt memory of a completely different Old Testament text being compared with John's vision of the heavenly Jerusalem. In Carruthers's terms, an image of the Transfiguration becomes the *phantasma*, the visualized memory which is enough to evoke recall of Isaiah 12 through its similarity to Revelation 21 and 22. An image of the Transfiguration becomes the aide-mémoire which enables a young monk to remember the words of Isaiah 12.

The Transfiguration in ivory: Victoria and Albert Museum Inventory No. 254-1867

A series of complex hermeneutic connections can also be seen in a pair of ninth-century ivories found at the Victoria and Albert Museum, numbered 254-1867. These two ivory plaques depict the Transfiguration and the Ascension, and evoke Revelation 21 and 22 in ways similar to those which we observed in Santa Prassede and the Utrecht Psalter.

The ivory is probably of late antique origin and has been used twice by different artists. On the back of the Transfiguration scene is an older depiction of the Last Judgement, and the reverse side of the Ascension is decorated with scenes of plants and animals. Paul Williamson dates the Ascension and Transfiguration scenes, the last to be inscribed on the ivory, to the late ninth century (850–870) and sees them as of French origin.[146] Their last use was as the two outer bindings of a book, but before that, it seems the original purpose of the Transfiguration and Ascension scenes was to serve as the doors to a casket, reliquary or tabernacle, shown by the markings left on them by an old lock and hinges.[147]

---

145. Indeed, Horst, *The Utrecht Psalter in Medieval Art*, 81, points to Carruthers's work in the light of the possibility that the Utrecht Psalter images could be a series of mnemonic devices.

146. Paul Williamson, *Medieval Ivory Carvings: Early Christian to Romanesque* (London: V&A Publishing, 2010), 191.

147. Ibid; see also W. Maskell, *A Description of the Ivories Ancient and Mediaeval in the South Kensington Museum* (London: Chapman & Hall for the Science and Art Department of the Committee of Council on Education, 1872), 99–100.

The Earliest Depiction of the Transfiguration

Figure 20 Ivory, Victoria and Albert Museum, Catalogue number 253-1867.
Source: © The Victoria and Albert Museum.

One of the most significant points which these images make, and which expresses a similar interpretation as that which we saw in Santa Prassede and Santa Maria in Domnica, is a comparison of the Transfiguration and Ascension as parallel entries into heaven. An intriguing element of this Transfiguration image is the appearance above the disciples of the three huts Peter suggests, along with a rather curious-looking tree. The only points of comparison for us here are a depiction of the Transfiguration from a similar period (870–880) held by the Victoria and Albert Museum (Inv. No. 255-1867),[148] and a slightly older (920–925) ivory image of the Transfiguration held at the British Museum (Inv. No. 1856,0623.15),[149] both of which omit the tabernacles and tree.[150] So few images of the Transfiguration in this medium exist from this period that comparison with these two images from the Victoria and Albert and the British museums may have limited worth. However, they show that the presence of the tabernacles and tree in Inv. No. 254-1867 could be distinct and somewhat unusual.

It is unclear whether the three huts simply represent Peter's words or whether they show Peter, James and John to have actually entered the place of heavenly tabernacles. In other words, this pair of ivories could be a depiction of the disciples having entered heaven and seeing at the moment of the Transfiguration the dwellings of the righteous, such as one sees in the *Apoc. Pet.* 16-18, or in 1 *Enoch* 39.[151] If that is the case, then it could be that the small tree depicted by the huts is, in fact, the Tree of Life, which is found on either side of the river of the water of life in Rev. 22.2. It strikes me as possible that we see again the influence of Revelation 22 in this image of the Transfiguration through the presence of what is possibly the Tree of Life, and that the image points to the disciples as having entered the place of heavenly dwellings in a way not dissimilar to the interpretation displayed in the Utrecht Psalter.

Of further significance is the theory, proposed by Williamson,[152] that these two images could have been chosen to adorn the doors of a tabernacle or reliquary in an Anglo-Saxon or Carolingian church. The use of these plaques as reliquary doors would chime with the theological concatenation we have noted elsewhere, particularly in Sant'Apollinare in Classe and Paschal I's Roman churches between imagery of the Transfiguration and Ascension and the relics of the saints signifying sacred space. Even more fascinating is the possibility

---

148. Williamson, *Medieval Ivory Carvings*, 194–5.

149. I. Goldschmidt, *Die Elkenbeinskulpturen aus der Zeit der karolongischen und sächsischen Kaiser VIII-XI Jahrhundert* (Berlin: Elfenbeinskulpturen I, 1914), no. 103; I. Goldschmidt, *Ars Sacra 800–1200* (Harmondsworth: Penguin Books, 1972), pl. 70.

150. Williamson, *Medieval Ivory Carvings*, 194–5.

151. In other words, the sort of interpretation Heil and Lohmeyer have suggested, that the dwellings of the just, such as are seen in 1 Enoch 39, are suggested through the New Testament narratives' use of language appertaining to tabernacles and tents. See, John Paul Heil, *The Transfiguration of Jesus: Narrative Meaning and Function of Mark 9:2-8, Matt 17:1-8 and Luke 9:28-36* (Rome: Editrice Pontificio Istituto Biblico, 2000), 115–27; Lohmeyer, 'Die Verklärung Jesu nach dem Markus-Evangelium', *Zeitschrift für Neutestamentliche Wissenschaft* 21 (1922): 194.

152. Williamson, *Medieval Ivory Carvings*, 191.

that the ivories were used as the doors of a tabernacle. Their being the entry point to proximity to the Blessed Sacrament would have echoed in a Christian church the Holy of Holies of the Jerusalem Temple and communicated the notion of a particular place as the locus of God's presence. The opening of those doors would have represented an entry point to God's presence embodied in the consecrated host of the Mass. Choosing these two images for the two doors of a tabernacle makes a strong theological point and, in the light of the evidence marshalled in this chapter, should not be seen as mere coincidence. Access to, and reception of, the Blessed Sacrament for those worshipping before a tabernacle decorated with these doors was to be seen as a similar experience as the Transfiguration and Ascension, a moment of entry into a heavenly realm and into God's presence.

Connections have been drawn between this pair of ivory plaques and the Utrecht Psalter by art historians, but only on artistic and stylistic grounds. John Beckwith[153] argued for a later provenance for the ivories, claiming them to be the product of later-tenth-century Anglo Saxon artists influenced by the Utrecht Psalter.[154] This theory has generally not been supported by scholars of the period.[155] I am not in a position to make a verdict on questions of dating and will leave that to academics more highly skilled in Anglo Saxon and Carolingian art history. However, the *theological* reading of this pair of ivories I outline above shares with the Utrecht image a drawing on imagery from Revelation 22. My reading does not claim to offer decisive historical evidence for Beckwith's theory but does produce a theological rationale which shows that reading these ivories in the light of the Utrecht Psalter could make sense. I cannot prove whether they pre- or post-date the Utrecht image, but I do argue that they display a similar theological reading of the Transfiguration as an entry into heaven and as evoking Revelation 22, a point which many art historians' discussion overlooks.

In both the Utrecht Psalter and this Victoria and Albert Museum pair of ivories, we see further examples of Revelation 21 and 22 and the Ascension being evoked

---

153. John Beckwith, *Ivory Carvings in Early Medieval England* (London: Harvey, Miller and Medcalf, 1972), 43–8.

154. See also Margaret Helen Longhurst, *Catalogue of Carvings in Ivory*, 2 vols (London: Published under the authority of the Board of Education, 1927), 64; Perette Michelli, 'Beckwith Revisited', in *Anglo-Saxon Styles*, ed. Catherine Karkov and George Brown (New York: State University of New York Press, 2003), 103–6, 109–11; Westwood, *A Descriptive Catalogue of the Fictile Ivories in the South Kensington Museum*, 116.

155. Danielle Gaborit-Chopin, *Ivoires du Moyen Age* (Fribourg: Office du Livre, 1978), 66; Fillitz Hermann, 'Rezensionen (book review of Beckwith's Ivory Carvings in Early Medieval England)', *Kunstchronik* 27, no. 12 (1974): 433–4; P. Lasko, 'Medieval Ivory Carvings at the Victoria and Albert Museum', *Burlington Magazine* 116 (1974): 429; A. L. Vandersall, 'Two Carolingian Ivories from the Morgan Collection in the Metropolitan Museum of Art', *Metropolitan Museum Journal*, no. 6 (1972): 25, 29; Williamson, *Medieval Ivory Carvings*, 191–3.

in connection with depiction of the Transfiguration, and, in the former case, of this being used to link the Transfiguration with Isaiah 12.

'Visionary visual exegesis'

In order to draw together some of the threads explored in this chapter, I wish to reflect on a number of questions appertaining to the Transfiguration's status as a visionary episode in the light of the work of scholars such as David Chidester,[156] Jane Ralls Baun,[157] O'Hear,[158] Kovacs, and Rowland.[159]

We have noted in Chapter 1 the importance of Chidester's work in the realm of human sense perception in antiquity. He points to the way in which verbal discourse oriented to reading and hearing a narrative was felt to express ideas in terms of precedence, order and sequence. He shows that the faculty of sight, by contrast, was capable of apprehending ideas and narratives with a stronger sense of simultaneity, creative overlap and connection. Visual depiction for Chidester resists prioritization and categorization, and rejoices in making connections between narratives in sometimes more allusive ways. The apse in Sant'Apollinare in Classe embodies this *par excellence*. Different commentators have seen a wide range of themes present such as Golgotha, the Transfiguration, the Ascension, the Exaltation of the Cross and the Parousia of Christ in glory, and have tried to argue for one to the exclusion of all others. Chidester's work shows that attitude to be misconceived and that the ancient mind considered the visionary experience of the Transfiguration as able to evoke simultaneously a range of motifs at the same time. Such a view would support my reading of the Classe mosaic as presenting the Transfiguration in the context of a series of visionary motifs linked with apocalyptic heavenly ascent, such as we also see in the *Apocalypse of Peter*. The triumphal arch in Santa Prassede also depends on a dynamic of simultaneity in the way in which it holds together images from very different portions of the New Testament, but which are presented as depicting a similar reality. The juxtaposing of the Transfiguration with images of Moses in St Catherine's Monastery, Sinai, or in Santi Nereo e Achilleo with images evoking Isaiah 7 also presents the viewer

---

156. David Chidester, *Word and Light: Seeing, Hearing, and Religious Discourse* (Urbana: University of Illinois Press, 1992).

157. Jane Ralls Baun, *Tales from another Byzantium: Celestial Journey and Local Community in the Medieval Greek Apocrypha* (Cambridge: Cambridge University Press, 2007).

158. Natasha O'Hear, *Contrasting Images of the Book of Revelation in Late Medieval and Early Modern Art: A Case Study in Visual Exegesis*, Oxford Theological Monographs (Oxford: Oxford University Press, 2011).

159. Judith Kovacs and Christopher Rowland, *Revelation: The Apocalypse of Jesus Christ* (Oxford: Blackwell, 2004).

with a single simultaneous apprehension of a series of incidents, which when viewed together are shown to share fundamental connections and similarities.

Chidester reveals the act of viewing a series of images in the ancient world to have involved a presupposition of continuity, simultaneity, cohesion and compatibility in the way in which they relate to each other. It was less concerned with the forensic diagnosing of origins, the pinpointing of one single theme to the exclusion of others, or the spotting of inconsistencies and theological tensions, in the way that modern comment on those images sometimes is.

A second point to make concerns the frequent connection we have seen emerge between the Western depiction of the Transfiguration and the book of Revelation. I want to suggest, in the light of insights provided by O'Hear's work, that there might be something characterizing this connection which stems from their both purporting to be the fruit of visionary experience. We noted in Chapter 1 the way in which O'Hear reveals the idiom of visual depiction to be particularly suited to expressing the visionary character of certain apocalyptic and prophetic narratives. She explores this dynamic, which she coins 'visionary visual exegesis', in relation to the book of the Apocalypse, and she shows that visual depiction of the text is able to 'connect the viewer with the visionary essence of the Book of Revelation'.[160] I want to suggest that, within O'Hear's terms, Paschal I was engaged in visionary visual exegesis when he created the triumphal arch mosaic scenes in both Santa Prassede and Santa Maria in Domnica. By combining Revelation 21 with elements from the Transfiguration narratives, he points to a quality or character within both texts which can be articulated *visually* and which is *visionary* in origin. In other words, both Revelation 21 and the Transfiguration narratives should be seen as reporting in words a visionary experience of a visual nature. A very similar thing can also be said about the image in Sinai and the comparison made between the Transfiguration and the images it is surrounded by of Moses's experience of the Burning Bush and receiving of the Law. The mosaicist interprets the gospel Transfiguration narratives as being characterized by the same fundamental mechanic as the Exodus narratives concerning Moses. There exists behind the text a visionary experience, recounted, possibly imperfectly by a narrative, which the artist chooses now to express using a visual medium. By doing this, the artist judges the character of the two narratives to be defined not just by imagery which may be expressed or depicted visually but also that this visual character stems from a similar or parallel visionary experience.

A third point I want to make in the light of O'Hear's and Chidester's ideas concerns what one might describe, using Kovacs' and Rowland's terminology,[161] a process of 'actualization' which takes place in the liturgy. Kovacs and Rowland understand 'actualization' in the context of the book of Revelation to refer to readers who use the text as a heuristic lens through which to comprehend and contextualize their experience, rather than as a text needing 'decoding' in order

---

160. O'Hear, *Contrasting Images of the Book of Revelation*, 226.
161. Kovacs and Rowland, *Revelation*, 7–11.

to find an unchanging, allegorical message. All of the mosaic cycles we have examined are found in liturgical spaces. I argue that they undergo just such a process of 'actualization' during the celebration of the liturgy. The eschatological and physical divide between the life of heaven and earth is held to be broken down by those worshipping below. Both Elsner and Simson have pointed to the importance of this liturgical context in Classe and Sinai. For Elsner, the Transfiguration image at Sinai depicts the ascent of the human soul to God, but also exemplifies and embodies it through the process of vision. The liturgy becomes for him a key moment within which the image presented before its viewers is understood to be experienced, or 'actualized', in the present-day lives of worshippers. However, this dynamic is also surely the case with the other images we have looked at in this chapter, such as Santi Nereo e Achilleo, Santa Maria in Domnica and the St Zeno Chapel in Santa Prassede, along with the liturgical use of sacred objects such as the Victoria and Albert ivory image which may have formed the doors of a tabernacle.

This apprehension is often perpetuated beyond the temporal span of the liturgy by the presence of the saints' remains, such as is seen in Santa Prassede or Sant'Apollinare in Classe. As a result of these relics' presence, the church is characterized as sacred space in which God is found dwelling amongst his saints. This 'actualization' of Revelation 21 and the Transfiguration narratives, particularly in Santa Prassede, finds its expression, therefore, in a broader political agenda in which, as Goodson argues,[162] the papal liturgy taking place in Santa Prassede was intended to point to the whole of Rome as sacred space, as a heavenly city in which God dwells, and in whose name and presence its bishop rules. The twin visions of the Transfiguration narratives and Revelation 21 held together become a lens through which those worshipping in ninth-century Rome interpret their experience of the liturgy and conceive of the political and spiritual status of the city they dwell in.

Conclusion

This chapter has shown that the emergence of visual depiction brings many new and intriguing perspectives to bear on the Transfiguration narratives, and that many of these revolve around the episode's status as an account of purported visionary experience.

I hope one contribution to knowledge this chapter has made is to focus on a number of images within the Western tradition which have otherwise often been overlooked by commentators and which display a considerable degree of complexity and creativity. A number of scholarly conventions have also been challenged, such as the assumption that the image in Classe has no influence on

---

162. Goodson, *The Rome of Paschal I*, 197–256.

later images, or the assumption that the Sinai image lays the foundations for the later template of the Eastern icon of the Transfiguration.

Second, we have shown several of the theological strands present in Latin written comment outlined in Chapter 7 to be present in later visual depiction. These include the propensity to interpret the Transfiguration in terms of a more corporate vision of heaven and to compare the Transfiguration with passages from other portions of the scriptures such as the book of Revelation, Luke's birth and infancy narratives, and Isaiah 7 and 12. This chapter has also shown the recurrence of the priestly and temple motifs which we have noted to be present in patristic comment. We have found it to be the case that the Lucan narrative exerts influence over many depictions of the Transfiguration, especially in connection with ideas to do with ascent into heaven.

Third, this chapter presents the argument that many ancient artists saw visual depiction of the Transfiguration as offering meditation in a special way on the visionary character of the episode recounted in the synoptic gospels. I have argued visual depiction in the ancient world to be able to hold together in one simultaneous presentation many different and complex ideas, motifs and theological assertions, and to show them to be mutually enriching perspectives. I have also argued that the images we have discussed could be seen as examples of visionary visual exegesis and as expressing in visual form the visionary character of the Transfiguration. In addition, the critical character of the liturgical context in which the images laid before worshippers were 'actualized' has been emphasized. The Transfiguration became a model for a number of ways in which ascent to the divine was understood to take place and was also exploited politically to exert and express the power of several bishops.

A fourth point to note is the way in which the Transfiguration assumes a particular role in Western interpretation that sees it as a nexus of hermeneutic and mnemonic connection with other scriptural texts. The Transfiguration is the mnemonic key to understanding how Revelation 21 and Isaiah 12 are linked in the Utrecht Psalter. The Transfiguration is regularly seen in a number of contexts which we have examined as exemplifying the unity of the New and Old Testaments and the processes by which scripture can be used to interpret scripture.

This chapter marks, in many respects, the culmination of my survey of the reception history of the Transfiguration in the patristic era. We see many of the interpretations we have encountered in written comment emerge and be explored in visual depiction. However, visual depiction of the Transfiguration also enables a number of artists to explore many of the complexities I have shown to exist in previous patristic comment, such as precisely how the Transfiguration was to be understood as a vision and how that related to the vision of ordinary Christians. A crucial part of that exploration, however, continues to be dependent on elements within Luke's narrative, such as his linking of the Transfiguration with the Ascension, with the cultic associations of the word 'glory' and a conception of the Transfiguration as an entry into the tabernacle dwelling of God. I have also shown the Western iconographic tradition to be capable of considerable creativity and to be orientated to hermeneutic concerns focused on interpretation of the

Transfiguration in the light of other portions of scripture. The emergence of Transfiguration images in Rome and Ravenna from the sixth century onwards marks a fascinating new chapter in the history of its interpretation, whose significance has often been overlooked or fundamentally misconstrued by those who have commented on it.

Chapter 9

CONCLUSION

'Seeing is metamorphosis, not mechanism.'[1] These intriguing words from James Elkins's work *The Object Stares Back* sum up the convincing thesis he proposes that the processes of human seeing and vision are far more complex than the simple mechanistic assumptions modernity has inherited from the Enlightenment. He aptly highlights the paradox that to see is not coldly to observe from a distance but to be changed, altered and shaped by that process. Our survey of early interpretation of the Transfiguration narratives shows that for ancient readers, the Transfiguration spoke to them deeply in just such a way about human connection, participation in the divine and the life of the imagination. Patristic writers include the Transfiguration is a wide-ranging series of discourses about subjects as diverse as salvation and theosis, apprehension of the divine and human inspiration, growth in virtue, definitions of reason and madness, scriptural hermeneutics and the processes of visualized thought that make up human memory. One of the most pronounced differences between patristic and modern comment is the focus which ancient writers continually place on the actualization of the narrative in the lives of hearers/listeners. By contrast, modern historical-critical scholars reflect seldom on broader metaphoric or allegorical questions of sight and vision in their focus on the historic 'origins of our story', which, to use Ulrich Luz's words, they often see as 'alien' and characterized by 'strangeness'.

This study has sought to overcome this gap between the scopic regime of modernity and that of antiquity by revealing how patristic writers, preachers, commentators and artists interpreted the Transfiguration narratives. For a truly worthwhile account of the Transfiguration narratives to be able to account satisfactorily for the 'origins of our story', it needs to take patristic comment into account in order better to understand the cultural milieu from which our text comes.

In its exploration of the scopic regime within which the Transfiguration narratives were first written down, transmitted and interpreted, this study has revealed ancient comment to be not only critically attentive to the biblical text but also immensely creative in its interpretation, depiction and hermeneutic use of

1. James Elkins, *The Object Stares Back* (New York: Simon and Shuster, 1996), 12.

it. As a conclusion to this study of patristic reception of the Transfiguration, I lay out here the broad conclusions the evidence points to and begin with a series of different categories into which various understandings of the disciples' vision of the Transfiguration falls.

Transfiguration and vision

Throughout our survey of patristic comment on the Transfiguration narratives, we have noted a wide range of different understandings of the disciples' vision, which I have ordered here in five broad categories.

Category 1: Altered vision

Many of the writers we have surveyed understand the disciples as able to witness the Transfiguration as a result of having their own vision altered. We see evidence of this in the earliest reception, in 2 Peter, where the writer uses language of Peter's status as an 'eyewitness', which could be capable of evoking comparison with the ecstatic, privileged vision of participants in the Greek mystery cults. The *Apocalypse of Peter* also describes Peter's eyes being 'opened' so that he might be enabled to enter heaven and witness a vision of God's heavenly tabernacle. Tertullian interpreted Peter's vision in terms of a dreamlike form of ecstasy, akin to that of the prophets Zechariah and Isaiah, in which the soul visualized an image of the reality God wished to reveal. Anastasius of Sinai also sees Luke's description of Peter as revealing him to be in a state of ecstasy, which prompts a vision of the heavens. For Origen, the disciples were only able to witness the Transfiguration because of a coming together of an alteration in their vision which was in proportion to their spiritual maturity, and an accompanying withholding by God of his full glory. Origen's ideas exert considerable influence over later Greek comment, which emphasizes the need for an alteration of the disciples' vision and describes an awakening of the eyes of the minds in which the soul 'sees' a reality which the physical eyes cannot. I have shown in Chapter six, however, that different emphases and understandings within this basic principle exist in Greek comment: Anastasius I of Antioch, Maximus and Andrew of Crete hold that the disciples' vision was altered to *prevent* the overwhelming of their mortal vision; Cyril, by contrast, argues their mortal vision *is* overwhelmed, whilst Basil and Eusebius argue the disciples' altered vision enabled them only to see a *partial* vision of divine glory.

Category 2: Unaltered mortal vision

Others we have encountered, especially Latin writers, insist that vision of the Transfiguration required little alteration of physical sight in order for it to be witnessed. Chrysostom is the only writer in the East I found to advocate a similar position. He sees this mortal vision as the springboard for an imaginative visualizing of heaven. Many Latin writers, including Hilary, Jerome, Leo, Gregory, Bede and Ambrose Autpert, emphasize the disciples' vision as mortal and their witnessing of the Transfiguration as needing no alteration in their faculties of sight. Broadly speaking, Latin commentators tend to insist that any human subject present on the mountain could see the Transfiguration and emphasize the communal, corporate vision at the Eschaton by the faithful, which this signifies. As a result of this, notions to do with transformation of the mind are connected by Latin commentators less with the disciples' vision and more often with entry into the overshadowing cloud, which is frequently associated with the action of the Holy Spirit.

Category 3: Vision prompting greater vision

A further tradition of interpretation we have examined revolves around the Transfiguration as an experience which prompts the visualizing of a greater vision of heaven. The first example of this we encounter is the *Apocalypse of Peter*, in which Peter's eyes are 'opened' to reveal a vision of God's 'tabernacle not made by human hands', where he dwells with his elect. Anastasius of Sinai and Chrysostom both understand the Transfiguration to prompt a further vision, but for them this is within those who heard the words of their sermons on the subject. Anastasius of Sinai urges his hearers to embrace a similar ecstasy and witness a glorious vision of God's heavenly Kingdom. Chrysostom advocates a more imaginative and tropological process in which reading the Transfiguration prompts the mind to visualize God's heavenly dwelling as a judge revealed in a courtroom or a theatre full of gloriously apparelled people.

Category 4: Vision as metaphor for ascent to God

A further important impulse is interpretation which uses the Transfiguration as a metaphor for intellectual apprehension of the divine and of ascent to God. Origen is the first proponent of this understanding. He sees in the disciples' vision of the Transfiguration a model for ascetic reading of the scriptures in which the mind of those who are spiritually mature metaphorically 'sees' God. Seeing the Transfiguration as a model for ascent to God through the spiritual life more generally, through monastic observance, or through ascetic practices becomes a widespread interpretative approach, especially in Greek comment. However, I have shown that there remain a number of tensions in the precise way in which various commentators reconcile what the disciples experience on the mountain, what the faithful Christian experiences through ascesis in this life and how the saved will witness Christ's glory in the Parousia: Anastasius I of Antioch, Maximus and Andrew of Crete hold the vision of the Transfiguration and the Parousia to be essentially the same thing, and to necessitate a change in the disciples' vision; Cyril, by contrast, holds that they are essentially the same thing but that this is precisely why the disciples' vision *is* overwhelmed by divine glory; in counterdistinction to this, Basil and Eusebius speak of the Transfiguration as only being a *partial* experience of heavenly glory. Both Anastasius of Sinai and Chrysostom point to connections between the Transfiguration and human vision of God before the Parousia but see a role for ecstatic and imaginative processes to bridge that eschatological gap. By contrast with the East, Latin commentators tend to see the disciples' vision as only a partial version of that witnessed at the Parousia but emphasize the corporate and communal nature of the vision to which the Transfiguration points forward.

Category 5: Vision to be compared with other visions and prophecy

A strong impulse found in Latin comment is a tendency to interpret the Transfiguration in the light of other visionary episodes in the New Testament and Old Testament prophetic utterance. This impulse starts with Tertullian, who suggests that the vision the disciples had at the Transfiguration was similar to the prophetic vision experienced by Habbakkuk and Zechariah. I have also shown Ambrose and Jerome to argue that the Transfiguration fulfils Isaiah 7. A tradition of interpretation is seen in Bede and Autpert which reads the Transfiguration in the light of Revelation 21 and 22, and Hebrews 12. We have seen that many of these traditions come to be expressed visually in artistic depictions. I have offered an explanation of some elements of the mosaics found in Santi Nereo e Achilleo in Rome based on Ambrose's and Jerome's comment and have shown a repeated theme of Paschal I's Transfiguration mosaics in Santa Prassede and Santa Maria in Domnica to be depiction of the Transfiguration which draws on Revelation 21. I argue this tendency to be present in an ivory depiction of the Transfiguration created at the same time as the mosaics in Santa Prassede. In addition, I have shown that a perceived connection between the Transfiguration and Revelation 21 was used by the creator of the Utrecht Psalter to create an aide-mémoire for the memorizing of Isaiah 12. Imagery of the Transfiguration may also have been capable of evoking the Ascension as a similar entry into the heavenly realm. This may be the case in the imagery on the Brescia Casket and is certainly present in Paschal I's mosaic creations in Santa Prassede and Santa Maria in Domnica.

To use the terminology coined by Martin Jay and developed by Stephen Pattison, this study has revealed the 'scopic regime' from within which the Transfiguration emerges. It is a regime in which close connections are perceived by readers between the Transfiguration and their own life of faith. It is a context in which the Transfiguration is seen fruitfully to interpret visionary and prophetic texts, and a cultural milieu in which sacred space and liminal liturgical locations contribute to the power of visual imagery to communicate what are seen as deep truths about Christian experience of the divine. It is a regime in which claims to ecstatic vision had a fundamentally different cultural significance from our own. In short, the scopic regime of antiquity involved a richer, more creative, more imaginative understanding of sight and vision than the narrower, desiccated interpretation of our own age.

The importance of Luke's narrative

Throughout our exploration of early reception of the Transfiguration and the scopic regime within which it emerges, we have repeatedly noticed the Lucan version of the narrative playing a decisively significant role in influencing Western Latin comment and early depiction. Details only present in Luke's narrative have repeatedly played a particularly important role in much of the discussion we have outlined concerning the visionary character of the Transfiguration, the disciples' *participation* in it and, therefore, the actualization of the narrative in the lives of hearers/readers.

Entry into the cloud

The question of who enters into the cloud, and Luke's distinct assertion that the disciples do, prompts reflection on the way in which the Transfiguration is conceived of as an entry into a divine tabernacle. The different sense of space I have pointed to as present in Luke's version could also underpin some comparisons made between the Transfiguration and entry into an enclosed space. Anastasius of Antioch describes Peter looking into a vestibule or porch, whilst Chrysostom compares the vision he hopes the Transfiguration will prompt in his hearers to be like looking into a theatre or a courtroom. The notion that this vocabulary stems from Luke's narrative is difficult to prove conclusively but is offered here as a plausible possibility. I have also suggested that Luke's entry into the cloud could be one of the principal dynamics being evoked by the creators of the Transfiguration mosaic at St Catherine's monastery on Sinai. Latin writers such as Ambrose and Hilary associate the cloud with the working of the Holy Spirit. Indeed, Jerome, Augustine, Bede and Autpert read the disciples' entry into the cloud as akin to entry into a heavenly tabernacle. The question of who enters the cloud is commented upon more widely by Latin writers. Most read the Lucan text as implying entry by all the disciples. The only exception to this, which I have been able to find, is Autpert, who sees the cloud as hiding Moses and Elijah and leaving the disciples outside it. We have noted that debate about who enters the cloud continues to be reflected in visual depiction. I have suggested that some of the more perplexing elements within the Transfiguration image in the St Zeno Chapel in Santa Prassede may stem from lack of clarity as to whether the disciples' should be included within the glorious cloud.

'Glory' and 'exodus'

I have shown Luke's language of 'glory' to be a crucial connection used repeatedly by patristic writers in the East and West to link the Transfiguration with a series of Old Testament epiphanies, experiences of God's cultic presence and the life of the Jerusalem Temple. However, I have argued in Chapter 8 that this is a particularly important connection for artists who draw connections between the Transfiguration and Revelation 21 and 22 in Santa Prassede, the Utrecht Psalter and the ivory diptych we examined. I have also argued that the images in Santa Prassede and Santa Maria in Domnica present the Transfiguration as a foretaste of what Luke describes as the 'exodus' Jesus was to accomplish in Jerusalem at his Ascension and glorification.

Connections with the Ascension

Luke's connecting of the Transfiguration to the Ascension described in Acts is accomplished through shared use of the phrase 'behold two men' (ἰδοὺ ἄνδρες δύο) (Lk. 9.30; cf. Acts 1.10). Links with the Ascension are very pronounced in the *Apocalypse of Peter* which locates its transfiguration scene on Mount Olivet and actually turns the incident into an ascension in which Moses, Jesus and Elijah are taken into heaven. I have argued that the *Apocalypse of Peter* draws on many Lucan details and echoes Luke's language concerning 'two men'. These Lucan connections with the Ascension are particularly evident in the depictions we have examined in ninth-century Rome, in Santa Prassede and in Santa Maria in Domnica, in which we see a concatenation of imagery from the Transfiguration with imagery drawn from Acts 1 showing Jesus entering heaven accompanied by two angelic figures. In addition to his, the Victoria and Albert Museum ivory diptych we studied presents the Transfiguration side by side with the Ascension and strongly evokes one in the depiction of the other.

Sleep

Both Anastasius of Sinai and Chrysostom see significance in the sleepiness of the disciples described by Luke. For Anastasius, it is a consequence of their ecstatic vision and evidence of exhausted rapture. Chrysostom interprets this entirely to the contrary. He sees the sleepy exhaustion as a sign of the weakness of the mortal faculties of sight and as proof that no form of ecstasy is entered into. This is an impulse shared by many later Latin writers, such as Ambrose of Milan and Ambrose Autpert, who connect the disciples' sleepiness with a state of joyful forgetfulness. More broadly, it is clear that early Western depictions of the Transfiguration draw on this Lucan motif of sleepiness more often than has been realized. The Matthean narrative places the falling of the disciples on their faces at the *end* of the incident at the moment when the vision draws to a close. It is Luke who uses a mention of sleepiness to signal the *beginning* of the disciples' vision. An image showing the disciples on the floor looking up at the Transfiguration must, therefore, be significantly influenced by Luke's account and his order of events rather than Matthew's or Mark's.

Peter's not knowing what he said

Luke's mention of Peter not knowing what he said is most notably pointed to as revealing an ecstatic state by Origen and Tertullian. For Tertullian, this is a positive example of the sort of Montanist prophetic activity he seeks to defend, and he argues the disciples' experience to be similar to that of the prophets of the Old Testament. Origen also sees Peter's not understanding what he said to be a sign of ecstatic vision, but one which is prompted by demonic possession. For Origen, Peter's state of mind is a hindrance to understanding the Transfiguration, whereas for Tertullian it is a crucial prerequisite. Anastasius I of Antioch echoes elements of Tertullian's judgement. For Anastasius, Peter's not knowing what he said is evidence of ecstasy and a positive example of the sort of vision available for his hearers. By contrast with this, there emerges a consistent impulse within later Latin interpretation seen in Ambrose, Leo, Bede, Augustine and Autpert to show that whilst Peter was somehow beside himself, it was purely in a sense of joyous excitement, or elated forgetfulness, and led to no state of epistemically altered consciousness or ecstasy.

Priestly, tabernacle and temple themes

It is also the case that a number of readings which present the Transfiguration as an entry into a temple space compare it with God's heavenly tabernacle or see Jesus as a high priestly figure, frequently draw on Lucan elements. The *Apocalypse of Peter* is one of the most important examples of this sort of interpretation. It locates the Transfiguration on Sion, mentions the Lucan theme of ascending the mountain in order to pray and echoes Luke's language of 'glory' and the phrase 'behold two men' in its description of a heavenly scene full of priestly figures. I have argued that this text influences later depictions of the Transfiguration in Classe, which is replete with priestly themes. Origen describes the transfigured Jesus as a High Priest and roots this in Luke's mention of Jesus' ascent of the mountain being in order to pray. He also describes the cloud as a tabernacle and points to the processes of ascending to the divine, which he sees the Transfiguration to stand for, as akin to entry into a Holy of Holies. I have shown that this temple understanding of the Transfiguration allows Origen to connect the Transfiguration to a number of temple incidents in Luke's gospel, through use of Philippians 2. Anastasius of Sinai has been shown both to draw on Luke's version of the narrative and to produce a number of readings in which the Transfiguration is compared with the feast of tabernacles, and the transfigured Christ is described as the new Christian temple established in the New Jerusalem. I have also argued that in the depictions found in Santa Prassede, in the Utrecht Psalter and in the ivory diptych we examined, details from the Lucan narrative are crucial to the connections which are drawn between the Transfiguration and the temple city of Revelation 21. These include the notion of 'glory', connections with the Ascension and meditation on the 'exodus' Jesus was to accomplish in Jerusalem.

Reappraisal of Latin traditions of Transfiguration interpretation

I hope this study contributes to a reappraisal of the vitality and creativity of Western traditions of Transfiguration interpretation. I have shown that early artists in Rome, Ravenna and France displayed great creativity in the way in which they juxtaposed imagery from the Transfiguration with other visionary incidents from the scriptures. These emphasized entry into God's heavenly tabernacle, such as Revelation 21 and 22 and Hebrews 12, or are prophetic texts from the Old Testament such as Isaiah 7, Habakkuk and Zechariah. In addition to this, the connections between the Transfiguration and the heavenly Jerusalem of Revelation 21 were felt to be so widely held by the author of the Utrecht Psalter that that it was used as an aide-mémoire for the memorizing of Isaiah 12. We have also pointed to examples of these connections having an impact on the liturgical and political experience of those who worshipped beneath these images. Paschal I's placing of many saints' remains under his mosaic in Santa Prassede reveals his attempts to 'actualize' the image he presented not just during the liturgy but also as a way of extending notions of sacred space to the whole city he presided over as bishop. In addition to this, the presence of the Transfiguration in the St Zeno Chapel of Santa Prassede may have contributed to local traditions which held the space to be like a paradisal garden, or Holy of Holies, and to be a place Pope Paschal I was himself held by local tradition to have experienced a vision of heaven. In many of these depictions, we see a frequent insistence within Latin discourse on the corporate and communal character of the vision which the Transfiguration points forward to. It is possible that this stems from the insistence of many Latin writers that the disciples' vision was not altered and that anyone present could have seen the Transfiguration. This contrasts with a greater emphasis in the East on the restricted nature of the vision which the Transfiguration stands for, reserved for the ascetically trained, those who lead the monastic life or those have received the wisdom needed to read and contemplate the scriptures correctly.

The importance of visual interpretation and depiction

A second contribution to knowledge which emerges out of this study is a renewed emphasis on the importance of visual interpretation within accounts of the reception history of scriptural texts. The study I have offered of mainly Western Transfiguration images has shown that many of the interpretative strands we have seen in written comment come to be expressed in different ways in visual depiction. I have argued that we see the sort of interpretation Natasha O'Hear has described as 'visionary visual exegesis'. The frequent comparison of the Transfiguration with portions of the book of Revelation, along with the influence of the *Apocalypse of Peter*, brings to the fore not just their shared status as the purported fruit of visionary experience but also the visual character of the subject those texts depict. Comparison of the Transfiguration with prophetic texts from the Old Testament, such as we see with Isaiah 7 in Santi Nereo e Achilleo, or in Tertullian's comment on the Transfiguration, also asserts an understanding of prophetic utterance which is rooted in the visualizing of imagery. It is also the case that a number of interpretations which are less pronounced in written comment are sometimes more emphasized in visual depiction. The presence of priestly or temple-centred themes, for example, becomes more pronounced in many of the depictions we have examined than it is in written comment, and it expresses the spatial dynamic inherent in ideas to do with entry into the divine presence and the place of God's dwelling. It is also the case that many of the depictions of the Transfiguration which we have examined succeed in holding several images, ideas and scriptural references together in one simultaneous presentation. I have used Chidester's work to show how visual depiction enables this in a way which resists the prioritizing of one reference over others and which can be more allusive or suggestive in the way in which it communicates a sense of relationship between images. Visual depiction also opens up opportunities for biblical texts to be 'actualized' in the lives of those who behold them, and who may indeed be illiterate, through the liturgical context in which they are set. Many of the themes explored in images of the Transfiguration such as vision of God, a sense of the presence of heavenly individuals, experience of Jesus' glorious presence or a looking forward to the Parousia are key dynamics within the celebration of the Mass, which will have taken place under them. Indeed, the communion of saints is often emphasized physically by the presence of the bones of the saints. What is depicted in Transfiguration depictions as a one-off event in the life of Jesus becomes a narrative participated in time and time again by those who feel they experience the reality it expresses every time they celebrate the Liturgy.

***

My reappraisal of the New Testament Transfiguration narratives and their interpretation in the patristic period has shown that a normative way of reading that narrative for something approaching almost half of Christian history is one which took very seriously the visionary character of the incident and which used that metaphor of sight and vision to actualize the narrative in the life of hearer/readers. The point of this study has not been to show that modern historical-critical comment on the Transfiguration has no use. I have simply shown where gaps and uncertainties within modern scholarship exist. I have tried to fill and clarify them by ranging across comment produced by people who inhabit a 'scopic regime' very different from that of modernity. As such, this study is useful to historical-critical scholars who want to explore how the sort of vision described in the Transfiguration narratives was understood by the gospels' writers and their first readers in antiquity. However, it is also of use to those interested in the significance of our texts' history of interpretation and the ways in which they have been interpreted in a number of contexts throughout a significant period of Christian history. Patristic commentators frequently saw the Transfiguration as a paradigm for the metaphorical sight, prophetic utterance, inspired dream and ecstatic vision, which characterize human existence, ascetic growth, liturgical worship and intellectual reflection. Especially in the West, it was compared in both written and artistic reflection with a broad range of apocalyptic and prophetic texts, and was often seen to embody an entry into the divine presence understood to be akin to the heavenly tabernacle of God, or the Holy of Holies. Luke's gospel played an especially pivotal role in discourse concerning the visionary status of the incident. This contrasts with the focus of much modern critical scholarship, which revolves around a smaller number of questions to do with the literary origin of the Transfiguration narratives, is ambivalent or uncertain about how to interpret the visionary claims of the texts and has frequently overlooked both the significance of visual reception, and the distinct character of Luke's narrative. By examining a number of artists and commentators who inhabit a 'scopic regime' much closer to that of the writers of the New Testament, we have shown the potential which many elements in our narrative have to provoke discourse concerning its visionary status. I have shown Luke's version to be particularly replete with such detail, and I have argued for a re-evaluation of the creativity of Western theological and artistic traditions' handling of the Transfiguration.

Far from being theologically naïve, or critically worthless, the patristic hermeneutic reflection we have examined is highly attentive to complexities present within the biblical text and sensitive to the different ways in which those complexities might be read or understood. My study is not intended to reveal the insights of modern critical scholarship on the Transfiguration to be worthless but rather that they stand on the shoulders of a much older body of reflection which is capable of significant hermeneutic sensitivity, creativity and originality.

BIBLIOGRAPHY

Allison, Dale C. *The New Moses: A Matthean Typology.* Edinburgh: T&T Clark, 1993.
Andreopoulos, Andreas. *Metamorphosis: The Transfiguration in Byzantine Theology and Iconography.* Crestwood, NY: St Vladimir's Seminary Press, 2005.
Baggley, John. *Doors of Perception: Icons and Their Spiritual Significance.* London: Mowbray, 1987.
Baggley, John. *Festival Icons for the Christian Year.* London: Cassell, 2000.
Baldracco, G. 'La cripta della chiesa di Santa Prassede'. *Revista di Archeologia Cristiana* 18 (1941): 277–96.
Baltensweiler, Heinrich. *Die Verklärung Jesu; historisches Ereignis und Synoptische Berichte.* Zürich: Zwingli-Verlag, 1959.
Balz, Horst, and Gerhard Schneider. *Exegetical Dictionary of the New Testament.* Grand Rapids, MI: Eerdmans, 1990.
Barker, Margaret. *On Earth as It Is in Heaven: Temple Symbolism in the New Testament.* Edinburgh: T&T Clark, 1995.
Barker, Margaret. *The Lost Prophet: The Book of Enoch and Its Influence on Christianity.* Sheffield: Sheffield Phoenix Press, 2005.
Barker, Margaret. *The Hidden Tradition of the Kingdom of God.* London: SPCK, 2007.
Barker, Margaret. *Temple Themes in Christian Worship.* London: T&T Clark, 2007.
Barker, Margaret. *The Gate of Heaven: The History and Symbolism of the Temple in Jerusalem.* Sheffield: Sheffield Phoenix Press, 2008.
Barnes, Timothy David. *Tertullian: A Historical and Literary Study.* Oxford: Clarendon Press, 1985.
Bauckham, Richard. *Jude, 2 Peter.* Word Biblical Commentary. Waco, TX: Word Books, 1983.
Bauckham, Richard. 'The Two Fig Tree Parables in the Apocalypse of Peter'. *Journal of Biblical Literature* 104, no. 2 (1985): 269–87.
Bauckham, Richard. 'The Apocalypse of Peter: A Jewish Christian Apocalypse from the Time of Bar Kokhba'. *Apocrypha* 5, no. 1 (1994): 7–112.
Bauckham, Richard. *The Fate of the Dead: Studies on the Jewish and Christian Apocalypses.* Supplements to Novum Testamentum. Leiden: Brill, 1998.
Bauckham, Richard. 'Jews and Jewish Christians in the Land of Israel at the Time of the Bar Kochba War with Special Reference to the Apocalypse of Peter'. In *Tolerance and Intolerance in Early Judaism and Christianity,* edited by Graham Stanton and Guy Stroumsa, 228–35. Cambridge: Cambridge University Press, 1998.
Baun, Jane Ralls. *Tales from another Byzantium: Celestial Journey and Local Community in the Medieval Greek Apocrypha.* Cambridge: Cambridge University Press, 2007.
Baur, Ferdinand Christian. *Kritische Untersuchungen über die kanonischen Evangelien.* Tübingen: L.F. Fues, 1847.
Beckwith, John. *Ivory Carvings in Early Medieval England.* London: Harvey, Miller and Medcalf, 1972.

Best, Ernest. *The Temptation and the Passion: The Markan Soteriology*. Cambridge: Cambridge University Press, 1965.
Berger, Klaus. 'Die Verklärung Jesu'. *IKaZ* 37 (2008): 3–9.
Betz, Hans Dieter. 'Jesus as Divine Man'. In *Jesus and the Historian: Written in Honor of Ernest Cadman Colwell*, edited by Thomas Trotter, 114–33. Philadelphia: Westminster, 1968.
Bierbrauer, Judith, in Joachim Plotzek and Ulrika Surmann. *Biblioteca Apostolica Vaticana: Liturgie und Andacht im Mittelalter*, entry no 7. Stuttgart: Belser, 1992.
Bigg, Charles. *A Critical and Exegetical Commentary on the Epistles of St. Peter and St. Jude*. Edinburgh: T&T Clark, 1902.
Bilby, Mark G. 'Pliny's Correspondence and the Acts of the Apostles: An Intertextual Relationship'. In *Luke on Jesus, Paul and Christianity: What Did He Really Know?*, edited by Joseph Verheyden and John S. Kloppenborg, 171–89. BTS 29. Leuven: Peeters, 2017.
Bilby, Mark G. 'The First Dionysian Gospel: Imitational and Redactional Layers in Luke and John'. In *Classical Models of the Gospels and Acts: Studies in Mimesis Criticism*, edited by Mark G. Bilby, Michael Kochenash and Margaret Froelich. Claremont Studies in New Testament and Christian Origins 3. Claremont, CA: Claremont Press, 2018.
Bischof, F. A. 'Zur Function and zur Datierung des Utrecht Psalters'. *Idea: Jahrbuch der Hamburger Kunsthalle* 4 (1985): 43–51.
Blinzler, Joseph. *Die neutestamentlichen Berichte über die Verklärung Jesu*. Münster: Aschendorff, 1937.
Boobyer, G. H. *St. Mark and the Transfiguration Story*. Edinburgh: T&T Clark, 1942.
Bourget, Pierre du. *Early Christian Art*. London: Weidenfeld and Nicholson, 1972.
Bovini, Giuseppe. *Ravenna, Art and History*. Ravenna: Longo Publisher, 1991.
Bovon, François. *Das Evangelium nach Lukas*. Evangelisch-Katholischer Kommentar Zum Neuen Testament. Zurich: Benziger, 1989.
Bovon, François. *Luke 1: A Commentary on the Gospel of Luke 1:1-9:50*. Minneapolis, MN: Fortress Press, 2002.
Boxall, Ian. *Patmos in the Reception History of the Apocalypse*. Oxford Theology and Religion Monographs. Oxford: Oxford University Press, 2013.
Braunfels, Wolfgang, and Engelbert Kirschbaum. *Lexikon der christlichen Ikonographie*, 8 vols. Rome: Herder, 1968.
Brown, Raymond Edward. *The Gospel According to John*. The Anchor Bible. Garden City, NY: Doubleday, 1966.
Buchholz, Dennis D. *Your Eyes Will Be Opened: A Study of the Greek (Ethiopic) Apocalypse of Peter*. Society of Biblical Literature. Atlanta: Scholars Press, 1988.
Bultmann, Rudolf. *The History of the Synoptic Tradition*, 2nd edn. Oxford: Blackwell, 1968.
Burkert, Walter. *Ancient Mystery Cults*. Cambridge, MA: Harvard University Press, 1987.
Burkett, Delbert. 'The Transfiguration of Jesus (Mark 9:2-8): Epiphany or Apotheosis?' *JBL* 138 (2019): 413–32.
Canty, Aaron. *Light and Glory: The Transfiguration of Christ in Early Fransiscan and Dominican Theology*. Washington, DC: Catholic University of America Press, 2011.
Carlston, C. 'Transfiguration and Resurrection'. *Journal of Biblical Literature* 80 (1961): 233–40.
Cartlidge, D. R. 'Transfigurations and Metamorphosis Traditions in the Acts of John, Thomas and Peter'. *Semeia* 38 (1986): 53–66.

Carruthers, Mary J. *The Craft of Thought: Meditation, Rhetoric, and the Making of Images, 400–1200.* Cambridge Studies in Medieval Literature. Cambridge: Cambridge University Press, 1998.

Carruthers, Mary J. *The Book of Memory: A Study of Memory in Medieval Culture*, 2nd edn. Cambridge Studies in Medieval Literature. Cambridge: Cambridge University Press, 2008.

Cecchelli, Carlo. *The Rabbula Gospels, Facsimile Edition of the Minatures of the Syriac Manuscript Plut. 56 in the Medicaean-Laurentian Library.* Olten: Urs Graf Verlag, 1959.

Chase, F. H. 'Peter, Second Epistle'. In *Dictionary of the Bible*. New York: Schibner and Sons, 1900.

Chidester, David. *Word and Light: Seeing, Hearing, and Religious Discourse.* Urbana: University of Illinois Press, 1992.

Chilton, Bruce. 'The Transfiguration: Dominical Assurance and Apostolic Vision'. *New Testament Studies* 27 (1980): 115–24.

Collins, Adela Yarbro. *Mark: A Commentary.* Minneapolis, MN: Fortress Press, 2007.

Conzelmann, Hans. *An Outline of the Theology of the New Testament.* London: S.C.M. Press, 1969.

Cornford, Francis. *Plato's Cosmology: The Timaeus of Plato.* London: Routledge and Kegan Paul, 1937.

Coune, Michel. *Grace de la Transfiguration d'après les Pères d'Occident.* Vie Monastique no. 24. Bégrolles-en-Mauges: Abbaye de Bellefontaine, 1990.

Coune, Michel. *Joie de la Transfiguration d'après les Pères d'Orient.* Spiritualité Orientale no. 39. Bégrolles-en-Mauges: Abbaye de Bellefontaine, 1985.

Cranfield, C. E. B. *The Gospel According to Saint Mark.* Cambridge: Cambridge University Press, 1963.

Curzi, Gaetano. 'La decorazione musiva della basilica dei Santi Nereo e Achilleo in Roma: materiali e ipotesi'. *Arte Medievale* 7, no. 2 (1993): 145–235.

Dailey, Brian E., S.J. *Light on the Mountain: Greek Patristic and Byzantine Homilies on the Transfiguration of the Lord.* Yonkers, NY: St Vladimir's Seminary Press, 2013.

Dabrowski, Eugeniusz. *La Transfiguration de Jésus.* Scripta Pontificii Instituti Biblici. Rome: Pontifical Biblical Institute, 1939.

D'Angelo, Mary Rose. 'The ANHP Question in Luke-Acts: Imperial Masculinity and the Deployment of Women in the Early Second Century'. In *A Feminist Companion to Luke*, edited by Amy-Jill Levine, 44–69. Sheffield: Sheffield Academic Press, 2002.

Daniélou, Jean. 'Les sources bibliques de la mystique d'Origène'. *Revue d'ascetique et de la mystique* 23 (1947): 126–41.

Daniélou, Jean. *Origène.* Paris: La Table Ronde, 1948.

Danker, Frederick W. *A Greek-English Lexicon of the New Testament and Other Early Christian Literature*, 3rd edn. Chicago: University of Chicago Press, 2000.

Davies, J. G. 'Prefigurement of the Ascension in the Third Gospel'. *Journal of Theological Studies* 6, no. 2 (1955): 229–33.

Davies, W. D., and Dale C. Allison. *A Critical and Exegetical Commentary on the Gospel According to Saint Matthew.* Edinburgh: T&T Clark, 1988.

Deichmann, Friedrich Wilhelm. *Ravenna: Hauptstadt des spätantiken Abendlandes*, vol. 2. Stuttgart: Franz Steiner, 1958.

Delbrück, Richard. 'Notes on the Wooden Doors of Santa Sabina'. *Art Bulletin* 34 (1952): 139–45.

Delbrück, Richard. *Probleme der Lipsanothek in Brescia.* Bonn: Peter Hanstein Verlag, 1952.

DeWald, Ernest T. *The Illustrations of the Utrecht Psalter*. Illuminated Manuscripts of the Middle Ages. Princeton, NJ: Princeton University Press, 1932.
Dibelius, Martin. *From Tradition to Gospel*. London: Ivor Nicholson and Watson, 1934.
Dibelius, Martin. *Die Geschichte der urchristlichen Literatur*. Munich: Chr. Kaiser, 1975.
Dietrich, Wolfgang. *Das Petrusbild der lukanischen Schriften*. Beiträge zur Wissenschaft vom alten und neuen Testament. Stuttgart: W. Kohlhammer, 1972.
Dinkler, Erich. *Das Apsismosaik von S. Apollinare in Classe*. Wissenschaftliche Abhandlungen der Arbeitsgemeinschaft für Forschung des Landes Nordrhein-Westfalen. Köln: Westdeutscher Verlag, 1964.
Dittenberger, Wilhelm. *Sylloge Inscriptionum Graecarum*. Lipsiae: apud S. Hirzelium, 1898.
Divry, Edouard. *La Transfiguration selon l'orient et l'occident*. Croire et Savoir vol. 54. Paris: Pierre Tequi, 2009.
Dodd, C. H. *The Coming of Christ: Four Broadcast Addresses for the Season of Advent*. Cambridge: Cambridge University Press, 1951.
Dodd, C. H. 'Appearances of the Risen Christ: An Essay in Form-Criticism of the Gospels'. In *Studies in the Gospels: Essays in Memory of R. H. Lightfoot*, edited by D. Nineham, 9–35. Oxford: Blackwell, 1955.
Driscoll, Jeremy. 'The Transfiguration in Hilary of Poitiers' Commentary on Matthew'. *Augustinianum* 29 (1984): 395–420.
Dufrenne, Suzy. *Les Illustrations du psautier d'Utrecht: Sources et apport carolingien*. Association des publications près les universités de Strasbourg. Paris: Ophrys, 1978.
Eichinger, Matthias. *Die Verklärung Christi bei Origines. Die Bedeutung des Menschen Jesus in seiner Christologie*. Vienna: Herder, 1969.
Elior, Rachel. *The Three Temples: On the Emergence of Jewish Mysticism*. Oxford: Littman Library of Jewish Civilization, 2004.
Elkins, James. *The Object Stares Back: On the Nature of Seeing*. New York: Simon and Schuster, 1996.
Elliott, J. K., and M. R. James. *The Apocryphal New Testament: A Collection of Apocryphal Christian Literature in an English Translation*. Oxford: Clarendon Press, 1993.
Ellis, E. E. 'The Composition of Luke 9 and the Source of Its Christology'. In *Current Issues in Biblical and Patristic Interpretation: Studies in Honour of Merrill C. Tenney*, edited by Gerald F. Hawthorne, 120–7. Grand Rapids, MI: Eerdmans, 1975.
Ellis, E. Earle. *The Gospel of Luke*. The Century Bible. London: Oliphants, 1974.
Elsner, Jas. *Art and the Roman Viewer: The Transformation of Art from the Pagan World to Christianity*. Cambridge: Cambridge University Press, 1995.
Elsner, Jas. 'Between Mimesis and Divine Power'. In *Visuality Before and Beyond the Renaissance: Seeing as Others Saw*, edited by Robert Nelson, 45–69. Cambridge: Cambridge University Press, 2000.
Evans, Craig A. *Mark 8:27-16:20*. Nashville: Thomas Nelson, 2001.
Evdokimov, Paul. *L'art de l'icône: théologie de la beauté*. Paris: Desclée De Brouwer, 1970.
Fasola, Umberto M. *The Catacomb of Domitilla and the Basilica of Saints Nereus and Achilleus*. The Churches of Rome Illustrated. Rome: Marietti, 1966.
Feuillet, A. 'Les perspectives propres à chaque évangéliste dans les récits de la Transfiguration'. *Biblica* 39 (1958): 281–301.
Fitzmyer, Joseph A. *The Gospel According to Luke (I-IX)*. The Anchor Bible. Garden City, NY: Doubleday, 1981.
Fletcher-Louis, Crispin. 'The Worship of Divine Humanity as God's Image and the Worship of Jesus'. In *The Jewish Roots of Christological Monotheism: Papers from the St.*

Andrews Conference on the Historical Origins of the Worship of Jesus, edited by Carey C. Newman, James R. Davila and Gladys S. Lewis, 112–28. Leiden: Brill, 1999.

Fletcher-Louis, Crispin. 'The Revelation of the Sacral Son of Man: The Genre, History of Religions Context, and Meaning of the Transfiguration'. In *Auferstehung-Resurrection: 4th Durham-Tübingen Research Symposium: Resurrection, Transfiguration, and Exaltation in the Old Testament, Ancient Judaism, and Early Christianity*, edited by H. Lichtenberger, 247–98. Tübingen: Mohr Siebeck, 2001.

Fletcher-Louis, Crispin. 'Jesus as the High Priestly Messiah Part 1'. *Journal for the Study of the Historical Jesus* 4, no. 2 (2006): 155–75.

Fletcher-Louis, Crispin. 'Jesus as the High Priestly Messiah Part 2'. *Journal for the Study of the Historical Jesus* 5, no. 1 (2007): 57–79.

Flusser, David. *Jesus*. New York: Herder, 1969.

Fornberg, Tord. *An Early Church in a Pluralistic Society: A Study of 2 Peter*. Uppsala: CWK Gleerup, 1977.

Fossum, J. E. 'Ascensio, Metamorphosis: The Transfiguration of Jesus in the Synoptic Gospels'. In *The Image of the Invisible God: Essays on the Influence of Jewish Mysticism on Early Christology*, edited by J. E. Fossum, 71–97. Göttingen: Vandenhoeck & Ruprecht, 1995.

France, R. T. *The Gospel of Mark: A Commentary on the Greek Text*. The New International Greek Testament Commentary. Grand Rapids, MI: Eerdmans, 2002.

Frank, Georgia. 'The Pilgrim's Gaze in the Age before Icons'. In *Visuality before and beyond the Renaissance: Seeing as Others Saw*, edited by Robert Nelson, 98–109. Cambridge: Cambridge University Press, 2000.

Freeland, Jane Patricia, and Agnes Josephine Conway. *Sermons*. Fathers of the Church. Washington, DC: Catholic University of America Press, 1996.

Frenschkowski, Marco. *Offenbarung und Epiphanie*. WUNT2/79–80. Tübingen: Mohr Siebeck, [1995] 1997.

Frey, Jörg, Matthijs den Dulk and Jan van der Watt, eds. *2 Peter and the Apocalypse of Peter: Towards a New Perspective*. Leiden: Brill, 2019.

Gaborit-Chopin, Danielle. *Ivoires du Moyen Age*. Fribourg: Office du Livre, 1978.

Gaddoni, Vanda Frattini. *The Basilica of St Apollinare in Classe, an Illustrated Art Guide*, translated by Annie Vancini. The Vallombrosian Benedictine monks of the monastery of St Apollinare in Classe.

Gallio, Paola. *The Basilica of Saint Praxedes*. Rome: Monaci Benedettini Vallombrosani, 2009.

Garrett, Susan. 'Exodus from Bondage: Luke 9.31 and Acts 12.1-24'. *Catholic Biblical Quarterly* 52 (1990): 656–80.

Garruchi, Raffaele. *Storia del'arte Cristiana*. Prato: Guasti, 1877.

Gerber, W. 'Die Metamorphose Jesu, Mk9.2f'. *Theologische Zeitschrift* 23 (1967): 385–95.

Gilmour, Michael J. *The Significance of Parallels between 2 Peter and Other Early Christian Literature*. Atlanta: Society of Biblical Literature, 2002.

Giunta, D. 'I mosaici dell'arco absidale della basilica dei Santi Nereo e Achilleo e l'erresia adozionista del sec. VII'. In *Roma e l'eta carolingia*, 195–200. Rome, 1976.

Glare, P. G. W., ed. *Oxford Latin Dictionary*. Oxford: Oxford University Press, 2012.

Gnilka, Joachim. *Das Evangelium nach Markus*. Zürich: Benziger, 1978.

Goetz, K. G. *Petrus als Gründer und Oberhaupt der Kirche und Schauer von Gesichten nach den altchristlichen Berichten und Legenden*. Leipzig: J.C. Hinrichs, 1927.

Goguel, Maurice. *La foi à la résurrection de Jésus dans le christianisme primitif*. Paris: Leroux, 1933.

Goldschmidt, I. *Die Elkenbeinskulpturen aus der Zeit der karolongischen und sächsischen Kaiser VIII-XI Jahrhundert*. Berlin: Elfenbeinskulpturen I, 1914.
Goldschmidt, I. *Ars Sacra 800-1200*. Harmondsworth: Penguin Books, 1972.
Goodson, Caroline. *The Rome of Paschal I: Papal Power, Urban Renovation, Church Building, and Relic Translation 817-824*. Cambridge: Cambridge University Press, 2010.
Goulder, M. D. *Type and History in Acts*. London: SPCK, 1964.
Gourdain, Jean-Louis. 'Jerome Exégète de la Transfiguration'. *Revue des Etudes Augustiniennes* 40 (1994): 365–73.
Grabar, André. *Martyrium: Recherches sur le culte des reliques et l'art chrétien antique*, vol. 2. Paris: Collège de France, 1946.
Green, Bernard. *The Soteriology of Leo the Great*. Oxford: Oxford University Press, 2008.
Green, Michael. *The Second Epistle General of Peter and the General Epistle of Jude: An Introduction and Commentary*. Tyndale New Testament Commentaries. London: Tyndale Press, 1968.
Gregory, Andrew F. *The Reception of Luke and Acts in the Period before Irenaeus: Looking for Luke in the Second Century*. Wissenschaftliche Untersuchungen Zum Neuen Testament, 2 Reihe. Tübingen: Mohr Siebeck, 2003.
Grundmann, Walter. *Der Brief des Judas und der Zweite Brief des Petrus*. Theologischer Handkommentar Zum Neuen Testament. Berlin: Evangelische Verlagsanstalt, 1974.
Grundmann, Walter, and Friedrich Hauck. *Das Evangelium nach Lukas*. Theologischer Handkommentar Zum Neuen Testament. Berlin: Evangelische Verlagsanstalt, 1964.
Guerrieri, Agnese. *La chiesa dei Ss. Nereo Ed Achilleo*. Collezione 'Amici Delle Catacombe'. Città del Vaticano: Società Amici Catacombe presso Pontificio Istituto di Archeologia Cristiana, 1951.
Guillou, André. 'Le monastère de la Théotokos au Sinaï. Origènes; Épiclèse; Mosaïque de la Transfiguration; Homélie inedite d'Anastase le Sinaïte sur la Transfiguration (Étude Critique)'. *Mélanges d'archéologie et d'histoire* 67 (1955): 215–56.
Habra, Georges. *La Transfiguration selon les pères grecs*. Paris: Editions S.O.S, 1974.
Hagner, Donald Alfred. *Matthew 14-28*. Word Biblical Commentary. Dallas, TX: Word Books, 1995.
Hahn, Ferdinand. *The Titles of Jesus in Christology: Their History in Early Christianity*. New York: World, 1969.
Harnack, Adolf von. *Geschichte der altchristlichen Literatur bis Eusebius*. Leipzig: J. C. Hinrichs, 1893.
Harnack, Adolf von. *Marcion: Das Evangelium vom Fremden Gott: eine Monographie zur Geschichte der Grundlegung der katholischen Kirche*. Texte und Untersuchungen zur Geschichte der altchristlichen Literatur. Leipzig: J.C. Hinrichs'sche Buchhandlung, 1921.
Harnack, Adolf von. 'Die Verklärung Jesu, der Bericht des Paulus (1kor 15,3)'. In *Sitzung Der Philosophisch-Historischen Klasse Vom 2. März, 1922*. Sitzungen der Königlichen Preussischen Akademie der Wissenschaften, Berlin, 1922.
Harrington, Daniel J. *The Gospel of Matthew*. Sacra Pagina Series. Collegeville, MN: Liturgical Press, 1991.
Hart-Hasler, J. N. 'Bede's Use of Patristic Sources: The Transfiguration'. In *Papers Presented to the Eleventh International Patristic Conference held in Oxford, 1991*, 197–204. Leuven: Peeters, 1993.
Hausherr, Irénée. 'L'origine de la doctrine occidentale des huit péchés capitaux'. *Orientalia Christiana Analecta* 30 (1930): 164–75.

Heil, John Paul. *The Transfiguration of Jesus: Narrative Meaning and Function of Mark 9:2-8, Matt 17:1-8 and Luke 9:28-36*. Rome: Editrice Pontificio Istituto Biblico, 2000.
Heisenberg, August E. K. *Grabeskirche und Apostelkirche, zwei Basiliken Konstantins*. Leipzig: J.C. Hinrichs, 1908.
Hermann, Fillitz. 'Rezensionen (book review of Beckwith's Ivory Carvings in Early Medieval England)'. *Kunstchronik* 27, no. 12 (1974): 429-34.
Hilgenfeld, Adolf. *Kritische Untersuchungen über die Evangelien Justin's, der clementinischen Homilien und Marcion's*. Halle: C.A. Schwetschke, 1850.
Horst, K. van der, William Noel and Wilhelmina C. M. Wüstefeld. *The Utrecht Psalter in Medieval Art: Picturing the Psalms of David*. Utrecht: HES in conjunction with Harvey Miller, 1996.
Humphrey, Edith McEwan. *And I Turned to See the Voice: The Rhetoric of Vision in the New Testament*. Grand Rapids, MI: Baker Academic, 2007.
Ihm, Christa. *Die Programme der christlichen Apsismalerei vom Vierten Jahrhundert bis zur Mitte des Achten Jahrhunderts*. Forschungen Zur Kunstgeschichte Und Christlichen Archäologie. Wiesbaden: Steiner, 1960.
Jakab, A. 'The Reception of the Apocalypse of Peter in Ancient Christianity'. In *The Apocalypse of Peter*, edited by Jan N. Bremmer and Istvan Czachesz, 174-86. Leuven: Peeters, 2003.
James, M. R. 'A New Text of the Apocalypse of Peter'. *Journal of Theological Studies* 13, no. 4 (1911): 573-83.
James, M. R. *The Second Epistle General of Peter and the General Epistle of Jude*. Cambridge: Cambridge University Press, 1912.
James, M. R. 'The Rainer Fragment of the Apocalypse of Peter'. *Journal of Theological Studies* 32, no. 127 (1931): 270-9.
Jay, Martin. 'Scopic Regimes of Modernity'. In *Vision and Visuality*, edited by Hal Foster, 3-23. Seattle: Bay Press, 1988.
Jay, Martin. *Downcast Eyes: The Denigration of Vision in Twentieth Century Thought*. Berkeley: University of California Press, 1993.
Jeremias, Gisela. *Die Holztür der Basilika S. Sabina in Rom*. Tübingen: Verlag Ernst Wasmuth, 1980.
Johnson, Luke Timothy. *The Literary Function of Possessions in Luke-Acts*. Missoula, MT: Scholars Press, 1977.
Johnson, Luke Timothy, and Daniel J. Harrington. *The Gospel of Luke*. Collegeville, MN: Liturgical Press, 1991.
Jonas, Hans. 'The Nobility of Sight: a Study in the Phenomenology of the Senses'. *Philosophy and Phenomenological Research* 14, no. 4 (June 1954): 507-19.
Kähler, Ernst. *Studien zum Te Deum und zur Geschichte des 24. Psalms in der alten Kirche*. Veröffentlichungen der evangelischen Gesellschaft für Liturgieforschung. Göttingen: Vandenhoeck & Ruprecht, 1958.
Kaufmann, Carl Maria. *Handbuch der christlichen Archäologie*. Paderborn: F. Schoningh, 1913.
Kee, H. C. 'The Transfiguration in Mark: Epiphany or Apocalyptic Vision?' In *Understanding the Sacred Text*, edited by J. Reumann, 135-52. Valley Forge: Judson, 1972.
Kelly, J. N. D. *A Commentary on the Epistles of Peter and of Jude*. London: Black, 1969.
Kitzinger, Ernst, and W. EugeneKleinbauer. *The Art of Byzantium and the Medieval West: Selected Studies*. Bloomington: Indiana University Press, 1976.

Klausner, Joseph. *Jesus of Nazareth: His Life, Times, and Teaching*. London: George Allen & Unwin, 1925.
Klinghardt, Matthias. 'Markion vs. Lukas: Plädoyer für die Wideraufnahme eines alten Falles'. *NTS* 52, no. 4 (2006): 484–513.
Klinghardt, Matthias. 'The Marcionite Gospel and the Synoptic Problem: A New Suggestion'. *NT* 50 (2008): 1–27.
Kloppenborg, John S. 'Literate Media in Early Christ Groups: The Creation of a Christian Book Culture'. *JECS* 22, no. 1 (2014): 21–59.
Klostermann, Erich. 'Zur Petrusapokalypse'. In *Hundert Jahre A. Marcus und E. Webers Verlag*, edited by A. Marcus and E. Webers Verlag, 77ff. Bonn: A. Marcus und Webers Verlag, 1921.
Klostermann, Erich. *Das Markusevangelium Erklärt*. Handbuch zum Neuen Testament. Tübingen: J.C.B. Mohr, 1950.
Knox, John. *Marcion and the New Testament: An Essay in the Early History of the Canon*. Chicago: University of Chicago Press, 1942.
Kollwitz, J. *Die Lisanothek von Brescia*. Berlin: de Gruyter, 1933.
Kovacs, Judith, and Christopher Rowland. *Revelation: the Apocalypse of Jesus Christ*. Oxford: Blackwell, 2004.
Kraus, Franz. *Geschichte der christlichen Kunst*. Freiburg in Breisgau: Herder, 1896.
Kraus, Thomas J., and Tobias Nicklas. *Das Petrusevangelium und die Petrusapokalypse: die griechischen Fragmente mit Deutscher und Englischer Übersetzung*. Griechischen Christlichen Schriftsteller Der Ersten Jahrhunderte, Neue Folge. Berlin: Walter de Gruyter, 2004.
Krautheimer, Richard. *Rome: Profile of a City, 312-1308*. Princeton, NJ: Princeton University Press, 2000.
Krautheimer, Richard, Spencer Corbett and Volfango Frankl. *Corpus Basilicarum Christianarum Romae: Le Basiliche Cristiane Antiche di Roma (Sec. IV-IX)*, 5 vols. Monumenti di Antichità Cristiana. Città del Vaticano: Pontificio istituto di archeologia cristiana; Institute of Fine Arts, 1937.
Kremer, Jacob, *Lukasevangelium*. Neue Echter Bibel. Würzburg: Echter, 1988.
Krüger, Manfred. *Die Verklärung auf dem Berge: Erkenntnis und Kunst*. Hildesheim: Georg Olms Verlag, 2003.
Kühl, Ernst Richard T. *Die Briefe Petri und Judae*. Göttingen: Kritischexegetischer Kommentar über das Neue Testament, Vandenhoeck & Ruprecht, 1897.
Kümmel, Werner Georg. *The Theology of the New Testament: According to Its Major Witnesses, Jesus, Paul, John*. London: S.C.M. Press, 1974.
Künzi, Martin. *Das Naherwartungslogion Markus 9,1*. Tübingen: Mohr, 1977.
Kurth, Julius. *Die Mosaiken Der Christlichen Ära*. Leipzig: Deutsche Bibelgesellschaft, 1902.
Labriolle, Pierre Champagne de. *La Crise Montaniste*. Paris: Leroux, 1913.
Lalleman, P. *The Acts of John*. Leuven: Peeters, 1998.
Lalleman, P. 'The Relation between the Acts of John and the Acts of Peter'. In *The Apochryphal Acts of Peter*, edited by Jan Bremmer, 161–8. Leuven: Peeters, 1998.
Lampe, Geoffrey. *A Patristic Greek Lexicon*. Oxford: Clarendon Press, 1961–8.
Lane Fox, Robin. *Pagans and Christians*. London: Penguin, 1988.
Lasko, P. 'Medieval Ivory Carvings at the Victoria and Albert Museum'. *Burlington Magazine* 116, no. 856 (1974): 426–30.
Leaney, A. R. C. *A Commentary on the Gospel According to St. Luke*, 2nd edn. Black's New Testament Commentaries. London: Black, 1966.

Leclercq, Henri. *Dictionnaire d'archéologie chrétienne et de liturgie*. Paris: Letouzey et Ané, 1953.
Leclercq, Jean. *Regards Monastiques sur le Christ au Moyen Age*. Jésus et Jésus-Christ, no 56. Paris: Mame-Desclée, 1993.
Leclercq, Jean, and Rene Dolle. *Sermons*, 4 vols. Sources Chrétiennes. Paris: Editions du Cerf, 1949.
Lee, Simon S. *Jesus' Transfiguration and the Believers' Transformation: A Study of the Transfiguration and Its Development in Early Christian Writings*. Wissenschaftliche Untersuchungen Zum Neuen Testament. Tübingen: Mohr Siebeck, 2009.
Lewis, Charlton. *A Latin Dictionary Revised by C. T. Lewis and C. Short*. Oxford, 1958.
Lewy, Yochanan. *Sobria Ebrietas: Untersuchungen zur Geschichte der Antiken Mystik*. Beihefte zur Zeitschrift für die neutestamentliche Wissenschaft und die Kunde der älteren Kirche. Giessen: A. Töpelmann, 1929.
Liddell, Henry. A Lexicon Abridged from Liddell and Scott's Greek-English Lexicon. Oxford: Clarendon Press, 1909.
Liefeld, Walter. 'Theological Motifs in the Transfiguration Narrative'. In *New Dimensions in New Testament Study*, edited by R. N. Logenecker and M. C. Tenney, 162–79. Grand Rapids, MI: Zondervan, 1974.
Liefeld, Walter. *Luke*. The Expositor's Bible Commentary. Grand Rapids, MI: Regency Reference Library, 1984.
Lienhard, Joseph T. *Homilies on Luke: Fragments on Luke*. Fathers of the Church. Washington, DC: Catholic University of America Press, 1996.
Lierman, John. *The New Testament Moses: Christian Perceptions of Moses and Israel in the Setting of Jewish Religion*. Wissenschaftliche Untersuchungen zum Neuen Testament, 2 Reihe. Tübingen: Mohr Siebeck, 2004.
Lindberg, David C. *Theories of Vision from Al-Kindi to Kepler*. Chicago: University of Chicago Press, 1976.
Lipsius, Richard, ed. *Acta Apostolorum Apocrypha*. Hildesheim: Georg Olms Verlag, 1959.
Litwa, M. David. *Iesus Deus: The Early Christian Depiction of Jesus as a Mediteraenean God*. Minneapolis, MN: Fortress Press, 2014.
Lohmeyer, E. 'Die Verklärung Jesu nach dem Markus-Evangelium'. *Zeitschrift für Neutestamentliche Wissenschaft* 21 (1922): 185–215.
Longhurst, Margaret Helen. *Catalogue of Carvings in Ivory*, 2 vols. London: Published under the authority of the Board of Education, 1927.
Lossky, Vladimir. *The Vision of God*. Library of Orthodox Theology. London: Faith Press, 1963.
Louth, Andrew. 'St Augustine's Interpretation of the Transfiguration of Christ'. *Studia Ephemerides Augustinianum* 68 (2000): 375–82.
Louth, Andrew. *The Origins of the Christian Mystical Tradition: From Plato to Denys*, 2nd edn. Oxford: Oxford University Press, 2007.
Luz, Ulrich. *Matthew 8-20*. Minneapolis, MN: Fortress Press, 2001.
MacDermot, Violet. *The Cult of the Seer in the Ancient Middle East: A Contribution to Current Research on Hallucinations Drawn from Coptic and Other Texts*. Publications of the Wellcome Institute of the History of Medicine. London: Wellcome Institute of the History of Medicine, 1971.
Mach, Michael. 'Christus Mutans: Zur Bedeutung der Verklärung Jesu im Wechsel von jüdischer Messianität zur neute stamentlichen Christologie'. In *Messiah and Christos*, edited by Ithamar Grunwald, 177–98. Tübingen: Mohr Siebeck, 1992.

Mâle, Emile. *The Early Churches of Rome*. London: Ernest Benn, 1960.
Manek, J. 'The New Exodus in the Books of Luke'. *Novum Testamentum* 2 (1958): 8–23.
Marcus, Joel. *The Way of the Lord: Christological Exegesis of the Old Testament in the Gospel of Mark*. Louisville: Westminster/John Knox Press, 1992.
Marcus, Joel. *Mark 8-16: A New Translation with Introduction and Commentary*. The Anchor Yale Bible. New Haven, CT: Yale University Press, 2009.
Marshall, I. Howard. *The Gospel of Luke: A Commentary on the Greek Text*. Exeter: Paternoster, 1978.
Maskell, W. *A Description of the Ivories Ancient and Mediaeval in the South Kensington Museum*. London: Chapman & Hall for the Science and Art Department of the Committee of Council on Education, 1872.
Matthews, Shelly. *Perfect Martyr: The Stoning of Stephen and the Construction of Christian Identity*. Oxford: Oxford University Press, 2010.
Matthiae, Guglielmo. *S. Maria in Domnica*. Chiese di Roma Illustrate. Rome: Marietta, 1960.
Matthiae, Guglielmo. *Le chiese di Roma dal IV al X Secolo*. Roma Cristiana. Bologna: Cappelli, 1962.
Matthiae, Guglielmo. *Mosaici Medioevali delle Chiese di Roma*, 2 vols. Rome: Istituto Poligrafico dello Stato, Libreria dello Stato, 1967.
Mauck, Marchita. 'The Mosaic of the Triumphal Arch of S. Prassede: A Liturgical Interpretation'. *Speculum* 62, no. 4 (1987): 813–28.
Mauser, Ulrich. *Christ in the Wilderness: The Wilderness Theme in the Second Gospel and Its Basis in the Biblical Tradition*. London: SCM, 1963.
Mayor, Joseph B. *The Epistle of St Jude and the Second Epistle of St Peter: Greek Text*. London: Macmillan, 1907.
McCurley, F. ' "And after Six Days," (Mark 9.2): A Semitic Literary Device'. *Journal of Biblical Literature* 93 (1971): 67–81.
MacDonald, Dennis R. 'Which Came First? Intertextual Relationships amongst the Apocryphal Acts of the Apostles'. *Semeia* 80 (1997): 11–41.
MacDonald, Dennis R. *The Gospels and Homer*. Lanham, MD: Rowman & Littlefield, 2015.
MacDonald, Dennis R. *Luke and Vergil*. Lanham, MD: Rowman & Littlefield, 2015.
McGinn, Bernard. *The Foundations of Mysticism*. The Presence of God: A History of Western Christian Mysticism. London: SCM, 1992.
McGuckin, John Anthony. *The Transfiguration of Christ in Scripture and Tradition*. Lewiston, NY: Edwin Mellen Press, 1986.
McGuckin, John Anthony. 'The Changing Forms of Jesus'. In *Origeniana Quarta: die Referate des 4. internationalen Origeneskongress, 1985*, edited by Lothar Lies, 215–22. Innsbrück: Tyrolia-Verlag, 1987.
Meeks, Wayne A. *The Prophet-King: Moses Traditions and the Johannine Christology*. Leiden: Brill, 1967.
Meyendorff, John, and George Lawrence. *A Study of Gregory Palamas*. London: Faith Press, 1964.
Michaelis, Wilhelm. 'Ἐπόπτης'. In *Theological Dictionary of the New Testament*, vol. 5, translated and edited by Geoffrey Bromley. Grand Rapids, MI: Eerdmans, 1964.
Michaelis, Wilhelm. 'Εἰσ–'Ἐξ– Διεξοδος'. In *Theological Dictionary of the New Testament*, vol. 5, translated and edited by Geoffrey Bromley. Grand Rapids, MI: Eerdmans, 1964.
Michelli, Perette. 'Beckwith Revisited'. In *Anglo-Saxon Styles*, edited by Catherine Karkov and George Brown, 101–14. New York: State University of New York Press, 2003.

Miller, J. 'Source Criticism and the Limits of Certainty'. *Ephemerides Theologicae Lovanienses* (1998): 127–44.
Miller, John B. F. *Convinced That God Had Called Us: Dreams, Visions and the Perception of God's Will in Luke-Acts*. Biblical Interpretation Series. Leiden: Brill, 2007.
Miller, Robert. 'Is There Independent Attestation for the Transfiguration in 2 Peter?' *New Testament Studies* 42 (1996): 620–5.
Millet, Gabriel. *Recherches sur l'iconographie de l'évangile aux XIV, XV, et XVI siècles: D'après les monuments de Mistra, de la Macédoine et du Mont-Athos*. Paris: E. de Boccard, 1960.
Moessner, David. 'Luke 9.1-50: Luke's Preview of the Journey of the Prophet Like Moses of Deuteronomy'. *Society of Biblical Literature* 102 (1983): 575–605.
Moessner, David. 'Jesus and the "Wilderness Generation": The Death of the Prophet Like Moses According to Luke'. In *SBL 1982 Seminar Papers*, edited by Kent Richards, 319–40. Chico, CA: Scholars, 1982.
Moll, Sebastian. *The Arch-Heretic Marcion*. Wissenschaftliche Untersuchungen zum neuen Testament. Tübingen: Mohr Siebeck, 2010.
Moses, A. D. A. *Matthew's Transfiguration Story and Jewish-Christian Controversy*. Sheffield: Sheffield Academic Press, 1996.
Moss, Candida. 'The Transfiguration: An exercise in Marcan Accommodation'. *BibInt* 12 (2004): 69–89.
Mount, Christopher. *Pauline Christianity: Luke-Acts and the Legacy of Paul*. NovTSup 104. Leiden: Brill, 2002.
Müller, Claudia. 'Das Apsismosaik von S. Apollinare in Classe: Eine Strukturanalyse'. *Römische Quartalschrift* 75 (1980): 11–50.
Murphy-O'Connor, J., 'What Really Happened at the Transfiguration?' *Biblical Revue*, 3 (1987): 8–21.
Nasrallah, Laura Salah. *An Ecstasy of Folly: Prophecy and Authority in Early Christianity*. Cambridge, MA: Harvard Theological Studies, Harvard Divinity School, 2003.
Nasrallah, Laura Salah. 'The Acts of the Apostles, Greek Cities, and Hadrian's Panhellenion'. *JBL* 127, no. 3 (2008): 533–66.
Nees, Lawrence. 'On Carolingian Book Painters: The Ottobani Gospels and Its Transfiguration Master'. *Art Bulletin* 83 (June 2001): 209–39.
Neirynck, F. 'Minor Agreements Matthew-Luke in the Transfiguration Story'. In *Orientierung an Jesus: zur Theologie der Synoptiker: für Josef Schmidt*, edited by Paul Hoffman, Norbert Brox and Wilhelm Pesch, 253–66. Freiburg: Herder, 1973.
Nes, Solrunn, and Arlyne Moi. *The Uncreated Light: An Iconographical Study of the Transfiguration in the Eastern Church*. Grand Rapids, MI: Eerdmans, 2007.
Neyrey, Jerome H. 'The Apologetic Use of the Transfiguration in 2 Peter 1.16-21'. *Catholic Biblical Quarterly* 42 (1980): 504–19.
Neyrey, Jerome H. *2 Peter, Jude: A New Translation with Introduction and Commentary*. The Anchor Bible. Garden City, NY: Doubleday, 1993.
Ni Riain, Ide M. *Commentary of Saint Ambrose on the Gospel According to Saint Luke*. Dublin: Halcyon Press, 2001.
Nickelsburg, George. 'Enoch, Levi, and Peter: Recipients of Revelation in Upper Galilee'. *Journal of Biblical Literature* 100, no. 4 (1981): 575–600.
Noble, Thomas. 'Topography, Celebration, and Power: The Making of a Papal Rome in the Eighth and Ninth Centuries'. In *Topographies of Power in the Early Middle Ages*, edited by Mayke De Jong, 45–91. Leiden: Brill, 2001.

Nolland, John. *Luke*. Word Biblical Commentary. Dallas, TX: Word Books, 1989.
Nordström, Carl Otto. *Ravennastudien; Ideengeschichtliche und Ikonographische Untersuchungen über die Mosaiken von Ravenna*. Stockholm: Almqvist & Wiksell, 1953.
Norris, Frederick. 'The Transfiguration of Christ: The Transformation of the Church'. In *Reading in Christian Communities: Essays on Interpretation in the Early Church*, edited by Charles Bobert, 188–98. Notre Dame, IN: University of Notre Dame Press, 2002.
O'Hear, Natasha. *Contrasting Images of the Book of Revelation in Late Medieval and Early Modern Art: A Case Study in Visual Exegesis*. Oxford Theological Monographs. Oxford: Oxford University Press, 2011.
Oakeshott, Walter. *The Mosaics of Rome from the Third to the Fourteenth Centuries*. London: Thames & Hudson, 1967.
Odorici, Frederico. *Antichita Cristiane di Brescia*. Brescia: Pio Instituto in S. Barnaba, 1845.
Öhler, M. 'Die Verklärung (Mk 9.1-8): Die Ankunft der Herrschaft Gottes auf der Erde'. *Novum Testamentum* 38 (1996): 197–217.
Onasch, Konrad. *Icons*. London: Faber and Faber, 1963.
Öpke, Albrecht. 'Νεφέλη'. In *Theological Dictionary of the New Testament*, vol. 4, edited by Gerhard Kittel. Grand Rapids, MI: Eerdmans, 1969.
Osborn, Eric Francis. *Tertullian, First Theologian of the West*. Cambridge: Cambridge University Press, 1997.
Otto, Randall, E. 'The Fear Motivation in Peter's Offer to build Τρεῖς Σκηνάς'. *WTJ* 59 (1997): 101–12.
Ouspensky, Leonide, and Vladimir Lossky. *The Meaning of Icons*. Boston: Boston Book and Art Shop, 1969.
Park, David. *The Fire Within: A Historical Essay on the Nature and Meaning of Light*. Princeton, NJ: Princeton University Press, 1997.
Panazza, Gaetano. *I musei e la pinacotecca di Brescia*. Bergamo: Instituto Italiano d'Arti Grafiche, 1959.
Pao, David W. *Acts and the Isaianic New Exodus*. Tübingen: Mohr Siebeck, 2000.
Pattison, Stephen. *Seeing Things: Deepening Relations with Visual Artefacts*. London: SCM Press, 2007.
Perrin, Norman. *The Kingdom of God in the Teaching of Jesus*. New Testament Library. London: SCM Press, 1963.
Pervo, Richard I. *Dating Acts: Between the Evangelists and the Apologists*. Santa Rosa, CA: Polebridge Press, 2006.
Pervo, Richard I. *Acts: A Commentary*. Hermeneia. Minneapolis, MN: Fortress Press, 2009.
Peterson, Erik. *Frühkirche, Judentum und Gnosis; Studien und Untersuchungen*. Rome: Herder, 1959.
Pettis, Jeffrey B. *Seeing the God: Ways of Envisioning the Divine in Ancient Mediterranean Religion*. Perspectives on Philosophy and Religious Thought. Piscataway, NJ: Gorgias Press, 2013.
Pfaff, Richard. *New Liturgical Feasts in Later Medieval England*. Oxford: Clarendon Press, 1970.
Pincherle, Alberto. 'Intorno a un celebre mosaico Ravennate'. *Byzantion* 36 (1966): 491–534.
Porter, M. *The Message of the Apocalyptical Writers*. London, 1905.

Pricop, Cosmin. *Die Verwandlung Jesu Christi, historisch-kritische und patristische Studien.* Wissenschaftliche Untersuchungen zum Neuen Testament, 2 Reihe. Tübingen: Mohr Siebeck, 2016.
Prumm, K. 'De Genuine Apocalysis Petri Textu Examen Testium Ian Notorum Et Novi Fragmenti Raineriani'. *Biblica* 10 (1929): 62–80.
Puech, Henri-Charles. 'Un livre récent sur la livre mystique d'Origène'. *Revue d'histoire et de philosophie religieuse* 13 (1933): 508–36.
Quasten, Johannes. *Patrology*, 4 vols. Westminster, MD: Spectrum, 1950.
Rahner, Karl. 'La doctrine des sens spirituels chez Origène'. *Revue d'ascetique et de la mystique* (1932): 113–45.
Ramsey, Michael. *The Glory of God and the Transfiguration of Christ.* London: Longmans, Green, 1949.
Reid, Barbara E. *The Transfiguration: A Source- and Redaction- Critical Study of Luke 9: 28-36.* Cahiers De La Revue Biblique. Paris: Gabalda, 1993.
Rengstorf, Karl Heinrich, *Das Evangelium Nach Lukas.* Neue Testament Deutsch. Göttingen: Vandenhoeck & Ruprecht, 1962.
Riesenfeld, Harald. *Jésus Transfiguré: L'arrière-plan récit évangélique de la Transfiguration de Notre-Seigneur.* Copenhagen: E. Munksgaard, 1947.
Ringe, S. H. 'Luke 9.28-36: The Beginning of an Exodus'. *Semeia* 28 (1983): 81–99.
Ritschl, Albrecht. *Das Evangelium Marcions und das kanonische Evangelium des Lucas: Eine kritische Untersuchung.* Tübingen: Ostander, 1846.
Robeck, Cecil M. *Prophecy in Carthage: Perpetua, Tertullian, and Cyprian.* Cleveland, OH: Pilgrim Press, 1992.
Robinson, J. Armitage, and M. R. James. *The Gospel According to Peter, and the Revelation of Peter.* London: C. J. Clay, 1892.
Rossi, Giovanni Battista de. *Musaici cristiani e saggi dei parimenti delle chiese di Roma anteriori al secolo XV., tavole cromo-litografiche con cenni storici et critici, con tr. Francese.* Rome: Librera Spithöver di Guglierlmo Haass, 1872.
Roth, Dieter T. 'Marcion's Gospel and Luke: The History of Research in Current Debate'. *Journal of Biblical Literature* 127 (2008): 513–27.
Roth, Dieter T. 'Marcion and the Early New Testament Text'. In *The Early Text of the New Testament*, edited by Charles E. Hill and Michael Kruger, 302–12. Oxford: Oxford University Press, 2012.
Roth, Dieter T. *The Text of Marcion's Gospel.* Leiden: Brill, 2015.
Rowland, Christopher, and Christopher R. A. Morray-Jones. *The Mystery of God: Early Jewish Mysticism and the New Testament.* Leiden: Brill, 2009.
Sabbe, M. 'La rédaction du récit de la Transfiguration'. In *La venue du messie: messianisme et eschatologie*, edited by E. Massaux, 65–100. Bruges: Desclée de Brouwer, 1962.
Sanday, W. *Inspiration: Eight Lectures on the Early History and Origin of the Doctrine of Biblical Inspiration, being the Bampton Lecture for 1983.* London: Longmans, Green, 1894.
Schelkle, Karl Hermann. *Die Petrusbriefe; Der Judasbrief: Auslegung.* Freiburg: Herder, 1961.
Schenke, Ludger. 'Gibt es im Markusevangelium eine Präexistenzchristologie?'. *ZNW* 91 (2000): 45–71.
Schiller, Gertrud. *Iconography of Christian Art.* London: Lund Humphries, 1971.
Schmithals, W. 'Der Markusschluss, die Verklärungsgeschichte und die Sendung der Zwölf'. *Zeitschrift für Theologie und Kirche* 95 (1976): 79–96.

Schneider, G. *Das Evangelium nach Lukas*, vol. 1. Ökumenischer Taschenbuchkommentar zum neuen Testament. Güttersloh: G. Mohn, 1977.

Schrage, Wolfgang. *Die 'Katholischen' Briefe: Die Briefe des Jakobus, Petrus, Johannes und Judas*. Neue Testament Deutsch. Göttingen: Vandenhoeck & Ruprecht, 1993.

Schramm, Tim. *Der Markus-Stoff bei Lukas: Eine literakritische und redaktionsgeschichtliche Untersuchung*. Cambridge: Cambridge University Press, 1971.

Schürmann, Heinz. *Das Lukasevangelium*. Herders Theologischer Kommentar zum Neuen Testament. Freiburg: Herder, 1969.

A Select Library of the Nicene and Post-Nicene Fathers of the Christian Church. 14 vols. Grand Rapids, MI: T&T Clark, 1988.

Senior, Donald, and Daniel J. Harrington. *1 Peter, Jude and 2 Peter*. Sacra Pagina Series. Collegeville, MN: Liturgical Press, 2003.

Shellard, Barbara. *New Light on Luke: Its Purpose, Sources and Literary Context*. London: Sheffield Academic Press, 2002.

Sidaway, Janet. *The Human Factor: 'Deification' as Transformation in the Theology of Hilary of Poitiers: 6 (Studia Patristica Supplements)*. Leuven: Peeters, 2016.

Simms, A. E. 'Second Peter and the Apocalypse of Peter'. *Expositor* 8, Fifth Series (1898): 460–71.

Simson, Otto Georg von. *Sacred Fortress: Byzantine Art and Statecraft in Ravenna*. Chicago: University of Chicago Press, 1948.

Smith, Dennis, and Joseph B Tyson, eds. *Acts and Christian Beginnings: The Acts Seminar Report*. Salem: Polebridge, 2013.

Smith, Morton. *Clement of Alexandria and a Secret Gospel of Mark*. Cambridge, MA: Harvard University Press, 1973.

Smith, Morton. 'The Origin and History of the Transfiguration Story'. *Union Seminary Quarterly Review* 36 (1980): 39–44.

Smith, Morton. 'Ascent to the Heavens and the Beginnings of Christianity'. *Eranos* 50 (1981): 403–29.

Smith, Terence V. *Petrine Controversies in Early Christianity: Attitudes towards Peter in Christian Writings of the First Two Centuries*. Wissenschaftliche Untersuchungen Zum Neuen Testament, 2 Reihe. Tübingen: J.C.B. Mohr, 1985.

Soper, A. C. 'The Italo-Gallic School of Early Christian Art'. *Art Bulletin* 20 (1938): 145–92.

Spieser, Jean-Michel. 'Le programme iconographique des portes de Sainte-Sabine'. *Journal des Savants* 1 (1991): 47–82.

Spitta, F. 'Die evangelische Geschichte von der Verklärung Jesu'. *Zeitschrift für Wissenschaftliche Theologie* 53 (1911): 97–167.

Spitta, F. 'Die Petrusapokalypse und der zweite Petrusbrief'. *Zeitschrift für Neutestamentliche Wissenschaft* 12 (1911): 237–43.

Stafford, Barbara. *Looking Good – Essays on the Virtues of Images*. Cambridge, MA: MIT Press, 1998.

Stegner, William. 'The Use of Scripture in Two Early Narratives of Early Jewish Christianity (Mt 4.1-11; Mk 9.2-8)'. In *Early Christian Interpretation of the Scriptures of Israel: Investigations and Proposals*, edited by Craig A. Evans and James Sanders. JSNT Suppl. 148, SSEJC 5, 98–120. Sheffield: Sheffield University Press, 1997.

Stein, R. 'Is the Transfiguration (Mark 9.2-8) a Misplaced Resurrection Account?' *Journal of Biblical Literature* 95, no. 1 (1976): 79–96.

Steinmann, Jean. *Tertullien*. Collection parole et Tradition. Lyon: Éditions du Chalet, 1967.

Stevenson, Kenneth. *Rooted in Detachment: Living the Transfiguration*. London: Darton, Longman and Todd, 2007.
Stevenson, Kenneth. *Liturgy and Interpretation*. London: SCM Press, 2011.
Stoops, R. F. 'The Acts of Peter in Intertextual Context'. *Semeia* 80 (1997): 57–86.
Strauss, David Friedrich, George Eliot, and Otto Pfleiderer. *The Life of Jesus, Critically Examined*, 2nd edn. London: S. Sonnenschein; Macmillan, 1892.
Stuhlfauth, H. G. *Die altchristliche Elfenbeinplastik*. Freiburg-Leipzig: Mohr, 1894.
Svizzereto, Floriana. 'Il Mosaico absidale, manifesto iconoduluo: proposta di interpretazione'. In *Caulius I: Santa Maria in Domnica, San Tommaso in Formis e il Clivus Scauri*, edited by Alia Englen. Rome: Palensesti Romani, 2003.
Swete, Henry Barclay. *The Gospel According to St. Mark*. London: Macmillan, 1927.
Sybel, Ludwig von. *Christliche Antike: einführung in die altchristliche Kunst*, vol. 2. Marburg: N.G. Elwert, 1909.
Taylor, Vincent. *The Formation of the Gospel Tradition*. London: Macmillan, 1949.
Taylor, Vincent. *The Gospel According to St Mark: The Greek Text*. London: Macmillan, 1966.
Teeple, Howard Merle. *The Mosaic Eschatological Prophet*. Philadelphia: Society of Biblical Literature, 1957.
Thackeray, St J. *Josephus*, vol. 1. Loeb Classical Library. Cambridge, MA: Harvard University Press, 1958.
Theissen, Gerd. *The Miracle Stories of the Early Christian Tradition*. Edinburgh: T&T Clark, 1983.
Thrall, M. 'Elijah and Moses in Mark's Account of the Resurrection'. *New Testament Studies* 16 (1969–70): 305–17.
Tkacz, Catherine Brown. *The Key to the Brescia Casket: Typology and the Early Christian Imagination*. Collection des études augustiniennes: Série antiquité. Notre Dame, IN: University of Notre Dame Press, 2002.
Toesca, P. *Il Medioevo*, vol. 1. Turin: Unione Tipographico-Editrice Torinese, 1927.
Tompkins, Matthew. *The Spectacle of Illusion: Magic, the Paranormal, and the Complicity of the Mind*. London: Thames and Hudson, 2019.
Toynbee, J. M. C. 'Review of Delbrück, *Probleme der Lipsanothek in Brescia*'. *Antiquaries Journal* 35 (1955): 238–40.
Trevett, Christine. *Montanism: Gender, Authority and the New Prophecy*. Cambridge: Cambridge University Press, 1996.
Tsutsui, Kenji. 'Das Evangelium Marcions: Ein neuer Versuch der Textrekonstruktion'. *Annual of the Japenese Biblical Institute* 18 (1992): 67–132.
Turner, Seth. 'Revelation 11:1-13: History of Interpretation'. DPhil. diss., University of Oxford, 2004.
Tyson, Joseph B. 'The Date of Acts: A Reconsideration'. *Forum* 5, no. 1 (2002): 33–51.
Tyson, Joseph B. 'Why Dates Matter: The Case of the Acts of the Apostles'. *The Fourth R* 18, no. 2 (2005): 8–14.
Tyson, Joseph B. *Marcion and Luke-Acts: A Defining Struggle*. Columbia: University of South Carolina Press, 2006.
Uehli, Ernst. *Die Mosaiken von Ravenna: mit 45 Abbildungen*. Basel: B. Schwabe, 1954.
Van Berchem, Marguerite, and Étienne Clouzot. *Mosaïques chrétiennes du IVme au Xme siècle*. Genève: Les presses de l'imprimerie du 'Journal de Genève', 1924.
Van Minnen, P. 'The Greek Apocalypse of Peter'. In *The Apocalypse of Peter*, edited by Jan N. Bremmer and Istvan Czachesz, 15–39. Leuven: Peeters, 2003.

Vandersall, A. L. 'Two Carolingian Ivories from the Morgan Collection in the Metropolitan Museum of Art'. *Metropolitan Museum Journal*, no. 6 (1972): 17-57.

Veniamin, Christopher N. 'The Transfiguration of Christ in Greek Patristic Literature: From Irenaeus of Lyons to Gregory Palamas'. DPhil. diss., University of Oxford, 1991.

Venturi, Adolfo. *Storia dell'arte italiana*, vol. 1. Milan: Ulrico Hoepli, 1901.

Viller, Marcel. 'Aux sources de la spiritualité de S. Maxime le Confesseur: Les ouevres d' 'Evagre le Pontique'. *Revue d'ascetique et de la mystique* 30 (1930): 156-84, 239-68, 331-6.

Volbach, W. *Early Christian Art*. New York: h. Abrams, 1962.

Volckmar, G. 'Über das Lukas-Evangelium nach seinem Verhältnis zu Marcion und seinem dogmatischen Charakter, mit besonderer Beziehung auf die kritischen Untersuchungen F. Ch. Baur's und A. Ritschl's'. *Theologische Jahrbücher* 9 (1850): 110-38, 185-223.

Völker, Walther. *Das Vollkommenheitsideal des Origenes: Eine Untersuchung zur Geschichte der Frömmigkeit und zu den Anfängen christlicher Mystik*. Beiträge zur historischen Theologie. Tübingen: J.C.B. Mohr, 1931.

Waal, A. de. 'Zur Ikonographie der Transfiguratio in der älteren Kunst'. *Romische Quartalschrift* 16 (1902): 25-40.

Walther, Ingo. *Codices Illustres: The World's Most Famous Illuminated Manuscripts 400-1600*. Köln: Taschen, 2001.

Wasson, R. Gordon, Carl A. P. Ruck and Albert Hofmann. *The Road to Eleusis: Unveiling the Secret of the Mysteries*. Los Angeles: William Dailey Rare Books, 1998.

Watson, Carolyn. 'The Program of the Brescia Casket'. *Gesta* 20 (1981): 283-98.

Weeden, Theodore J. *Mark: Traditions in Conflict*. Philadelphia: Fortress Press, 1971.

Weitzmann, Kurt. *The Icon: Holy Images, Sixth to Fourteenth Century*. London: Chatto & Windus, 1978.

Wellhausen, Julius. *Das Evangelium Marci*. Berlin: Reimer, 1909.

Westwood, John Obadiah. *A Descriptive Catalogue of the Fictile Ivories in the South Kensington Museum. With an Account of the Continental Collections of Classical and Medieval Ivories*. London: Eyre & Spottiswoode, 1876.

Wiefel, Wolfgang. *Das Evangelium Nach Lukas*. Theologischer Handkommentar Zum Neuen Testament. Berlin: Evangelische Verlagsanstalt, 1988.

Wiefel, Wolfgang. *Das Evangelium Nach Matthäus*. Leipzig: Evangelische Verlagsanstalt, 1998.

Wiegand, J. *Das altchristliche Hauptportal und der Kirche der Hl. Sabina*. Trier: Paulinus Druckerei, 1900.

Williams, D. S. 'Reconsidering Marcion's Gospel'. *Journal of Biblical Literature* 108 (1989): 477-96.

Williams, Frank. *The Panarion of Epiphanius of Salamis Books 2-3 (Sections 47-80)*, translated by Frank Williams. Nag Hammadi Studies. Leiden: E.J. Brill, 1987.

Williams, Frank. *The Panarion of Epiphanius of Salamis. Book I (Sections 1-46)*, 2nd edn. Nag Hammadi and Manichaean Studies. Leiden: Brill, 2009.

Williamson, Paul. *Medieval Ivory Carvings: Early Christian to Romanesque*. London: V&A Publishing, 2010.

Willoughby, Harold R. *Pagan Regeneration: A Study of Mystery Initiations in the Graeco-Roman World*. Chicago: University of Chicago Press, 1929.

Wilpert, Josef, and Walter Nikolaus Schumacher. *Die römischen Mosaiken der kirchlichen Bauten vom IV.-XIII. Jahrhundert*. Freiburg im Breisgau: Herder, 1976.

Wisskirchen, Rotraut. *Das Mosaikprogramm von S. Prassede in Rom: Ikonographie und Ikonologie*. Jahrbuch für Antike und Christentum Ergänzungsband. Münster: Aschendorff, 1990.

Wisskirchen, Rotraut. 'Leo III und die Mosaikprogramme von S. Apollinaris in Classe in Ravenna und Santi Nereo e Achilleo in Rom'. *Jahrbuch für Antike und Christentum* 34 (1991): 139–51.

Wisskirchen, Rotraut. *Die Mosaiken der Kirche Santa Prassede in Rom*. Mainz am Rhein: Verlag Philipp von Zabern, 1992.

Zajonc, Arthur. *Catch the Light: The Entwined Story of Light and Mind*. New York: Oxford University Press, 1995.

Zeller, Dieter. 'Die Menschwerdung des Sohnes Gottes im neuen Testament und die antike Religionsgeschichte'. In *Menschwerdung Gottes – Vergöttlichung Von Menschen*, edited by D. Zeller, 141–76. Göttingen: Vandenhoeck & Ruprecht, 1988.

Zeller, Dieter. 'Le Métamorphose de Jésus comme Épiphanie (Mc 9,2-8)'. In *L'évangile Exploré*, edited by Alain Marchendour, 167–86. Paris: Cerf, 1996.

Zeller, Dieter. 'Bedeutung und religionsgeschichtlicher Hintergrund der Verwandlung Jesu'. In *Authenticating the Activities of Jesus*, edited by Bruce Chilton and Craig A. Evans, 303–21. Leiden: Brill, 1999.

Ziesler, J. A. 'The Transfiguration Story and the Markan Soteriology'. *ExpTim* 81 (1970): 263–8.

INDEX

Acts of Peter 65–8
Acts of John 65–8
actualization 201
Allison, Dale 40
Ambrose of Milan 126, 133, 137, 139, 142, 171
Ambrose Autpert 130, 135, 138, 140, 147, 148
amentia 78–82, 88
Anastasius I of Antioch 105
Anastasius of Sinai 110–15
Andreopoulos, Andreas 152, 159, 160, 161
Andrew of Crete 106
Annunciation of the Blessed Virgin Mary 170, 174
Apocalypse of Peter 53–65, 160–4, 198, 200
Artistic depiction of biblical narratives 2
Ascension of Jesus 163, 210
 see also Transfiguration: 'Behold Two Men'
Ascension of Isaiah 143, 145
Augustine of Hippo 12, 135, 137, 140, 146

Baltensweiler, Heinrich 36, 42
Balz, Horst 51
Barker, Margaret 45
Basil of Caesarea 108
Baun, Jane 14, 200
Bauckham, Richard 42, 50, 56, 58
Beckwith, John 199
Bede the Venerable 130, 134, 138, 140, 147
Biblical reception history 2
Bischof, F. A. 194
Boobyer, G. H. 42, 56
Booths, *see* 'Tabernacles'
Bovini, Giuseppe 160
Bremmer, Jan 57
Brescia Casket 152
Buchholz, Dennis 60–2
Bultmann, Rudolf 37, 55

Burkett, Delbert 43
Burning Bush 154

Callan, Terrance 57
Carruthers, Mary 11–12, 120–1, 196
Cartlidge, D. R. 67
Chidester, David 10, 15–16, 200
churches
 Sant'Apollinare in Classe, Ravenna 152, 158–65, 200
 St Catherine's Monastery, Sinai 154–7, 200
 Santa Maria in Domnica 187–92, 201–2
 Santi Nereo e Achilleo, Rome 145, 168–75, 178, 200, 202
 St Paul's Outside the Walls 167
 Santa Prassede, Rome 175–87, 201–2
  St. Zeno Chapel 184–7, 202
 Santa Restituta, Naples 166
 Santa Sabina, Rome 152
 Santa Stephania, Naples 165–6
Collins, Adela 40
Conzelmann, Hans 39
Clement of Alexandria 51
Curzi, Gaetano 170
Cyril of Alexandria 107
 Commentary on Luke 107
 Commentary on the Gospel according to John 107

Davies, W. D. 40
Daniélou, Jean 95
Deichmann, Friedrich 160, 164
Delbrück, Richard 153
Descartes, Rene 9
Dinkler, Erich 153, 160, 161, 163
Dibelius, Martin 55
Driscoll, Jeremy 127

ecstasy 78–82, 86–9, 93–6
Eichinger, Matthias 92

Eleusinian mysteries 51
Elior, Rachel 45
Elkins, James 205
Elsner, Jas 13–14, 155–6
Emmaus 152
Enoch 43, 45
Epiphanius' Anti-Phrygian Source 86–8
eyewitness (c.f. 2 Pet 1.16) 50–2

Figura 86
Finding in the Temple 97
Fletcher Louis, Crispin 44
Fossum, J. E. 43
Frey, Jörg 57

Gadamer, Hans-Georg 16
Gaddoni, Vanda 160
Gallio, Paola 187
Gerber, W. 40, 43
Gilmour, Michael 50
Giunta, D. 170
Goodson, Caroline 175, 202
Gospel of Thomas 44
Gourdain, Jean-Louis 126
Grabar, André 162, 164
Gregory of Nyssa 156
Gregory the Great 129
Grünstäudl, Wolfgang 57
Guerrieri, Agnese 171

Habakkuk 84–7
Habitus 85
Hadrian I 175
Haptic vision 8–9
Harnack, Adolf von 36, 73, 75
Hart-Hasler, J. N. 126
Heil, John Paul 46
Hilary of Poitiers 127, 129, 137, 139
Hilgenfeld, Adolf 73
Homer 40
Horst, van der, K. 194
Humphrey, Edith 46

Ihm, Christa 160, 166
Isaac, sacrifice of 22
Isaiah 188
Ivory, V & A Museum Inventory No. 254–1867 196–200

Jakab, Attila 64
Jay, Martin 10
Jeremiah 188
Jeremias, Gisela 152
Jerome 126, 128, 137, 139, 142, 144, 171
John the Baptist 24, 188
John Chrysostom 115–22
　Ad Theodorum Lapsum 116, 118
　Commentary on Matthew's Gospel 116, 119
　Homily on the Transfiguration 115
　Homily 21, 116
Jonas, Hans 10

Kee, H.C. 40, 42
Kelly, J. N. D. 53
Knox, John 73
Kovacs, Judith 14, 200–1
Krüger, Manfred 159–60
Kümmel, Werner 39
Kurth, Julius 159

Lalleman, P. J. 67
Lee, Simon 46, 56
Leo the Great 128, 134
Leo III 167, 168
Lierman, John 41
Locke, John 9
Lohmyer, E. 39
Lossky, Vladimir 104
Louth, Andrew 95, 126, 146
Luz, Ulrich 3–5

MacDermot, Violet 28
MacDonald, Dennis 40
Mâle, Emile 187
Mauck, Marchita 179
McGinn, Bernard 95
McGuckin, John Anthony 98, 104, 128
Mach, Michael 42, 43
Marcion's gospel 72–6
Mary's virginity *in partu* 144
Maximus the Confessor 106
Medieval theories of memory 11–12
Merleau-Ponty, Maurice 11
Miller, John 38
Miller, Robert 50
Moll, Sebastian 73

Moses and Elijah 21, 23, 24, 82–3, 138, 142, 153, 182, 188
Moses, A. D. A. 42
Mount Carmel 20
Mount Hermon 20
Mount Sinai 20
Mount Tabor 20
Müller, Claudia 164
Murphy O'Connor, Jerome 38

Nasrallah, Laura 78
Neirynck, Frans 38
Nelson, Robert 14
Nes, Solrunn 160, 161
Neyrey, Jerome 51
Nickelsburg, George 43, 44
Noble, Thomas 175
Nordtröm, Carl 160, 162, 164
Norris, Frederick 4

Oakeshott, Walter 171
O'Hear, Natasha 15–16, 200–1
Öhler, M. 43
Origen 90–100, 126, 144
  Cloud as tabernacle 97
  Finding in the Temple 97
  High Priestly, temple and tabernacle motifs 96–7, 137
  Origen and ecstasy 93–5
  Presentation in the Temple 98
  'sober drunkenness' of the soul 95
  Use of Phil 2.7, 98
  Com. Mat 40, 93, 144
  Com. Mat. 38, 93
  Contra Cels. 7.3–4, 95, 144
  Frag. Luc. 140, 96–7
  Hom. Lev. 7, 95
  Hom. Luc. 18, 98
  Hom. Nom. 7, 95

Paschal I 175, 201
Pattison, Stephen 7–11
Pearl of Great Price 153
Pincherle, Alberto 159–60
Plotinus 156
Polymorphy 67
Pope Paschal I 152
Presentation in the Temple 98
Pricop, Cosmin 5

Protoevangelium of James 143, 171, 174
Puech, Henri-Charles 94

Rabbula Gospels 152, 153
Reid, Barbara 38
'Religious' or 'ritual' viewing 12–13, 155–6
Riesenfeld, Harald 44
Robeck, Cecil 78
Roth, Dieter 75
Rowland, Christopher 14, 43, 200–1

Sabbe, M. 43, 57
Sartre, Jean-Paul 11
Schneider, Gerhard 51
'Scopic regime' 7–11
Sidaway, Janet 127
Simson, Otto von 160, 164
Sleep 80–1
Smith, Morton 44
Son of Man (Dan. 7) 44
Spieser, Jean-Michel 152
Spitta, F. 56
Stein, Robert 37
Stevenson, Kenneth 6
Sukkoth 21, 27, 44, 113

Tabernacles 21, 24, 183
Tabernacles, Feast of, *see* 'Sukkoth'
Teeple, Howard 42
Tent of Meeting 21, 41
Tents, *see* 'Tabernacles'
Tertullian 72–90, 126
  Amentia and ecstasy 76–8, 79–82
  Old Testament prophecy 82–6
  Reconstruction of his understanding of the Transfiguration 88–90
  Adv. Marc. 4.22, 72, 76
  Adv. Prax. 15, 77, 88–9
  De Anima 9, 88–9
  De Anima 45, 81, 89
Testament of Levi 43
Traditio Legis 152
Transfiguration
  Academic approaches and questions
    Angelomorphism 43
    Eschatological and apocalyptic readings 42
    Hellenistic epiphany 39–40

Historical-critical scholarship
2–3, 36–8
Lucan Transfiguration source
theory 37
Minor agreements, Mt & Lk
against Mk 37
Misplaced resurrection account 37
Moses and Sinai analogies 41
Rhetorical and narrative-critical
readings 46
Temple and High Priestly motifs 21,
44–6, 113, 164–5, 182–3, 211
Visual depiction of 212
*Elements in the Transfiguration
narrative*
'Behold two men' 27, 162, 191
Cloud 97, 125, 136–41, 180
Disciples falling on faces 24
'Exodus' 27, 181, 209
Entry into the cloud 32, 156, 209
Glory 27, 180, 209
Jesus' prayer 27, 96
Moses' and Elijah's conversation 76
Mountain top vision 179
Overshadowing cloud 22, 171
Peter not knowing what he was
saying 31, 76, 77, 93–4, 110–12,
117, 131–6, 211
Sleepiness of disciples 27–9, 112, 117,
125, 131, 210
Transfiguration taking place at night
33, 117, 130.
Voice from cloud 22, 24
Hermeneutic connections with:
Annunciation 141
Hebrews 12, 125
Isaiah 7.14, 125, 141–5
Rev 21–21, 125

Transfiguration as:
Altered vision 206
Compared with prophetic vision 208
Dangerous to sight 77, 116
Discussed in Greek comment 104–10
Discussed in Latin comment 125–43,
146–50
Metaphor for ascent to God 207
Mortal vision 206
Partial vision of eschatological
glory 108
Prompting greater vision of
heaven 207
Transformation of the human
subject 4
Vision of the Parousia 104–5, 159
Vision overwhelming to mortal
sight 107–8
Trevett, Christine 78
Turner, Seth 61
Tyson, Joseph, B. 73

Uehli, Ernst 160
Utrecht Psalter 192–6

'Visionary visual exegesis' 15–16, 200–1
Völker, Walther 94
Volckmar, G. 73

Walter, Ingo 194
Wellhausen, Julius 37
Williams, D. S 74
Williamson, Paul 196
Wiegand, J. 152
Wisskirchen, Rotraut 167, 168, 170, 179

Zechariah 84–7
Zeller, Dieter 39

INDEX OF BIBLICAL REFERENCES

Genesis
Gen. 28   114

Deuteronomy
Det. 18.15   41, 83

Exodus
Exod. 24   41, 84
Exod. 33.20
Exod. 40.   34–8, 41

Numbers
Num. 12.6-8

2 Chronicles
2 Chron. 5   144

Daniel
Dan. 7   44
Dan. 10   42

Wisdom
Wis. 3.2   28
Wis. 7.6   28

Psalms
Ps. 2.7   83
Ps. 24.6-9   58
Ps. 89.12   20
Ps. 150   195

Isaiah
Isa. 7.11   171, 200
Isa. 12   195
Isa. 50.10   83
Isa. 53.4   68
Isa. 60.19   179

Matthew,
Mt. 17.2   24

Mt. 17.5   24
Mt. 17.9   25, 145
Mt. 17.10-13   24
Mt. 17.19   24
Mt. 24.30   162

Mark
Mk 1.11   22
Mk 9.1   19
Mk 9.2   20
Mk 9.3   21
Mk 9.5   21
Mk 9.6   22
Mk 9.9   23
Mk 8.27   20

Luke
Lk. 1.35   171
Lk .9.20   26
Lk. 9.27   107
Lk. 9.29   27
Lk. 9.30   27
Lk. 9.31   27, 75, 94
Lk. 9.32   28, 29
Lk. 9.33   29, 30, 76, 139
Lk. 9.34   31, 156, 171
Lk. 9. 35   75
Lk. 9.36   75
Lk 9.51   26

John
John 21   153

Acts
Acts 1   162
Acts 1.10   182, 191
Acts 10.10   87

2 Corinthians
2 Cor. 3   46

Philippians
Phil. 2.6-11   68

Hebrews
Heb. 5.7   149
Heb. 12   114
Heb. 12.1   149
Heb. 12.22   147–8

2 Peter
2 Pet. 1.15   28
2 Pet. 1.16   50
2 Pet. 16-18   49–53
2 Pet. 1.18   58

Revelation
Rev. 4   167, 177
Rev. 11.1-13   182
Rev. 11   61–2
Rev. 21   166, 177, 195
Rev. 21.3   183
Rev. 21.9   180
Rev. 21.10   179
Rev. 21.11   180
Rev. 21.15   180, 182
Rev. 21.16   182
Rev. 21.22   147–8
Rev. 21.23   180
Rev. 21.24   179
Rev. 22   195
Rev. 22.3   195

1 Enoch   21, 198

Printed in the USA
CPSIA information can be obtained
at www.ICGtesting.com
LVHW051931120524
779928LV00002B/184

9 780567 699794